T0357881

A HANDBOOK OF
UNITED STATES COINS
2026
R.S. YEOMAN

83RD EDITION

JEFF **GARRETT**
SENIOR EDITOR

JOHN **FEIGENBAUM**
PUBLISHER

A Handbook of United States Coins™

OFFICIAL BLUE BOOK and OFFICIAL BLUE BOOK
OF UNITED STATES COINS are registered
trademarks of Whitman-CDN Publishing, LLC.

SINCE 1934
©2025 Whitman®
4001 Helton Dr., Florence, AL 35630
whitman.com

Printed in China

For a complete catalog of numismatic reference books, supplies, and storage products, visit Whitman.com.

If you enjoy United States coins, visit Greysheet.com for up-to-date news, pricing, and research.

The precious-metal spot prices in use for this edition are as follows:

Silver	$30
Gold	$2,670
Platinum	$960
Palladium	$980

Per industry practice, the actual weights of precious metals within coins are given in troy ounces.

CONTENTS

BLUE BOOK 2026 ADVISORY PANEL

Senior Editor: Jeff Garrett.
Editors Emeritus: Kenneth Bressett and Q. David Bowers.
Creative Director and Cover Designer: Matt Jeffirs.
Coordinating Editor: Diana Plattner. Graphic Design and Layout: Matthew Heller.
Pricing Editors: John Feigenbaum and Patrick Ian Perez.
Advertising Coordinator: Billie Blattel.

2026 ADVISORY PANEL

John Agre	Bill Fivaz	Greg Roberts
John Albanese	Gerry Fortin	Greg Rohan
Ted Ancher	Pierre Fricke	Allen Rowe
Justin Atkins	Ronald J. Gillio	P. Scott Rubin
Russell Augustin	Rusty Goe	Ian Russell
Bjorn Bergstrom	Ron Guth	David Ryder
Mark Borckardt	James Halperin	Stephanie Sabin
Q. David Bowers	Stephen Hayden	Mark Salzberg
Ken Bressett	Brian Hodge	Scott Schechter
William Bugert	Todd Imhoff	Jeff Shevlin
Roger Burdette	Steve Ivy	Craig Sholley
John Butler	Donald H. Kagin	Roger Siboni
H. Robert Campbell	Bradley S. Karoleff	Richard Snow
Seth Chandler	John Kraljevich	Laura Sperber
Elizabeth Coggan	Kevin Lipton	Jon Sullivan
Marc Crane	Andy Lustig	Saul Teichman
Adam Crum	Dwight N. Manley	Anthony Terranova
John Dannreuther	Olivia Marino	Scott Thomas
Charles Davis	David McCarthy	Troy Thoreson
Dan Decker	Joshua McMorrow-	Rick Tomaska
Blake Duncan	Hernandez	Tom Uram
Kenny Duncan Jr.	Harry Miller	Tom Warren
Steven Ellsworth	Lee S. Minshull	
David Fanning	Robert Rhue	

The following organizations have contributed to this edition: American Numismatic Association, American Numismatic Society, Central States Numismatic Society, Colonial Coin Collectors Club (C4), Florida United Numismatists, Pennsylvania Association of Numismatists, Professional Numismatists Guild, Rittenhouse Society

Special photo credits are due to the following: CAC Grading, GreatCollections, Heritage Auctions, NGC, PCGS, Smithsonian Institution, Stack's Bowers Galleries, United States Mint

Since 1942, annually revised editions of the *Official Blue Book of United States Coins* have aided thousands of people who have coins to sell or are actively engaged in collecting United States coins. The popular coin-folder method of collecting by date has created ever-changing premium values, based on the supply and demand of each date and mint. Through its panel of contributors, the *Blue Book* has, over the years, reported these changing values. It also serves as a source of general numismatic information to all levels of interest in the hobby.

The values shown are representative prices paid by dealers for various United States coins. These are averages of prices assembled from many widely separated sources. On some issues slight differences in price among dealers may result from proximity to the various mints or heavily populated centers. Other factors, such as local supply and demand or dealers' stock conditions, may also cause deviations from the prices listed. While many coins bring no premium in circulated grades, they usually bring premium prices in Mint State and Proof. Extremely rare and valuable coins are usually sold at public auction, and prices vary according to current demand.

THIS BOOK LISTS PRICES MANY COIN DEALERS WILL PAY.

Premium prices are the average amount dealers will pay for coins (according to condition) if required for their stock. This book is not a retail price list.

IF YOU HAVE COINS TO SELL

Chances are that the dealer from whom you purchased this book is engaged in the buying and selling of rare coins—contact them first. In the event that you purchased this book from a source other than a numismatic establishment, check the phone book or the web for the names of coin dealers (they will be found sometimes under the heading of "Stamp and Coin Dealers"). If you live in a city or town that does not have any coin dealers, obtain a copy of one of the trade publications (such as *Coin World* [www.coinworld.com] or *Numismatic News* [www.numismaticnews.net]) or check the Internet for the names and addresses of many of the country's leading dealers. Coin dealers who belong to the congressionally chartered American Numismatic Association (and who must abide by its code of ethics) are listed at www.money.org.

You will find current average *retail* valuations of American coins (the prices you can expect to pay a professional coin dealer) in the latest edition of *A Guide Book of United States Coins* by R.S. Yeoman, edited by Jeff Garrett. Coin collectors popularly call this the *Red Book*. Pricing in even greater detail is included in Mega Red—*A Guide Book of United States Coins, Expanded Deluxe Edition.*

HOW TO READ THE CHARTS

A dash in a price column indicates that a coin may or may not exist in that grade, and if it does, there are no current sales or auction records in that grade (which does not necessarily mean that the coin is especially rare). Italicized prices indicate unsettled or speculative values. A number of listings of rare coins do not have prices or dashes in certain grades. This indicates that they are not available or not believed to exist in those grades.

Mintages of Proof coins are listed in parentheses.

Italicized mintages are estimates.

Numismatics or coin collecting is one of the world's oldest hobbies, dating back several centuries. Coin collecting in America did not develop to any extent until about 1840, as our pioneer forefathers were too busy carving a country out of wilderness to afford the luxury of a hobby. The discontinuance of the large-sized cent in 1857 encouraged many people to attempt to accumulate a complete set of the pieces while they were still in circulation. One of the first groups of collectors to band together for the study of numismatics was the American Numismatic Society, founded in 1858 and still a dynamic part of the hobby (www.numismatics.org). Lack of an economical method to house a collection held the number of devotees of coin collecting to a few thousand until Whitman Publishing and other manufacturers placed low-priced coin boards and folders on the market in the 1930s. Since that time, the number of Americans collecting coins has increased many-fold.

THE PRODUCTION OF COINS

To collect coins intelligently it is necessary to have some knowledge of the manner in which they are produced. Coins are made in factories called "mints." The Mint of the United States was established at Philadelphia by a resolution of Congress dated April 2, 1792. The act also provided for the coinage of gold eagles ($10), half eagles, and quarter eagles; silver dollars, half dollars, quarter dollars, dimes (originally spelled "disme"), and half dismes or half dimes; and copper cents and half cents. The first coins struck were one-cent and half-cent pieces, in March of 1793 on a hand-operated press. Most numismatic authorities consider the half disme of 1792 the first United States coinage, quoting the words of George Washington as their authority. Washington, in his annual address, November 6, 1792, said, "There has been a small beginning in the coining of the half dimes, the want of small coins in circulation calling the first attention to them." Though the half disme is considered America's first coinage, it was not the first coinage produced by the Mint; these coins were produced off premises in July of 1792 before the mint was completed. In the new Philadelphia Mint are a number of implements from the original mint, and some coins discovered when the old building was wrecked. These coins included half dismes, and the placard identifying them states that Washington furnished the silver and gave some of the pieces to his friends as souvenirs.

Prior to the adoption of the Constitution, the Continental Congress arranged for the issuance of copper coins under private contract. These are known as the 1787 *Fugio coppers* from their design, which shows a sundial and the Latin word "fugio"—"I Fly" or, in connection with the sundial, "Time Flies." The ever-appropriate motto "Mind Your Business" is also on the coin.

In the manufacture of a coin, the first step is die preparation. Dies for early federal coinage were prepared by hand; generally, letters and numbers were added with punches, while portraits and other designs were engraved into the die. Eventually, eagles, Liberty heads, and the like were also added with hubs and punches. After about 1836, many dies were made from masters, which contained all elements except the date and, if applicable, the mintmark. The addition of an element to a master die ensured its consistent placement throughout the life of the die. Today, many design tasks are performed with three-dimensional computer graphics. Mint artists are either sculptor-engravers or medallic sculptors, and their work takes place mainly at the Philadelphia Mint. The dies are made of soft steel, which is hardened after the impression is received. The die is then dressed or finished to remove imperfections and make it suitable for coining. A typical die for production coinage can be used to strike hundreds of thousands of pieces. Dies for special issues such as Proofs are replaced more often.

COLLECTING COINS

The hand method of cutting dies accounts for the many die varieties of early United States coins. Where the amount of coinage of a given year was large enough to wear out many dies, each new die placed in the coining press created another die variety of that year. The dies being cut by hand, no two were exactly alike in every detail, even though some of the major elements such as the head or wreath, were sunk into the die by individual master punches. Of the cents dated 1794, more than sixty different die varieties have been discovered.

Thousands of dies are now used by the mints of the United States each year, but they are all made from one master die, which is produced in the following manner:

After the design is settled upon, the plaster of paris or wax model is prepared several times the actual size of the coin. When this model is finished an electrotype (an exact duplicate in metal) is made and prepared for the reducing lathe. The reducing lathe is a machine that works on the principle of the pantograph, only in this case the one point traces or follows the form of the model while another much smaller point in the form of a drill cuts away the steel and produces a reduced-size die of the model. The die is finished and details are sharpened or worked over by an engraver with chisel and graver. The master die is used to make duplicates in soft steel which are then hardened and ready for the coining press. To harden dies, they are placed in cast-iron boxes packed with carbon to exclude the air, and when heated to a bright red are cooled suddenly with water.

In the coinage operations the first step is to prepare the metal. Among the alloys that have been used are the following: silver coins, 90% silver and 10% copper; five-cent pieces, 75% copper and 25% nickel; one-cent pieces, 95% copper and 5% zinc. (The 1943 cent consists of steel coated with zinc; and the five-cent piece of 1942–1945 contains 35% silver, 56% copper, and 9% manganese.) Under the Coinage Act of 1965, the composition of dimes, quarters, and half dollars was changed to eliminate or reduce the silver content of these coins. The copper-nickel "clad" dimes, quarters, half dollars, and dollars are composed of an outer layer of copper-nickel (75% copper and 25% nickel) bonded to an inner core of pure copper. The silver clad half dollar and dollar have an outer layer of 80% silver bonded to an inner core of 21% silver, with a total content of 40% silver. Current cents are made from a core of 99.2% zinc, 0.8% copper, with a plating of pure copper. Dollars are composed of a pure copper core with outer layers of manganese-brass.

Alloys are melted in crucibles and poured into molds to form ingots. The ingots are in the form of thin bars and vary in size according to the denomination of the coin. The width is sufficient to allow three or more coins to be cut from the strips.

The ingots are next put through rolling mills to reduce the thickness to required limits. The strips are then fed into cutting presses which cut circular blanks of the approximate size of the finished coin. The blanks are run through annealing furnaces to soften them; next they move through tumbling barrels, rotating cylinders containing cleaning solutions which clean and burnish the metal; and finally into centrifugal drying machines.

The blanks are next fed into a milling machine which produces the raised or upset rim. The blank, now called a *planchet,* is now ready for the coining press.

The planchet is held firmly by a collar, as it is struck under heavy pressure varying from 40 tons for the one-cent pieces and dimes to 170 tons for silver dollars. Upper and lower dies impress the design on both sides of the coin. The pressure is sufficient to produce a raised surface level with that of the milled rim. The collar holding the blank for silver or clad coins is grooved. The pressure forces the metal into the grooves of the collar, producing the "reeding" on the edge of the finished coin.

HOW A PROOF COIN IS MADE

Selected dies are inspected for perfection and are highly polished and cleaned. They are again wiped clean or polished after every 15 to 25 impressions and are replaced frequently to avoid imperfections from wear. Coinage blanks are polished and cleaned to assure high quality in striking. They are then hand fed into the coinage press one at a time, each blank receiving two blows from the dies to bring up sharp, high-relief details. The coinage operation is done at slow speed. Finished Proofs are individually inspected and are handled by gloves or tongs. They also receive a final inspection by packers before being sonically sealed in special plastic cases.

Certain coins, including Lincoln cents, Buffalo nickels, quarter eagles, half eagles, eagles, and double eagles, between the years 1908 and 1916, were made with Matte Proof (nickel and silver) and Sand Blast and Satin Proof (gold) finishes. These later Proofs have a dull frosted surface which was either applied to the dies, or produced by special treatment after striking.

MINTS AND MINTMARKS

In addition to the Philadelphia Mint, the U.S. government has from time to time established branch mints in various parts of the country. At present, branch mints operate in Denver, West Point, and San Francisco. Starting in 1968, Proof sets as well as some of the regular coins were produced at the San Francisco Mint and Assay Office. The Denver Mint has operated since 1906. A mint was operated at New Orleans from 1838 to 1861 and again from 1879 to 1909. Mints were also in service at Carson City, Nevada, from 1870 to 1893; at Charlotte, North Carolina, from 1838 to 1861; at Dahlonega, Georgia, from 1838 to 1861; and at San Francisco since 1854. The U.S. government also supplied a mint in the Philippines (M mintmark) in the early 1900's.

Coins struck at Philadelphia before 1979 (except 1942 to 1945 five-cent pieces) do not bear a mintmark. Historically the mintmark was used only for branch mints. Modern exceptions include the 2017-P Lincoln cent and the Kennedy half dollar, which both use the P for Philadelphia. All circulating coins struck after 1967 have the mintmark on the obverse. The letters signifying the various mints are as follows:

C—Charlotte, North Carolina (gold coins only; 1838–1861)
CC—Carson City, Nevada (1870–1893)
D—Dahlonega, Georgia (gold coins only; 1838–1861)
D—Denver, Colorado (1906 to date)
O—New Orleans, Louisiana (1838–1861; 1879–1909)
P—Philadelphia, Pennsylvania (1793 to date; P not used in early years)
S—San Francisco, California (1854 to date)
W—West Point, New York (1984 to date)

The mintmark is of utmost importance to collectors because, historically, coinage of the branch mints has often been much smaller than quantities struck at Philadelphia. Many early coins of the branch mints are very scarce.

SLABBED VERSUS UNSLABBED COINS

In this handbook, values from under $1 up to several hundred dollars are for "raw" coins—that is, coins that have not been graded and encapsulated by a professional third-party grading service. Coins valued near or above $500 are assumed to be third-party graded. A high-value coin that has not been professionally certified as authentic, graded, and encapsulated by an independent firm is apt to be valued lower than the prices indicated.

The general effect of third-party grading and authentication has been to increase buyers' and sellers' comfort levels with the perceived quality of rare coins in the marketplace.

Coins in high grades that have been certified (professionally graded and guaranteed authentic) and encapsulated ("slabbed") may be valued significantly higher than similar coins that have not been so treated. In today's marketplace, "raw" or non-certified coins, are usually valued at less, except for modern U.S. Mint and bullion products.

DISTINGUISHING MARKS

The illustrations and explanations in this section will help the collector identify certain well-known varieties.

Half Cents of 1795–1796 Showing Location of Pole to Cap

The end of the pole lies parallel with the lines of the bust, which is pointed. On some coins, the pole is missing due either to engraver error (while cutting the die) or to an error in "relapping" (when the die is ground to remove wear, clash marks, etc.).

Pole to Cap   No Pole to Cap

Stemless Wreath Variety of Half Cents and Large Cents

For this variety, the difference is on the reverse side. Illustrations show both Stemless and Stems to Wreath types for comparison—stemless wreath found on the 1804, 1805, and 1806 half cents; and on the 1797, 1802, and 1803 large cents.

Stemless Wreath   Stems to Wreath

1864 Bronze Indian Head Cent With "L" on Ribbon

A small "L," the initial of the designer James B. Long-acre, was added to the Indian Head design late in 1864 and was continued through 1909. For coins in less than Fine condition, this small letter will often be worn away. The point of the bust is rounded on the 1864 variety without "L"; the bust is pointed on the variety with "L." The initial must be visible, however, for the 1864 variety to bring the higher premium. If the coin is turned slightly so that the portrait faces the observer, the highlighted details will usually appear to better advantage.

Designer Initials, Overstrikes, Die-Doublings, and Date Varieties

During 1909, initials appeared on the reverse of the Lincoln cent. Starting in 1918, they appear below the shoulder.

Prior to 1990, mintmarks for all mints were usually applied directly to working dies at Philadelphia in a hand-punching operation. Occasionally, a die was accidentally marked with one letter on top of another.

Dies are produced by impressing the raised coin design of a hub into the end of a cylinder of steel. In early years the Mint made use of old dies by repunching the dates on their dies with new numbers. That practice was stopped prior to 1909. Since that time, all overdated coins have been the result of errors that occur when two different-dated hubs have been used in die preparation, and one is impressed over the other by accident.

**1938-D, D Over S,
Buffalo Nickel**

**1918-S, 8 Over 7,
Standing Liberty Quarter**
*A variety of this kind is rarely found
in coinage of the 20th century.*

**1942, 2 Over 1,
Mercury Dime**

**1955, Doubled-Die Obverse
Lincoln Cent**

**Large Date Cent
(1960)**

**Small Date Cent
(1960)**

**Large Date Cent
(1982)**

**Small Date Cent
(1982)**

COUNTERFEIT COINS

Recognizing a spurious coin can be made easier through the use of common sense and an elementary knowledge of the techniques used by counterfeiters. It is well to keep in mind that the more popular a coin is among collectors and the public, the more likely it is that counterfeits and replicas will abound. Until recently, collector coins valued at under $100 were rarely replicated because of the high cost of making such items. The same was true of counterfeits made to deceive the public. Few counterfeit coins were made because it was more profitable for the fakers to print paper money. Today, however, counterfeiters in Asia and elsewhere create fakes of a surprising variety of coins, most notably silver dollar types, but also other denominations.

Coin dealers will rarely buy coins of exceptional rarity or value without being 100% certain of authenticity. Professional authentication of rare coins for a fee is offered by commercial grading services, and by some dealers.

Replicas

Reproductions of famous and historical coins have been distributed for decades by marketing firms and souvenir vendors. Most replicas are poorly made by the casting method, and are virtually worthless. They can sometimes be identified by a seam that runs around the edge of the piece where the two halves of the casting mold were joined together.

Counterfeits

For many centuries, counterfeiters have produced base-metal forgeries of gold and silver coins to deceive the public in the normal course of trade. These pieces are usually crudely made and easily detected on close examination. Crudely cast counterfeit copies of older coins are the most prevalent. These can usually be detected by the casting bubbles or pimples that can be seen with low-power magnification. Pieces struck from handmade dies are more deceptive, but the engravings do not match those of genuine Mint products.

Die-struck gold coin counterfeits have been mass produced overseas since 1950. Forgeries exist of most U.S. gold coins dated between 1870 and 1933, as well as all issues of the gold dollar and three-dollar gold piece. Most of these are very well made, as they were intended to pass the close scrutiny of collectors. Many gold coins of earlier dates have been counterfeited, and all coins dated before 1930 should be carefully examined.

Silver dollars dated 1804, Lafayette dollars, several of the low-mintage commemorative half dollars, and the 1795 half dimes have been forged in quantity. Minor-coin forgeries made in recent years are the 1909-S V.D.B.; 1914-D and 1955 doubled-die Lincoln cents; 1877 Indian Head cents; 1856 Flying Eagle cents; and, on a much smaller scale, a variety of dates of half cents and large cents. Nineteenth-century copies of colonial coins are also sometimes encountered.

Alterations

Coins are occasionally altered by the addition, removal, or change of a design feature (such as a mintmark or date digit) or by the polishing, sandblasting, acid etching, toning, or plating of the surface of a genuine piece. Among U.S. gold coins, only the 1927-D double eagle is commonly found with a spuriously added mintmark. On $2.50 and $5 gold coins, 1839 through 1856, New Orleans O mintmarks have been deceptively altered to C (for Charlotte, North Carolina) in a few instances.

Over a century ago, five-dollar gold pieces were imitated by gold plating 1883 Liberty Head five-cent coins without the word CENTS on the reverse. Other coins commonly created fraudulently through alteration include the 1799 large cent and the 1909-S; 1909-S V.D.B.; 1914-D; 1922, No D; and 1943, Copper, cents. The 1913 Liberty Head nickel has been extensively replicated by alteration of 1903 and 1912 nickels. Scarce, high-grade Denver and San Francisco Buffalo nickels of the 1920's; 1916-D and 1942, 42 Over 41, dimes; 1918-S, 8 Over 7, quarters; 1932-D and -S quarters; and 1804 silver dollars have all been made by the alteration of genuine coins of other dates or mints.

Detection

The best way to detect counterfeit coins is to compare suspected pieces with others of the same issue. Look at the photographs in this book for comparisons. Carefully check size, color, luster, weight, edge devices, and design details. Replicas generally have less detail than their genuine counterparts when studied under magnification. Modern struck counterfeits made to deceive collectors are an exception to this rule. Any questionable gold coin should be referred to an expert for verification.

Cast forgeries are usually poorly made and of incorrect weight. Base metal is often used in place of gold or silver, and the coins are lightweight and often incorrect in color and luster. Deceptive cast pieces have been made using real metal content and modern dental techniques, but these too usually vary in quality and color. Detection of alterations sometimes involves comparative examination of the suspected areas of a coin (usually mintmarks and date digits) at magnification ranging from 10x to 40x.

MISINFORMATION IN NUMISMATICS

Much misinformation that circulates on the Internet is confusing for anyone trying look up the value of a coin. This has been taken to new level recently, as posts on social media and elsewhere make outrageous claims about the value of common coins.

A recent one noted online that a 1976 Bicentennial quarter could be worth millions. The purpose of these crazy claims is to get the reader to click through and be exposed to the ads—a classic "click-bait" maneuver. Anyone with a coin shop or web presence hates this spreading of misinformation. Among other issues, they'll be fielding calls from some of the millions of individuals with a 1976 Bicentennial quarter who want to know if they've won the lottery.

There are also companies that claim to have an app for taking a picture of a coin and determining value. The ads for these apps often show a modern coin with a grossly inflated value. One dubious review for such an app stated, "Though I haven't taken my coins to an expert or had them appraised by anyone, I feel the app served me well, with a better understanding and invaluable amount of knowledge that I didn't have otherwise." The use of artificial intelligence might one day make this a reality, but we are very far from being able to determine the value of a coin by snapping a picture with a cellphone and loading it into an app.

Besides the flood of misinformation and fake news that circulates on the Internet about rare coins, legitimate news can be very confusing to anyone trying to determine value by doing a web search. A 1964 Kennedy half dollar graded MS-68 recently sold for about $57,600 in a major auction. Although the coin is a spectacular, high-grade example, and one of the finest circulation strikes seen for the date, the aggressive auction price was probably the result of two set-registry bidders doing battle.

The problem this creates is that someone who finds this information on the Internet is confused because they might have a roll of 20 Kennedys that look identical to the uneducated eye. It's really hard to explain to someone on the phone why *any* example of a 1964 Kennedy half dollar might be worth nearly $60,000.

We often have this problem with veteran collectors who think they may have coins of this caliber. Every week our company has to explain to people why they shouldn't waste grading fees on coins with no shot of achieving unrealistic results. I talked to one young intern for a major grading company who recently graded for a week, and said he was amazed by how many submissions contained basic pocket change.

Probably the most prolific topic that confuses the general public are error coins, or what people think are error coins. Many individuals can be confused by damage on a coin that they believe to be a mint-caused error. The value of minor mint errors is grossly overestimated by the general public. This edition of *A Guide Book of United States Coins* (a.k.a. the *Red Book*) contains a chapter on error coinage that can clear up much of this confusion. The *Red Book*—which is the best-selling annual guide to the prices collectors are paying for U.S. coins—contains an incredible amount of information that is especially helpful for those who are new to the hobby.

The next time you read a story about a relatively modern coin selling for tens of thousands of dollars, seek advice from an expert before spending money for grading fees. Having your coins pre-screened at the nearest coin shop can save you so much time and money. You can also have your coins checked at the many coin shows held around the country.

And an important tip for anyone who seeks information on the value of something: do not argue with the experts. This can lead to confrontation

Rare Bicentennial Quarter Worth More Than $2.2 Billion!

Scores of click-bait articles and YouTube videos have recently touted a "rare Bicentennial quarter" worth millions—or as in this ad, billions. In reality, the auction record for any Bicentennial quarter is $19,200.

or being hung-up on. Be patient and trust those who have devoted decades of their lives to studying coins and following the coin market.

We are all inundated by suspicious news every day, and coins stories are no different. Don't let the lure of instant riches perpetuated by misinformation lead you on a wild goose chase that will never materialize. Rare coins are exciting, and anything is, technically, possible—but the odds are not in your favor for finding instant riches in your pocket.

CONDITIONS OF COINS
Essential Elements of the Official ANA Grading System

Proof—A specially made coin distinguished by sharpness of detail and usually with a brilliant, mirrorlike surface. *Proof* refers to the method of manufacture and is not a condition, but normally the term implies nearly perfect condition unless otherwise noted.

Perfect Proof (PF-70)—The perfect coin, with strike and surface of the highest quality. No contact marks are visible under magnification. There are absolutely no hairlines, scuff marks, or defects.

Gem Proof (PF-65)—Brilliant surfaces with no noticeable blemishes or flaws. A few scattered, barely noticeable marks or hairlines.

Choice Proof (PF-63)—Reflective surfaces with only a few blemishes in secondary focal places. No major flaws.

Proof (PF-60)—Surface may have several contact marks, hairlines, or light rubs. Luster may be dull and eye appeal lacking.

Mint State—The terms *Mint State (MS)* and *Uncirculated (Unc.)* are used interchangeably to describe coins showing no trace of wear. Such coins may vary to some degree because of blemishes, toning, or slight imperfections, as described in the following subdivisions:

Perfect Uncirculated (MS-70)—Perfect new condition, showing no trace of wear. The finest quality possible, with no evidence of scratches, handling, or contact with other coins.

Gem Uncirculated (MS-65)—An above average Uncirculated coin that may be brilliant or lightly toned and that has very few contact marks on the surface or rim. MS-67 through MS-62 indicate slightly higher or lower grades of preservation.

Choice Uncirculated (MS-63)—Has some distracting contact marks or blemishes in prime focal areas. Luster may be impaired.

Uncirculated (MS-60)—Has no trace of wear but may show a number of contact marks, and surface may be spotted or lack some luster.

Choice About Uncirculated (AU-55)—Evidence of friction on high points of design. Most of the mint luster remains.

About Uncirculated (AU-50)—Traces of light wear on many of the high points. At least half of the mint luster is still present.

Choice Extremely Fine (EF-45)—Light overall wear on highest points. All design details are very sharp. Some of the mint luster is evident.

Extremely Fine (EF-40)—Light wear on design throughout, but all features sharp and well defined. Traces of luster may show.

Choice Very Fine (VF-30)—Light, even wear on the surface and highest parts of the design. All lettering and major features are sharp.

Very Fine (VF-20)—Moderate wear on high points. All major details are clear.

Fine (F-12)—Moderate to considerable even wear. Entire design is bold with overall pleasing appearance.

Very Good (VG-8)—Well worn with main features clear and bold, although rather flat.

Good (G-4)—Heavily worn, with design visible but faint in areas. Many details are flat.

About Good (AG-3)—Very heavily worn with portions of lettering, date, and legend worn smooth. The date may be barely readable.

A star (or similar notation) in the grade on a slab means "exceptional quality."

Important: Damaged coins, such as those that are bent, corroded, scratched, holed, nicked, stained, or mutilated, are worth less than those without defects. Flawless Uncirculated coins are generally worth more than values quoted in this book. Slightly worn coins ("sliders") that have been cleaned and conditioned ("buffed") to simulate Uncirculated luster are worth considerably less than perfect pieces.

Unlike damage inflicted after striking, manufacturing defects do not always lessen values. Examples include colonial coins with planchet flaws and weakly struck designs; early silver and gold with weight-adjustment "file marks" (parallel cuts made prior to striking); and coins with "lint marks" (surface marks due to the presence of dust or other foreign matter during striking).

Brief guides to grading are placed before each major coin type. Grading standards are not scientific and often vary among collectors, dealers, and certification services. For more on grading, consult the *Official ANA Grading Standards for United States Coins.*

PRESERVING AND CLEANING COINS

Most say, "Never clean a coin," and it is good advice! Cleaning coins almost always reduces their value. Collectors prefer coins in their original condition.

Some effort should be made to protect Uncirculated and Proof coins so they won't need cleaning. Tarnish on a coin is purely a chemical process caused by oxygen in the air acting on the metal, or by chemicals with which the coin comes in contact. One of the most common chemicals causing tarnish is sulphur; most paper, with the exception of specially manufactured "sulfur-free" kinds, contains sulfur due to the sulfuric acid that is used in paper manufacture; therefore do not wrap coins in ordinary paper. Also keep Uncirculated and Proof coins away from rubber bands (a rubber band placed on a silver coin for a few days will eventually produce a black stripe on the coin where the band touched). The utmost in protection is obtained by storing the coin in an airtight box, away from moisture and humidity, and by using holders made of inert materials.

Many coins become marred by careless handling. Always hold the coin by the edge. The accompanying illustration shows the right and wrong way to handle numismatic specimens. It is a breach of numismatic etiquette to handle another collector's coin except by the edge, even if it is not an Uncirculated or Proof piece.

STARTING A COLLECTION

One may start a collection of United States coins with very little expense by systematically assembling the various dates and mintmarks of all the types and denominations that are now in general circulation, using Whitman's many different coin folders and albums, especially those for quarters and dollars with various designs.

With the exception of the price paid for the coin folder, collecting coins received in everyday business transactions entails no expense whatsoever; a Jefferson nickel taken out of circulation, for example, can always be spent for five cents if the occasion arises. Filling an album or two with coins found in circulation is probably the best method of determining whether coin collecting appeals to you. Not everyone can be a successful coin collector. It requires patience, intelligence of a high order, and a certain desire to know the meaning behind a lot of things that at first glance appear meaningless. You may not be cut out to be a collector but you'll never know until you look further into the subject, and if by the time an album or two of coins are collected you have no burning desire to acquire many more different coins, you will probably never be a collector. However, chances are that you will be, because if you have read this far in this book, it shows that you are interested in the subject.

High quality is the goal of every endeavor and coin collecting is no exception. After an album has been filled with circulated specimens, the next step will be to replace them with coins in Uncirculated condition, or perhaps to start collecting an obsolete series; in either case, it will be necessary to purchase some coins from dealers or other collectors. The most logical way to keep abreast of the market, or obtain the addresses of the country's leading dealers, is to subscribe to one or more of the trade publications. These magazines carry advertisements of various dealers listing coins for sale. Moreover, through these sources the beginner may obtain price lists and catalogs from the dealers.

There are several good reference books available at reasonable prices which will be helpful to the collector who wishes to know more about U.S. coins and paper money. R.S. Yeoman's *A Guide Book of United States Coins*™ (the *Red Book*) lists retail values of all regular U.S. coins and also lists all coins of the U.S. colonial period and private and territorial gold coins, plus tokens, pattern pieces, errors, and other numismatic collectibles.

Most coin, book, and hobby dealers can supply the following titles:

The Official Red Book: A Guide Book of United States Coins—R.S. Yeoman, edited by Jeff Garrett

The Official Red Book: A Guide Book of United States Coins, Expanded Deluxe Edition—R.S. Yeoman, edited by Jeff Garrett

A Guide Book of Morgan Silver Dollars—Q. David Bowers

The Expert's Guide to Collecting and Investing in Rare Coins—Q. David Bowers

Coin Collecting: A Beginner's Guide to the World of Coins—Kenneth Bressett

History of the United States Mint and Its Coinage—David W. Lange

The Official ANA Grading Standards for United States Coins—Kenneth Bressett, et al.

A Guide Book of United States Type Coins—Q. David Bowers

Join a Coin Club

Beginners should join a coin club if they live in a city which has one. Associating with more experienced collectors will be of great benefit. Practically all larger cities have one or more clubs and they are being rapidly organized in smaller towns. Trade publications carry information about coin clubs and events such as coin shows and conventions.

The American Numismatic Association is a national organization that collectors can join. The ANA website (www.money.org) has a list of member coin clubs throughout the United States. Contact the ANA by email at pr@money.org; by mail at 818 North Cascade Avenue, Colorado Springs, CO 80903; or by phone at 800-367-9723.

WHAT TO DO WITH INHERITED COINS

Have you inherited some coins, tokens, medals, paper money, or other collectibles, and are you thinking of selling? If you've inherited a group of coins that someone else collected, and you don't know much about them, you're at a disadvantage when starting the process of selling them. The following overview will help level the playing field. Based on advice from Beth Deisher, author of *Cash In Your Coins: Selling the Rare Coins You've Inherited*; *Blue Book* senior editor Jeff Garrett; and other professional numismatists, it will help you identify your coins, estimate their current market value, and explore your options for selling them.

One of the most important things to first consider is, what kind of collector was the friend or family member who gifted you the coins?

An *accumulator* or *casual collector* saves coins in a random fashion. Many of these collectors save coins from circulation, and started in the 1960's when silver coins were eliminated from production. They also bring coins home from overseas trips, sometimes when in the military. Quite a few started with State quarters in 1999 when that program began. One of the most common traits of a casual collector is that they purchase coins on a regular basis from the United States Mint, usually commemorative coins, Mint Sets, and Proof Sets. More recently, casual collectors are those who have bought coins seen on TV or through other mass-media outlets.

A *numismatist*, often described as a "serious" or "advanced" collector, is more knowledgeable about the history and science of coinage. A numismatist might have broad collecting interests among many coin types, or might specialize, focusing their study, research, and collecting on particular coins or series. These are collectors who pay for coins as opposed to finding them in circulation. A serious numismatist is much more likely to have valuable coins that need research to determine value. Numismatists and other, more serious collectors often keep meticulous records of where and when they bought their coins, and for how much. These records can be useful when establishing values.

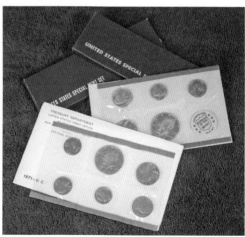

Inherited coin collections may hold a wide array of items, depending on the collector and their area of interest. Items in Mint-sealed packaging, like these unopened sets, are best left unopened prior to selling them.

DECIDING ON YOUR FIRST STEPS

There are two major approaches to handling inherited coins: try to determine basic values on your own, or trust an expert to appraise your coins. Both steps require time and patience to accomplish properly, but for many, the subject of numismatics is too bewildering to know where to start. The following offers basic guidance on how to get a handle on the value of the coins you have inherited. Later sections will discuss in detail how find someone you can trust to appraise your collection.

Option 1: Establishing Values on Your Own

Advice on Examining Your Coins

You might inherit coins in small manila envelopes with notes written on them. Keep these, as they can hold important information such as the coin's purchase price or a comment on its rarity. You might also find coins in blue Whitman coin folders, or larger coin albums, both a popular way of organizing a collection by date and mintmark. Your coins might be stored in cigar boxes, zipper bags, or other ad hoc containers. Coins and coin sets in U.S. Mint packaging should be left in their original government boxes, plastic capsules, and envelopes.

Some coins might be "slabbed" in sonically sealed plastic holders. Professional grading and certification by third-party firms (so called because they are neither the owner nor the potential buyer of the coin) started in the mid-1980's. The three largest and most well-established third-party grading firms are Numismatic Guaranty Company (NGC), Professional Coin Grading Service (PCGS), and Certified Acceptance Corporation Grading (CACG). Their tamper-resistant holders are sealed with labels that tell the coin's date and grade. There are also dozens of other third-party grading companies who may have holdered the coins you have inherited. Many of these companies use less-stringent grading standards, and the coins they certify have lower resale values.

To start to understand how much your coins are worth, you must first examine them. While you do so, **never clean your coins!** This might be the most important piece of advice. Cleaning coins can destroy the value, and should be done only by highly trained professionals.

Keep all packaging, envelopes, receipts, handwritten notes, correspondence, and such
with the coins. An experienced collector or dealer can glean important information
from these items (and some even have value as collectibles in their own right).

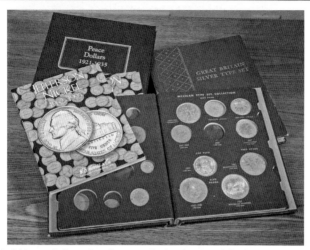

Coin folders and albums have been popular for storage and display since the 1930s.

Carefully lay your coins on a table or desk with enough space to comfortably examine everything. Have a magnifying glass or loupe handy. A handheld magnifier with 5x magnification is sufficient.

Make sure you have good lighting so you can see the details that impact a coin's value. Always hold a coin by the edge, rather than gripping it by its surfaces.

As you identify your coins, separate them and store them in tubes, folders, cardboard holders, albums, or other inert (chemically non-reactive) holders to protect them from damage. You can find many types and brands of holders at hobby and coin shops, or online from sellers of coin supplies.

Also keep a coin price guide handy—such as this edition of the *Blue Book*, which shows the average prices coin dealers pay for coins in various grades.

For grading instructions, consult the book *Official American Numismatic Association Grading Standards for United States Coins*, edited by Kenneth Bressett, or *Grading Coins by Photographs*, by Q. David Bowers.

Holders ("slabs") from NGC, PCGS, and CACG.

The Basics of Sorting and Identifying Your Coins

If you have a large group of coins to identify—say, a hundred or more—sort them first by metallic composition, and then by denomination. This will give you an understanding of the size of the collection, and will provide a basic structure for organizing your work and estimating the time it will take to identify and inventory your coins.

Step 1: Sort by color. U.S. coins are one of three basic colors: brown, white, or yellow. These correspond to copper (and bronze), silver, and gold (with some exceptions, noted below).

Copper and bronze coins are bright orange when they're freshly minted. Then they react with oxygen and begin to turn brown. This color change speeds up as the coins react to the oil and acid in our skin, as they pass from hand to hand in circulation.

Silver coins are free of color, and appear white when newly minted. Silver reacts with oxygen, sulfur, and other elements in the environment, and over time silver coins will naturally tarnish with a range of colors from light yellow to steel-blue or even dark gray.

Nickel coins might be mistaken for silver because of their "white" appearance. Nickel does not tarnish as quickly as silver. Modern five-cent coins are made of an alloy of copper and nickel. Modern dimes and quarters minted after 1964, and half dollars minted after 1970, are made of a copper core layered with an alloy of copper-nickel.

Steel coins—in particular, Lincoln cents minted in 1943 to conserve copper during World War II—were coated with a layer of zinc. This composition tarnished easily, so 1943 steel cents are commonly found with spots of rust.

Platinum and palladium coins look like silver—white in appearance. Modern bullion and collector pieces (American Platinum Eagles and American Palladium Eagles) are identified by *PLATINUM* or *Pd* (for *palladium*) on the coin.

Gold coins range in color from a light yellow to a deep orange-gold. Note, however, that *manganese-brass coins* (modern dollar coins, like Presidential and Native American dollars) are made of an alloy that is golden in color but contains no actual gold. This alloy turns brown over time, when exposed to oxygen and the oils and acid in our hands.

Step 2: Sort by denomination. After you've organized your coins by color, further sort them by denomination.

Circulation Coins (Minted for Commerce)

Metal or Alloy	Denominations
copper and bronze	half cents, cents, and two-cent pieces
silver	three-cent pieces (1851–1873), five-cent coins (1943–1945), and half dimes; before 1965: dimes, twenty-cent pieces, quarter dollars, half dollars (also struck in a 40% silver alloy from 1965 to 1970), and dollars
copper-nickel	three-cent pieces (1865–1889) and five-cent coins (except 1943–1945); since 1965: dimes, quarters, and dollars of 1971 to 1999; since 1971: half dollars
steel	cents (1943)
gold	$1, $2.50, $3, $5, $10, and $20
manganese-brass	dollars (since 2000)

Commemorative Coins

These special coins are minted to celebrate a person, place, event, or anniversary. Most U.S. commemorative coins have been issued in silver or gold. *Classic commemoratives* (1892 to 1954) are mostly half dollars, although there was one quarter dollar and a silver dollar, as well as a few gold dollars and $2.50 coins, and large $50 gold coins. *Modern commemoratives* (1982 to date) include many silver dollars, but also silver half dollars and copper-nickel half dollars, in addition to $5 and $10 gold coins.

Bullion Coins

The Mint has produced silver and gold bullion coins (and related limited-edition collector coins) since 1986. Its platinum bullion coins debuted in 1997, and palladium in 2017. These are illustrated in the "Bullion" chapter.

Metal or Alloy	Denominations
silver	quarter dollar (5-ounce America the Beautiful series) and $1 (American Silver Eagle)
gold	$5, $10, $25, and $50 (American Gold Eagle, American Gold Buffalo, First Spouse)
platinum	$10, $25, $50, and $100 (American Platinum Eagle)
palladium	$25 (American Palladium Eagle)

Create an Inventory

Now that you've sorted your coins in a first pass, you can make informed decisions on how to further identify them and then create an inventory.

In a random accumulation of common coins—such as a jug full of Wheat cents (minted 1909 to 1958)—there *might* be a key date or rare variety, but it's unlikely. Often with such a hoard it isn't worth your time and effort to inventory every individual coin. A fair wholesale price for common Wheat cents is about $0.02 to $0.03 per coin, so you can expect a coin dealer to offer about $3.65 per pound, or $1.25 per roll of 50 coins.

On the other hand, sorting every coin in an accumulation can be fun and profitable if you have the time and interest.

Secure the more valuable metals (silver, gold, platinum, and palladium) in particular, keeping them in a safe or a bank box if you have one.

Identify each coin by its design type, using a guide like the *Blue Book* to match the sorted coins to their photographs.

Remember that the *mintmark* can be as important as the *date* on a coin. For example, a 1916-D Mercury dime (struck at the Denver Mint) is much scarcer than a regular 1916 dime (with no mintmark, indicating it was struck at the Philadelphia Mint).

Now, make an inventory of your coins by denomination, date, mintmark, and quantity. Include a column for purchase price (how much the collector paid for each coin, if that information is available) and a column for current value. You can also include columns for design type (e.g., Liberty Seated, Barber, Mercury, Roosevelt, etc.), date acquired, grade, or other information you want to capture.

Microsoft Excel is a useful program for making spreadsheets, but if you prefer pen and paper, a legal pad will suffice.

Figuring Out Grades and Values

After you determine the denomination, design type, date, and mintmark of the coins you want to sell, you can grade them, and from this information estimate their value.

A coin's *grade* is a way of classifying its physical condition—how much wear it has received. Such wear might come from being transported in a bag from the coinage press to a storage vault, or from being circulated hand to hand in everyday business transactions.

When you examine your coins for circulation wear, look for slight changes in color, surface texture, and sharpness of fine details. Signs of handling and abrasion are first seen on the highest parts of a coin's design. They become rounded or flattened, with fine details merging together in small spots. More and more circulation wears away the coin's mint luster (its brilliant shiny surface), starting on the highest areas, then the flat fields, and finally the recessed areas. The high details of the design continue to merge together, the coin's rim smooths away, and finally the entire surface flattens.

A coin's grade is perhaps the single most important factor that affects its relative value. Supply (rarity) and demand are important, too, of course. But those factors being equal, an attractive, higher-grade coin of a particular type and date/mintmark will be worth more than a lower-grade example. Look at the 1901 Morgan silver dollar as an example. In Very Fine condition, a dealer might pay $32 for the coin. In About Uncirculated, its wholesale value jumps to $160. And in MS-63, you can expect to receive $8,500 or more.

Grading Case Study: Morgan Dollars

The following descriptions and enlarged photographs show you examples of grades for Morgan dollars, one of the most popular and widely collected coin types. (A general discussion of grades and grading can be found earlier in this chapter under "Conditions of Coins"; the grade descriptions here are specific to Morgan dollars.) Understanding the level of wear in your coins will help you evaluate the offers you get from coin dealers when the time comes to sell.

MS-65 (Mint State)

MS-65 (Gem Uncirculated)—Only light, scattered contact marks that are not distracting. Strong luster, good eye appeal.

MS-64 (Uncirculated)—A few scattered contact marks. Good eye appeal and attractive luster.

MS-63 (Choice Uncirculated)

MS-63 (Choice Uncirculated)—No trace of wear; full mint luster; few noticeable surface marks.

MS-60 (Uncirculated)—No trace of wear. Full mint luster is present, but may be noticeably marred by scuff marks or bag abrasions.

AU-50 (About Uncirculated)—Slight trace of wear on the bust shoulder and the hair to the left of the forehead, as well as on the eagle's breast and top edges of the wings.

EF-40 (Extremely Fine)—All hair lines are strong, and the ear is bold. The eagle's feathers are all plain, but with slight wear on the breast and wing tips.

VF-20 (Very Fine)

VF-20 (Very Fine)—Two-thirds of the hair lines from the top of Liberty's forehead to the ear are visible. The ear is well defined. The feathers on the eagle's breast are worn.

Option 2: Finding an Expert to Appraise Your Coins
Finding a Reputable Coin Dealer

If you're trying to sell an inherited coin or collection, seek someone whose advice you can trust. This includes finding someone with the right credentials for the material you're selling. For an accumulation or casual collection, described earlier, most local coin shops will serve the purpose of liquidation. **IMPORTANT TIP—Consider bringing a small sample of the coins you think might be the most valuable to multiple dealers for offers.** This often will give you enough information to know who you should be dealing with. If the person you inherited coins from was a serious collector, you should take the same care selling as the collector did assembling the coins in the first place.

Check with the Better Business Bureau to learn whether there are any outstanding complaints with the dealer you're considering working with. Ask the dealer if the company's owners or staff are members in good standing of the Professional Numismatists Guild (PNG, at www.pngdealers.com) and the American Numismatic Association (ANA, at www.money.org), both of which maintain dealer-member listings online. Members of these organizations are required to follow a code of ethics, and both organizations offer a process for resolving complaints if disputes arise. It is also important to check the online reviews of the company you are dealing with—these can be very revealing.

If you live in a small town or city, you should consider having your coins appraised in a larger city nearby as well. Take your sample group for offers to the largest and most well-established dealer in your area of the country. The trip can be well worth the effort.

Getting Your Coins Graded by a Third-Party Grading Company

If you have coins that have been valued above about $500, you should consider having them professionally graded by a third-party grading company such as NGC, PCGS, or CACG. Submitting coins for grading is complicated and should be done by someone with experience. Most coin dealers are members of the grading companies and will assist you with the process. The exact grade of a coin is vital for establishing value, and having the coin graded is usually worth the cost. An important service that most dealers can provide is to prescreen coins for grading submission. Once the coin is graded, it will be much easier to determine the fair wholesale value of the coin you are selling.

DECIDING HOW TO SELL YOUR COINS
Dos and Don'ts When You Sell

A few simple tips, similar to those for selecting a professional to appraise your coins, will help you prepare for when it's time to sell:

- Check the dealer's credentials.
- Identify the types of coins the dealer buys and sells. Many coin shops are just buying locations, and the dealer may lack true expertise. Check the company's online presence as well.
- Call or email to make an appointment to meet with the dealer.
- Be prepared to transport the coins in an inconspicuous briefcase or secure boxes.
- Take your inventory list with you.
- Get offers from two or more dealers.
- Get offers in writing, and itemized if possible.
- For extremely large transactions, you might also consider asking for references, such as from a bank officer of the company in question.
- Don't sell to jewelers, pawn shops, estate attorneys, or others not knowledgeable about coins and their current market values.
- Don't invite strangers into your home to examine coins.

Selling at a Coin Show

Local, state, regional, and national coin shows are good places to buy and sell coins. Coin clubs frequently sponsor smaller, regularly scheduled shows, often over a weekend and with several dozen dealers in attendance. State and regional shows are larger. National shows typically attract more than 500 dealers, and are conducted over the course of several days or a full week, often with educational programs and events.

Most coin shows are free for the public. At a coin show you have the chance to talk with many dealers in a single day or even within an hour or two. If you have specialized or rare coins, a regional or national show can provide more competition than a smaller show might. Dealers who advertise in numismatic newspapers and magazines (such as *Coin World*, the *Numismatist*, *Greysheet*, and *Red Book Quarterly*) attend the larger coin shows. Look at these publications to find dealers who advertise the kinds of coins you have; chances are they also buy those types. You can call ahead or check a dealer's website to see if they'll be at an upcoming show within driving distance of you.

The ANA maintains information on local, state, regional, and national coin shows at its website, www.money.org.

For best results, decide in advance which dealers would be best to approach,
especially if you'll have to travel a long way or you're interested in a narrow specialty.

Selling by Public Auction

In recent years, many important collections of rare coins have been sold at public auction, rather than changing hands privately. If you have rare coins with significant value, selling at a public auction can bring you prices that are higher than wholesale, sometimes even surpassing current retail. Auctions make your coins available to a wide audience of eager collectors. However, be aware that auction firms charge a fee for their services (which can include researching your coins, professionally grading them, photographing them, and marketing them), and this usually is 15% to 25% of the net sale price. These fees are negotiable, and you should get multiple proposals from different auction firms. It is important to note that after fees are considered, the net auction proceeds can sometimes be less than an outright sale to another dealer. Bullion-related numismatic material is usually not suitable for public auctions, as the fees are more than the commission most dealers would charge. Other downsides to auctions include the uncertainty of the market, the fact that a sale might not be scheduled immediately, and the fact that payment can often take 45 days or more. Public auctions are best suited for specialized collections that collectors will aggressively compete for. For some collections, the results can be astounding.

Selling by Mail

Many companies around the country would be interested in buying your coins, but can't make accurate offers without seeing the coins. Shipping a large collection can be very difficult and involves risk. Packages can be lost (common these days), and proper insurance is vital. If you decide to send your coins to a dealer for offers, be sure to work with the dealer carefully and follow their instructions to avoid losses.

FINAL ADVICE

As mentioned earlier in this chapter, you should take time with the coins you have inherited. Many collections were assembled over decades, and selling them properly is a responsibility. Use tools such as the *Blue Book* and other Whitman publications to educate yourself about the coins you inherited. The time will most certainly be worth the effort, and is your way of honoring the person who collected the coins.

Values for the *Blue Book* are derived directly from Greysheet®, the industry-standard in wholesale coin pricing. Learn more and subscribe to access over 1.1 million prices at **greysheet.com**.

POWERED BY
G GREYSHEET

Early American coins are rare in conditions better than those listed and consequently dealers pay much more for them.

BRITISH NEW WORLD ISSUES
Sommer Islands (Bermuda)

This coinage, issued around 1616, was the first struck for England's colonies in the New World. The coins were known as "Hogge Money" or "Hoggies."

The pieces were made of copper lightly silvered, in four denominations: shilling, sixpence, threepence, and twopence, indicated by Roman numerals. The hog is the main device and appears on the obverse side of each. SOMMER ISLANDS is inscribed within beaded circles. The reverse shows a full-rigged galleon with the flag of St. George on each of four masts.

Shilling

	VG-8	F-12	VF-20	EF-40	AU-50
Twopence	$9,750	$14,000	$24,000	$41,000	—
Threepence	—	—	121,500	144,000	—
Sixpence	—	14,000	28,000	46,500	$73,500
Shilling	11,500	24,000	31,500	55,000	171,000

Massachusetts
"New England" Coinage (1652)

In 1652 the General Court of Massachusetts ordered the first metallic currency to be struck in the British Americas, the New England silver threepence, sixpence, and shilling. These coins were made from silver bullion procured principally from the West Indies. Joseph Jenks made the punches for the first coins at his Iron Works in Saugus, Massachusetts, close to Boston where the mint was located. John Hull was appointed mintmaster; his assistant was Robert Sanderson.

NE Shilling (1652)

	F-12	VF-20	EF-40	AU-50	MS-60
NE Threepence *(2 known)*	—	—	—	—	—
NE Sixpence *(8 known)*	—	—	$360,000	—	—
NE Shilling	$55,000	$60,500	97,000	$117,000	$247,500

Willow Tree Coinage (1653–1660)

The simplicity of the design on the N.E. coins invited counterfeiting and clipping of the edges. Therefore, they were soon replaced by the Willow Tree, Oak Tree, and Pine Tree series. The Willow Tree coins were struck from 1653 to 1660, the Oak Trees 1660 to 1667, and the Pine Trees 1667 to 1682. All of them (with the exception of the Oak Tree twopence) bore the date 1652. Many varieties of all of these coins exist. Values shown are for the most common types.

Sixpence

	VG-8	F-12	VF-20	EF-40	AU-50	MS-60
1652 Willow Tree Threepence *(3 known)*	—	—	—	—	$495,000	—
1652 Willow Tree Sixpence *(14 known)*	—	$29,000	$60,000	$108,000	198,000	—
1652 Willow Tree Shilling.	$15,000	28,000	50,500	87,500	112,500	$144,000

Oak Tree Coinage (1660–1667)

Twopence   Threepence

	VG-8	F-12	VF-20	EF-40	AU-50	MS-60	MS-63
1652 Oak Tree Twopence	$1,000	$1,250	$1,500	$2,600	$3,050	$6,750	$11,500
1652 Oak Tree Threepence	1,300	1,850	2,650	5,000	8,500	24,000	39,500
1652 Oak Tree Sixpence	1,150	1,550	2,300	4,300	5,500	15,000	31,500
1652 Oak Tree Shilling.	1,550	1,800	2,100	3,550	5,250	9,500	19,000

Pine Tree Coinage (1667–1682)

The first Pine Tree coins were minted on the same size planchets as the Oak Tree pieces. Subsequent issues of the shilling were narrower and thicker, to conform to the size of English coins.

Shilling, Large Planchet (1667–1674)   Shilling, Small Planchet (1675–1682)

See next page for chart.

	VG-8	F-12	VF-20	EF-40	AU-50	MS-60	MS-63
1652 Pine Tree Threepence	$975	$1,400	$1,750	$3,700	$5,750	$9,500	$26,000
1652 Pine Tree Sixpence	—	1,800	2,100	3,050	3,350	9,500	26,000
1652 Pine Tree Shilling, Large Planchet	1,600	1,750	2,250	4,100	6,250	12,000	26,000
1652 Pine Tree Shilling, Small Planchet	1,300	2,050	2,600	3,550	7,500	12,000	26,000

Maryland
Lord Baltimore Coinage

In 1659, Cecil Calvert, Lord Baltimore and Lord Proprietor of Maryland, had coinage struck in England for use in Maryland. There were four denominations: shilling, sixpence, fourpence (groat) in silver, and copper penny (denarium). The silver coins have the bust of Lord Baltimore on the obverse, and the Baltimore family arms with the denomination in Roman numerals on the reverse.

Fourpence (groat) Lord Baltimore Shilling

	F-12	VF-20	EF-40	AU-50	MS-60
Denarium, copper *(extremely rare)*	—	—	$92,000	—	—
Fourpence	—	$8,500	16,500	$28,000	$60,000
Sixpence	—	6,250	7,500	11,000	32,500
Shilling	$8,000	9,500	12,000	16,500	44,500

New Jersey
St. Patrick or Mark Newby Coinage

Mark Newby, who came to America from Dublin, Ireland, in November 1681, brought copper pieces believed by numismatists to have been struck in England circa 1663 to 1672. These are called St. Patrick coppers. The coin received wide circulation in the New Jersey Province, having been authorized to pass as legal tender by the General Assembly in May 1682. The smaller piece, known as a farthing, was never specifically authorized for circulation in the colonies.

St. Patrick Farthing

	F-12	VF-20	EF-40	AU-50
St. Patrick "Farthing"	$330	$395	$600	$925
St. Patrick "Halfpenny"	500	925	2,600	7,000

COINAGE AUTHORIZED BY BRITISH ROYAL PATENT
American Plantations Tokens

These pieces struck in nearly pure tin were the first royally authorized coinage for the British colonies in America. They were made under a franchise granted in 1688 to Richard Holt. Restrikes were made circa 1828 from original dies.

	VF-20	EF-40	AU-50	MS-60	MS-63
(1688) James II Plantation Token Farthing..................					
1/24 Part Real....................................	$460	$1,050	$1,400	$1,850	$4,650
1/24 Part Real, Restrike...........................	—	435	500	700	1,500

Coinage of William Wood
Rosa Americana Coins

William Wood, an Englishman, obtained a patent from King George I to make coins for Ireland and the American colonies. The Rosa Americana pieces were issued in three denominations—halfpenny, penny, and twopence—and were intended for use in America.

Penny

	VG-8	F-12	VF-20	EF-40	AU-50	MS-60
(No Date) Twopence, Motto in Ribbon	—	$330	$415	$600	$725	$1,150
1722 Halfpenny, DEI GRATIA REX UTILE DULCI ...	$135	200	275	425	550	1,650
1722 Penny............................	110	180	255	330	500	1,100
1722 Twopence........................	160	240	320	440	550	1,300

Halfpenny

	VG-8	F-12	VF-20	EF-40	AU-50	MS-60
1723 Halfpenny........................	$160	$215	$315	$485	$600	$1,400

Entry continued on next page.

Twopence

	VG-8	F-12	VF-20	EF-40	AU-50	MS-60
1723 Penny...........................	$90	$130	$215	$375	$460	$775
1723 Twopence.......................	125	160	255	500	750	1,000

Wood's Hibernia Coinage

The type intended for Ireland had a seated figure with a harp on the reverse side and the word HIBERNIA. Denominations struck were the halfpenny and the farthing with dates 1722, 1723, and 1724. Although these have no association with the Americas, because of the connection with William Wood many American collectors desire to obtain them.

1722, Hibernia
Halfpenny

First Type

Second Type

	VG-8	F-12	VF-20	EF-40	AU-50	MS-60	MS-63
1722 Farthing, First Type.............	—	—	$2,050	$4,450	—	—	$14,000
1722 Halfpenny, First or Second Type.....	$70	$90	130	190	$225	$460	1,000

1723, Hibernia Farthing

1724, Hibernia Halfpenny

	VG-8	F-12	VF-20	EF-40	AU-50	MS-60	MS-63
1723 Farthing	$70	$85	$105	$150	$180	$330	$440
1723 Halfpenny......................	55	65	110	150	170	220	370
1724 Farthing	—	160	215	315	825	2,400	4,650
1724 Halfpenny......................	70	80	110	180	265	550	1,100

Virginia Halfpennies

In 1773, coinage of a copper halfpenny was authorized for Virginia by the British Crown. The style is similar to the regular English coinage. These pieces did not arrive in Virginia until 1775, but after then they did circulate on a limited basis. Most examples known today are Uncirculated, by virtue of a hoard of several thousand pieces that came to light in the 19th century and was distributed in numismatic channels.

	VF-20	EF-40	AU-50	MS-60	MS-63	MS-65
1773 Halfpenny	$145	$265	$320	$575	$825	$1,500

EARLY AMERICAN AND RELATED TOKENS

Elephant Tokens

London Elephant Tokens

The London Elephant tokens were struck circa 1672 to 1694. Although they were undated, two examples are known to have been struck over 1672 British halfpennies. Most are struck in copper, but one is made of brass. The legend on this piece, GOD PRESERVE LONDON, is probably just a general plea for divine aid and not a specific reference to the outbreak of plague in 1665 or the great fire of 1666.

These pieces were not struck for the colonies, and probably did not circulate in America, although a few may have been carried there by colonists. They are associated with the 1694 Carolina and New England Elephant tokens, through a shared obverse die.

	VG-8	F-12	VF-20	EF-40	AU-50	MS-60
(1694) Halfpenny, GOD PRESERVE LONDON, Thick or Thin Planchet	$345	$415	$650	$925	$1,300	$2,550

Carolina Elephant Tokens

Although no law is known authorizing coinage for Carolina, very interesting pieces known as Elephant tokens were made with the date 1694. These copper tokens were of halfpenny denomination. The reverse reads GOD PRESERVE CAROLINA AND THE LORDS PROPRIETERS 1694.

The Carolina pieces were probably struck in England and perhaps intended as advertising to heighten interest in the Carolina Plantation.

	F-12	VF-20	EF-40	AU-50	MS-60
1694 CAROLINA	$17,000	$20,500	$24,000	$28,000	$37,000

New England Elephant Tokens

Like the Carolina Tokens, the New England Elephant tokens were believed to have been struck in England as promotional pieces to increase interest in the American colonies.

	VG-8	F-12
1694 NEW ENGLAND	$77,500	$99,000

New Yorke in America Token

Little is known about the origin of this token. The design of a heraldic eagle on a regulated staff with oak leaf finials is identical to the crest found on the arms of William Lovelace, governor of New York, 1668 to 1673. It seems likely that this piece is a token farthing struck by Lovelace for use in New York.

	F-12	VF-20	EF-40	AU-50
(Undated), brass or copper	$7,500	$14,000	$33,500	$42,000
(Undated), pewter	—	—	—	—

Gloucester Tokens

This token appears to have been a private coinage by a merchant of Gloucester (county), Virginia. The only specimens known are struck in brass. The exact origin and use of these pieces are unknown.

	F-12
1714 Shilling, brass *(2 known)*	$83,000

Higley or Granby Coppers

The Higley coppers were private issues. All the pieces were made of pure copper. There were seven obverse and four reverse dies. The first issue, in 1737, bore the legend THE VALUE OF THREEPENCE. After a time the quantity exceeded the local demand, and a protest arose against the stated value of the piece. The inscription was changed to VALUE ME AS YOU PLEASE.

	F-12	VF-20	VF-30	EF-40
1737, THE VALVE OF THREE PENCE, CONNECTICVT, 3 Hammers	$60,500	$77,500	$99,000	—
1737, THE VALVE OF THREE PENCE, I AM GOOD COPPER, 3 Hammers......	—	—	—	—
1737, VALUE ME AS YOU PLEASE, I AM GOOD COPPER, 3 Hammers	46,500	69,000	94,500	$153,000
(1737), VALUE ME AS YOU PLEASE, J CUT MY WAY THROUGH, Broad Axe ...	46,500	69,000	94,500	153,000
1739, VALUE ME AS YOU PLEASE, J CUT MY WAY THROUGH, Broad Axe	—	60,500	—	—

Hibernia–Voce Populi Coins

These coins, struck in the year 1760, were made in Dublin. Although these have no connection with America, they have been listed in numismatic publications in the United States for a long time and are collected by tradition.

Farthing (1760)   **Halfpenny (1760)**

	F-12	VF-20	EF-40	AU-50	MS-60	MS-63
1760 Farthing	$700	$925	$1,150	$1,500	$2,800	$4,650
1760 Halfpenny.......................	90	170	330	415	725	2,250

Pitt Tokens

British politician William Pitt is the subject of these pieces, probably intended as commemorative medalets. He was a friend to the interests of America. The so-called halfpenny served as currency in England during a shortage of regular coinage.

	F-12	VF-20	EF-40	AU-50	MS-60
1766 Farthing	$4,650	$8,000	$17,000	$24,000	—
1766 Halfpenny	460	725	975	1,550	$4,100

Rhode Island Ship Medals

Although this medal has a Dutch inscription, the spelling and design indicate an English or Anglo-American origin. It is believed that this token was struck in England circa 1779 for the Dutch market. Specimens are known in brass and pewter. As with many colonial issues, modern copies exist.

1778–1779, Rhode Island Ship Medal

Values shown are for brass pieces. Those struck in pewter are rare and valued higher.

	VF-20	EF-40	AU-50	MS-60
Rhode Island Ship Medal	$975	$1,450	$1,850	$3,550

John Chalmers Issues

John Chalmers, a silversmith, struck a series of silver tokens at Annapolis in 1783. Certain of the dies were by Thomas Sparrow, who also engraved bank-note plates. As most examples show wear today, these pieces seem to have served well in commerce.

	F-12	VF-20	EF-40	AU-50
1783 Threepence	$4,200	$6,250	$10,500	$12,000

	VG-8	F-12	VF-20	EF-40	AU-50
1783 Sixpence	$2,800	$3,700	$6,250	$23,500	—
1783 Shilling	825	2,050	2,800	7,000	$9,500

FRENCH NEW WORLD ISSUES

None of the coins of the French regime is strictly American. They were all general issues for the French colonies of the New World. The copper of 1717 to 1722 was authorized by edicts of 1716 and 1721 for use in New France, Louisiana, and the French West Indies.

Copper Sou or Nine Deniers

	VG	F	VF	EF
1721-B (Rouen)	$275	$550	$1,800	$4,000
1721-H (La Rochelle)	60	125	450	1,350
1722-H	60	125	450	1,350

French Colonies in General

Coined for use in the French colonies, these circulated only unofficially in Louisiana, along with other foreign coins and tokens. Most were counterstamped RF (République Française) for use in the West Indies. The mintmark A signifies the Paris Mint.

	VG	VF	EF	AU
1767 French Colonies, Sou	$55	$125	$375	$1,000
1767 French Colonies, Sou, counterstamped RF	50	100	165	350

CONTINENTAL CURRENCY PIECES

The Continental Currency pieces may have been experimental coins or patterns, possibly proposed as a paper-money substitute, or even commemorative medals. The exact nature of their monetary role, if any, is uncertain. They may have been struck in Philadelphia from dies

engraved by Elisha Gallaudet, or even made in Europe many years after 1776. As with many early pieces, numerous replicas exist.

	F-12	VF-20	EF-40	AU-50	MS-60	MS-63
1776, CURENCY, pewter *(2 varieties)*	$16,500	$19,500	$23,500	$28,000	$42,000	$86,500
1776, CURENCY, silver *(2 known)*	—	—	1,305,000	—	—	—
1776, CURRENCY, pewter	16,000	18,500	22,000	25,500	41,000	83,000
1776, CURRENCY, EG FECIT, pewter	16,500	19,500	23,500	28,000	42,000	86,500

SPECULATIVE ISSUES, TOKENS, AND PATTERNS

Nova Constellatio Coppers

The Nova Constellatio pieces were struck supposedly by order of Gouverneur Morris. Evidence indicates that they were all struck in Birmingham, England, and imported for American circulation as a private business venture.

1783, CONSTELLATIO, Pointed Rays

1783, CONSTELLATIO, Blunt Rays

1785, CONSTELLATIO, Blunt Rays

1785, CONSTELLATIO, Pointed Rays

	F-12	VF-20	EF-40	AU-50	MS-60	MS-63
1783, CONSTELLATIO, Pointed Rays	$180	$275	$625	$800	—	$3,900
1785, CONSTELATIO, Blunt Rays.	245	415	700	1,200	—	7,000
1785, CONSTELLATIO, Pointed Rays	225	415	700	925	$1,500	2,900
1783, CONSTELATIO, Blunt Rays.	225	415	800	1,600	3,700	8,500

Immune Columbia Pieces

Nearly all of these are very rare. Many if not most seem to be unofficial, including pieces produced at the private Machin's Mills mint in Newburgh, New York.

**1785, Copper,
Star Reverse**

**1785, George III
Obverse**

	F-12	VF-20	EF-40	AU-50	MS-60
1785, Copper, Stars Reverse.	—	—	$23,500	$31,500	$69,000
1785, GEORGE III Obverse.	$13,000	$15,500	33,500	42,000	—

1787, IMMUNIS COLUMBIA, Eagle Reverse

	F-12	VF-20	EF-40	AU-50	MS-60
1785, VERMON AUCTORI Obverse, IMMUNE COLUMBIA	$7,500	$22,500	—	—	—
1787, IMMUNIS COLUMBIA, Eagle Reverse.	1,150	2,050	$2,700	$4,650	$14,000

Confederatio Coppers

The Confederatio and associated coppers have patriotic motifs and were made in small quantities for circulation. The die with the CONFEDERATIO legend was also combined with other designs such as a bust of George Washington, Libertas et Justitia of 1785, Immunis Columbia of 1786, the New York "Excelsiors," Inimica Tyrannis Americana, and others. In all there were 12 dies struck in 13 combinations. There are two types of the Confederatio reverse. In one instance the stars are contained in a small circle; in the other, larger stars are in a larger circle.

Typical Obverse	Small Circle Reverse		Large Circle Reverse	

	VF-20	VF-30	EF-40	EF-45	AU-50
1785, Stars in Small Circle, various obverses.............	$24,000	$26,000	$37,000	$44,500	$55,000
1785, Stars in Large Circle, various obverses.............	37,000	55,000	83,000	88,500	99,000

Speculative Patterns

1786, IMMUNIS COLUMBIA	Eagle Reverse	Shield Reverse

	VF	EF
1786, IMMUNIS COLUMBIA, Eagle Reverse	$35,000	$50,000
1786, IMMUNIS COLUMBIA, Shield Reverse......................................	27,500	35,000
(No date) (1786) Washington Obverse, Shield Reverse.............................	60,000	
1786, Eagle Obverse, Shield Reverse..	40,000	
1786, Washington Obverse, Eagle Reverse *(2 known)*	—	

COINAGE OF THE STATES AND VERMONT
Vermont

Reuben Harmon Jr. was granted permission to coin copper pieces for the Republic of Vermont beginning July 1, 1785. (Vermont would not become a state until 1791.) The franchise was extended for eight years in 1786, but in 1787 production was shifted to Machin's Mills, Newburgh, New York, in which Harmon had a proprietary interest. Although the Vermont coins were legally issued there, most other products of Machin's Mills were counterfeits, some dies for which were combined with Vermont pieces, creating several illogical pieces below, including the 1785 Immune Columbia and the 1788 Georgivs III Rex.

1785, IMMUNE COLUMBIA   **1785–1786, Plow Type**

1786, Baby Head

	VG-8	F-12	VF-20	EF-40	AU-50
1785, IMMUNE COLUMBIA	$6,250	$14,000	$23,500	$46,500	—
1785, VERMONTS	415	725	1,450	2,300	$3,700
1786, VERMONTENSIUM	225	460	1,100	2,050	3,250
1786, Baby Head	—	925	1,850	5,750	11,500

1786–1787, Bust Left   **1787, BRITANNIA**

1787, Bust Right

	VG-8	F-12	VF-20	EF-40	AU-50
1786, Bust Left	$460	$825	$1,300	$2,300	—
1787, Bust Left	13,000	17,000	22,500	—	—
1787, BRITANNIA	—	145	225	675	$1,150
1787, Bust Right *(several varieties)*	180	225	435	1,350	2,050

1788, Bust Right   **1788, GEORGIVS III REX**

See next page for chart.

	VG-8	F-12	VF-20	EF-40	AU-50
1788, Bust Right *(several varieties)*	$170	$200	$415	$1,050	$1,650
1788, GEORGIVS III REX...........................	370	700	1,250	2,600	—

Note: This piece should not be confused with the common British halfpence with similar design and reverse legend BRITANNIA.

New Hampshire

New Hampshire was the first of the states to consider the subject of coinage following the Declaration of Independence.

William Moulton was empowered to make a limited quantity of coins of pure copper, authorized by the State House of Representatives in 1776.

	G-6	VG-8	VG-10
1776 New Hampshire Copper...	$55,000	$60,000	$66,000

Massachusetts

The coinage of Massachusetts copper cents and half cents in 1787 and 1788 was under the direction of Joshua Witherle. These were the first coins bearing the denomination *cent* as later established by Congress. Many varieties exist, the most valuable being the cent with arrows in the eagle's right talon (on the left side of the coin).

1787 Half Cent   **1787 Cent**

1788 Half Cent   **1788 Cent**

	VG-8	F-12	VF-20	EF-40	AU-50	MS-60
1787 Half Cent	$255	$330	$405	$750	$1,050	$1,650
1787 Cent, Arrows in Right Talon............	12,000	19,000	30,000	40,000	78,000	—
1787 Cent, Arrows in Left Talon *(illustrated)*....	245	275	370	925	1,300	3,000
1788 Half Cent	205	300	370	700	975	1,850
1788 Cent.............................	160	255	370	725	1,400	2,800

Connecticut

Authority for establishing a mint near New Haven was granted by the state to Samuel Bishop, Joseph Hopkins, James Hillhouse, and John Goodrich in 1785. Today, well over 300 different die varieties are known of Connecticut coppers dated from 1785 to 1788. These pieces circulated widely and effectively; most are seen with significant evidence of circulation.

1785, Bust
Facing Right

1785, Bust
Facing Left

1786–1787, Mailed
Bust Facing Right

1786–1787, Mailed
Bust Facing Left

1787, Draped
Bust Facing Left

1788, Mailed
Bust Facing Right

1788, Mailed
Bust Facing Left

1788, Draped
Bust Facing Left

See next page for chart.

	VG-8	F-12	VF-20	EF-40	AU-50	MS-60	MS-63
1785, Bust Facing Left.	$330	$525	$825	$3,700	$6,500	—	—
1785, Bust Facing Right	110	160	240	525	925	$2,300	$8,500
1786, Mailed Bust Facing Right. . . .	110	160	240	525	925	—	—
1786, Mailed Bust Facing Left.	90	180	260	700	875	2,800	5,750
1787, Mailed Bust Facing Right. . . .	275	370	550	1,200	2,800	7,500	—
1787, Mailed Bust Facing Left.	110	160	210	320	650	2,100	—
1787, Draped Bust Facing Left	70	105	180	460	600	1,500	4,650
1788, Mailed Bust Facing Right. . . .	225	255	275	500	925	5,750	24,000
1788, Mailed Bust Facing Left.	90	135	275	460	1,200	2,800	5,750
1788, Draped Bust Facing Left	110	180	255	330	925	2,700	8,500

New York and Related Issues
Brasher Doubloons

Perhaps the most famous pieces coined before the establishment of the U.S. Mint at Philadelphia were those produced by a well-known goldsmith and jeweler, Ephraim Brasher of New York.

Brasher produced a gold piece weighing about 408 grains, approximately equal in value to a Spanish doubloon (about $15.00 in New York currency).

The punch-mark EB appears in either of two positions as illustrated. This mark is found on some foreign gold coins as well, and probably was so used by Brasher as evidence of his testing of their value. Many modern forgeries exist.

	AU-50	AU-55	MS-63	MS-65
1787 New York doubloon, gold, E.B on Breast	$5,490,000	—	—	—
1787 New York doubloon, gold, E.B on Wing.	—	$2,250,000	$3,600,000	$8,415,000

New York Copper Coinage

No coinage was authorized by the State of New York following the Revolutionary War, although several propositions were considered. The only coinage laws passed were those regulating coins already in use. Private mints struck several unauthorized coppers.

	VG-8	F-12	VF-20	EF-40	AU-50	AU-55
1786, NON VI VIRTUTE VICI	$9,000	$11,500	$13,000	$19,000	$24,000	$37,000

	F-12	VF-20	EF-40	AU-50	AU-55
1787 EXCELSIOR, Eagle on Globe Facing Right	$8,500	$11,500	$24,000	$42,000	—
1787 EXCELSIOR, Eagle on Globe Facing Left	8,000	11,500	19,000	24,000	$37,000

1787, George Clinton and New York Arms

1787, Indian and New York Arms

1787, Indian and Eagle on Globe

	VG-8	F-12	VF-20	EF-40	AU-50
1787, George Clinton.............................	$23,500	$55,000	$77,500	$157,500	—
1787, Indian and New York Arms.....................	21,500	28,000	31,500	39,000	$44,500
1787, Indian and Eagle on Globe.....................	—	11,500	15,000	51,500	69,000

Georgivs/Britannia
"Machin's Mills" Copper Halfpennies Made in America

During the era of American state coinage, James F. Atlee and other coiners minted unauthorized, lightweight, imitation British halfpence. These American-made false coins have the same devices, legends, and, in some cases, dates as genuine regal halfpence, but contain less copper. Overall quality of these pieces is similar to that of British-made imitations, but details are more often poorly rendered or missing. Identification of American-made imitations has been confirmed by identifying punch marks and matching them to those of known engravers.

Dates used on these pieces were often evasive, and are as follows: 1771, 1772, and 1774 through 1776 for the first group; 1747 and 1787 for the second group; and 1776, 1778, 1787, and 1788 for the third group. Pieces generally attributed to Atlee can be identified by a single outline in the crosses (British Union) of Britannia's shield and large triangular dentils along the coin circumference. The more-valuable American-made pieces are not to be confused with the similar English-made George III counterfeits (some of which have identical dates), or with genuine British halfpence dated 1770 to 1775.

Group I coins dated 1771, 1772, and 1774 through 1776 have distinctive bold designs but lack the fine details of the original coins. Planchets are generally of high quality. Group II coins dated 1747 and 1787 are generally poorly made. The 1 in the date is not J-shaped, and the dentils are of various sizes. There are no outlines to the stripes in the shield. Group III coins dated 1776, 1778, 1787, and 1788, struck at Machin's Mills in Newberg, New York, are similar to coins of Group II, with their triangular-shaped dentils. Most have wide dates and berries in the wreath.

	VG-8	F-12	VF-20	EF-40	AU-50	MS-60
1747, GEORGIVS II, Group II.............	$345	$435	$825	$3,500	$5,750	—
1771, GEORGIVS III, Group I.............	215	370	550	1,500	—	—
1772, GEORGIVS III, Group I.............	575	825	1,750	4,200	—	—
1772, GEORGIUS III, Group I.............	—	2,800	—	—	—	—
1774, GEORGIVS III, Group I.............	240	350	460	2,550	—	—
1774, GEORGIVS III, Group I.............	315	—	550	—	—	—
1775, GEORGIVS III, Group I.............	215	275	415	1,200	—	—
1776, GEORCIVS III, Group III, Small Date......	5,500	6,750	9,000	15,000	—	—
1778, GEORGIVS III, Group III.............	145	200	240	700	1,400	$5,250
1784, GEORGIVS III	575	825	1,850	3,350	—	—
1787, GEORGIVS III, Group II and III.........	110	125	170	415	650	2,250
1788, GEORGIVS III, Group III.............	135	260	370	850	1,150	3,700

Note: Values shown are what coin dealers pay for the most common varieties in each category. Rare pieces can be worth significantly more. Also see related George III combinations under Connecticut, Vermont, and New York.

Nova Eborac Coinage for New York

1787, NOVA EBORAC Reverse,	1787, NOVA EBORAC Reverse,
Seated Figure Facing Right	Seated Figure Facing Left

	G-4	VG-8	F-12	VF-20	EF-40	AU-50
1787, NOVA EBORAC, Seated Figure Facing Right ...	$110	$145	$240	$370	$725	$1,300
1787, NOVA EBORAC, Seated Figure Facing Left	160	200	240	350	650	775

New Jersey

On June 1, 1786, the New Jersey General Assembly granted to Thomas Goadsby, Albion Cox, and Walter Mould authority to coin some three million coppers no later than June 1788, on condition that they delivered to the treasurer of the state "one-tenth part of the full sum they shall strike and coin," in quarterly installments. These coppers were to pass current at 15 to the shilling. Produced in significant quantities, these coins are often seen in the market today and are widely collectible, although certain varieties can be rare and especially valuable.

Narrow Shield   **Wide Shield**

	G-4	VG-8	F-12	VF-20	EF-40	AU-50
1786, Narrow Shield.	$110	$160	$240	$460	$775	$1,200
1786, Wide Shield.	100	120	260	460	1,000	1,500

Small Planchet

	G-4	VG-8	F-12	VF-20	EF-40	AU-50
1787, Horse's Head Facing Right	$110	$135	$180	$320	$725	$1,700

Fox Before Legend

	G-4	VG-8	F-12	VF-20	EF-40	AU-50
1788, Horse's Head Facing Right	$110	$135	$180	$320	$725	$1,700
1788, Similar, Fox in Legend.	200	295	460	1,300	3,000	4,000
1788, Horse's Head Facing Left	370	500	925	2,400	9,500	22,500

PRIVATE TOKENS AFTER CONFEDERATION
North American Tokens

This piece was struck in Dublin, Ireland. The obverse shows the seated figure of Hibernia facing left. Although dated 1781, it is believed to have been struck early in the next century.

	VG-8	F-12	VF-20	EF-40	AU-50
1781, Copper or Brass	$75	$110	$125	$200	$500

Bar Coppers

The Bar copper is undated and of uncertain origin. It has 13 parallel and unconnected bars on one side. On the other side is the large roman-letter USA monogram. The design was supposedly copied from a Continental Army uniform button.

	F-15	VF-20	EF-40	AU-50	MS-60
(Undated) (Circa 1785) Bar Copper	$4,550	$5,250	$7,000	$8,500	$17,000

Auctori Plebis Tokens

This token is sometimes included with the coins of Connecticut as it greatly resembles issues of that state. It was struck in England by an unknown maker.

	VG-8	F-12	VF-20	EF-40	AU-50	MS-60
1787, AUCTORI PLEBIS	$105	$145	$215	$315	$405	$2,400

Mott Store Cards

This 19th century store card has long been considered an early token because of its date (1789). Most scholars believe it was most likely produced circa 1830 as a commemorative of the founding of the Mott Company, and probably served as a business card.

	F-12	VF-20	EF-40	AU-50	MS-60	MS-63
"1789," Mott Token	$135	$160	$225	$305	$500	$725

Standish Barry Threepence

Standish Barry, a Baltimore silversmith, circulated a silver threepence in 1790. The tokens were believed to have been an advertising venture at a time when small change was scarce.

	F-12	VF-20	EF-40	EF-45	AU-50
1790 Threepence	$9,750	$11,500	$22,500	$25,500	$30,000

Kentucky Tokens

These tokens were struck in England about 1795. Each star in the triangle represents a state, identified by its initial letter. These pieces are usually called *Kentucky cents* because the letter K (for Kentucky) happens to be at the top. In the 19th century these were often called *triangle tokens,* from the arrangement of the stars. Values are for the normal issue with plain edge; lettered-edge varieties exist and are scarcer.

	VF-20	EF-40	AU-50	MS-60	MS-63
(1792–1794), Plain Edge	$135	$205	$310	$415	$600

Franklin Press Tokens

This piece is an English tradesman's token, but, being associated with Benjamin Franklin, has accordingly been included in American collections.

	VF-20	EF-40	AU-50	MS-60	MS-63
1794, Franklin Press Token	$240	$295	$370	$575	$925

Talbot, Allum & Lee Cents

Talbot, Allum & Lee, engaged in the India trade and located in New York, placed a large quantity of English-made coppers in circulation during 1794 and 1795. ONE CENT appears on the 1794 issue and on the edge of the 1795 issue.

1794 Cent,
With NEW YORK

1795 Cent

	VG-8	F-12	VF-20	EF-40	AU-50	MS-60
1794 Cent, With NEW YORK	$90	$180	$205	$295	$350	$625
1794 Cent, Without NEW YORK	—	1,150	1,500	2,250	4,400	—
1795 Cent.................................	—	—	—	215	260	460

WASHINGTON PORTRAIT PIECES

An interesting series of coins and tokens dated from 1783 to 1795 bear the portrait of George Washington. The likenesses in most instances were faithfully reproduced and were designed to honor Washington. Many of these pieces were of English origin and made later than the dates indicate.

1783,
Military Bust

1783,
Draped Bust

	F-12	VF-20	EF-40	AU-50	MS-60
1783, Military Bust	$115	$160	$315	$370	$875
1783, Draped Bust	125	150	330	370	650

1783, UNITY STATES

	VG-8	F-12	VF-20	EF-40	AU-50	MS-60
1783, UNITY STATES	$95	$125	$155	$240	$305	$725

Undated Double-Head Cent

	VG-8	F-12	VF-20	EF-40	AU-50	MS-60
(Undated) Double-Head Cent	$110	$125	$180	$275	$370	$1,000

Obverse — Large Eagle Reverse — Small Eagle Reverse

	F-12	VF-20	EF-40	AU-50	MS-60
1791 Cent, Large Eagle (Date on Obverse)	$370	$550	$800	$1,050	$1,500
1791 Cent, Small Eagle (Date on Reverse)	300	370	650	925	1,500

	F-12	VF-20	EF-40	AU-50
1791 Liverpool Halfpenny, Lettered Edge	$875	$975	$1,550	$2,250

	VF-20	EF-40	AU-50
1792, Eagle With Stars, Copper	$8,500	$14,000	$20,500
1792, Eagle With Stars, Silver	—	157,500	—
1792, Eagle With Stars, Gold *(unique)*	—	1,575,000	—

**(1792) Undated Cent,
WASHINGTON BORN VIRGINIA**

**1792 Cent,
WASHINGTON PRESIDENT**

	VF-20	EF-40	AU-50
(1792) Cent, WASHINGTON BORN VIRGINIA, Copper	$2,400	$5,000	$6,000
1792, WASHINGTON PRESIDENT, Plain Edge	8,500	14,000	20,500

1792 Getz Pattern

1793 Ship Halfpenny

1795 Halfpenny, Grate Token

	VG-8	F-12	VF-20	EF-40	AU-50	MS-60
1792, Getz Pattern, Copper	$8,500	$9,750	$11,500	$20,500	$28,000	$78,000
1793 Ship Halfpenny, Lettered Edge	180	240	275	500	625	1,650
1795, Grate Token, Lettered Edge	—	255	305	415	525	700
1795, Grate Token, Reeded Edge	95	115	170	275	300	370

	F-12	VF-20	EF-40	AU-50	MS-60
1795 LIBERTY AND SECURITY Halfpenny, Plain Edge	$180	$240	$345	$460	—
1795 LIBERTY AND SECURITY Halfpenny, Lettered Edge	190	215	285	460	$1,250
(1795), LIBERTY AND SECURITY Penny	215	300	415	550	900

	VG-8	F-12	VF-20	EF-40	AU-50
(1795), NORTH WALES Halfpenny	$160	$170	$200	$350	$825

	F-12	VF-20	EF-40	AU-50	MS-60
SUCCESS Medal, Large, Plain or Reeded Edge	$225	$345	$925	$1,100	$1,600
SUCCESS Medal, Small, Plain or Reeded Edge	260	330	825	1,000	1,400

FUGIO CENTS

The first coins issued by authority of the United States were the 1787 "Fugio" coppers. The legends have been credited to Benjamin Franklin by many, and the coins, as a consequence, have been referred to as *Franklin cents.*

| | **1787, With Pointed Rays** | | **1787, With Club Rays** | | | |

	F-12	VF-20	EF-40	AU-50	MS-60	MS-63
Pointed Rays, STATES UNITED at Side of Circle						
(illustrated)	$575	$875	$1,400	$1,850	$2,300	$3,050
Pointed Rays, UNITED STATES at Side of Circle	650	1,050	1,600	2,050	2,450	3,050
Club Rays, Rounded Ends	675	1,150	1,850	3,850	7,000	—

The half cent was authorized to be coined April 2, 1792. Originally the weight was to have been 132 grains, but this was changed to 104 grains by the Act of January 14, 1793, before coinage commenced. The weight was again changed to 84 grains January 26, 1796, by presidential proclamation in conformity with the Act of March 3, 1795. Coinage was discontinued by the Act of February 21, 1857. All were coined at the Philadelphia Mint.

LIBERTY CAP (1793–1797)

AG-3 About Good: Clear enough to identify.
G-4 Good: Outline of bust of Liberty clear, no details. Date readable. Reverse lettering incomplete.
VG-8 Very Good: Some hair details. Reverse lettering complete.
F-12 Fine: Most of hair detail visible. Leaves worn, but all visible.
VF-20 Very Fine: Hair near ear and forehead worn, other areas distinct. Some details in leaves visible.
EF-40 Extremely Fine: Light wear on highest parts of head and wreath.
AU-50 About Uncirculated: Only a trace of wear on Liberty's face.

Head Facing Left (1793)

	Mintage	AG-3	G-4	VG-8	F-12	VF-20	EF-40	AU-50
1793 35,334		$2,300	$3,700	$4,650	$6,750	$11,000	$15,500	$21,500

Head Facing Right (1794–1797)

Pole to Cap   Punctuated Date   No Pole to Cap

	Mintage	AG-3	G-4	VG-8	F-12	VF-20	EF-40	AU-50
1794 81,600		$295	$450	$875	$1,300	$2,000	$4,350	$8,000
1795, All kinds. 139,690								
1795, Lettered Edge, With Pole		305	440	875	1,300	2,050	5,500	11,000
1795, Lettered Edge, Punctuated Date		330	495	1,050	1,450	2,300	6,250	12,000
1795, Plain Edge, Punctuated Date . . .		300	430	775	1,350	2,000	4,350	7,500
1795, Plain Edge, No Pole		275	405	725	1,150	1,750	3,900	6,000
1796, With Pole 5,090		11,000	15,500	23,500	29,000	37,000	55,000	87,500
1796, No Pole 1,390		28,000	42,000	54,000	87,500	135,000	189,000	234,000

1797, 1 Above 1, Plain Edge   **1797, Plain Edge**

	Mintage	AG-3	G-4	VG-8	F-12	VF-20	EF-40	AU-50
1797, All kinds 127,840								
1797, 1 Above 1, Plain Edge		$275	$405	$725	$1,150	$1,750	$3,900	$4,950
1797, Plain Edge		350	485	1,100	1,500	2,050	4,650	13,000
1797, Lettered Edge		1,100	1,850	3,250	6,500	9,500	22,500	46,500
1797, Gripped Edge		60,000	83,000	117,000	—	—	—	—

DRAPED BUST (1800–1808)

AG-3 About Good: Clear enough to identify.
G-4 Good: Outline of bust of Liberty clear, few details, date readable. Reverse lettering worn and incomplete.
VG-8 Very Good: Some drapery visible. Date and legends complete.
F-12 Fine: Shoulder drapery and hair over brow worn smooth.
VF-20 Very Fine: Only slight wear in previously mentioned areas. Slight wear on reverse.
EF-40 Extremely Fine: Light wear on highest parts of head and wreath.
AU-50 About Uncirculated: Wear slight on hair above forehead.

1st Reverse   **2nd Reverse**

	Mintage	AG-3	G-4	VG-8	F-12	VF-20	EF-40	AU-50
1800 202,908		$60	$80	$100	$145	$240	$625	$1,050
1802, 2 Over 0 20,266		650	975	1,500	3,250	6,750	15,500	27,000
1803 92,000		60	85	115	165	275	725	1,550

Plain 4   **Crosslet 4**   **Stems to Wreath**   **Stemless Wreath**

	Mintage	AG-3	G-4	VG-8	F-12	VF-20	EF-40	AU-50
1804, All kinds 1,055,312								
1804, Plain 4, Stems to Wreath		$80	$135	$225	$370	$500	$1,200	$2,300
1804, Plain 4, Stemless Wreath		43	70	80	105	140	280	460
1804, Crosslet 4, Stemless Wreath . . .		55	75	95	125	170	295	525
1804, Crosslet 4, Stems to Wreath . . .		43	80	90	125	180	385	725

| 1804, "Spiked Chin" | | Small 5 | | Large 5 | | | |

	Mintage	AG-3	G-4	VG-8	F-12	VF-20	EF-40	AU-50
1804, "Spiked Chin" ....*		$47	$85	$110	$145	$215	$480	$800
1805, All kinds............. 814,464								
1805, Medium 5, Stemless Wreath ...		60	70	90	145	200	425	875
1805, Small 5, Stems to Wreath		460	725	1,250	2,150	5,500	12,500	26,000
1805, Large 5, Stems to Wreath		47	80	95	145	260	405	725

* Included in "1804, All kinds" mintage (previous page).

| Small 6 | | Large 6 | | 1808, 8 Over 7 | | Normal Date | |

	Mintage	AG-3	G-4	VG-8	F-12	VF-20	EF-40	AU-50
1806, All kinds............. 356,000								
1806, Small 6, Stems to Wreath		$80	$160	$320	$600	$975	$2,000	$3,250
1806, Small 6, Stemless Wreath		43	70	80	105	140	280	440
1806, Large 6, Stems to Wreath		43	70	80	105	140	280	440
1807.................... 476,000		47	80	95	120	180	405	875
1808, Normal Date 400,000		60	85	110	145	205	550	1,500
1808, 8 Over 7 ....*		115	180	260	500	1,500	4,650	9,750

* Included in number above.

CLASSIC HEAD (1809–1836)

G-4 Good: LIBERTY only partly visible on hair band. Lettering, date, and stars worn but visible.
VG-8 Very Good: LIBERTY entirely visible on hair band. Lower curls worn.
F-12 Fine: Only partial wear on LIBERTY, and hair at top worn in spots.
VF-20 Very Fine: Lettering clear-cut. Hair only slightly worn.
EF-40 Extremely Fine: Light wear on highest points of hair and leaves.
AU-50 About Uncirculated: Sharp hair detail with only a trace of wear on higher points.
MS-60 Uncirculated: Typical brown to red surface. No trace of wear.
MS-63 Choice Uncirculated: Well-defined color, brown to red. No traces of wear.

| 1828, 13 Stars | 1828, 12 Stars |

Dealers often pay more than the prices shown for brilliant or red Uncirculated coins, and less for spotted, cleaned, or discolored pieces.

	Mintage	G-4	VG-8	F-12	VF-20	EF-40	AU-50	MS-60	MS-63
1809 1,154,572		$60	$65	$80	$90	$125	$275	$625	$1,300
1810 215,000		85	85	170	305	725	1,000	1,650	2,600
1811 63,140		275	600	925	1,350	3,250	6,500	28,000	62,500

Chart continued on next page.

	Mintage	G-4	VG-8	F-12	VF-20	EF-40	AU-50	MS-60	MS-63	PF-63
1825 63,000		$65	$70	$85	$100	$160	$295	$650	$1,500	
1826 234,000		60	65	80	90	110	160	390	825	
1828, 13 Stars 606,000		60	65	80	90	100	125	200	405	
1828, 12 Stars . . . . *		60	65	80	100	150	275	775	1,550	
1829 487,000		60	65	80	90	120	150	310	460	
1831 2,200		7,000	9,500	12,000	19,000	30,000	44,000	64,500	—	$55,000
1832 51,000		60	65	80	90	100	125	200	405	11,500
1833 103,000		60	65	80	90	100	125	200	405	6,000
1834 141,000		60	65	80	90	100	125	200	405	5,000
1835 398,000		60	65	80	90	100	125	200	405	4,550
1836										6,750

* Included in number above.

BRAIDED HAIR (1840–1857)

VG-8 Very Good: Beads in hair uniformly distinct. Hair lines visible in spots.
F-12 Fine: Hair lines above ear worn. Beads sharp.
VF-20 Very Fine: Lowest curl worn; hair otherwise distinct.
EF-40 Extremely Fine: Light wear on highest points of hair and on leaves.
AU-50 About Uncirculated: Very slight trace of wear on hair above Liberty's ear.
MS-60 Uncirculated: No trace of wear. Clear luster.
MS-63 Choice Uncirculated: No trace of wear.
PF-63 Choice Proof: Nearly perfect; only light blemishes.

Dealers often pay more than the prices shown for brilliant or red Uncirculated coins, and less for spotted, cleaned, or discolored pieces.

	PF-63			PF-63
1840, Original	$6,250		1845, Original	$13,000
1840, Restrike	5,750		1845, Restrike	4,450
1841, Original	5,750		1846, Original	7,500
1841, Restrike	6,000		1846, Restrike	5,750
1842, Original	7,500		1847, Original	6,000
1842, Restrike	3,050		1847, Restrike	4,450
1843, Original	6,750		1848, Original	9,000
1843, Restrike	6,000		1848, Restrike	3,050
1844, Original	9,750		1849, Original, Small Date	9,300
1844, Restrike	5,500		1849, Restrike, Small Date	4,550

Small Date

Large Date

	Mintage	G-4	VG-8	F-12	VF-20	EF-40	AU-50	MS-60	MS-63	PF-63
1849, Large Date 39,864		$65	$70	$75	$90	$125	$200	$385	$700	$26,000
1850 39,812		80	125	180	275	460	550	975	2,250	6,000
1851 147,672		65	70	75	85	95	110	160	305	—
1852										—
1853 129,694		65	70	75	85	95	110	160	305	
1854 55,358		65	70	75	85	95	110	160	305	6,000
1855 56,500		65	70	75	85	95	110	160	305	3,050
1856 40,430		65	70	75	85	95	110	160	305	3,050
1857 35,180		65	70	75	90	120	180	275	460	3,050

Cents and half cents were the first coins struck at the United States Mint. Coinage began in 1793 with laws stating that the cent should weigh exactly twice as much as the half cent. Large cents are dated every year from 1793 to 1857 with the exception of 1815, when a lack of copper prevented production. All were coined at the Philadelphia Mint. Varieties listed are those most significant to collectors. Numerous other die varieties may be found, as each of the early dies was individually made.

FLOWING HAIR (1793)

AG-3 About Good: Date and devices clear enough to identify.
G-4 Good: Lettering worn but readable. No detail on bust.
VG-8 Very Good: Date and lettering distinct, some details of head visible.
F-12 Fine: About half of hair and other details visible.
VF-20 Very Fine: Ear visible, most details visible.
EF-40 Extremely Fine: Wear evident on highest points of hair and back of temple.

Chain Reverse (1793)

	AMERI. Reverse			AMERICA Reverse		
Mintage	**AG-3**	**G-4**	**VG-8**	**F-12**	**VF-20**	**EF-40**
1793, Chain, All kinds 36,103						
1793, AMERI. in Legend	$4,800	$6,500	$9,500	$16,500	$22,500	$48,500
1793, AMERICA	4,300	6,000	8,500	15,000	20,500	44,500

Wreath Reverse (1793)

Strawberry Leaf Variety

	Mintage	AG-3	G-4	VG-8	F-12	VF-20	EF-40
1793, Wreath, All kinds 63,353							
1793, Vine and Bars Edge	$1,650	$2,400	$3,350	$5,000	$8,250	$18,000
1793, Lettered Edge	1,650	2,400	3,350	5,000	8,250	18,000
1793, Strawberry Leaf. . . . . *(4 known)*	—	315,000	405,000	648,000	—	—

LIBERTY CAP (1793–1796)

1793, Vine and Bars Edge
Chain and Wreath types only.

Lettered Edge (1793–1795)
ONE HUNDRED FOR A DOLLAR

Entry continued on next page.

Beaded Border (1793)

Head of 1793 (1793–1794)
Head in high, rounded relief.

Head of 1794 (1794)
Well-defined hair;
hook on lowest curl.

Head of 1795 (1794–1796)
Head in low relief;
no hook on lowest curl.

	Mintage	AG-3	G-4	VG-8	F-12	VF-20	EF-40
1793, Liberty Cap	11,056	$4,450	$5,750	$7,500	$15,000	$30,000	$87,500
1794, All kinds	918,521						
1794, "Head of 1793"		825	1,100	1,850	5,750	9,500	15,000
1794, "Head of 1794"		215	345	500	775	1,550	3,000
1794, "Head of 1795"		215	345	550	775	1,250	3,500
1795, Lettered Edge	37,000	215	345	500	775	1,400	3,350
1795, Plain Edge	501,500	215	345	500	775	1,250	2,800
1796, Liberty Cap	109,825	245	380	600	1,000	1,850	5,250

DRAPED BUST (1796–1807)

AG-3 About Good: Clear enough to identify.
G-4 Good: Lettering worn, but clear; date clear. Bust lacking in detail.
VG-8 Very Good: Drapery on Liberty partly visible. Less wear in date and lettering.
F-12 Fine: Hair over brow smooth; some detail showing in other parts of hair.
VF-20 Very Fine: Hair lines slightly worn. Hair over brow better defined.
EF-40 Extremely Fine: Hair above forehead and left of eye outlined and detailed. Only slight wear on olive leaves.

LIHERTY Error

	Mintage	AG-3	G-4	VG-8	F-12	VF-20	EF-40
1796, Draped Bust	363,375	$110	$180	$320	$825	$1,150	$3,250
1796, LIHERTY Error	*	600	825	1,200	2,400	3,700	9,500

* Included in number above.

Gripped Edge	With Stems	Stemless

	Mintage	AG-3	G-4	VG-8	F-12	VF-20	EF-40
1797, All kinds.	.897,510						
1797, Gripped Edge, 1795-Style Reverse . . .		$135	$260	$320	$700	$1,200	$3,250
1797, Plain Edge, 1795-Style Reverse.		180	225	415	1,100	1,650	6,750
1797, 1797 Reverse, With Stems.		90	160	275	550	975	2,050
1797, 1797 Reverse, Stemless		135	225	500	650	1,400	5,750

1798, 8 Over 7	1799, 9 Over 8	1800 Over 1798	1800, 80 Over 79

	Mintage	AG-3	G-4	VG-8	F-12	VF-20	EF-40
1798, All kinds.	1,841,745						
1798, 8 Over 7		$170	$320	$500	$725	$1,500	$3,050
1798		70	100	200	375	500	1,300
1799, 9 Over 8 . . . . *		2,700	5,500	9,000	19,000	41,000	105,500
1799, Normal Date . . . . *		2,450	4,200	8,500	18,000	24,000	92,000
1800, All kinds.	2,822,175						
1800, 1800 Over 1798		50	70	125	275	650	3,250
1800, 80 Over 79		50	70	110	200	460	2,300
1800, Normal Date		50	70	120	255	460	2,150

* Included in "1798, All kinds," mintage.

Fraction 1/000	Corrected Fraction	1801 Reverse, 3 Errors

	Mintage	AG-3	G-4	VG-8	F-12	VF-20	EF-40
1801, All kinds.	1,362,837						
1801, Normal Reverse.		$50	$70	$120	$255	$390	$1,500
1801, 3 Errors: 1/000, One Stem, and IINITED		100	255	550	1,200	2,800	7,000
1801, Fraction 1/000.		70	110	215	390	925	3,700
1801, 1/100 Over 1/000		90	135	275	500	1,100	4,200
1802, All kinds.	3,435,100						
1802, Normal Reverse.		60	80	110	190	355	925
1802, Fraction 1/000.		60	90	135	320	485	1,650
1802, Stemless Wreath		70	110	180	300	500	1,000

1803, Small Date, Blunt 1	1803, Large Date, Pointed 1	Small Fraction	Large Fraction

See next page for chart.

	Mintage	AG-3	G-4	VG-8	F-12	VF-20	EF-40
1803, All kinds.	3,131,691						
1803, Small Date, Small Fraction.		$50	$70	$100	$215	$355	$825
1803, Small Date, Large Fraction		50	70	105	225	390	875
1803, Large Date, Small Fraction		3,250	7,500	12,000	14,000	32,500	92,000
1803, Large Date, Large Fraction		135	225	370	925	2,050	7,000
1803, 1/100 Over 1/000		90	145	295	500	975	2,050
1803, Stemless Wreath		60	90	135	255	390	925

Broken Dies

All genuine 1804 cents have crosslet 4 in date and a large fraction.
The 0 in date is in line with O in OF on reverse.

	Mintage	AG-3	G-4	VG-8	F-12	VF-20	EF-40
1804 (a)	96,500	$1,100	$1,850	$3,250	$6,000	$9,500	$18,000
1805	941,116	50	70	100	200	385	775
1806	348,000	50	70	120	300	460	1,450

a. Values shown are for coins with normal or broken dies.

Small 1807, 7 Over 6 **Large 1807, 7 Over 6**
(Blunt 1) **(Pointed 1)**

	Mintage	AG-3	G-4	VG-8	F-12	VF-20	EF-40
1807, All kinds.	829,221						
1807, Small 7 Over 6, Blunt 1		$1,750	$2,250	$2,900	$7,500	$21,000	$55,000
1807, Large 7 Over 6		70	135	190	345	600	1,000
1807, Small Fraction		70	90	160	275	925	7,500
1807, Large Fraction		50	70	95	185	415	925

CLASSIC HEAD (1808–1814)

AG-3 About Good: Details clear enough to identify.
G-4 Good: Legends, stars, and date worn, but plain.
VG-8 Very Good: LIBERTY all readable. Liberty's ear visible. Details worn but plain.
F-12 Fine: Hair on forehead and before ear nearly smooth. Ear and hair under ear sharp.
VF-20 Very Fine: Some detail in all hair lines. Slight wear on leaves on reverse.
EF-40 Extremely Fine: All hair lines sharp. Very slight wear on high points.

LARGE CENTS

	Mintage	G-4	VG-8	F-12	VF-20	EF-40	AU-50
1808	1,007,000	$100	$180	$370	$675	$1,250	$2,150
1809	222,867	215	495	1,000	1,400	2,800	3,900

1810, 10 Over 09

1810, Normal Date

1811, Last 1 Over 0

1811, Normal Date

	Mintage	G-4	VG-8	F-12	VF-20	EF-40	AU-50
1810, All kinds	1,458,500						
1810, 10 Over 09		$115	$205	$425	$825	$2,250	$4,950
1810, Normal Date		110	200	405	750	1,400	2,800
1811, All kinds	218,025						
1811, Last 1 Over 0		295	485	825	1,350	6,750	14,000
1811, Normal Date		150	275	435	1,000	2,050	3,550
1812	1,075,500	100	180	370	675	1,250	2,150
1813	418,000	100	180	370	675	1,250	2,150
1814	357,830	100	180	370	675	1,250	2,150

CORONET HEAD (1816–1857)

G-4 Good: Details on Liberty's head partly visible. Even wear in date and legends.
VG-8 Very Good: LIBERTY, date, stars, and legends clear. Part of hair cord visible.
F-12 Fine: All hair lines visible. Hair cords uniformly visible.
VF-20 Very Fine: Hair cords only slightly worn. Hair lines only partly worn, all well defined.
EF-40 Extremely Fine: Both hair cords stand out sharply. All hair lines sharp.
AU-50 About Uncirculated: Only traces of wear on hair and highest points on leaves and bow.
MS-60 Uncirculated: Typical brown surface. No trace of wear.
MS-63 Choice Uncirculated: Some distracting contact marks or blemishes in prime focal areas. Impaired luster possible.

1817, 13 Stars

1817, 15 Stars

Dealers often pay more than the prices shown for brilliant or red Uncirculated coins, and less for spotted, cleaned, or discolored pieces.

	Mintage	G-4	VG-8	F-12	VF-20	EF-40	AU-50	MS-60	MS-63
1816	2,820,982	$22	$27	$36	$75	$215	$320	$600	$800
1817, 13 Stars	3,948,400	23	32	50	100	215	390	600	925
1817, 15 Stars	*	29	36	60	135	550	925	2,250	4,650
1818	3,167,000	16	23	31	55	135	200	375	650

* Included in number above.

1819, 9 Over 8   **1820, 20 Over 19**

Mintage	G-4	VG-8	F-12	VF-20	EF-40	AU-50	MS-60	MS-63
1819 2,671,000	$16	$23	$31	$55	$135	$275	$460	$775
1819, 9 Over 8 . . . . *	16	23	37	70	255	460	1,050	1,850
1820 4,407,550	16	23	31	55	160	240	330	550
1820, 20 Over 19 . . . . *	22	27	40	70	320	550	1,100	1,850
1821 (a) 389,000	36	55	145	320	1,000	1,550	7,500	19,000
1822 2,072,339	22	31	55	110	275	500	925	1,850

* Included in number above. **a.** Wide and closely spaced AMER varieties are valued the same.

1823, 3 Over 2   **1824, 4 Over 2**   **1826, 6 Over 5**

Mintage	G-4	VG-8	F-12	VF-20	EF-40	AU-50	MS-60	MS-63
1823, 3 Over 2 . . . . *	$90	$200	$390	$725	$1,850	$5,250	$16,500	—
1823, Normal Date . . . . *	110	180	415	700	2,250	4,650	15,000	$21,500
1824, 4 Over 2 . . . . *	90	110	160	320	700	2,300	4,650	19,000
1824, Normal Date . 1,262,000	45	90	135	225	415	550	2,300	4,100
1825 1,461,100	36	55	75	110	275	600	1,500	3,150
1826, 6 Over 5 . . . 1,517,425	90	110	180	320	775	1,400	3,000	6,250
1826, Normal Date . . . . **	36	55	85	110	215	425	825	1,600
1827 2,357,732	45	70	90	125	165	275	825	2,050

* Included in number below. ** Included in number above.

Date Size, Through 1828   **Date Size, 1828 and Later**

Mintage	G-4	VG-8	F-12	VF-20	EF-40	AU-50	MS-60	MS-63
1828, Large Narrow Date 2,260,624	$27	$40	$55	$70	$255	$370	$925	$1,850
1828, Small Wide Date . . . . *	75	110	160	225	370	550	1,850	2,800
1829 1,414,500	45	70	90	110	225	415	925	1,850
1830 1,711,500	22	36	50	70	165	275	700	1,850
1831 3,359,260	22	32	40	65	110	200	415	725
1832 2,362,000	22	36	50	70	110	200	460	1,150
1833 2,739,000	22	40	55	80	145	225	500	875
1834 1,855,100	22	32	55	90	160	275	600	825
1835 3,878,400	22	36	55	65	125	200	650	1,000

* Included in number above.

LARGE CENTS

1839, 1839 Over 1836

Dealers often pay more than the prices shown for brilliant or red Uncirculated coins, and less for spotted, cleaned, or discolored pieces.

	Mintage	G-4	VG-8	F-12	VF-20	EF-40	AU-50	MS-60	MS-63
1836	2,111,000	$22	$36	$50	$70	$110	$320	$460	$775
1837	5,558,300	16	23	31	55	105	170	265	500
1838	6,370,200	16	23	31	55	105	170	265	550
1839	3,128,661	16	23	31	55	135	225	370	600
1839, 1839 Over 1836, Plain Cords	*	390	600	1,100	2,400	6,750	13,000	—	—

* Included in number above.

Braided Hair (1837–1857)

"Head of 1840"
Petite Head (1839–1843)

"Head of 1844"
Mature Head (1843–1857)

Small Letters

Large Letters

G-4 Good: Considerably worn. LIBERTY readable.
VG-8 Very Good: Hairlines smooth but visible; outline of ear clearly defined.
F-12 Fine: Hairlines at top of head and behind ear worn but visible. Braid over brow plain; ear clear.
VF-20 Very Fine: All details sharper than for F-12. Only slight wear on hair over brow.
EF-40 Extremely Fine: Hair above ear detailed, but slightly worn.
AU-50 About Uncirculated: Trace of wear on high points of hair above ear and eye and on highest points on leaves and bow.
MS-60 Uncirculated: Typical brown surface. No trace of wear.
MS-63 Choice Uncirculated: Some distracting contact marks or blemishes in prime focal areas. Impaired luster possible.

	Mintage	G-4	VG-8	F-12	VF-20	EF-40	AU-50	MS-60	MS-63
1839, Braided Hair, Type of 1840	*	$27	$36	$60	$70	$160	$345	$725	$1,650
1840	2,462,700	17	20	34	65	110	200	500	925
1841	1,597,367	22	45	70	100	125	180	650	1,050
1842	2,383,390	17	19	24	36	70	180	425	825
1843, Petite, Small Letters	2,425,342	17	19	24	36	70	160	460	775
1843, Petite, Large Letters	**	25	32	45	70	200	315	525	925
1843, Mature, Large Letters	**	25	30	40	65	325	430	550	1,250
1844, Normal Date	2,398,752	17	19	24	36	70	180	460	1,100
1844, 44 Over 81	**	70	90	110	180	370	700	1,400	2,800
1845	3,894,804	17	18	22	27	41	100	215	370
1846	4,120,800	17	18	22	27	50	110	240	415
1847	6,183,669	17	18	22	45	70	125	275	370
1847, 7 Over "Small 7"	**	45	70	90	110	225	320	1,000	1,700

* Included in 1839 listing (see prior chart). ** Included in number above.

Mintage	G-4	VG-8	F-12	VF-20	EF-40	AU-50	MS-60	MS-63
1848 6,415,799	$17	$18	$22	$45	$70	$135	$250	$415
1849 4,178,500	17	18	22	45	70	180	300	525
1850 4,426,844	17	18	22	27	41	100	155	255

1844, 44 Over 81

1851, 51 Over 81

1847, 7 Over "Small" 7

Dealers often pay more than the prices shown for brilliant or red Uncirculated coins, and less for spotted, cleaned, or discolored pieces.

Mintage	G-4	VG-8	F-12	VF-20	EF-40	AU-50	MS-60	MS-63
1851, Normal Date . . 9,889,707	$17	$18	$22	$27	$41	$100	$145	$210
1851, 51 Over 81 . . . . *	45	70	90	110	160	330	495	1,000
1852 5,063,094	17	18	22	27	41	100	145	210
1853 6,641,131	17	18	22	27	41	100	145	210
1854 4,236,156	17	18	22	27	41	100	145	210

* Included in number above.

1855, Upright 5's

1855, Slanting 5's

1855, Knob on Ear

Mintage	G-4	VG-8	F-12	VF-20	EF-40	AU-50	MS-60	MS-63
1855, All kinds. 1,574,829								
1855, Upright 5's.	$17	$18	$22	$27	$41	$100	$145	$210
1855, Slanting 5's	36	45	70	90	110	200	320	700
1855, Slanting 5's, Knob on Ear.	17	18	22	27	41	100	145	210
1856, Upright 5 2,690,463	17	18	22	27	41	100	145	210
1856, Slanting 5 . . . . *	17	18	22	27	41	100	145	210

* Included in number above.

1857, Large Date

1857, Small Date

Mintage	G-4	VG-8	F-12	VF-20	EF-40	AU-50	MS-60	MS-63
1857, Large Date. . . . 333,546	$45	$85	$115	$135	$165	$200	$320	$500
1857, Small Date. . . . . *	45	95	125	180	255	300	390	600

* Included in number above.

FLYING EAGLE (1856–1858)

The Act of February 21, 1857, provided for the coinage of the new copper-nickel small cent. The 1856 Flying Eagle cent was not an authorized Mint issue, as the law governing the new-size coin was enacted after the date of issue. It is believed that nearly 1,000 original strikings and 1,500 or more restrikes were made of the 1856. They are properly referred to as *patterns*.

G-4 Good: All details worn, but readable.
VG-8 Very Good: Details in eagle's feathers and eye evident, but worn.
F-12 Fine: Eagle-head details and feather tips sharp.
VF-20 Very Fine: Considerable detail visible in feathers in right wing and tail.
EF-40 Extremely Fine: Slight wear, all details sharp.
AU-50 About Uncirculated: Slight wear on eagle's left wing and breast.
MS-60 Uncirculated: No trace of wear. Light blemishes.
MS-63 Choice Uncirculated: Some distracting contact marks or blemishes in prime focal areas. Some impairment of luster possible.
PF-63 Choice Proof: Nearly perfect.

| 1858, 8 Over 7 | 1856–1858, Large Letters | 1858, Small Letters |

Dealers often pay more than the prices shown for brilliant Uncirculated and Proof coins, and less for spotted, cleaned, or discolored pieces.

	Mintage	G-4	VG-8	F-12	VF-20	EF-40	AU-50	MS-60	MS-63	PF-63
1856	*(1,000–1,500)* **(a)**	$6,750	$7,500	$8,500	$9,500	$10,500	$11,500	$13,500	$19,500	$15,000
1857	17,450,000	18	27	36	55	120	250	460	850	
. . . .	*(100)*									4,650
1858, Large Letters . .	24,600,000	18	27	36	55	120	250	460	850	
. . . .	*(100)*									4,650
1858, 8 Over 7 . . . . *		90	135	140	160	200	305	500	950	
1858, Small Letters . . . .*		18	27	36	55	120	250	525	1,000	
. . . .	*(200)*									4,650

* Included in mintage for 1858, Large Letters. **a.** Most of those seen are Proofs; a small number have been designated circulation strikes.

INDIAN HEAD (1859–1909)

The small cent was redesigned in 1859, and a representation of Liberty wearing a Native American war bonnet was adopted as the obverse device. The 1859 reverse was also changed to represent a laurel wreath. In 1860 the reverse was modified to display an oak wreath with a small shield at the top. From 1859 into 1864, cents were struck in copper-nickel. In 1864 the composition was changed to bronze, although copper-nickel cents were also struck during that year.

G-4 Good: No LIBERTY visible.
VG-8 Very Good: At least some letters of LIBERTY readable on head band.
F-12 Fine: LIBERTY mostly visible.
VF-20 Very Fine: Slight but even wear on LIBERTY.
EF-40 Extremely Fine: LIBERTY sharp. All other details sharp. Only slight wear on ribbon end.
AU-50 About Uncirculated: Very slight trace of wear above the ear and the lowest curl of hair.
MS-60 Uncirculated: No trace of wear. Light blemishes.
MS-63 Choice Uncirculated: Some distracting contact marks or blemishes in prime focal areas. Impaired luster possible.
PF-63 Choice Proof: Nearly perfect.

Without Shield at Top of Wreath (1859 Only)

With Shield on Reverse (1860–1909)

Variety 1 – Copper-Nickel, Laurel Wreath Reverse (1859)

Dealers often pay more than the prices shown for brilliant Uncirculated coins, and less for spotted, cleaned, or discolored pieces.

	Mintage	G-4	VG-8	F-12	VF-20	EF-40	AU-50	MS-60	MS-63	PF-63
1859 . . . . . . *(800)* . . .	36,400,000	$9.00	$11.50	$16	$34	$100	$150	$305	$625	$1,400

Variety 2 – Copper-Nickel, Oak Wreath With Shield (1860–1864)

	Mintage	G-4	VG-8	F-12	VF-20	EF-40	AU-50	MS-60	MS-63	PF-63
1860 . . . . . . *(1,000)* . .	20,566,000	$8.00	$11.50	$14.50	$32	$47	$70	$165	$340	$625
1861 . . . . . . *(1,000)* . .	10,100,000	21.00	22.00	32.00	45	70	110	165	340	1,100
1862 . . . . *(550)* . .	28,075,000	7.75	8.50	11.00	22	40	65	145	295	625
1863 . . . . *(460)* . .	49,840,000	7.75	8.50	11.00	22	40	65	145	295	625
1864 . . *(800–1,000)* . .	13,740,000	17.00	20.00	25.00	30	60	90	125	325	625

Variety 3 – Bronze (1864–1909)

1864, Indian Head Cent With "L"

	Mintage	G-4	VG-8	F-12	VF-20	EF-40	AU-50	MS-60	MS-63	PF-63
1864, All kinds	39,233,714									
1864, No L *(150)*		$16.00	$22.00	$26	$30	$60	$90	$180	$330	$625
1864, With L *(20)*		37.00	60.00	105	135	170	225	305	390	24,000
1865 . . . . *(500)* . .	35,429,286	11.00	13.50	22	27	36	55	70	125	275
1866 . . . . *(725)* . .	9,826,500	40.00	50.00	65	95	115	170	275	370	180
1867 . . . . *(625)* . .	9,821,000	40.00	55.00	70	90	120	170	245	320	180
1868 . . . . *(600)* . .	10,266,500	40.00	55.00	70	95	135	180	235	315	200
1869 . . . . *(600)* . .	6,420,000	65.00	90.00	160	200	320	395	550	650	600
1870 . . . . . . *(1,000)* . .	5,275,000	45.00	95.00	135	180	310	370	470	525	460
1871 . . . . *(960)* . .	3,929,500	60.00	85.00	135	160	345	415	500	600	205
1872 . . . . *(850)* . .	4,042,000	75.00	105.00	160	260	340	405	600	725	460
1873 *(1,500–2,000)* . .	11,676,500	16.00	32.00	50	65	125	160	225	330	
1874 . . . . *(700)* . .	14,187,500	16.00	27.00	45	50	70	95	140	190	295
1875 . . . . *(700)* . .	13,528,000	16.00	27.00	45	50	90	120	165	210	300
1876 . . . . . . *(1,150)* . .	7,944,000	25.00	34.00	60	100	140	190	235	260	300
1877 . . . . *(900)*	852,500	400.00	575.00	825	1,100	1,650	2,100	3,550	4,650	2,750

Dealers often pay more than the prices shown for brilliant or red Uncirculated coins, and less for spotted, cleaned, or discolored pieces.

	Mintage	G-4	VG-8	F-12	VF-20	EF-40	AU-50	MS-60	MS-63	PF-63
1878 .... (2,350)...	5,797,500	$22.00	$29.00	$55.00	$110.00	$140.00	$190.00	$250	$275	$170
1879 .... (3,200)..	16,228,000	5.50	7.25	13.50	27.00	45.00	55.00	65	115	170
1880 .... (3,955)..	38,961,000	2.60	2.60	5.50	8.50	21.00	32.00	45	70	170
1881 .... (3,575)..	39,208,000	2.60	2.60	5.50	6.25	18.00	25.00	39	65	170
1882 .... (3,100)..	38,578,000	2.60	2.60	5.50	7.25	18.00	25.00	39	70	170
1883 .... (6,609)..	45,591,500	2.60	2.60	4.30	6.25	15.50	22.00	39	75	170
1884 .... (3,942)..	23,257,800	3.40	5.50	5.50	11.50	22.00	30.00	47	75	170
1885 .... (3,790)..	11,761,594	8.00	9.00	11.00	22.00	50.00	65.00	90	125	170
1886 .... (4,290)..	17,650,000	4.30	8.00	14.50	48.00	115.00	135.00	155	195	200
1887 .... (2,960)..	45,223,523	2.20	2.20	3.00	4.10	15.50	23.00	38	75	170
1888 .... (4,582)..	37,489,832	2.60	2.60	2.80	5.75	16.00	18.00	55	120	170
1889 .... (3,336)..	48,866,025	0.90	1.70	2.20	3.40	9.00	18.00	38	60	170
1890 .... (2,740)..	57,180,114	0.90	1.70	2.20	2.80	7.25	18.00	39	60	170
1891 .... (2,350)..	47,070,000	0.90	1.70	2.20	2.80	8.00	18.00	39	65	170
1892 .... (2,745)..	37,647,087	1.70	1.90	2.60	3.40	9.00	18.00	39	80	170
1893 .... (2,195)..	46,640,000	1.50	1.70	2.20	3.00	7.25	18.00	39	75	170
1894 .... (2,632)..	16,749,500	4.10	5.50	11.00	14.50	34.00	45.00	70	110	170
1895 .... (2,062)..	38,341,574	0.90	1.30	1.50	2.20	4.30	20.00	34	70	170
1896 .... (1,862)..	39,055,431	0.90	1.30	1.50	2.20	4.30	18.00	34	65	170
1897 .... (1,938)..	50,464,392	0.90	1.30	1.50	2.20	4.30	18.00	34	60	170
1898 .... (1,795)..	49,821,284	0.90	1.30	1.50	2.20	4.30	15.50	30	60	170
1899 .... (2,031)..	53,598,000	0.90	1.30	1.50	2.20	4.30	15.50	30	60	170
1900 .... (2,262)..	66,831,502	0.90	1.30	1.50	2.20	4.30	15.50	30	60	170
1901 .... (1,985)..	79,609,158	0.90	1.30	1.50	2.20	4.30	15.50	30	60	170
1902 .... (2,018)..	87,374,704	0.90	1.30	1.50	2.20	4.30	15.50	30	60	170
1903 .... (1,790)..	85,092,703	0.90	1.30	1.50	2.20	4.30	15.50	30	60	170
1904 .... (1,817)..	61,326,198	0.90	1.30	1.50	2.20	4.30	15.50	30	60	170
1905 .... (2,152)..	80,717,011	0.90	1.30	1.50	2.20	4.30	15.50	30	60	170
1906 .... (1,725)..	96,020,530	0.90	1.30	1.50	2.20	4.30	15.50	30	60	170
1907 .... (1,475).	108,137,143	0.90	1.30	1.50	2.20	4.30	15.50	30	60	170

Location of Mintmark S on Reverse of Indian Head Cent (1908 and 1909 Only)

	Mintage	G-4	VG-8	F-12	VF-20	EF-40	AU-50	MS-60	MS-63	PF-63
1908 .... (1,620)...	32,326,367	$0.90	$1.30	$1.50	$2.20	$4.30	$15.50	$30	$60	$170
1908S	1,115,000	55.00	65.00	70.00	90.00	120.00	155.00	225	370	
1909 .... (2,175)...	14,368,470	3.40	5.50	6.25	8.00	13.50	22.00	30	60	170
1909S	309,000	210.00	225.00	290.00	320.00	450.00	550.00	850	1,200	

LINCOLN, WHEAT EARS REVERSE (1909–1958)

Victor D. Brenner designed this cent, which was issued to commemorate the 100th anniversary of Abraham Lincoln's birth. The designer's initials (V.D.B.) appear on the reverse of a limited quantity of cents of 1909. Later in the year they were removed from the dies but restored in 1918 as very small incuse letters beneath the shoulder. The Lincoln type was the first cent to have the motto IN GOD WE TRUST.

G-4 Good: Date worn but apparent. Lines in wheat heads missing. Full rims.
VG-8 Very Good: Half of lines visible in upper wheat heads.
F-12 Fine: Wheat lines worn but visible.
VF-20 Very Fine: Lincoln's cheekbone and jawbone worn but separated. No worn spots on wheat heads.
EF-40 Extremely Fine: Slight wear. All details sharp.
AU-50 About Uncirculated: Slight wear on cheek and jaw and on wheat stalks.
MS-60 Uncirculated: No trace of wear. Light blemishes. Brown or red-brown color.
MS-63 Choice Uncirculated: No trace of wear. Slight blemishes. Red-brown color.
MS-65 Gem Uncirculated: No trace of wear. Barely noticeable blemishes. Nearly full red color.
PF-63 Choice Proof: Reflective surfaces with only a few blemishes in secondary focal places. No major flaws.

Location of mintmark S or D on obverse of Lincoln cent.

Designer's Initials V.D.B. (1909 Only)

No V.D.B. on Reverse (1909–1958)

Dealers often pay more than the prices shown for brilliant Uncirculated coins, and less for spotted, cleaned, or discolored pieces.

	Mintage	VG-8	F-12	VF-20	EF-40	AU-50	MS-60	MS-63	MS-65	MATTE PF-63
1909, V.D.B. . . . . (1,194). . .27,995,000		$3.00	$5.50	$6.25	$8.00	$9.00	$15.50	$22	$55	$12,000
1909S, V.D.B. 484,000		625.00	725.00	850.00	1,050.00	1,250.00	1,550.00	1,900	2,700	
1909 . . . (2,618). . .72,702,618		1.30	1.70	2.20	4.30	8.00	11.50	18	40	525
1909S 1,825,000		60.00	75.00	85.00	110.00	145.00	240.00	305	500	
1910 . . . (4,083). .146,801,218		0.30	0.30	0.40	2.80	6.75	12.50	18	65	485
1910S 6,045,000		11.00	14.50	18.00	35.00	55.00	70.00	90	200	
1911 . . . (1,725). .101,177,787		0.30	0.90	1.30	5.50	7.75	12.50	20	90	485
1911D 12,672,000		5.00	7.75	18.00	40.00	50.00	65.00	100	300	
1911S 4,026,000		25.00	30.00	36.00	50.00	70.00	130.00	225	725	
1912 . . . (2,172). . .68,153,060		1.30	1.70	3.90	10.00	19.00	22.00	32	75	485
1912D 10,411,000		7.25	8.00	22.00	55.00	75.00	120.00	200	415	
1912S 4,431,000		12.50	15.50	27.00	47.00	75.00	125.00	180	600	
1913 . . . (2,983). . .76,532,352		0.40	1.30	2.40	14.50	21.00	24.00	40	110	485
1913D 15,804,000		1.70	2.20	5.75	36.00	45.00	70.00	145	415	
1913S 6,101,000		8.00	11.00	18.00	40.00	70.00	140.00	200	775	
1914 . . . (1,365). . .75,238,432		0.60	1.30	4.30	13.50	29.00	38.00	50	110	550
1914D **(a)** 1,193,000		155.00	195.00	255.00	575.00	1,050.00	1,950.00	2,800	4,650	
1914S 4,137,000		13.50	16.00	21.00	60.00	105.00	245.00	415	1,300	
1915 . . . (1,150). . .29,092,120		2.20	2.80	8.00	32.00	36.00	60.00	70	150	600
1915D 22,050,000		2.40	4.30	8.00	22.00	32.00	50.00	70	180	
1915S 4,833,000		11.50	17.00	22.00	55.00	70.00	200.00	460	925	
1916 . . . (1,050). .131,833,677		0.30	0.50	1.70	5.75	10.00	13.50	18	70	1,300
1916D 35,956,000		0.60	1.70	2.60	9.00	22.00	65.00	75	320	
1916S 22,510,000		1.30	2.20	9.00	20.00	34.00	75.00	140	495	
1917 196,429,785		0.20	0.30	1.10	3.20	10.00	11.50	22	110	
1917D 55,120,000		0.90	2.20	3.40	27.00	32.00	50.00	90	275	
1917S 32,620,000		0.40	0.90	1.70	8.00	18.00	55.00	110	435	

a. Beware of altered date or mintmark. No V.D.B. on shoulder of genuine 1914-D cent.

SMALL CENTS

Designer's initials placed on Lincoln's
shoulder next to rim, starting in 1918.

For brilliant Unc. coins before 1934, dealers usually pay more than the prices shown. They pay less for spotted, cleaned, or discolored pieces.

	Mintage	VG-8	F-12	VF-20	EF-40	AU-50	MS-60	MS-63	MS-65
1918	288,104,634	$0.20	$0.30	$0.40	$3.00	$6.50	$9.00	$14.50	$160.00
1918D	47,830,000	0.60	0.90	2.60	11.50	25.00	55.00	100.00	345.00
1918S	34,680,000	0.50	0.90	2.20	7.75	23.00	50.00	135.00	500.00
1919	392,021,000	0.20	0.30	0.30	0.90	3.40	5.50	12.50	60.00
1919D	57,154,000	0.90	1.10	2.60	7.25	19.00	45.00	75.00	225.00
1919S	139,760,000	0.20	0.60	1.70	3.90	12.50	36.00	80.00	295.00
1920	310,165,000	0.10	0.30	0.60	1.70	5.50	11.00	15.50	55.00
1920D	49,280,000	0.30	0.90	1.70	9.00	25.00	50.00	80.00	345.00
1920S	46,220,000	0.30	0.90	1.70	9.00	25.00	75.00	125.00	525.00
1921	39,157,000	0.30	0.50	1.70	7.75	15.50	31.00	45.00	125.00
1921S	15,274,000	1.30	2.60	4.30	27.00	48.00	75.00	160.00	775.00
1922D	7,160,000	15.50	16.00	20.00	30.00	50.00	70.00	160.00	370.00
1922, No D **(b)**	*	500.00	600.00	725.00	1,400.00	2,800.00	8,250.00	17,000.00	62,500.00
1923	74,723,000	0.20	0.20	0.70	4.30	7.75	10.00	14.50	90.00
1923S	8,700,000	5.50	6.25	8.00	40.00	75.00	180.00	415.00	1,100.00
1924	75,178,000	0.20	0.30	0.50	3.40	7.25	12.50	27.00	65.00
1924D	2,520,000	23.00	32.00	34.00	75.00	100.00	190.00	415.00	1,000.00
1924S	11,696,000	0.90	1.70	3.40	23.00	60.00	80.00	240.00	1,300.00
1925	139,949,000	0.10	0.20	0.30	1.70	4.30	6.25	11.00	55.00
1925D	22,580,000	0.40	1.30	1.70	11.00	22.00	45.00	90.00	240.00
1925S	26,380,000	0.40	1.30	1.70	8.00	27.00	100.00	160.00	825.00
1926	157,088,000	0.10	0.20	0.30	0.90	3.40	5.50	7.25	18.00
1926D	28,020,000	0.90	1.90	3.90	11.00	23.00	75.00	115.00	460.00
1926S	4,550,000	8.00	9.00	11.50	27.00	55.00	180.00	390.00	2,550.00
1927	144,440,000	0.10	0.20	0.30	0.90	3.40	5.50	8.00	27.00
1927D	27,170,000	0.60	0.90	1.70	5.50	18.00	40.00	55.00	240.00
1927S	14,276,000	0.60	0.90	1.70	11.00	30.00	75.00	150.00	1,250.00
1928	134,116,000	0.10	0.20	0.30	0.70	2.60	5.50	11.00	36.00
1928D	31,170,000	0.50	0.90	1.50	4.30	13.50	32.00	55.00	180.00
1928S	17,266,000	0.40	0.90	1.70	6.25	22.00	70.00	80.00	275.00
1929	185,262,000	0.10	0.20	0.20	1.70	3.40	4.30	6.25	18.00
1929D	41,730,000	0.50	0.80	1.70	3.90	9.50	17.00	36.00	110.00
1929S	50,148,000	0.50	1.20	1.70	4.30	10.50	13.50	18.00	55.00
1930	157,415,000	0.10	0.10	0.30	0.70	1.70	2.60	3.40	15.50
1930D	40,100,000	0.10	0.20	0.30	1.30	3.40	7.25	11.00	25.00
1930S	24,286,000	0.10	0.30	0.70	0.90	4.30	6.25	7.25	18.00
1931	19,396,000	0.40	0.40	1.10	2.60	7.25	13.50	16.00	32.00
1931D	4,480,000	3.90	4.30	5.50	9.00	24.00	35.00	55.00	145.00
1931S	866,000	50.00	60.00	65.00	70.00	80.00	100.00	120.00	310.00
1932	9,062,000	1.10	1.70	2.20	4.30	9.00	12.50	15.50	22.00
1932D	10,500,000	1.10	1.10	1.70	2.60	8.00	12.50	20.00	32.00
1933	14,360,000	1.10	1.50	1.70	4.30	8.00	11.50	14.50	20.00
1933D	6,200,000	2.60	3.40	5.50	9.00	13.50	17.00	21.00	32.00

* Included in number above. **b.** 1922 cents with a weak or missing mintmark were made from extremely worn dies that originally struck normal 1922-D cents. Three different die pairs were involved; two of them produced "Weak D" coins. One die pair (no. 2, identified by a "strong reverse") is acknowledged as striking "No D" coins. Weak D cents are worth considerably less. Beware of removed mintmark.

Chart continued on next page.

	Mintage	VG-8	F-12	VF-20	EF-40	AU-50	MS-60	MS-63	MS-65	PF-63
1934	219,080,000	$0.02	$0.10	$0.10	$0.10	$0.10	$0.90	$3.40	$7.25	
1934D	28,446,000	0.30	0.40	0.50	0.60	0.90	2.60	7.25	13.50	
1935	245,388,000	0.02	0.10	0.10	0.10	0.10	0.90	3.40	7.25	
1935D	47,000,000	0.02	0.10	0.10	0.10	0.10	1.70	5.50	9.00	
1935S	38,702,000	0.10	0.10	0.20	0.30	0.40	3.40	7.25	18.00	
1936 . . . . (5,569)	309,632,000	0.10	0.10	0.20	0.30	0.30	0.90	1.50	2.60	$305
1936D	40,620,000	0.10	0.10	0.20	0.30	0.30	0.90	1.50	3.40	
1936S	29,130,000	0.10	0.10	0.20	0.30	0.40	1.30	1.70	4.30	
1937 . . . . (9,320)	309,170,000	0.02	0.10	0.10	0.10	0.10	0.90	1.50	2.60	40
1937D	50,430,000	0.02	0.10	0.10	0.10	0.10	0.90	1.50	2.60	
1937S	34,500,000	0.10	0.10	0.20	0.30	0.40	1.30	1.70	3.40	
1938 . . . (14,734)	156,682,000	0.02	0.10	0.10	0.10	0.10	0.90	1.50	2.60	32
1938D	20,010,000	0.20	0.20	0.20	0.30	0.40	1.10	1.70	3.40	
1938S	15,180,000	0.20	0.20	0.20	0.30	0.40	1.30	2.20	3.40	
1939 . . . (13,520)	316,466,000	0.02	0.10	0.10	0.10	0.10	0.90	1.50	2.60	32
1939D	15,160,000	0.20	0.20	0.20	0.30	0.40	1.10	1.70	2.60	
1939S	52,070,000	0.10	0.10	0.20	0.30	0.40	1.30	1.70	3.40	
1940 . . . (15,872)	586,810,000	0.02	0.10	0.10	0.10	0.10	0.90	1.50	2.60	27
1940D	81,390,000	0.10	0.10	0.10	0.20	0.30	0.90	1.50	2.60	
1940S	112,940,000	0.10	0.10	0.10	0.20	0.30	0.90	1.50	2.60	
1941 . . . (21,100)	887,018,000	0.02	0.10	0.10	0.10	0.10	0.90	1.50	2.60	27
1941D	128,700,000	0.10	0.10	0.10	0.20	0.30	0.90	1.50	2.60	
1941S	92,360,000	0.10	0.10	0.10	0.20	0.40	1.30	1.70	3.40	
1942 . . . (32,600)	657,796,000	0.02	0.10	0.10	0.10	0.10	0.90	1.50	2.60	22
1942D	206,698,000	0.02	0.10	0.10	0.10	0.10	0.90	1.50	2.60	
1942S	85,590,000	0.10	0.10	0.10	0.20	0.40	1.30	3.00	5.50	

Variety 2 – Zinc-Coated Steel (1943)

	Mintage	F-12	VF-20	EF-40	AU-50	MS-60	MS-63	MS-65
1943	684,628,670	$0.10	$0.10	$0.10	$0.20	$0.90	$1.70	$9
1943D	217,660,000	0.10	0.10	0.10	0.20	0.90	1.70	9
1943S	191,550,000	0.10	0.20	0.30	0.40	1.70	3.40	18

Variety 1 (Bronze) Resumed (1944–1958)

1944-D, D Over S   1955, Doubled-Die Obverse

	Mintage	VF-20	EF-40	AU-50	MS-60	MS-63
1944	1,435,400,000	$0.02	$0.02	$0.10	$0.10	$0.20
1944D	430,578,000	0.02	0.02	0.10	0.10	0.20
1944D, D Over S	*	85.00	105.00	170.00	240.00	300.00
1944S	282,760,000	0.10	0.10	0.10	0.20	0.50

* Included in number above.

	Mintage	VF-20	EF-40	MS-60	MS-63	PF-65
1945	1,040,515,000	$0.02	$0.02	$0.10	$0.20	
1945D	266,268,000	0.02	0.02	0.10	0.20	
1945S	181,770,000	0.10	0.10	0.20	0.50	
1946	991,655,000	0.02	0.02	0.10	0.20	
1946D	315,690,000	0.10	0.10	0.20	0.50	
1946S	198,100,000	0.02	0.02	0.20	0.50	
1947	190,555,000	0.10	0.10	0.20	0.50	
1947D	194,750,000	0.10	0.10	0.20	0.50	
1947S	99,000,000	0.10	0.10	0.20	0.50	
1948	317,570,000	0.02	0.02	0.10	0.20	
1948D	172,637,500	0.10	0.10	0.20	0.50	
1948S	81,735,000	0.10	0.10	0.20	0.50	
1949	217,775,000	0.02	0.02	0.10	0.20	
1949D	153,132,500	0.10	0.10	0.20	0.50	
1949S	64,290,000	0.10	0.10	0.20	0.50	
1950 (51,386)	272,635,000	0.02	0.02	0.10	0.20	$38.00
1950D	334,950,000	0.02	0.02	0.10	0.20	
1950S	118,505,000	0.10	0.10	0.20	0.50	
1951 (57,500)	284,576,000	0.10	0.10	0.20	0.90	32.00
1951D	625,355,000	0.02	0.02	0.10	0.20	
1951S	136,010,000	0.10	0.10	0.20	0.50	
1952 (81,980)	186,775,000	0.10	0.10	0.20	0.50	16.00
1952D	746,130,000	0.02	0.02	0.10	0.20	
1952S	137,800,004	0.10	0.10	0.20	0.50	
1953 (128,800)	256,755,000	0.10	0.10	0.20	0.50	12.50
1953D	700,515,000	0.02	0.02	0.10	0.20	
1953S	181,835,000	0.10	0.10	0.20	0.50	
1954 (233,300)	71,640,050	0.02	0.02	0.10	0.20	5.50
1954D	251,552,500	0.02	0.02	0.10	0.20	
1954S	96,190,000	0.10	0.10	0.20	0.50	
1955 (378,200)	330,958,200	0.02	0.02	0.10	0.20	5.50
1955, Doubled-Die Obverse	*	1,050.00	1,300.00	2,150.00	3,000.00	
1955D	563,257,500	0.02	0.02	0.10	0.20	
1955S	44,610,000	0.10	0.10	0.20	0.50	
1956 (669,384)	420,745,000	0.02	0.02	0.10	0.20	1.70
1956D	1,098,201,100	0.02	0.02	0.10	0.20	
1957 (1,247,952)	282,540,000	0.02	0.02	0.10	0.20	1.30
1957D	1,051,342,000	0.02	0.02	0.10	0.20	
1958 (875,652)	252,525,000	0.02	0.02	0.10	0.20	1.70
1958D	800,953,300	0.02	0.02	0.10	0.20	

* Included in number above.

LINCOLN, MEMORIAL REVERSE (1959–2008)

Small Date — Large Date

	Mintage	MS-63	MS-65	PF-65
1959 (1,149,291)	609,715,000	$3.40	$9.00	$1.90

1969-S, Doubled-Die
Obverse

Small Date,
Numbers
Aligned at Top

Large Date,
Low 7 in Date

Enlarged Detail of 1972
Doubled-Die Obverse

	Mintage	MS-63	MS-65	PF-65
1959D	1,279,760,000	$2.60	$5.50	
1960, Lg Dt	586,405,000	2.60	7.25	
	(1,691,602)			$1.10
1960, Sm Dt	*	2.60	4.30	
	*			9.00
1960D, Lg Dt	1,580,884,000	2.60	5.50	
1960D, Sm Dt	*	2.60	7.25	
1961	753,345,000	2.60	6.25	
	(3,028,244)			1.70
1961D	1,753,266,700	1.70	7.25	
1962	606,045,000	2.60	6.25	
	(3,218,019)			1.70
1962D	1,793,148,140	1.70	5.50	
1963	754,110,000	1.70	5.50	
	(3,075,645)			1.70
1963D	1,774,020,400	1.70	7.25	
1964	2,648,575,000	1.70	4.30	
	(3,950,762)			1.70
1964D	3,799,071,500	0.60	2.60	
1965	1,497,224,900	0.60	3.40	
1966	2,188,147,783	0.60	3.40	
1967	3,048,667,100	0.60	2.60	
1968	1,707,880,970	0.60	3.40	
1968D	2,886,269,600	0.60	3.70	
1968S	258,270,001	0.60	2.60	
	(3,041,506)			2.60
1969	1,136,910,000	0.60	3.70	
1969D	4,002,832,200	0.60	2.60	
1969S	544,375,000	2.60	4.30	
	(2,934,631)			2.60
1969S, DDO	*	33,500	108,000	
1970	1,898,315,000	0.50	2.60	
1970D	2,891,438,900	0.50	2.60	
1970S, Sm Dt (High 7)	(a)	20.00	36.00	
	(b)			70.00
1970S, Lg Dt (Low 7)	690,560,004	0.60	3.40	
	(2,632,810)			2.60

	Mintage	MS-63	MS-65	PF-65
1971	1,919,490,000	$0.50	$2.60	
1971D	2,911,045,600	0.50	2.60	
1971S	525,133,459	0.50	5.50	
	(3,220,733)			$2.60
1972, DDO	**	255.00	320.00	370.00
1972	2,933,255,000	0.50	2.60	
1972D	2,665,071,400	0.50	2.60	
1972S	376,939,108	0.50	5.50	
	(3,260,996)			2.60
1973	3,728,245,000	0.50	2.60	
1973D	3,549,576,588	0.50	2.60	
1973S	317,177,295	0.50	5.50	
	(2,760,339)			2.60
1974	4,232,140,523	0.50	2.60	
1974D	4,235,098,000	0.50	2.60	
1974S	409,426,660	0.50	5.50	
	(2,612,568)			2.60
1975	5,451,476,142	0.50	2.60	
1975D	4,505,275,300	0.50	2.60	
1975S	(2,845,450)			2.60
1976	4,674,292,426	0.50	2.60	
1976D	4,221,592,455	0.50	2.60	
1976S	(4,149,730)			2.60
1977	4,469,930,000	0.50	2.60	
1977D	4,194,062,300	0.50	2.60	
1977S	(3,251,152)			2.60
1978	5,558,605,000	0.50	2.60	
1978D	4,280,233,400	0.50	2.60	
1978S	(3,127,781)			2.60
1979	6,018,515,000	0.50	2.60	
1979D	4,139,357,254	0.50	2.60	
1979S, Variety 1	(3,677,175)			2.60
1979S, Variety 2	*			2.60
1980	7,414,705,000	0.50	2.60	
1980D	5,140,098,660	0.50	2.60	
1980S	(3,554,806)			2.60
1981	7,491,750,000	0.50	2.60	
1981D	5,373,235,677	0.50	2.60	
1981S, Variety 1	(4,063,083)			2.60
1981S, Variety 2	*			7.25

* Included in number above. ** Included in number below. **a.** Included in circulation-strike mintage for 1970-S, Large Date (Low 7). **b.** Included in Proof mintage for 1970-S, Large Date (Low 7).

Large Date

Small Date

	Mintage	MS-63	MS-65	PF-65
1982, Lg Dt.	10,712,525,000	$0.50	$5.50	
1982, Sm Dt	.............*	3.40	11.00	

* Included in number above.

	Mintage	MS-63	MS-65	PF-65
1982D, Lg Dt.	6,012,979,368	$0.50	$2.60	
1982S	(3,857,479)			$2.60

Copper-Plated Zinc (1982–2008)

Close AM

Wide AM

1995, Doubled Die showing strong doubling on word LIBERTY.

	Mintage	MS-63	MS-65	PF-65
1982, Lg Dt	.............*	$0.50	$2.60	
1982, Sm Dt	.............*	0.90	5.50	
1982D, Lg Dt.	.............*	0.50	2.60	
1982D, Sm Dt	...........*	0.50	2.60	
1983	7,752,355,000	0.50	2.60	
1983D	6,467,199,428	0.50	2.60	
1983S	(3,279,126)			$2.60
1984	8,151,079,000	0.50	2.60	
1984, Dbl Ear	..........**	140.00	160.00	
1984D	5,569,238,906	0.50	2.60	
1984S	(3,065,110)			2.60
1985	5,648,489,887	0.50	2.60	
1985D	5,287,339,926	0.50	2.60	
1985S	(3,362,821)			2.60
1986	4,491,395,493	0.50	2.60	
1986D	4,442,866,698	0.50	2.60	
1986S	(3,010,497)			2.60
1987	4,682,466,931	0.50	2.60	
1987D	4,879,389,514	0.50	2.60	
1987S	(4,227,728)			2.60
1988	6,092,810,000	0.50	2.60	
1988D	5,253,740,443	0.50	2.60	
1988S	(3,262,948)			2.60
1989	7,261,535,000	0.50	2.60	
1989D	5,345,467,111	0.50	2.60	
1989S	(3,220,194)			2.60
1990	6,851,765,000	0.50	2.60	
1990D	4,922,894,533	0.50	2.60	
1990S	(3,299,559)			2.60
1990, Pf, No S	..........**			1,800.00
1991	5,165,940,000	0.50	2.60	

	Mintage	MS-63	MS-65	PF-65
1991D	4,158,446,076	$0.50	$2.60	
1991S	(2,867,787)			$2.60
1992	4,648,905,000	0.50	2.60	
1992, Close AM **(a)**	.... **	16,500.00	23,500.00	
1992D	4,448,673,300	0.50	2.60	
1992D, Close AM **(a)**	... **	3,100.00	6,750.00	
1992S	(4,176,560)			2.60
1993	5,684,705,000	0.50	2.60	
1993D	6,426,650,571	0.50	2.60	
1993S	(3,394,792)			2.60
1994	6,500,850,000	0.50	2.60	
1994D	7,131,765,000	0.50	2.60	
1994S	(3,269,923)			2.60
1995	6,411,440,000	0.50	2.60	
1995, DblDie Obv	..... **	32.00	45.00	
1995D	7,128,560,000	0.50	2.60	
1995S	(2,797,481)			2.60
1996	6,612,465,000	0.50	2.60	
1996D	6,510,795,000	0.50	2.60	
1996S	(2,525,265)			2.60
1997	4,622,800,000	0.50	2.60	
1997D	4,576,555,000	0.50	2.60	
1997S	(2,796,678)			2.60
1998	5,032,155,000	0.50	2.60	
1998, Wide AM **(b)**	..... **	22.00	45.00	
1998D	5,225,353,500	0.50	2.60	
1998S	(2,086,507)			2.60
1998S, Close AM **(a)**	... **			65.00
1999	5,237,600,000	0.50	2.60	
1999, Wide AM **(b)**	..... **	130.00	145.00	
1999D	6,360,065,000	0.50	2.60	

* Included in previous section's mintages. ** Included in number above. **a.** The circulation-strike hub adopted in 1993, with AM almost touching, was accidentally used on these cents. **b.** Varieties were made using Proof dies that have a wide space between AM in AMERICA. The letters nearly touch on other Uncirculated cents.

Chart continued on next page.

73

	Mintage	MS-63	MS-65	PF-65
1999S . . . . (3,347,966)				$2.60
1999S, Close AM (a) . . . . . **				36.00
2000 5,503,200,000	$0.50	$2.60		
2000, Wide AM (b) . . . . **	7.25	13.50		
2000D 8,774,220,000	0.50	2.60		
2000S . . . . (4,047,993)			2.60	
2001 4,959,600,000	0.50	2.60		
2001D 5,374,990,000	0.50	2.60		
2001S . . . . (3,184,606)			2.60	
2002 3,260,800,000	0.50	2.60		
2002D 4,028,055,000	0.50	2.60		
2002S . . . . (3,211,995)			2.60	
2003 3,300,000,000	0.50	2.60		
2003D 3,548,000,000	0.50	2.60		
2003S . . . . (3,298,439)			2.60	

	Mintage	MS-63	MS-65	PF-65
2004 3,379,600,000	$0.50	$2.60		
2004D 3,456,400,000	0.50	2.60		
2004S . . . . (2,965,422)				$2.60
2005 3,935,600,000	0.50	2.60		
2005D 3,764,450,500	0.50	2.60		
2005S . . . . (3,344,679)				2.60
2006 4,290,000,000	0.50	2.60		
2006D 3,944,000,000	0.50	2.60		
2006S . . . . (3,054,436)				2.60
2007 3,762,400,000	0.50	2.60		
2007D 3,638,800,000	0.50	2.60		
2007S . . . . (2,577,166)				2.60
2008 2,558,800,000	0.50	2.60		
2008D 2,849,600,000	0.50	2.60		
2008S . . . . (2,169,561)				2.60

** Included in number above. **a.** The circulation-strike hub adopted in 1993, with AM almost touching, was accidentally used on these cents. **b.** Varieties were made using Proof dies that have a wide space between AM in AMERICA. The letters nearly touch on other Uncirculated cents.

LINCOLN, BIRTH BICENTENNIAL (2009)

One-cent coins issued during 2009 are a unique tribute to President Abraham Lincoln, recognizing the bicentennial of his birth and the 100th anniversary of the first issuance of the Lincoln cent. These coins use four different design themes on the reverse to represent the four major aspects of President Lincoln's life. The obverse of each of these coins carries the traditional portrait of Lincoln that has been in use since 1909.

Those issued for commercial circulation are made of the exact same copper-plated composition used since 1982. Special versions included in collector sets are made of the same metallic composition as was used for the original 1909 cents (95% copper, 5% tin and zinc), and have a Satin finish.

2009 Lincoln cent reverse designs

	Mintage	MS-65	MS-66	PF-67
2009, Birth and Early Childhood	284,400,000	$0.20	$4.30	
2009, Birth and Early Childhood, copper, Satin finish	784,614	1.50	3.40	
2009D, Birth and Early Childhood	350,400,000	0.20	3.40	
2009D, Birth and Early Childhood, copper, Satin finish	784,614	1.50	3.40	
2009S, Birth and Early Childhood . . . . (2,995,615)				$1.70
2009, Formative Years	376,000,000	1.70	6.00	
2009, Formative Years, copper, Satin finish	784,614	1.50	3.40	
2009D, Formative Years	363,600,000	0.20	5.50	
2009D, Formative Years, copper, Satin finish	784,614	1.50	3.40	
2009S, Formative Years . . . . (2,995,615)				1.70
2009, Professional Life	316,000,000	0.20	9.00	
2009, Professional Life, copper, Satin finish	784,614	1.50	3.40	
2009D, Professional Life	336,000,000	0.20	6.25	

	Mintage	MS-65	MS-66	PF-67
2009D, Professional Life, copper, Satin finish	784,614	$1.50	$3.40	
2009S, Professional Life	(2,995,615)			$1.70
2009, Presidency	129,600,000	0.20	5.50	
2009, Presidency, copper, Satin finish	784,614	1.50	3.40	
2009D, Presidency	198,000,000	0.20	4.30	
2009D, Presidency, copper, Satin finish	784,614	1.50	3.40	
2009S, Presidency	(2,995,615)			1.70

LINCOLN, SHIELD REVERSE (2010 TO DATE)

Since the conclusion of the 2009 Bicentennial One-Cent Program, one-cent coins feature a reverse that has "an image emblematic of President Lincoln's preservation of the United States of America as a single and united country." The Union Shield design is by Lyndall Bass, sculpted by Joseph Menna.

	Mintage	MS-65	PF-67
2010	1,963,630,000	$0.20	
2010D	2,047,200,000	3.40	
2010S	(1,689,216)		$1.70
2011	2,402,400,000	0.20	
2011D	2,536,140,000	0.20	
2011S	(1,673,010)		1.70
2012	3,132,000,000	0.20	
2012D	2,883,200,000	0.20	
2012S	(1,239,148)		1.70
2013	3,750,400,000	0.20	
2013D	3,319,600,000	0.20	
2013S	(1,274,505)		1.70
2014	3,990,800,000	0.20	
2014D	4,155,600,000	0.20	
2014S	(1,193,699)		1.70
2015	4,691,300,000	0.20	
2015D	4,674,000,000	0.20	
2015S	(1,099,182)		1.70
2016	4,698,000,000	0.20	
2016D	4,420,400,000	0.20	
2016S	(1,011,624)		1.70
2017P	4,361,220,000	0.20	
2017D	4,272,800,000	0.20	
2017S	(979,475)		1.70
2018	4,066,800,000	0.20	
2018D	3,736,400,000	0.20	

	Mintage	MS-65	PF-63
2018S	(901,072)		$1.70
2019	3,542,800,000	$0.20	
2019D	3,497,600,000	0.20	
2019S	(1,062,662)		1.70
2019W	346,257	2.60	
2019W, Proof	(601,327)		1.70
2019W, Reverse Proof	(412,708)		14.50
2020	3,560,800,000	0.20	
2020D	4,035,600,000	0.20	
2020S	(823,909)		1.70
2021	3,925,820,000	0.20	
2021D	3,982,800,000	0.20	
2021S	(868,644)		1.70
2022	3,129,200,000	0.20	
2022D	3,230,400,000	0.20	
2022S	(699,097)		1.70
2023	2,262,000,000	0.20	
2023D	2,260,800,000	0.20	
2023S	(593,245)		1.70
2024		0.20	
2024D		0.20	
2024S			1.70
2025		0.20	
2025D		0.20	
2025S			1.70

TWO-CENT PIECES (1864–1873)

The Act of April 22, 1864, which changed the copper-nickel cent to a lighter-weight bronze composition, included a provision for a new coin, the two-cent piece. Its weight was specified as 96 grains, and its bronze alloy the same as for the cent. The two-cent piece was the nation's first circulating coin to bear the motto IN GOD WE TRUST.

There are two varieties for 1864, the first year of issue: the scarcer Small Motto, and the Large Motto. The differences are illustrated in the close-ups below. On the Small Motto variety, the stem to the cluster of leaves below TRUST is plainly visible, the D in GOD is wide, the first T in TRUST is close to the ribbon crease, and the U in TRUST is squat. On the Large Motto variety there is no stem, the D is narrow, the first T is farther from the crease, and the U is tall and narrow.

1864, Small Motto

1864, Large Motto

G-4 Good: At least part of IN GOD visible.
VG-8 Very Good: WE weakly visible.
F-12 Fine: Complete motto visible. The word WE weak.
VF-20 Very Fine: WE is clear, but not strong.
EF-40 Extremely Fine: The word WE bold.
AU-50 About Uncirculated: Traces of wear visible on leaf tips, arrow points, and the word WE.
MS-60 Uncirculated: No trace of wear. Light blemishes.
MS-63 Choice Uncirculated: Some distracting contact marks or blemishes in prime focal areas. Some impairment of luster possible.
PF-63 Choice Proof: Reflective surfaces with only a few blemishes in secondary focal places. No major flaws.

Dealers often pay more than the prices shown for brilliant red choice Uncirculated and Proof coins, and less for cleaned or discolored pieces.

	Mintage	G-4	VG-8	F-12	VF-20	EF-40	AU-50	MS-60	MS-63	PF-63
1864, Small Motto . . . (20) . . . . *	$125.00	$170.00	$275	$370	$525	$750	$975	$1,100	$19,500
1864, Large Motto . . (100) . . 19,822,500	13.50	14.50	16	22	35	55	90	155	775
1865 . . . . (500) . . 13,640,000	13.50	14.50	16	22	35	55	90	155	375
1866 . . . . (725) . . 3,177,000	14.50	15.50	27	35	42	70	105	165	375
1867 . . . . (625) . . 2,938,750	14.50	15.50	27	35	42	70	105	160	375
1868 . . . . (600) . . 2,803,750	15.50	16.00	27	36	47	70	140	180	375
1869 . . . . (600) . . 1,546,500	19.00	21.00	32	40	65	90	120	180	375
1870 . . . . (1,000) 861,250	25.00	32.00	45	65	100	140	200	295	375
1871 . . . . (960) 721,250	29.00	35.00	50	75	115	145	225	300	375
1872 . . . . (950) 65,000	255.00	300.00	370	460	700	1,000	2,100	2,600	485
1873 . . . . (600)									2,100

* Included in number below.

SILVER THREE-CENT PIECES (TRIMES) (1851–1873)

This smallest of United States silver coins was authorized by Congress March 3, 1851. The first three-cent silver pieces had no lines bordering the six-pointed star. From 1854 through 1858 there were two lines, while issues of the last 15 years show only one line. Issues from 1854 through 1873 have an olive sprig over the III and a bundle of three arrows beneath.

G-4 Good: Star worn smooth. Legend and date readable.
VG-8 Very Good: Outline of shield defined. Legend and date clear.
F-12 Fine: Only star points worn smooth.
VF-20 Very Fine: Only partial wear on star ridges.
EF-40 Extremely Fine: Ridges on star points visible.
AU-50 About Uncirculated: Trace of wear visible at each star point. Center of shield possibly weak.
MS-60 Uncirculated: No trace of wear. Light blemishes.
MS-63 Choice Uncirculated: Some distracting contact marks or blemishes in prime focal areas. Some impairment of luster possible.
PF-63 Choice Proof: Reflective surfaces with only a few blemishes in secondary focal places. No major flaws.

Mintmark location.

No Outline Around Star (1851–1853)	Three Outlines to Star, Large Date (1854–1858)	Two Outlines to Star, Small Date (1859–1873)	1862, 2 Over 1

Dealers usually pay higher prices for well-struck examples.

	Mintage	G-4	VG-8	F-12	VF-20	EF-40	AU-50	MS-60	MS-63	PF-63
1851	5,447,400	$32	$38	$43	$50	$75	$115	$160	$215	—
1851O	720,000	50	60	70	95	180	345	650	1,000	
1852	18,663,500	32	38	43	50	75	115	160	215	—
1853	11,400,000	32	38	43	50	75	115	160	215	
1854	671,000	44	47	50	70	110	160	305	650	
1855	139,000	60	70	90	120	185	345	550	1,200	$4,650
1856	1,458,000	40	43	50	65	110	160	305	700	3,700
1857	1,042,000	37	40	49	60	110	165	350	650	2,550
1858 . . . . *(210)* . .	1,603,700	37	40	49	60	110	165	330	675	1,750
1859 . . . . . . *(800)*	364,200	37	40	45	50	85	125	200	340	775
1860 . . . . . .*(1,000)*	286,000	37	40	45	50	85	125	200	315	775
1861 . . . .*(1,000)*	497,000	37	40	45	50	85	125	200	315	775
1862, 2/1 . . . .*		37	40	45	50	85	125	200	315	775
1862 . . . . *(550)*	343,000	41	44	48	60	90	160	370	485	
1863 . . . . *(460)*	21,000	370	415	460	500	550	650	825	1,500	775
1864 . . . . *(470)*	12,000	370	415	460	500	550	650	925	1,100	850
1865 . . . . *(500)*	8,000	370	415	460	500	550	650	1,400	2,050	825
1866 . . . . *(725)*	22,000	415	460	525	575	700	750	1,000	1,650	775
1867 . . . . *(625)*	4,000	370	415	460	500	600	1,000	1,650	2,800	775
1868 . . . . *(600)*	3,500	600	700	825	1,100	1,500	2,150	3,950	5,750	775
1869, 9/9	4,500	370	415	460	500	600	875	1,200	1,750	
1869, 9/"8," Narrow Dt *(600)*										775
1870 . . . . . .*(1,000)*	3,000	370	415	500	550	700	875	1,400	1,700	775
1871 . . . . *(960)*	3,400	370	415	460	500	600	650	750	925	775
1872 . . . . *(950)*	1,000	500	650	825	1,100	1,500	1,850	2,900	3,650	775
1873, Closed 3, Proof only *(600)*										1,350

* Included in number below.

NICKEL THREE-CENT PIECES (1865–1889)

Three-cent pieces struck in a nickel alloy were intended to replace the earlier silver three-cent coins, which were hoarded by the public during the Civil War. The Mint struck more than 11 million three-cent coins of the new composition (75% copper and 25% nickel) in 1865, their first year of issue, compared to only 8,000 silver pieces. The nickel coins were all made at the Philadelphia Mint. They have a plain (non-reeded) edge.

G-4 Good: Date and legends complete though worn. III smooth.
VG-8 Very Good: III half worn. Rims complete.
VF-20 Very Fine: Three-quarters of hair details visible.
EF-40 Extremely Fine: Slight, even wear.
AU-50 About Uncirculated: Slight wear on hair curls, above forehead, and on wreath and numeral III.
MS-60 Uncirculated: No trace of wear. Light blemishes.
MS-63 Choice Uncirculated: Some distracting contact marks or blemishes in prime focal areas. Some impairment of luster possible.
PF-63 Choice Proof: Reflective surfaces with only a few blemishes in secondary focal places. No major flaws.

Dealers often pay more than the prices shown for brilliant choice Unc. and Proof coins, and less for spotted, cleaned, or discolored pieces.

	Mintage	G-4	VG-8	F-12	VF-20	EF-40	AU-50	MS-60	MS-63	PF-63
1865 . . . . *(500)* . . 11,382,000		$12.50	$13.50	$14.50	$19	$31	$47	$100	$155	$1,200
1866 . . . . *(725)* . . 4,801,000		11.00	11.50	12.50	17	29	47	100	155	240
1867 . . . . *(625)* . . 3,915,000		12.50	13.50	17.00	22	32	47	100	155	240
1868 . . . . *(600)* . . 3,252,000		11.00	11.50	12.50	17	29	47	100	155	240
1869 . . . . *(600)* . . 1,604,000		11.00	11.50	12.50	19	31	50	105	160	275
1870 . . . . . . *(1,000)* . . 1,335,000		12.50	13.50	14.50	19	31	50	105	165	240
1871 . . . . *(960)* 604,000		12.50	14.50	16.00	22	34	70	115	160	240
1872 . . . . *(950)* 862,000		12.50	13.50	16.00	21	33	75	125	200	240
1873 . . . . . . *(1,100)* . . 1,173,000		16.00	18.00	21.00	27	45	55	115	200	240
1874 . . . . *(700)* 790,000		12.50	13.50	16.00	21	32	55	110	180	240
1875 . . . . *(700)* 228,000		17.00	20.00	22.00	32	50	65	125	170	240
1876 . . . . . . *(1,150)* 162,000		23.00	27.00	32.00	43	65	90	180	275	240
1877, Pf only . . *(900)*		—	—	—	985	1,100	—	—	—	1,600
1878, Pf only (2,350)		—	—	—	575	595	—	—	—	600
1879 . . . . . . *(3,200)* 38,000		55.00	65.00	85.00	90	105	145	210	275	240
1880 . . . . . . *(3,955)* 21,000		80.00	95.00	115.00	125	150	165	255	370	240
1881 . . . . . . *(3,575)* . . 1,077,000		12.50	13.50	17.00	22	31	47	100	160	240
1882 . . . . . . *(3,100)* 22,200		105.00	125.00	150.00	165	200	260	290	460	240
1883 . . . . . . *(6,609)* 4,000		245.00	295.00	345.00	390	550	825	1,300	2,550	240
1884 . . . . . . *(3,942)* 1,700		600.00	725.00	1,000.00	1,200	1,650	3,000	3,950	6,000	240
1885 . . . . . . *(3,790)* 1,000		700.00	925.00	1,200.00	1,400	1,850	2,400	3,150	4,950	240
1886, Pf only (4,290)		—	—	—	290	295	—	—	—	300
1887 . . . . . . *(2,960)* 5,001		210.00	255.00	275.00	370	460	525	650	700	240
1887, 7/6 . . . . *		—	—	—	320	330	—	—	—	265
1888 . . . . . . *(4,582)* 36,501		43.00	48.00	55.00	60	75	115	200	260	240
1889 . . . . . . *(3,436)* 18,125		70.00	95.00	130.00	145	170	190	205	300	240

* Included in number above.

SHIELD (1866–1883)

The Shield type nickel was made possible by the Act of May 16, 1866. Its weight was set at 77-16/100 grains with the same composition as the nickel three-cent piece.

G-4 Good: All letters in motto readable.
VG-8 Very Good: Motto clear and stands out. Rims slightly worn but even. Part of shield lines visible.
F-12 Fine: Half of each olive leaf worn smooth.
EF-40 Extremely Fine: Slight wear to leaf tips and cross over shield.
AU-50 About Uncirculated: Traces of light wear on only the high design points. Half of mint luster present.
MS-60 Uncirculated: No trace of wear. Light blemishes.
MS-63 Choice Uncirculated: Some distracting blemishes in prime focal areas. Impaired luster possible.
PF-63 Choice Proof: Reflective surfaces. Only a few blemishes in secondary focal areas. No major flaws.

With Rays (1866–1867)

Without Rays (1867–1883)

1873, Close 3

1873, Open 3

Typical Example of
1883, 3 Over 2
Other varieties exist.

Dealers often pay more than the prices shown for brilliant choice Unc. and Proof coins, and less for spotted, cleaned, or discolored pieces.

	Mintage	G-4	VG-8	F-12	VF-20	EF-40	AU-50	MS-60	MS-63	PF-63
1866, Rays	*(600)* . .14,742,500	$22	$30	$45	$70	$115	$150	$285	$405	$1,250
1867, Rays	*(25)* . . .2,019,000	24	32	50	85	145	185	300	500	22,000
1867, Without Rays	*(600)* . .28,890,500	21	22	25	32	60	75	115	185	375
1868	*(600)* . .28,817,000	21	22	25	32	60	75	120	180	325
1869	*(600)* . .16,395,000	21	22	25	32	60	75	110	195	315
1870	*(1,000)* . . .4,806,000	23	27	43	55	70	110	170	320	330
1871	*(960)* 561,000	60	75	110	160	240	330	485	725	325
1872	*(950)* . . .6,036,000	32	40	70	80	85	110	155	190	325
1873, Closed 3 . . .	*(1,100)* 436,050	36	45	65	100	125	180	320	600	325
1873, Open 3	4,113,950	23	32	43	55	70	130	215	460	
1874	*(700)* . . .3,538,000	25	36	60	70	90	100	160	225	325
1875	*(700)* . . .2,097,000	38	50	70	100	135	160	215	300	305
1876	*(1,150)* . . .2,530,000	32	43	70	100	135	150	200	255	305
1877, Pf only	*(900)*	—	—	1,550	1,650	1,750	—	—	—	2,250
1878, Pf only	*(2,350)*	—	—	725	725	725	—	—	—	1,000
1879	*(3,200)* 25,900	415	550	625	725	1,300	1,550	2,400	3,000	305
1880	*(3,955)* 16,000	1,850	2,300	3,000	3,900	6,000	8,750	14,000	28,000	305
1881	*(3,575)* 68,800	190	275	330	370	485	600	875	1,100	305
1882	*(3,100)* . .11,472,900	21	22	25	32	60	75	110	170	305
1883	*(5,419)* . . .1,451,500	21	22	25	32	60	75	110	170	305
1883, 3 Over 2	*	180	255	405	575	700	750	1,200	1,500	

* Included in number above.

LIBERTY HEAD (1883–1913)

In 1883 the design was changed to the "Liberty head." This type first appeared without the word CENTS on the coin, merely a large letter V. These "CENTS-less" coins were goldplated by fraudsters and passed as $5 pieces. Later in that year the word CENTS was added.

G-4 Good: No details in head. LIBERTY obliterated.
VG-8 Very Good: Some letters in LIBERTY legible.
F-12 Fine: All letters in LIBERTY legible.
VF-20 Very Fine: LIBERTY bold, including letter L.
EF-40 Extremely Fine: LIBERTY sharp. Corn grains at bottom of wreath visible on reverse.
AU-50 About Uncirculated: Traces of light wear on only high points of design. Half of mint luster present.
MS-60 Uncirculated: No trace of wear. Contact marks possible. Surface may be spotted, or luster faded.
MS-63 Choice Uncirculated: No trace of wear. Light blemishes.
PF-63 Choice Proof: Reflective surfaces. Only a few blemishes in secondary focal areas. No major flaws.

Variety 1, Without CENTS (1883 Only)   Variety 2, With CENTS (1883–1913)   Mintmark Location

Dealers often pay more than the prices shown for brilliant choice Unc. and Proof coins, and less for spotted, cleaned, or discolored pieces.

	Mintage	G-4	VG-8	F-12	VF-20	EF-40	AU-50	MS-60	MS-63	PF-63
1883, Without CENTS . . (5,219) . . . 5,474,300		$4.30	$5.50	$6.25	$7	$10	$14	$38	$65	$215
1883, CENTS (6,783) . . 16,026,200		13.50	21.00	27.00	38	60	80	110	150	200
1884 . . . . . . (3,942) . . 11,270,000		14.00	23.00	27.00	40	60	95	135	205	200
1885 . . . . . . (3,790) . . 1,472,700		240.00	435.00	550.00	825	925	1,100	1,750	3,050	875
1886 . . . . . . (4,290) . . 3,326,000		115.00	160.00	260.00	315	460	575	975	1,650	405
1887 . . . . . . (2,960) . . 15,260,692		9.00	13.50	22.00	30	55	70	110	200	200
1888 . . . . . . (4,582) . . 10,167,901		19.00	30.00	45.00	85	120	160	215	275	200
1889 . . . . . . (3,336) . . 15,878,025		9.00	11.00	22.00	36	60	90	125	170	200
1890 . . . . . . (2,740) . . 16,256,532		5.50	11.00	18.00	27	45	75	110	160	200
1891 . . . . . . (2,350) . . 16,832,000		3.40	5.50	14.50	25	40	80	105	135	200
1892 . . . . . . (2,745) . . 11,696,897		3.40	5.50	14.50	27	45	80	110	170	200
1893 . . . . . . (2,195) . . 13,368,000		3.40	5.50	14.50	25	40	70	105	150	200
1894 . . . . . . (2,632) . . . 5,410,500		9.00	21.00	70.00	110	175	225	305	405	200
1895 . . . . . . (2,062) . . . 9,977,822		3.00	4.30	11.50	27	47	80	115	200	200
1896 . . . . . . (1,862) . . . 8,841,058		3.90	14.50	27.00	45	85	115	155	260	200
1897 . . . . . . (1,938) . . 20,426,797		1.30	2.40	5.50	14	32	55	70	130	200
1898 . . . . . . (1,795) . . 12,530,292		1.30	2.40	5.50	12	40	65	105	160	200
1899 . . . . . . (2,031) . . 26,027,000		0.90	1.40	2.60	6	22	38	70	115	200
1900 . . . . . . (2,262) . . 27,253,733		0.90	1.40	2.60	6	22	38	60	105	200
1901 . . . . . . (1,985) . . 26,478,228		0.90	1.40	2.60	6	22	38	60	110	200
1902 . . . . . . (2,018) . . 31,480,579		0.90	1.40	2.60	6	22	38	60	105	200
1903 . . . . . . (1,790) . . 28,004,935		0.90	1.40	2.60	6	22	38	60	105	200
1904 . . . . . . (1,817) . . 21,403,167		0.90	1.40	2.60	6	22	38	60	105	200
1905 . . . . . . (2,152) . . 29,825,124		0.90	1.40	2.60	6	22	38	60	105	200
1906 . . . . . . (1,725) . . 38,612,000		0.90	1.40	2.60	6	22	38	60	105	200
1907 . . . . . . (1,475) . . 39,213,325		0.90	1.40	2.60	6	22	38	60	105	200
1908 . . . . . . (1,620) . . 22,684,557		0.90	1.40	2.60	6	22	38	60	105	200

	Mintage	G-4	VG-8	F-12	VF-20	EF-40	AU-50	MS-60	MS-63	PF-63
1909 .... (4,763)... 11,585,763		$0.90	$1.40	$2.60	$6	$22	$38	$60	$105	$200
1910 .... (2,405)... 30,166,948		0.90	1.40	2.60	6	22	38	60	105	200
1911 .... (1,733)... 39,557,639		0.90	1.40	2.60	6	22	38	60	105	200
1912 .... (2,145)... 26,234,569		0.90	1.40	2.60	6	22	38	60	105	200
1912D 8,474,000		1.70	2.40	7.25	25	70	125	235	370	
1912S 238,000		80.00	95.00	135.00	330	725	1,050	1,300	1,500	
1913 Liberty Head *(5 known)*.										2,250,000

INDIAN HEAD OR BUFFALO (1913–1938)

The Buffalo nickel was designed by James E. Fraser, whose initial F is below the date. He modeled the bison after Black Diamond in the New York Central Park Zoo.

G-4 Good: Legends and date readable. Buffalo's horn does not show.
VG-8 Very Good: Horn worn nearly flat.
F-12 Fine: Horn and tail smooth but partially visible. Obverse rim intact.
VF-20 Very Fine: Much of horn visible. Indian's cheekbone worn.
EF-40 Extremely Fine: Horn lightly worn. Slight wear on Indian's hair ribbon.
AU-50 About Uncirculated: Traces of light wear on high points of design. Half of mint luster present.
MS-60 Uncirculated: No trace of wear. May have several blemishes.
MS-63 Choice Uncirculated: No trace of wear. Light blemishes.
Matte PF-63 Choice Proof: Crisp surfaces. Only a few blemishes in secondary focal areas. No major flaws.

Variety 1 – FIVE CENTS on Raised Ground (1913)

Dealers often pay more than the prices shown for brilliant choice Unc. coins, and less for spotted, cleaned, weakly struck, or discolored pieces.

	Mintage	G-4	VG-8	F-12	VF-20	EF-40	AU-50	MS-60	MS-63	MATTE PF-63
1913, Variety 1 .. (1,520) .. 30,992,000		$6	$8	$9	$11	$16	$17	$27	$55	$1,100
1913D, Variety 1 5,337,000		11	14	15	22	27	41	60	80	—
1913S, Variety 1 2,105,000		31	32	36	43	55	70	110	200	—

Variety 2 – FIVE CENTS in Recess (1913–1938)

Mintmark Below FIVE CENTS   **1916, Doubled-Die Obverse**   **1918-D, 8 Over 7**

	Mintage	G-4	VG-8	F-12	VF-20	EF-40	AU-50	MS-60	MS-63	MATTE PF-63
1913, Variety 2 29,857,186		$6	$9	$12	$13	$15	$16	$22	$47	
................(1,514)										$725
1913D, Variety 2 4,156,000		85	110	110	115	145	160	215	315	
1913S, Variety 2 1,209,000		140	190	255	300	350	425	625	875	
1914 20,664,463		11	13	15	16	19	25	41	90	
................(1,275)										650

Chart continued on next page.

Dealers often pay more than the prices shown for brilliant choice Unc. coins, and less for spotted, cleaned, weakly struck, or discolored pieces.

	Mintage	G-4	VG-8	F-12	VF-20	EF-40	AU-50	MS-60	MS-63	MATTE PF-63
1914D	3,912,000	$65.00	$70.00	$85.00	$110.00	$165	$220	$305	$370	
1914S	3,470,000	18.00	24.00	30.00	40.00	65	110	160	295	
1915	20,986,220	2.60	3.40	4.30	7.00	11	26	34	70	
. . . .	(1,050)									$775
1915D	7,569,000	13.50	20.00	27.00	40.00	80	100	180	240	
1915S	1,505,000	27.00	40.00	55.00	125.00	275	425	650	1,150	
1916	63,497,466	2.60	3.40	4.30	6.00	7	16	40	65	
. . . .	(600)									1,100
1916, DblDie Obv	* 3,700.00	5,250.00	7,500.00	9,500.00	14,000	19,500	46,500	94,500	
1916D	13,333,000	12.00	16.00	19.00	23.00	55	70	120	215	
1916S	11,860,000	7.25	10.00	15.00	23.00	55	90	150	275	
1917	51,424,019	2.60	3.40	4.30	5.50	9	22	47	145	
1917D	9,910,000	13.50	22.00	34.00	55.00	115	215	350	600	
1917S	4,193,000	16.00	29.00	65.00	90.00	150	275	800	1,300	
1918	32,086,314	3.00	3.40	4.30	5.50	16	43	125	260	

* Included in number above.

	Mintage	G-4	VG-8	F-12	VF-20	EF-40	AU-50	MS-60	MS-63
1918D, 8 Over 7 . . . . . . **	$550.00	$825.00	$1,650.00	$2,300.00	$6,750.00	$8,250	$22,500	$33,500
1918D	8,362,000	15.50	24.00	40.00	80.00	160.00	255	425	800
1918S	4,882,000	9.00	18.00	38.00	70.00	140.00	275	700	1,600
1919	60,868,000	1.30	2.20	2.60	4.30	9.00	23	47	110
1919D (a)	8,006,000	11.00	20.00	48.00	70.00	170.00	275	700	1,200
1919S (a)	7,521,000	5.50	13.50	34.00	70.00	170.00	305	625	1,200
1920	63,093,000	0.60	1.10	1.70	3.40	11.00	25	60	115
1920D (a)	9,418,000	5.75	13.00	24.00	70.00	185.00	275	525	1,100
1920S	9,689,000	2.60	6.25	14.50	55.00	135.00	195	500	1,050
1921	10,663,000	2.20	3.40	4.30	13.50	40.00	60	105	275
1921S	1,557,000	40.00	65.00	80.00	170.00	525.00	875	1,500	2,700
1923	35,715,000	1.10	1.90	2.60	4.30	9.00	27	50	125
1923S (a)	6,142,000	4.30	6.75	16.00	65.00	160.00	240	425	800
1924	21,620,000	0.60	0.90	1.70	4.30	14.50	31	75	160
1924D	5,258,000	5.25	7.50	20.00	55.00	170.00	275	405	875
1924S	1,437,000	11.00	27.00	60.00	180.00	550.00	1,100	2,050	3,200
1925	35,565,100	1.30	2.20	2.60	4.30	13.50	21	34	95
1925D (a)	4,450,000	6.50	14.00	29.00	60.00	125.00	275	385	725
1925S	6,256,000	2.40	6.00	13.50	50.00	135.00	215	525	1,250
1926	44,693,000	0.40	0.60	1.70	3.40	7.75	15	20	55
1926D (a)	5,638,000	6.50	12.00	20.00	60.00	120.00	170	265	415
1926S	970,000	16.00	36.00	55.00	120.00	625.00	1,550	3,900	7,000
1927	37,981,000	0.40	0.60	1.30	2.60	8.00	15	27	60
1927D	5,730,000	1.70	4.30	6.25	22.00	55.00	90	135	305
1927S	3,430,000	1.10	1.30	4.30	27.00	80.00	180	725	1,650
1928	23,411,000	0.40	0.60	1.30	2.60	8.00	16	27	60
1928D	6,436,000	0.40	0.60	2.20	10.00	29.00	34	45	90
1928S	6,936,000	0.40	0.60	1.70	7.75	20.00	65	210	495
1929	36,446,000	0.40	0.60	1.30	2.60	8.00	15	22	50
1929D	8,370,000	0.40	0.60	1.10	4.30	23.00	32	40	90
1929S	7,754,000	0.40	0.60	1.10	1.70	8.00	18	40	105

** Included in number below. **a.** Dealers pay considerably more for Uncirculated pieces with full, sharp details.

1937-D, "3-Legged" Variety　　　　**1938-D, D Over S**

Dealers often pay more than the prices shown for brilliant choice Unc. coins, and less for spotted, cleaned, weakly struck, or discolored pieces.

	Mintage	G-4	VG-8	F-12	VF-20	EF-40	AU-50	MS-60	MS-63	PF-63
1930	22,849,000	$0.40	$0.60	$1.30	$2.60	$7.75	$14.50	$22	$48	
1930S	5,435,000	0.40	0.60	1.70	2.60	11.00	29.00	65	115	
1931S	1,200,000	8.00	10.00	11.00	12.50	23.00	34.00	55	95	
1934	20,213,003	0.40	0.60	1.30	2.60	6.75	17.00	32	43	
1934D	7,480,000	0.40	0.60	2.60	6.25	14.50	32.00	55	85	
1935	58,264,000	0.40	0.60	0.70	0.90	1.70	5.00	16	25	
1935D	12,092,000	0.40	0.60	1.30	3.40	13.50	32.00	47	60	
1935S	10,300,000	0.40	0.60	0.70	1.10	1.70	15.00	33	43	
1936 . . . . (4,420) . .	118,997,000	0.40	0.60	0.70	0.90	1.70	5.00	16	31	$725
1936D	24,814,000	0.40	0.60	0.70	1.10	1.70	15.50	26	36	
1936S	14,930,000	0.40	0.60	0.70	1.30	1.70	7.25	23	29	
1937 . . . . (5,769) . . .	79,480,000	0.40	0.60	0.70	0.90	1.70	5.00	16	20	650
1937D	17,826,000	0.40	0.60	0.70	1.10	1.70	5.00	21	27	
1937D, 3-Legged . . . . *	360.00	395.00	460.00	575.00	725.00	975.00	2,050	4,450	
1937S	5,635,000	0.40	0.60	0.70	0.90	1.70	5.00	16	25	
1938D	7,020,000	1.30	1.50	1.70	2.20	2.80	5.00	16	18	
1938D, D Over S . . . . *	6.25	7.25	8.00	9.00	12.50	24.00	36	50	

* Included in number above.

JEFFERSON (1938–2003)

This nickel was originally designed by Felix Schlag. He won an award of $1,000 in a competition with some 390 artists. It established the definite public approval of portrait and pictorial rather than symbolic devices on our coinage. On October 8, 1942, the wartime five-cent piece composed of copper (56%), silver (35%), and manganese (9%) was introduced to eliminate nickel, a critical war material. A larger mintmark was placed above the dome. The letter P (Philadelphia) was used for the first time, indicating the change of alloy. The designer's initials FS were added below the bust starting in 1966. The mintmark position was moved to the obverse starting in 1968.

VG-8 Very Good: Second porch pillar from right nearly gone, other three still visible but weak.

F-12 Fine: Jefferson's cheekbone worn flat. Hair lines and eyebrow faint. Second pillar weak, especially at bottom.

VF-20 Very Fine: Second pillar plain and complete on both sides.

EF-40 Extremely Fine: Cheekbone, hair lines, eyebrow slightly worn but well defined. Base of triangle above pillars visible but weak.

MS-63 Select Uncirculated: No trace of wear. Slight blemishes.

MS-65 Choice Uncirculated: No trace of wear. Barely noticeable blemishes.

PF-65 Gem Proof: Brilliant surfaces. No noticeable blemishes or flaws. May have a few barely noticeable marks or hairlines.

Mintmark located at right of building.

Mintmark, starting in 1968.

See next page for chart.　　　　**83**

Coin dealers usually pay more than the Mint State prices shown for Uncirculated Jefferson nickels with fully struck steps visible in Monticello.

	Mintage	EF-40	AU-50	MS-60	MS-63	MS-65	PF-65
1938 . . . .(19,365).	19,496,000	$0.20	$0.40	$2.60	$5.50	$11.00	$70
1938D	5,376,000	0.90	1.30	2.60	4.30	7.25	
1938S	4,105,000	1.70	1.90	3.40	6.25	11.00	
1939 . . . .(12,535). . . .	120,615,000	0.40	0.60	1.70	6.25	18.00	70
1939D	3,514,000	3.40	11.00	27.00	34.00	41.00	
1939S	6,630,000	0.30	1.70	18.00	23.00	34.00	
1940 . . . .(14,158). . . .	176,485,000	0.10	0.10	0.90	2.60	6.25	55
1940D	43,540,000	0.10	0.10	1.70	3.00	6.25	
1940S	39,690,000	0.40	0.60	3.40	5.50	10.00	
1941 . . . .(18,720). . . .	203,265,000	0.40	0.60	1.30	2.60	8.00	40
1941D	53,432,000	1.10	1.90	2.60	4.30	6.25	
1941S	43,445,000	1.30	2.20	3.40	6.25	11.00	
1942 . . . .(29,600).	49,789,000	0.90	1.70	2.60	7.25	9.00	45
1942D	13,938,000	4.30	5.50	20.00	25.00	32.00	

Wartime Silver Alloy (1942–1945)

Mintmark Location

1943-P, 3 Over 2

	Mintage	EF-40	AU-50	MS-60	MS-63	MS-65	PF-65
1942P . . . .(27,600).	57,873,000	$1.30	$2.20	$6.25	$9.00	$16.00	$50
1942S	32,900,000	1.30	1.80	5.50	8.00	16.00	
1943P, 3 Over 2	*	1.30	1.60	2.60	5.50	11.00	
1943P	271,165,000	70.00	110.00	225.00	330.00	405.00	
1943D	15,294,000	1.30	1.60	2.60	5.50	11.00	
1943S	104,060,000	1.30	1.60	2.60	5.50	11.00	
1944P	119,150,000	1.30	1.60	2.60	5.50	15.50	
1944D	32,309,000	1.30	2.60	7.25	9.00	13.50	
1944S	21,640,000	1.30	2.60	6.25	9.00	13.50	
1945P	119,408,100	1.30	2.20	3.40	6.25	13.50	
1945D	37,158,000	1.30	1.60	2.60	5.50	12.50	
1945S	58,939,000	1.30	1.60	2.60	5.50	11.00	

* Included in number below.

Prewar Composition, Mintmark Style Resumed (1946–1965)

1954-S, S Over D

1955-D, D Over S

	Mintage	EF-40	AU-50	MS-60	MS-63	MS-65
1946	161,116,000	$0.30	$0.40	$0.90	$1.70	$7.25
1946D	45,292,200	0.30	0.40	1.00	1.50	7.25
1946S	13,560,000	0.30	0.40	0.60	0.90	7.25

NICKEL FIVE-CENT PIECES

	Mintage	EF-40	AU-50	MS-60	MS-63	MS-65	PF-65
1947	95,000,000	$0.30	$0.40	$0.80	$1.70	$7.25	
1947D	37,822,000	0.30	0.40	0.80	1.70	7.25	
1947S	24,720,000	0.30	0.40	0.90	1.70	8.00	
1948	89,348,000	0.30	0.40	0.60	2.60	9.00	
1948D	44,734,000	0.30	0.90	1.70	2.60	7.25	
1948S	11,300,000	0.20	0.40	1.10	2.60	6.25	
1949	60,652,000	0.40	1.90	3.40	6.25	10.00	
1949D	36,498,000	0.30	0.90	2.40	4.30	8.00	
1949D, D Over S	*	50.00	90.00	135.00	180.00	285.00	
1949S	9,716,000	0.30	0.90	1.90	3.40	16.00	
1950	(51,386) 9,796,000	0.20	0.40	1.00	1.70	12.50	$38.00
1950D	2,630,030	3.40	4.30	5.50	9.00	17.00	
1951	(57,500) 28,552,000	0.30	0.40	2.60	5.50	11.00	32.00
1951D	20,460,000	0.30	0.40	2.60	4.30	10.00	
1951S	7,776,000	0.30	0.60	2.60	5.50	11.00	
1952	(81,980) 63,988,000	0.20	0.30	1.30	3.40	17.00	25.00
1952D	30,638,000	0.20	0.60	2.40	5.50	12.50	
1952S	20,572,000	0.10	0.20	0.60	2.60	11.00	
1953	(128,800) 46,644,000	0.10	0.20	0.30	1.70	15.50	22.00
1953D	59,878,600	0.10	0.20	0.20	1.70	11.00	
1953S	19,210,900	0.10	0.20	0.40	2.60	18.00	
1954	(233,300) 47,684,050	0.20	0.30	0.60	3.40	15.50	12.50
1954D	117,183,060	0.10	0.10	0.30	3.40	33.00	
1954S	29,384,000	0.10	0.10	0.20	2.60	18.00	
1954S, S Over D	*	9.00	10.50	20.00	50.00	150.00	
1955	(378,200) 7,888,000	0.10	0.10	0.30	1.70	12.50	9.00
1955D	74,464,100	0.10	0.10	0.10	1.70	10.00	
1955D, D Over S	*	9.50	17.00	36.00	60.00	150.00	
1956	(669,384) 35,216,000	0.10	0.10	0.10	0.90	7.25	1.70
1956D	67,222,940	0.10	0.10	0.10	0.90	8.00	
1957	(1,247,952) 38,408,000	0.10	0.10	0.20	0.90	14.50	3.40
1957D	136,828,900	0.10	0.10	0.10	0.50	8.00	
1958	(875,652) 17,088,000	0.10	0.10	0.10	1.70	34.00	1.70
1958D	168,249,120	0.10	0.10	0.10	0.40	4.30	
1959	(1,149,291) 27,248,000	0.10	0.10	0.10	0.40	16.00	0.90
1959D	160,738,240	0.10	0.10	0.10	0.40	11.00	
1960	(1,691,602) 55,416,000	0.05	0.05	0.10	0.40	9.00	0.90
1960D	192,582,180	0.05	0.05	0.10	0.40	11.00	
1961	(3,028,144) 73,640,100	0.05	0.05	0.10	0.40	5.50	0.90
1961D	229,342,760	0.05	0.05	0.10	0.40	11.50	
1962	(3,218,019) 97,384,000	0.05	0.05	0.10	0.40	6.25	0.90
1962D	280,195,720	0.05	0.05	0.10	0.40	36.00	
1963	(3,075,645) 175,776,000	0.05	0.05	0.10	0.40	5.50	0.90
1963D	276,829,460	0.05	0.05	0.10	1.70	38.00	
1964	(3,950,762) 1,024,672,000	0.05	0.05	0.10	1.30	3.40	0.90
1964D	1,787,297,160	0.05	0.05	0.10	0.40	3.40	
1965	136,131,380	0.05	0.05	0.30	1.70	9.00	

* Included in number above.

1966 Through 2003

	Mintage	MS-60	MS-63	MS-65		Mintage	MS-60	MS-63	MS-65
1966	156,208,283	$0.90	$3.40	$18.00	1968D	91,227,880	$0.50	$1.50	$7.25
1967	107,325,800	0.30	0.40	8.00	1968S	100,396,004	0.40	1.30	4.30

Chart continued on next page.

	Mintage	MS-63	MS-65	PF-65
1968S, Proof	(3,041,506)			$0.90
1969D	202,807,500	$1.70	$10.00	
1969S	120,165,000	0.40	3.40	0.90
	(2,934,631)			
1970D	515,485,380	0.40	11.00	
1970S	238,832,004	0.90	11.00	0.90
	(2,632,810)			
1971	106,884,000	0.60	6.25	
1971D	316,144,800	0.40	2.60	
1971S	(3,220,733)			0.90

	Mintage	MS-63	MS-65	PF-65
1972	202,036,000	$1.10	$7.25	
1972D	351,694,600	0.90	6.25	
1972S	(3,260,996)			$0.90
1973	384,396,000	0.40	3.40	
1973D	261,405,000	0.40	2.60	
1973S	(2,760,339)			0.90
1974	601,752,000	0.90	8.00	
1974D	277,373,000	0.40	3.40	
1974S	(2,612,568)			0.90

	Mintage	MS-65	PF-65
1975	181,772,000	$3.40	
1975D	401,875,300	3.40	
1975S	(2,845,450)		$0.90
1976	367,124,000	4.30	
1976D	563,964,147	8.00	
1976S	(4,149,730)		0.90
1977	585,376,000	4.30	
1977D	297,313,422	3.40	
1977S	(3,251,152)		0.90
1978	391,308,000	13.50	
1978D	313,092,780	4.30	
1978S	(3,127,781)		0.90
1979	463,188,000	9.00	
1979D	325,867,672	7.25	
1979S, Variety 1	(3,677,175)		0.90
1979S, Variety 2	*		0.90
1980P	593,004,000	3.40	
1980D	502,323,448	4.30	
1980S	(3,554,806)		0.90
1981P	657,504,000	4.30	
1981D	364,801,843	3.40	
1981S, Variety 1	(4,063,083)		0.90
1981S, Variety 2	*		0.90
1982P	292,355,000	11.00	
1982D	373,726,544	6.25	
1982S	(3,857,479)		0.90
1983P	561,615,000	18.00	
1983D	536,726,276	13.50	
1983S	(3,279,126)		0.90
1984P	746,769,000	2.60	
1984D	517,675,146	3.40	
1984S	(3,065,110)		0.90
1985P	647,114,962	3.40	
1985D	459,747,446	3.40	
1985S	(3,362,821)		0.90
1986P	536,883,483	2.60	
1986D	361,819,140	2.60	
1986S	(3,010,497)		0.90
1987P	371,499,481	1.70	
1987D	410,590,604	2.60	

	Mintage	MS-65	PF-65
1987S	(4,227,728)		$0.90
1988P	771,360,000	$2.60	
1988D	663,771,652	2.60	
1988S	(3,262,948)		0.90
1989P	898,812,000	1.70	
1989D	570,842,474	3.40	
1989S	(3,220,194)		0.90
1990P	661,636,000	3.40	
1990D	663,938,503	5.50	
1990S	(3,299,559)		0.90
1991P	614,104,000	5.00	
1991D	436,496,678	2.60	
1991S	(2,867,787)		0.90
1992P	399,552,000	1.70	
1992D	450,565,113	2.60	
1992S	(4,176,560)		0.90
1993P	412,076,000	2.60	
1993D	406,084,135	2.60	
1993S	(3,394,792)		0.90
1994P	722,160,000	2.60	
1994D	715,762,110	2.60	
1994S	(3,269,923)		0.90
1995P	774,156,000	2.60	
1995D	888,112,000	2.60	
1995S	(2,797,481)		0.90
1996P	829,332,000	2.60	
1996D	817,736,000	2.60	
1996S	(2,525,265)		0.90
1997P	470,972,000	2.60	
1997D	466,640,000	2.60	
1997S	(2,796,678)		0.90
1998P	688,272,000	2.60	
1998D	635,360,000	3.40	
1998S	(2,086,507)		0.90
1999P	1,212,000,000	2.60	
1999D	1,066,720,000	4.30	
1999S	(3,347,966)		0.90
2000P	846,240,000	2.60	
2000D	1,509,520,000	2.60	
2000S	(4,047,993)		0.90

* Included in number above.

	Mintage	MS-65	PF-65
2001P	675,704,000	$2.60	
2001D	627,680,000	2.60	
2001S	(3,184,606)		$0.90
2002P	539,280,000	2.60	
2002D	691,200,000	2.60	

	Mintage	MS-65	PF-65
2002S	(3,211,995)		$0.90
2003P	441,840,000	$2.60	
2003D	383,040,000	2.60	
2003S	(3,298,439)		0.90

WESTWARD JOURNEY (2004–2005)

The Westward Journey Nickel Series commemorates the bicentennial of the Louisiana Purchase and the journey of Meriwether Lewis and William Clark to explore that vast territory. **2004**—*Obverse:* traditional portrait of Jefferson. *Reverses:* Louisiana Purchase / Peace Medal reverse, by Mint sculptor Norman E. Nemeth. Keelboat reverse, by Mint sculptor Al Maletsky. **2005**—*Obverse:* new portrait of Jefferson, designed by Joe Fitzgerald after a 1789 marble bust by Jean-Antoine Houdon, and rendered by Mint sculptor Don Everhart. *Reverses:* American Bison reverse, designed by Jamie Franki and produced by Norman E. Nemeth. "Ocean in View" reverse, designed by Joe Fitzgerald (based on a photograph by Andrew Cier) and produced by Mint sculptor Donna Weaver.

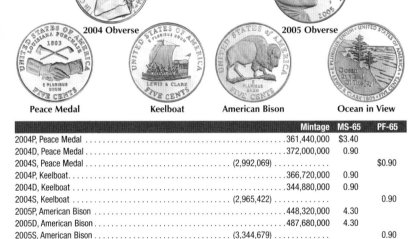

2004 Obverse   **2005 Obverse**

Peace Medal   **Keelboat**   **American Bison**   **Ocean in View**

	Mintage	MS-65	PF-65
2004P, Peace Medal	361,440,000	$3.40	
2004D, Peace Medal	372,000,000	0.90	
2004S, Peace Medal	(2,992,069)		$0.90
2004P, Keelboat	366,720,000	0.90	
2004D, Keelboat	344,880,000	0.90	
2004S, Keelboat	(2,965,422)		0.90
2005P, American Bison	448,320,000	4.30	
2005D, American Bison	487,680,000	4.30	
2005S, American Bison	(3,344,679)		0.90
2005P, Ocean in View	394,080,000	4.30	
2005D, Ocean in View	411,120,000	4.30	
2005S, Ocean in View	(3,344,679)		0.90

JEFFERSON MODIFIED (2006 TO DATE)

In 2006 the Monticello design of 1938 to 2003 was returned to the reverse of the nickel five-cent coin. A new obverse motif featured a facing portrait of Thomas Jefferson, designed by Jamie Franki and sculpted by Donna Weaver. These designs have continued in use to date.

Felix Schlag's initials moved to reverse

	Mintage	MS-65	PF-65
2006P	693,120,000	$0.40	
2006D	809,280,000	1.70	
2006S	(3,054,436)		$0.90
2007P	571,680,000	1.70	
2007D	626,160,000	1.70	
2007S	(2,577,166)		0.90
2008P	279,840,000	1.70	
2008D	345,600,000	1.70	
2008S	(2,169,561)		0.90
2009P	39,840,000	1.70	
2009D	46,800,000	1.70	
2009S	(2,179,867)		0.90
2010P	260,640,000	1.70	
2010D	229,920,000	0.40	
2010S	(1,689,216)		0.90
2011P	450,000,000	0.40	
2011D	540,240,000	0.40	
2011S	(1,673,010)		0.90
2012P	464,640,000	0.40	
2012D	558,960,000	0.40	
2012S	(1,239,148)		0.90
2013P	607,440,000	0.40	
2013D	615,600,000	0.40	
2013S	(1,274,505)		0.90
2014P	635,520,000	0.40	
2014D	570,720,000	0.40	
2014S	(1,193,699)		0.90
2015P	752,880,000	0.40	
2015D	846,720,000	0.40	
2015S	(1,099,182)		0.90
2016P	786,960,000	0.40	

	Mintage	MS-65	PF-63
2016D	759,600,000	$0.40	
2016S	(1,011,624)		$0.90
2017P	710,160,000	0.40	
2017D	663,120,000	0.40	
2017S	(979,475)		0.90
2018P	629,520,000	0.40	
2018D	626,880,000	0.40	
2018S	(901,072)		0.90
2019P	567,854,400	0.40	
2019D	527,040,000	0.40	
2019S	(1,061,558)		0.90
2020P	785,500,000	0.40	
2020D	798,000,000	0.40	
2020S	(824,332)		0.90
2020W	(465,080)		0.90
2020W, Reverse Proof	(313,184)		15.50
2021P	772,780,000	0.40	
2021D	798,000,000	0.40	
2021S	(868,644)		0.90
2022P	769,920,000	0.40	
2022D	777,600,000	0.40	
2022S	(699,097)		0.90
2023P	692,600,000	0.40	
2023D	734,800,000	0.40	
2023S	(593,245)		0.90
2024P		0.40	
2024D		0.40	
2024S			0.90
2025P		0.40	
2025D		0.40	
2025S			0.90

The half dime types present the same general characteristics as larger United States silver coins. Authorized by the Act of April 2, 1792, they were not coined until February 1795, although dated 1794. At first the weight was 20.8 grains, and fineness .8924. By the Act of January 18, 1837, the weight was slightly reduced to 20-5/8 grains and the fineness changed to .900. Finally, the weight was reduced to 19.2 grains by the Act of February 21, 1853.

FLOWING HAIR (1794–1795)

AG-3 About Good: Details clear enough to identify.
G-4 Good: Eagle, wreath, bust outlined but lack details.
VG-8 Very Good: Some details on face. All lettering legible.
F-12 Fine: Hair ends visible. Hair at top smooth.
VF-20 Very Fine: Hair lines at top visible. Hair about ear defined.
EF-40 Extremely Fine: Hair above forehead and at neck well defined but shows some wear.

AU-50 About Uncirculated: Slight wear on high waves of hair, near ear and face, and on head and tips of eagle's wings.
MS-60 Uncirculated: No trace of wear. Light blemishes.
MS-63 Choice Uncirculated: Some distracting marks or blemishes in prime focal areas. Some impairment of luster possible.

For Uncirculated examples, coin dealers usually pay less than the prices shown for pieces that are weakly struck.

	Mintage	AG-3	G-4	VG-8	F-12	VF-20	EF-40	AU-50	MS-60	MS-63
1792	*1,500 est.*	$34,500	$41,000	$50,500	$64,500	$79,000	$108,000	$126,000	$166,500	$270,000
1794	7,756	1,400	1,650	2,400	3,250	3,900	7,000	9,500	16,000	25,500
1795	78,660	825	1,150	1,500	2,000	2,600	4,450	5,250	8,000	10,500

DRAPED BUST (1796–1805)

AG-3 About Good: Details clear enough to identify.
G-4 Good: Date, stars, LIBERTY readable. Bust of Liberty outlined, but no details.
VG-8 Very Good: Some details visible.
F-12 Fine: Hair and drapery lines worn, but visible.
VF-20 Very Fine: Only left side of drapery indistinct.
EF-40 Extremely Fine: Details visible in all hair lines.
AU-50 About Uncirculated: Slight wear on bust, shoulder, and hair; wear on eagle's head and top of wings.
MS-60 Uncirculated: No trace of wear. Light blemishes.
MS-63 Choice Uncirculated: Some distracting marks or blemishes in prime focal areas. Impaired luster possible.

Small Eagle Reverse (1796–1797)

	Mintage	AG-3	G-4	VG-8	F-12	VF-20	EF-40	AU-50	MS-60	MS-63
1796, 6 Over 5	10,230	$1,300	$1,850	$2,300	$3,250	$4,200	$7,250	$11,500	$22,000	$28,000
1796, LIKERTY.............	*	925	1,250	1,650	2,800	3,600	6,000	8,000	17,500	28,000
1797, 15 Stars........	44,527	825	1,200	1,500	2,550	3,600	4,300	6,750	13,000	18,000
1797, 16 Stars.............	*	825	1,200	1,500	2,550	3,600	4,300	6,750	13,000	18,000
1797, 13 Stars.............	*	1,300	1,850	2,600	3,850	4,650	7,000	19,000	37,000	55,000

* Included in number above.

Heraldic Eagle Reverse (1800–1805)

1800 LIBEKTY

	Mintage	AG-3	G-4	VG-8	F-12	VF-20	EF-40	AU-50	MS-60	MS-63
1800	24,000	$825	$1,250	$1,450	$1,750	$2,400	$4,200	$6,000	$9,750	$14,500
1800, LIBEKTY	16,000	925	1,300	1,550	1,850	2,800	4,650	6,750	11,500	16,500
1801	27,760	925	1,350	1,550	1,900	2,650	4,450	6,250	14,500	20,500
1802	3,060	55,000	83,000	101,000	121,500	135,000	180,000	288,000	—	—
1803	37,850	825	1,250	1,450	1,750	2,400	4,200	6,000	10,500	28,000
1805	15,600	1,100	1,400	1,850	2,250	3,150	8,500	19,000	—	—

CAPPED BUST (1829–1837)

G-4 Good: Bust of Liberty outlined, no detail. Date and legend legible.
VG-8 Very Good: Complete legend and date plain. At least three letters of LIBERTY on edge of cap show clearly.
F-12 Fine: All letters in LIBERTY visible.
VF-20 Very Fine: Full rims. Ear and shoulder clasp show plainly.
EF-40 Extremely Fine: Ear very distinct; eyebrow and hair well defined.
AU-50 About Uncirculated: Traces of light wear on many of the high points. At least half of mint luster still present.
MS-60 Uncirculated: No trace of wear. Light blemishes.
MS-63 Choice Uncirculated: No trace of wear. Light blemishes. Attractive mint luster.

	Mintage	G-4	VG-8	F-12	VF-20	EF-40	AU-50	MS-60	MS-63
1829	1,230,000	$50	$65	$75	$100	$140	$200	$385	$725
1830	1,240,000	50	65	75	100	140	200	385	725
1831	1,242,700	50	65	75	100	140	200	385	725
1832	965,000	50	65	75	100	140	200	385	725
1833	1,370,000	50	65	75	100	140	200	385	725
1834	1,480,000	50	65	75	100	140	200	385	725
1835	2,760,000	50	65	75	100	140	200	385	725
1836	1,900,000	50	65	75	100	140	200	385	725
1837, Small 5 C.	871,000	90	110	135	180	275	550	1,550	2,100
1837, Large 5 C.	*	50	65	75	100	140	200	385	725

* Included in number above.

LIBERTY SEATED (1837–1873)

G-4 Good: LIBERTY on shield smooth. Date and letters legible.
VG-8 Very Good: At least three letters in LIBERTY visible.
F-12 Fine: Entire LIBERTY visible, weak spots.
VF-20 Very Fine: Entire LIBERTY strong and even.
EF-40 Extremely Fine: LIBERTY and scroll edges distinct.
AU-50 About Uncirculated: Traces of light wear on many of the high points. At least half of mint luster still present.
MS-60 Uncirculated: No trace of wear. Light blemishes.
MS-63 Choice Uncirculated: No trace of wear. Light blemishes. Attractive mint luster.

Variety 1 – No Stars on Obverse (1837–1838)

	Mintage	G-4	VG-8	F-12	VF-20	EF-40	AU-50	MS-60	MS-63
1837	1,405,000	$32	$50	$75	$125	$205	$350	$550	$875
18380, No Stars	70,000	135	200	415	775	2,000	3,250	5,000	9,500

Variety 2 – Stars on Obverse (1838–1853)

From 1838 through 1859 the mintmark was located above the bow on the reverse. Large, medium, or small mintmark varieties occur for several dates.

	Mintage	G-4	VG-8	F-12	VF-20	EF-40	AU-50	MS-60	MS-63
1838	2,255,000	$25	$29	$34	$50	$80	$145	$255	$425
1839	1,069,150	28	32	38	56	90	160	300	510
18390	1,100,000	27	31	38	60	110	300	725	1,500
1840	1,344,085	25	29	34	50	80	145	255	425
18400	935,000	85	125	175	240	440	550	1,500	4,100
1841	1,150,000	22	24	29	32	55	100	135	215
18410	815,000	60	85	120	160	240	320	925	1,950
1842	815,000	22	24	29	32	55	100	200	275
18420	350,000	60	100	160	330	500	775	1,150	1,650
1843	815,000	22	24	29	32	55	100	145	275
1844	430,000	23	26	31	40	75	135	225	370
18440	220,000	105	165	260	550	1,100	1,850	5,750	8,500
1845	1,564,000	22	24	29	32	55	100	150	275
1846	27,000	600	1,000	1,500	2,250	3,550	7,000	17,000	39,000
1847	1,274,000	22	24	29	32	55	100	135	225
1848	668,000	22	24	29	32	55	100	255	405
18480	600,000	26	33	42	75	160	275	460	725
1849, 9 Over 6 . . . .*		37	60	90	100	150	275	550	875
1849, 9 Over Widely Placed 6 . . . .*		37	60	90	105	150	275	650	1,150
1849, Normal Date . . .	1,309,000	22	24	29	32	55	100	180	370
18490	140,000	65	110	180	265	460	825	1,650	2,900
1850	955,000	22	24	29	32	55	100	135	215
18500	690,000	23	26	31	50	100	200	500	1,150
1851	781,000	22	24	29	32	55	100	160	275
18510	860,000	23	29	34	50	105	200	370	725
1852	1,000,500	22	24	29	32	55	100	135	215
18520	260,000	32	55	85	125	225	405	875	2,250
1853, No Arrows	135,000	34	60	100	145	240	435	550	775
18530, No Arrows	160,000	240	415	700	1,150	2,250	3,000	9,000	12,000

* Included in number below.

Variety 3 – Arrows at Date (1853–1855)

As on the dimes, quarters, and halves, arrows were placed at the sides of the date for a short period starting in 1853 to denote the reduction of weight.

	Mintage	G-4	VG-8	F-12	VF-20	EF-40	AU-50	MS-60	MS-63
1853	13,210,020	$22	$24	$29	$32	$50	$100	$145	$240
18530	2,200,000	22	26	31	37	80	135	330	825
1854	5,740,000	22	24	29	32	50	100	145	240

Chart continued on next page.

	Mintage	G-4	VG-8	F-12	VF-20	EF-40	AU-50	MS-60	MS-63
18540 1,560,000		$22	$24	$31	$37	$70	$150	$275	$650
1855 1,750,000		22	24	29	32	50	100	145	240
18550 600,000		22	26	31	47	95	145	460	775

Variety 2 Resumed, with Weight Standard of 1853 (1856–1859)

1858 Over Inverted Date

	Mintage	G-4	VG-8	F-12	VF-20	EF-40	AU-50	MS-60	MS-63	PF-63
1856 4,880,000		$22	$24	$29	$32	$55	$100	$135	$215	
18560 1,100,000		22	24	31	39	75	180	370	700	
1857 7,280,000		22	24	29	32	55	100	135	215	
18570 1,380,000		27	28	32	40	70	145	275	440	
1858 . . . . . . *(300)* 3,500,000		22	24	29	32	55	100	135	215	$825
1858, Over Inverted Date . . . .*		60	75	105	125	260	290	700	1,200	
18580 1,660,000		24	28	32	36	65	100	200	320	
1859 . . . . . . *(800)* 340,000		22	24	31	34	60	110	160	275	650
18590 560,000		23	28	48	70	110	160	275	370	

* Included in number above.

Variety 4 – Legend on Obverse (1860–1873)

	Mintage	G-4	VG-8	F-12	VF-20	EF-40	AU-50	MS-60	MS-63	PF-63
1860 . . . . . . (1,000) 798,000		$20	$23	$25	$27	$36	$65	$135	$215	$390
18600 1,060,000		22	27	31	34	60	100	225	370	
1861 . . . . . . (1,000) . . 3,360,000		25	27	29	31	36	65	135	215	390
1862 . . . .(550) . . 1,492,000		20	23	25	27	36	65	135	215	390
1863 . . . .(460) 18,000		145	185	270	310	395	485	600	675	390
1863S 100,000		27	50	90	115	180	320	600	775	
1864 . . . .(470) 48,000		260	405	625	700	900	975	1,000	1,100	390
1864S 90,000		75	105	150	210	370	525	725	1,100	
1865 . . . .(500) 13,000		225	345	525	600	725	775	875	1,000	460
1865S 120,000		37	60	90	130	225	460	875	1,850	
1866 . . . .(725) 10,000		220	330	490	550	625	650	700	825	390
1866S 120,000		24	35	50	85	160	275	415	875	
1867 . . . .(625) 8,000		345	420	600	625	700	800	925	1,250	390
1867S 120,000		37	60	90	110	160	210	460	800	
1868 . . . .(600) 88,600		41	70	110	140	215	320	460	650	390
1868S 280,000		20	23	27	33	50	105	265	425	
1869 . . . .(600) 208,000		20	23	27	39	65	85	160	215	390
1869S 230,000		20	23	27	43	80	100	260	700	
1870 . . . . . . (1,000) 535,000		20	23	25	27	36	65	135	215	390
1870S *(unique)*									2,700,000	
1871 . . . .(960) . . 1,873,000		20	23	25	27	36	65	135	215	390
1871S 161,000		22	25	30	42	65	125	190	305	
1872 . . . .(950) . . 2,947,000		20	23	25	27	36	65	135	215	390
1872S 837,000		22	26	28	30	40	70	150	240	
1873 . . . .(600) . . 7,126,000		20	23	25	27	36	65	135	215	390
1873S 324,000		20	23	27	32	41	65	135	215	

The designs of the dimes, first coined in 1796, follow closely those of the half dimes up through the Liberty Seated type. The dimes in each instance weigh twice as much as the half dimes.

DRAPED BUST (1796–1807)
Small Eagle Reverse (1796–1797)

AG-3 About Good: Details clear enough to identify.

G-4 Good: Date legible. Bust outlined, but no detail.

VG-8 Very Good: All but deepest drapery folds worn smooth. Hair lines nearly gone and curls lacking in detail.

F-12 Fine: All drapery lines visible. Hair partly worn.

VF-20 Very Fine: Only left side of drapery indistinct.

EF-40 Extremely Fine: Hair well outlined with details visible.

AU-50 About Uncirculated: Traces of light wear on many of the high points. At least half of mint luster still present.

MS-60 Uncirculated: No trace of wear. Light blemishes.

MS-63 Choice Uncirculated: Some distracting marks or blemishes in prime focal areas. Impaired luster possible.

1797, 16 Stars   **1797, 13 Stars**

	Mintage	AG-3	G-4	VG-8	F-12	VF-20	EF-40	AU-50	MS-60	MS-63
1796	22,135	$1,950	$2,600	$3,250	$3,650	$4,100	$6,750	$9,000	$16,000	$33,500
1797, All kinds	25,261									
1797, 16 Stars		1,950	2,600	3,250	3,650	4,100	7,500	11,500	31,500	48,000
1797, 13 Stars		2,150	2,850	3,600	5,250	6,500	12,000	17,500	44,500	69,000

Heraldic Eagle Reverse (1798–1807)

	Mintage	AG-3	G-4	VG-8	F-12	VF-20	EF-40	AU-50	MS-60	MS-63
1798, All kinds	27,550									
1798, 8 Over 7,										
16 Stars on Reverse		$725	$925	$1,300	$1,650	$2,050	$3,050	$3,900	$6,750	$14,000
1798, 8 Over 7,										
13 Stars on Reverse		2,600	3,550	5,750	7,500	9,500	14,000	23,500	32,500	162,000
1798		600	925	1,200	2,050	2,400	3,350	3,950	10,500	30,000
1800	21,760	495	725	925	1,400	1,850	3,000	6,500	13,000	28,000
1801	34,640	600	825	1,400	1,750	2,800	4,550	9,250	38,000	43,500
1802	10,975	1,000	1,250	1,850	2,400	3,050	5,500	12,500	28,000	87,500
1803	33,040	550	925	1,100	1,400	1,850	3,700	4,650	46,500	92,000
1804	8,265	2,900	3,700	5,250	8,500	14,000	25,000	50,500	—	—
1805	120,780	415	600	825	1,000	1,400	2,450	3,100	4,650	6,750
1807	165,000	415	600	825	1,000	1,400	2,450	3,100	4,650	6,750

CAPPED BUST (1809–1837)

G-4 Good: Date, letters, and stars discernible. Bust outlined, no details.
VG-8 Very Good: Legends and date plain. Some letters in LIBERTY visible.
F-12 Fine: Clear LIBERTY. Ear and shoulder clasp visible. Part of rim visible on both sides.
VF-20 Very Fine: LIBERTY distinct. Full rim. Ear and clasp plain and distinct.
EF-40 Extremely Fine: LIBERTY sharp. Ear distinct. Hair above eye well defined.
AU-50 About Uncirculated: Traces of light wear on only the high points of the design. Half of mint luster present.
MS-60 Uncirculated: No trace of wear. Light blemishes.
MS-63 Choice Uncirculated: Some distracting marks or blemishes in prime focal areas. Impaired luster possible.

Variety 1 – Large Planchet (1809–1828)

| 1823, 3 Over 2 | 1824, 4 Over 2 | 1828, Large Date | 1828, Small Date |

	Mintage	G-4	VG-8	F-12	VF-20	EF-40	AU-50	MS-60	MS-63
1809	51,065	$700	$925	$1,300	$1,850	$3,000	$3,700	$4,950	$8,500
1811, 11 Over 09	65,180	180	275	700	975	1,400	1,850	2,800	6,250
1814	421,500	55	85	120	180	385	485	1,000	1,750
1820	942,587	55	85	120	180	485	725	1,650	2,400
1821	1,186,512	55	85	120	180	385	525	1,200	1,750
1822	100,000	1,500	2,250	3,900	6,000	8,000	10,500	16,000	22,500
1823, 3 Over 2, All kinds	440,000								
1823, 3 Over 2, Small E's		70	110	180	320	550	675	1,200	2,800
1823, 3 Over 2, Large E's		70	135	180	260	500	600	1,850	3,250
1824, 4 Over 2	510,000	75	100	180	405	625	725	1,300	2,400
1825	*	55	85	120	180	385	485	1,100	1,950
1827	1,215,000	55	85	120	180	385	485	1,000	1,750
1828, Large Date, Curl-Base 2	125,000	110	150	215	425	1,000	1,650	3,900	9,500

* Included in number above.

Variety 2 – Small Planchet (1828–1837)

| 1829, Small 10 C. | 1829, Large 10 C. | 1830, 30 Over 29 |

	Mintage	G-4	VG-8	F-12	VF-20	EF-40	AU-50	MS-60	MS-63
1828, Small Date, Square-Base 2	*	$60	$100	$135	$180	$415	$700	$1,550	$2,800
1829, Small 10 C.	770,000	27	40	55	85	200	360	625	1,350
1829, Medium 10 C.	*	36	45	60	90	275	415	1,150	2,100
1829, Large 10 C.	*	45	60	110	160	370	575	1,100	2,800
1830, 30 Over 29	510,000	36	45	70	110	275	460	1,150	2,600

* Included in number above.

	Mintage	G-4	VG-8	F-12	VF-20	EF-40	AU-50	MS-60	MS-63
1830, Medium 10 C. . *		$27	$40	$55	$85	$200	$360	$625	$1,350
1830, Small 10 C. . . . *		27	40	55	85	200	360	1,050	1,700
1831 771,350		27	40	55	85	200	360	625	1,350
1832 522,500		27	40	55	85	200	360	650	1,350
1833 485,000		27	40	55	85	200	360	625	1,350
1834 635,000		27	40	55	85	200	360	625	1,350
1835 1,410,000		27	40	55	85	200	360	625	1,350
1836 1,190,000		27	40	55	85	200	360	625	1,350
1837 359,500		27	40	55	85	200	360	625	1,350

* Included in mintage for 1830, 30 Over 29 (previous page).

LIBERTY SEATED (1837–1891)
Variety 1 – No Stars on Obverse (1837–1838)

G-4 Good: LIBERTY on shield not readable. Date and letters legible.
F-12 Fine: LIBERTY visible, weak spots.
VF-20 Very Fine: LIBERTY strong and even.
EF-40 Extremely Fine: LIBERTY and scroll edges distinct.
AU-50 About Uncirculated: Wear on Liberty's shoulder and hair high points.
MS-60 Uncirculated: No trace of wear. Light blemishes.
MS-63 Choice Uncirculated: Some distracting marks or blemishes in focal areas. Impaired luster possible.

**No Drapery From Elbow
No Stars on Obverse**

Mintmarks on Liberty Seated dimes on reverse, within or below the wreath. Size of mintmark varies on many dates.

	Mintage	G-4	F-12	VF-20	EF-40	AU-50	MS-60	MS-63
1837 682,500		$50	$115	$180	$405	$600	$950	$1,650
18380 406,034		65	135	315	575	725	2,800	4,650

Variety 2 – Stars on Obverse (1838–1853)

No Drapery From Elbow, Tilted Shield (1838–1840)

1838, Small Stars

1838, Large Stars

Drapery From Elbow, Upright Shield (1840–1891)

	Mintage	G-4	F-12	VF-20	EF-40	AU-50	MS-60	MS-63
1838, All kinds. 1,992,500								
1838, Small Stars		$24.00	$60	$125	$290	$320	$550	$1,100
1838, Large Stars		13.50	25	65	160	225	425	725
1838, Partial Drapery		23.00	50	135	275	500	875	1,300
1839 1,053,115		13.50	25	65	160	225	425	725
18390 . . . . *1,288,000*		22.00	65	110	180	320	600	1,650
1840, No Drapery 981,500		13.50	25	65	165	225	425	725
18400, No Drapery 1,175,000		45.00	90	135	390	600	5,250	10,500
1840, Drapery 377,500		70.00	125	255	600	1,000	2,600	9,500

Chart continued on next page.

	Mintage	G-4	F-12	VF-20	EF-40	AU-50	MS-60	MS-63
1841	1,622,500	$11.00	$16.00	$25	$70	$130	$275	$550
1841O	2,007,500	18.00	36.00	60	110	200	650	1,100
1842	1,887,500	11.00	16.00	25	70	130	240	395
1842O	2,020,000	32.00	70.00	155	370	725	2,100	3,250
1843	1,370,000	11.50	16.00	25	70	130	320	600
1843O	150,000	135.00	425.00	1,000	2,300	8,250	55,000	112,500
1844	72,500	135.00	240.00	350	700	1,400	3,350	7,500
1845	1,755,000	12.50	16.00	25	70	130	300	485
1845O	230,000	50.00	180.00	440	1,000	2,550	10,500	26,000
1846	31,300	315.00	650.00	1,500	2,000	5,750	19,000	42,000
1847	245,000	27.00	39.00	70	135	300	1,100	2,500
1848	451,500	22.00	40.00	60	90	180	550	775
1849	839,000	18.00	27.00	36	70	180	370	625
1849O	300,000	22.00	55.00	120	295	550	1,850	3,350
1850	1,931,500	13.50	22.00	29	65	150	275	525
1850O	510,000	31.00	65.00	90	255	625	1,650	3,700
1851	1,026,500	13.50	17.00	28	60	160	320	525
1851O	400,000	22.00	55.00	95	225	825	2,100	2,800
1852	1,535,500	11.50	14.50	22	60	130	240	395
1852O	430,000	32.00	90.00	180	320	485	1,400	2,300
1853, No Arrows	95,000	150.00	315.00	390	700	825	1,100	1,650

Variety 3 – Arrows at Date (1853–1855)

	Mintage	G-4	F-12	VF-20	EF-40	AU-50	MS-60	MS-63
1853, With Arrows	12,173,000	$12.50	$14.50	$24	$60	$125	$260	$470
1853O	1,100,000	16.00	65.00	80	200	485	1,650	3,700
1854	4,470,000	12.50	14.50	24	60	125	260	470
1854O	1,770,000	27.00	70.00	90	110	180	320	650
1855	2,075,000	12.50	14.50	24	60	125	260	470

Variety 2 Resumed, With Weight Standard of Variety 3 (1856–1860)

Small Date, Arrows Removed (1856–1860)

	Mintage	G-4	F-12	VF-20	EF-40	AU-50	MS-60	MS-63
1856, All kinds	5,780,000							
1856, Large Date		$32.00	$70.00	$90	$135	$210	$500	$1,650
1856, Small Date		11.00	12.50	22	50	130	240	395
1856O	1,180,000	22.00	50.00	75	110	300	575	925
1856S	70,000	255.00	600.00	925	1,450	1,850	5,750	11,500

	Mintage	G-4	F-12	VF-20	EF-40	AU-50	MS-60	MS-63	PF-63
1857	5,580,000	$11.00	$12.50	$22	$50	$130	$240	$395	
1857O	1,540,000	14.50	22.00	32	55	140	305	460	
1858 . . . . *(300)*. . .	1,540,000	11.00	12.50	22	50	130	260	425	$1,050
1858O	200,000	20.00	40.00	85	150	275	700	1,650	
1858S	60,000	200.00	370.00	725	1,400	1,750	6,750	13,000	
1859 . . . . *(800)*. . . .	429,200	11.00	12.50	27	60	130	240	395	800
1859O	480,000	18.00	27.00	47	105	180	320	525	
1859S	60,000	200.00	370.00	925	2,300	4,200	14,000	23,500	
1860S	140,000	70.00	180.00	275	500	775	1,850	6,750	

Variety 4 – Legend on Obverse (1860–1873)

	Mintage	G-4	F-12	VF-20	EF-40	AU-50	MS-60	MS-63	PF-63
1860 . . . . *(1,000)* . .	606,000	$10.00	$12.50	$16	$44	$65	$165	$320	$525
1860O	40,000	700.00	1,450.00	1,750	4,200	8,500	16,000	33,500	
1861 . . . . *(1,000)*	1,883,000	10.00	13.50	17	27	55	115	225	485
1861S	172,500	135.00	320.00	500	725	925	3,700	14,000	
1862 . . . . . . *(550)* . .	847,000	12.50	15.50	20	32	60	125	275	485
1862S	180,750	110.00	225.00	415	775	1,850	3,250	7,500	
1863 . . . . *(460)* . . .	14,000	700.00	1,100.00	1,350	1,650	2,100	2,550	3,050	600
1863S	157,500	105.00	225.00	415	725	925	2,800	6,750	
1864 . . . . *(470)* . . .	11,000	525.00	850.00	1,100	1,500	1,650	2,250	2,800	485
1864S	230,000	100.00	180.00	310	600	800	1,200	1,650	
1865 . . . . *(500)* . . .	10,000	600.00	1,100.00	1,250	1,750	2,050	2,700	3,000	485
1865S	175,000	100.00	275.00	460	825	2,200	6,000	11,500	
1866 . . . . *(725)* . . .	8,000	600.00	1,100.00	1,250	1,550	1,850	2,300	2,600	650
1866S	135,000	100.00	275.00	360	550	1,100	2,800	5,750	
1867 . . . . *(625)* . . .	6,000	750.00	1,250.00	1,300	1,500	1,650	2,400	3,250	550
1867S	140,000	110.00	205.00	305	550	1,100	2,400	3,950	
1868 . . . . *(600)* . .	464,000	15.50	22.00	33	60	110	200	500	485
1868S	260,000	45.00	110.00	200	415	495	1,100	1,850	
1869 . . . . *(600)* . .	256,000	22.00	32.00	70	160	200	460	775	430
1869S	450,000	27.00	60.00	100	200	285	650	925	
1870 . . . . *(1,000)* . .	470,500	15.50	21.00	30	70	110	240	415	430
1870S	50,000	275.00	485.00	650	825	925	1,650	2,300	
1871 . . . . *(960)* . .	906,750	11.50	14.50	22	43	115	260	435	430
1871CC	20,100	2,800.00	5,750.00	7,000	13,000	17,000	35,000	103,500	
1871S	320,000	27.00	90.00	135	300	650	1,200	2,800	
1872 . . . . *(950)*	2,395,500	11.00	13.50	17	27	55	115	240	430
1872CC	35,480	1,300.00	2,400.00	3,250	8,500	19,000	83,000	306,000	
1872S	190,000	45.00	110.00	160	305	500	1,500	2,600	
1873, Closed 3 . . *(600)*	1,506,900	11.50	22.00	36	55	90	200	370	430
1873, Open 3 . . . . *		14.50	40.00	55	90	180	600	875	
1873CC *(unique)* . . . . **(a)**								3,150,000	

*Included in number above. **a.** Most of the original mintage of 12,400 was melted after the law of 1873 was passed.

Variety 5 – Arrows at Date (1873–1874)

In 1873, the dime was increased in weight from 2.49 grams to 2.50 grams. Arrows at the date in 1873 and 1874 indicate this change.

	Mintage	G-4	F-12	VF-20	EF-40	AU-50	MS-60	MS-63	PF-63
1873 . . . . (500). . . 2,377,700	$12.50	$20	$43	$115	$240	$350	$600	$600
1873CC 18,791	2,400.00	4,300	6,500	19,000	42,000	83,000	126,000	
1873S 455,000	18.00	27	60	140	370	700	1,250	
1874 . . . . (700). . . 2,940,000	12.50	20	43	115	240	350	600	600
1874CC 10,817	9,750.00	15,500	18,000	28,000	46,500	99,000	216,000	
1874S 240,000	36.00	90	115	275	600	925	1,650	

Variety 4 Resumed, With Weight Standard of Variety 5 (1875–1891)

	Mintage	G-4	F-12	VF-20	EF-40	AU-50	MS-60	MS-63	PF-63
1875 . . . . (700). . 10,350,000	$10.00	$12.50	$16	$22	$55	$115	$215	$430
1875CC 4,645,000	22.00	32.00	45	70	165	300	550	
1875S 9,070,000	10.00	12.50	16	22	55	115	215	
1876 . . . .(1,150). . 11,450,000	10.00	12.50	16	22	55	115	215	430
1876CC 8,270,000	27.00	41.00	55	110	180	370	600	
1876S 10,420,000	12.50	18.00	22	34	65	135	275	
1877 . . . . (510). . . 7,310,000	10.00	12.50	16	22	55	115	215	430
1877CC 7,700,000	22.00	25.00	39	100	170	255	600	
1877S 2,340,000	17.00	22.00	27	41	75	225	700	
1878 . . . . (800). . . 1,677,200	10.00	12.50	16	22	55	115	215	430
1878CC 200,000	160.00	225.00	275	370	825	1,300	2,050	
1879 . . . . . .(1,100). 14,000	135.00	195.00	275	370	435	485	550	430
1880 . . . . . .(1,355). 36,000	100.00	180.00	225	295	330	415	460	430
1881 . . . . (975). 24,000	110.00	190.00	245	315	390	550	825	430
1882 . . . . . .(1,100). . . 3,910,000	10.00	12.50	16	22	55	115	215	430
1883 . . . . . .(1,039). . . 7,674,673	10.00	12.50	16	22	55	115	215	430
1884 . . . . (875). . . 3,365,505	10.00	12.50	16	22	55	115	215	430
1884S 564,969	22.00	33.00	50	90	235	500	825	
1885 . . . . (930). . . 2,532,497	10.00	12.50	16	22	55	115	215	430
1885S 43,690	600.00	900.00	1,350	2,000	3,250	4,650	7,000	
1886 . . . . (886). . . 6,376,684	10.00	12.50	16	22	55	115	215	430
1886S 206,524	32.00	55.00	75	110	160	385	825	
1887 . . . . (710). . 11,283,229	10.00	12.50	16	22	55	115	215	430
1887S 4,454,450	10.00	12.50	16	22	65	130	245	
1888 . . . . (832). . . 5,495,655	10.00	12.50	16	22	55	115	215	430
1888S 1,720,000	12.50	16.00	22	32	70	255	485	
1889 . . . . (711). . . 7,380,000	10.00	12.50	16	22	55	115	215	430
1889S 972,678	18.00	27.00	40	60	100	255	625	
1890 . . . . (590). . . 9,910,951	10.00	12.50	16	22	55	115	215	430
1890S 1,423,076	11.00	16.00	30	50	100	180	415	
1891 . . . . (600). . 15,310,000	10.00	12.50	16	22	55	115	215	430
1891O 4,540,000	13.50	18.00	20	32	65	130	275	
1891S 3,196,116	10.00	12.50	16	22	55	115	260	

BARBER (1892–1916)

This type was designed by Charles E. Barber, chief engraver of the Mint. His initial B is at the truncation of the neck. He also designed the quarters and half dollars of the same period.

G-4 Good: Date and letters plain. LIBERTY obliterated.
VG-8 Very Good: Some letters visible in LIBERTY.
F-12 Fine: Letters in LIBERTY visible, though some weak.
VF-20 Very Fine: Letters of LIBERTY evenly plain.
EF-40 Extremely Fine: All letters in LIBERTY sharp, distinct. Headband edges distinct.
AU-50 About Uncirculated: Slight traces of wear on hair cheekbone and on leaf tips in wreath.
MS-60 Uncirculated: No trace of wear. Light blemishes.
MS-63 Choice Uncirculated: Some distracting blemishes in prime focal areas. Impaired luster possible.

Mintmark location is on reverse, below wreath.

	Mintage	G-4	VG-8	F-12	VF-20	EF-40	AU-50	MS-60	MS-63	PF-63
1892 .... (1,245)...12,120,000		$5.00	$7.25	$11.50	$15.50	$23	$50	$100	$140	$345
1892O 3,841,700		7.25	12.50	25.00	41.00	55	65	125	275	
1892S 990,710		55.00	110.00	165.00	200.00	240	275	405	650	
1893, 3/2 ....*		5.50	8.00	14.50	22.00	39	55	110	240	345
1893 ......(792)....3,339,940		115.00	160.00	215.00	260.00	415	575	1,150	1,650	8,000
1893O 1,760,000		21.00	32.00	70.00	80.00	110	180	240	460	
1893S **(a)** 2,491,401		9.00	16.00	29.00	41.00	70	110	260	600	
1894 ......(970)....1,330,000		16.00	32.00	90.00	110.00	135	160	205	330	345
1894O 720,000		36.00	60.00	155.00	200.00	370	650	1,650	3,700	
1894S ......(24) **(b)**										1,035,000
1895 ......(880)..... 690,000		65.00	115.00	260.00	345.00	390	445	550	700	345
1895O 440,000		395.00	495.00	775.00	1,150.00	1,950	2,700	4,400	11,000	
1895S 1,120,000		29.00	40.00	100.00	145.00	160	240	415	850	
1896 ......(762)....2,000,000		8.00	15.50	41.00	60.00	70	80	110	285	345
1896O 610,000		60.00	110.00	200.00	265.00	370	725	1,100	2,250	
1896S 576,056		75.00	150.00	215.00	275.00	375	500	725	1,300	
1897 ......(731)...10,868,533		4.20	4.70	6.00	12.50	28	50	100	140	345
1897O 666,000		45.00	95.00	210.00	265.00	315	415	825	1,100	
1897S 1,342,844		13.50	27.00	70.00	95.00	125	200	345	650	
1898 ......(735)...16,320,000		3.90	4.30	5.75	11.00	23	50	100	140	345
1898O 2,130,000		8.00	26.00	70.00	110.00	140	205	345	775	
1898S 1,702,507		5.50	10.00	25.00	38.00	80	125	405	1,100	
1899 ......(846)...19,580,000		3.90	4.10	5.50	11.00	22	50	100	140	345
1899O 2,650,000		5.50	20.00	55.00	75.00	135	170	305	725	
1899S 1,867,493		5.50	11.00	25.00	29.00	43	70	240	485	
1900 ......(912)...17,600,000		3.90	4.10	4.90	9.00	22	50	100	140	345

* Included in number below. **a.** Boldly doubled mintmark is valued slightly higher. **b.** Five of these were reserved for assay.

Chart continued on next page.

	Mintage	G-4	VG-8	F-12	VF-20	EF-40	AU-50	MS-60	MS-63	PF-63
1900O	2,010,000	$11.50	$27.00	$85.00	$115.00	$155	$200	$425	$925	
1900S	5,168,270	4.30	6.25	11.00	15.50	29	50	135	285	
1901 (813)	18,859,665	3.90	4.10	4.90	9.00	22	50	100	140	$345
1901O	5,620,000	4.30	6.25	14.50	29.00	60	120	500	725	
1901S	593,022	70.00	135.00	295.00	360.00	440	600	1,250	1,750	
1902 (777)	21,380,000	3.90	4.10	4.90	9.00	22	50	100	160	345
1902O	4,500,000	4.30	6.25	13.50	24.00	55	110	275	525	
1902S	2,070,000	9.00	19.00	41.00	70.00	95	140	275	625	
1903 (755)	19,500,000	3.90	4.10	4.90	11.00	22	50	100	140	345
1903O	8,180,000	4.30	6.25	11.50	22.00	46	70	160	355	
1903S	613,300	55.00	90.00	275.00	360.00	525	750	975	1,250	
1904 (670)	14,600,357	3.90	4.10	4.90	10.00	22	50	100	145	345
1904S	800,000	27.00	55.00	110.00	165.00	225	345	650	1,200	
1905 (727)	14,551,623	3.90	4.10	4.90	9.00	22	50	100	140	345
1905O	3,400,000	4.30	11.00	25.00	40.00	85	100	210	325	
1905S	6,855,199	4.30	6.25	8.00	16.00	37	70	125	175	
1906 (675)	19,957,731	3.90	4.10	4.90	9.00	22	50	100	140	345
1906D	4,060,000	4.30	6.25	8.00	11.00	30	55	110	255	
1906O	2,610,000	5.50	14.50	36.00	60.00	90	100	135	300	
1906S	3,136,640	4.30	6.25	11.00	21.00	47	100	200	350	
1907 (575)	22,220,000	3.90	4.10	4.90	9.00	22	50	100	140	345
1907D	4,080,000	4.30	6.25	9.00	18.00	37	75	180	525	
1907O	5,058,000	4.30	10.00	24.00	36.00	55	70	140	220	
1907S	3,178,470	4.30	7.25	14.50	29.00	60	105	255	500	
1908 (545)	10,600,000	3.90	4.10	4.90	9.00	22	50	100	140	345
1908D	7,490,000	3.90	4.10	4.90	11.00	27	50	100	160	
1908O	1,789,000	5.50	12.50	33.00	45.00	85	130	315	550	
1908S	3,220,000	4.70	6.25	11.00	15.50	47	120	260	550	
1909 (650)	10,240,000	3.90	4.10	4.90	9.00	22	50	100	140	345
1909D	954,000	10.00	19.00	45.00	70.00	95	155	370	625	
1909O	2,287,000	4.30	6.25	11.00	21.00	45	110	215	500	
1909S	1,000,000	9.00	26.00	65.00	95.00	130	210	370	925	
1910 (551)	11,520,000	3.90	4.10	4.90	9.00	22	50	100	160	345
1910D	3,490,000	4.30	6.25	8.00	18.00	43	70	145	275	
1910S	1,240,000	5.50	15.50	38.00	55.00	95	135	295	460	
1911 (543)	18,870,000	3.90	4.10	4.90	9.00	22	50	100	150	345
1911D	11,209,000	3.90	4.10	4.90	11.00	23	50	100	140	
1911S	3,520,000	4.30	6.25	8.00	16.00	40	70	135	255	
1912 (700)	19,349,300	3.90	4.10	4.90	9.00	22	50	100	140	345
1912D	11,760,000	3.90	4.10	4.90	9.00	22	50	100	140	
1912S	3,420,000	4.30	6.25	9.00	15.50	38	65	125	215	
1913 (622)	19,760,000	3.90	4.10	4.90	9.00	22	50	100	140	345
1913S	510,000	24.00	36.00	90.00	135.00	215	275	575	1,100	
1914 (425)	17,360,230	3.90	4.10	4.90	9.00	22	50	100	140	345
1914D	11,908,000	3.90	4.10	4.90	9.00	22	50	100	155	
1914S	2,100,000	4.50	6.25	8.00	15.50	36	65	115	225	
1915 (450)	5,620,000	3.90	4.10	4.90	9.00	22	50	100	140	345
1915S	960,000	7.25	12.50	25.00	36.00	60	90	160	260	
1916	18,490,000	3.90	4.10	4.90	9.00	22	50	100	140	
1916S	5,820,000	3.90	4.10	4.90	9.00	22	50	100	155	

MERCURY (WINGED LIBERTY HEAD) (1916–1945)

Although this coin is commonly called the *Mercury* dime, the main device is in fact a representation of Liberty. The wings crowning her cap are intended to symbolize liberty of thought. Designer Adolph Weinman's monogram, AW, is at the right of the neck. A centennial gold issue was struck in 2016.

G-4 Good: Letters and date clear. Lines and bands in fasces obliterated.
VG-8 Very Good: Half of sticks discernible in fasces.
F-12 Fine: All sticks in fasces defined. Diagonal bands worn nearly flat.
VF-20 Very Fine: Diagonal bands definitely visible.
EF-40 Extremely Fine: Only slight wear on diagonal bands. Braids and hair before ear clearly visible.
AU-50 About Uncirculated: Slight trace of wear. Most mint luster present.
MS-63 Choice Uncirculated: No trace of wear. Light blemishes. Attractive mint luster.
MS-65 Gem Uncirculated: Only light, scattered, non-distracting marks. Strong luster, good eye appeal.

Mintmark location is on reverse,
left of fasces.

The Mint State prices shown are what coin dealers pay for average Uncirculated pieces with minimum blemishes. For coins with sharp strikes and split horizontal bands on the reverse, they usually pay much more.

	Mintage	VG-8	F-12	VF-20	EF-40	AU-50	MS-60	MS-63	MS-65
1916	22,180,080	$4.30	$5.00	$5.50	$6.50	$11.00	$36	$70	$125
1916D	264,000	1,500.00	2,600.00	3,600.00	5,250.00	7,250.00	10,500	14,000	22,500
1916S	10,450,000	4.30	7.25	10.00	16.00	17.00	32	75	215
1917	55,230,000	2.60	2.80	3.00	4.30	7.25	19	40	135
1917D	9,402,000	5.50	11.00	20.00	50.00	70.00	115	200	600
1917S	27,330,000	4.30	5.50	6.25	10.00	22.00	85	150	285
1918	26,680,000	2.60	4.10	8.00	23.00	30.00	60	110	330
1918D	22,674,800	2.60	3.90	9.00	23.00	50.00	135	260	625
1918S	19,300,000	4.30	5.50	7.25	18.00	45.00	110	275	650
1919	35,740,000	2.60	2.80	3.40	7.25	20.00	45	125	315
1919D	9,939,000	4.30	7.25	16.00	40.00	80.00	245	500	1,050
1919S	8,850,000	3.40	9.00	14.50	29.00	75.00	275	650	1,500
1920	59,030,000	2.60	2.80	3.00	4.30	6.25	23	65	170
1920D	19,171,000	3.90	5.50	7.25	16.00	50.00	145	350	500
1920S	13,820,000	3.40	6.25	8.00	27.00	95.00	240	415	1,100
1921	1,230,000	65.00	90.00	180.00	405.00	675.00	1,250	1,850	2,800
1921D	1,080,000	95.00	135.00	255.00	485.00	925.00	1,450	1,900	2,550
1923	50,130,000	2.20	2.30	3.00	4.30	6.25	20	38	135
1923S	6,440,000	3.40	8.00	14.50	70.00	115.00	295	460	1,000
1924	24,010,000	2.60	2.60	3.00	9.00	20.00	49	90	160
1924D	6,810,000	2.60	6.25	16.50	45.00	70.00	215	370	825
1924S	7,120,000	3.50	5.50	16.00	60.00	110.00	275	415	1,450
1925	25,610,000	2.20	2.30	3.00	4.30	7.25	32	75	200
1925D	5,117,000	6.25	11.00	40.00	110.00	170.00	370	650	1,300
1925S	5,850,000	3.40	11.00	23.00	80.00	145.00	275	550	1,050
1926	32,160,000	2.20	2.30	3.00	4.30	7.25	27	55	180
1926D	6,828,000	2.60	3.00	11.00	25.00	50.00	150	215	460
1926S	1,520,000	13.50	29.00	60.00	240.00	320.00	1,350	2,000	3,000
1927	28,080,000	2.20	2.30	3.00	4.30	8.00	27	60	110
1927D	4,812,000	3.40	9.00	23.00	75.00	110.00	315	550	1,250

Chart continued on next page.

	Mintage	VG-8	F-12	VF-20	EF-40	AU-50	MS-60	MS-63	MS-65
1927S	4,770,000	$3.40	$4.30	$11.00	$32.00	$80.00	$330	$600	$1,150
1928	19,480,000	2.20	2.30	3.00	4.30	6.25	22	47	100
1928D	4,161,000	3.40	14.50	24.00	60.00	110.00	160	355	775
1928S	7,400,000	3.40	3.90	5.50	13.50	25.00	115	240	385
1929	25,970,000	2.20	2.30	3.00	4.30	6.25	18	25	60
1929D	5,034,000	2.20	2.30	3.00	4.30	6.25	20	29	90
1929S	4,730,000	2.70	2.80	3.20	4.30	6.25	27	49	160
1930	6,770,000	2.20	2.30	3.00	4.30	6.25	22	40	90
1930S	1,843,000	2.60	3.00	4.30	12.50	36.00	70	110	265
1931	3,150,000	2.30	3.20	3.40	6.25	14.50	36	75	135
1931D	1,260,000	6.75	11.50	17.00	36.00	45.00	85	120	305
1931S	1,800,000	3.70	4.30	9.00	22.00	45.00	90	135	285

	Mintage	F-12	VF-20	EF-40	AU-50	MS-60	MS-63	MS-65	PF-63
1934	24,080,000	$2.30	$3.00	$5.50	$8.00	$20.00	$25.00	$32	
1934D	6,772,000	2.50	3.00	11.50	21.00	41.00	47.00	65	
1935	58,830,000	2.30	3.00	3.50	3.60	8.00	12.50	27	
1935D	10,477,000	2.50	3.00	8.00	18.00	27.00	35.00	55	
1935S	15,840,000	2.50	3.00	4.30	6.25	18.00	22.00	27	
1936	(4,130) 87,500,000	2.30	3.00	3.50	3.60	7.25	10.00	20	$525
1936D	16,132,000	2.50	3.00	6.25	9.00	22.00	31.00	50	
1936S	9,210,000	2.50	3.00	4.30	8.00	20.00	25.00	31	
1937	(5,756) 56,860,000	2.30	3.00	3.50	3.60	6.25	9.00	17	265
1937D	14,146,000	2.30	3.00	4.30	5.50	17.00	22.00	36	
1937S	9,740,000	2.30	3.00	4.30	5.50	16.00	20.00	34	
1938	(8,728) 22,190,000	2.30	3.00	3.50	3.60	6.25	11.00	22	140
1938D	5,537,000	2.30	3.00	4.30	5.50	16.00	20.00	29	
1938S	8,090,000	2.30	3.00	4.30	5.50	16.00	22.00	31	
1939	(9,321) 67,740,000	2.30	3.00	3.50	3.60	6.25	9.00	17	115
1939D	24,394,000	2.30	3.00	4.30	5.50	16.00	20.00	28	
1939S	10,540,000	2.30	3.00	4.30	5.50	16.00	20.00	27	
1940	(11,827) 65,350,000	2.30	3.00	3.60	3.70	6.25	9.00	17	100
1940D	21,198,000	2.30	3.00	3.60	3.70	6.25	9.00	26	
1940S	21,560,000	2.30	3.00	3.60	3.70	6.25	11.50	26	
1941	(16,557) 175,090,000	2.30	2.70	3.20	3.30	6.25	9.00	17	100
1941D	45,634,000	2.30	2.70	3.20	3.30	6.25	11.50	20	
1941S	43,090,000	2.30	2.70	3.20	3.30	6.25	9.00	26	
1942	(22,329) 205,410,000	2.30	2.70	3.20	3.30	6.25	9.00	17	100
1942, 42 Over 41	*	340.00	405.00	525.00	825.00	2,400.00	4,200.00	8,000	
1942D	60,740,000	2.30	2.70	3.20	3.30	6.25	11.50	20	
1942D, 42 Over 41	*	330.00	370.00	460.00	825.00	2,400.00	4,650.00	9,500	
1942S	49,300,000	2.30	2.70	3.20	3.30	6.25	9.00	20	
1943	191,710,000	2.30	2.70	3.20	3.30	6.25	9.00	17	
1943D	71,949,000	2.30	2.70	3.20	3.30	6.25	11.00	17	
1943S	60,400,000	2.30	2.70	3.20	3.30	6.25	11.00	17	
1944	231,410,000	2.30	2.70	3.20	3.30	6.25	9.00	17	
1944D	62,224,000	2.30	2.70	3.20	3.30	6.25	11.00	17	
1944S	49,490,000	2.30	2.70	3.20	3.30	7.25	11.50	20	
1945	159,130,000	2.30	2.70	3.20	3.30	6.25	9.00	17	
1945D	40,245,000	2.30	2.70	3.20	3.30	6.25	9.00	17	
1945S	41,920,000	2.30	2.70	3.20	3.30	6.25	11.00	17	
1945S, Micro S	*	3.10	3.40	4.30	6.25	22.00	32.00	80	

* Included in number above.

ROOSEVELT (1946 TO DATE)

John R. Sinnock (whose initials, JS, are at the truncation of the neck) designed this dime showing a portrait of Franklin D. Roosevelt. The design has heavier lettering and a more modernistic character than preceding types.

VF-20 Very Fine: Moderate wear on high points of design. All major details are clear.

EF-40 Extremely Fine: All lines of torch, flame, and hair very plain.

MS-63 Choice Uncirculated: Some distracting contact marks or blemishes in prime focal areas. Impaired luster possible.

MS-65 Gem Uncirculated: Only light, non-distracting scattered marks. Strong luster, good eye appeal.

PF-65 Gem Proof: Nearly perfect.

Mintmark on reverse,
1946–1964.

Silver Coinage (1946–1964)

	Mintage	MS-63	MS-65	MS-66	PF-65
1946	255,250,000	$3.20	$8.00	$13.50	
1946D	61,043,500	3.20	10.00	17.00	
1946S	27,900,000	3.20	11.00	21.00	
1947	121,520,000	2.60	9.00	14.50	
1947D	46,835,000	3.90	8.00	18.00	
1947S	34,840,000	3.60	9.00	15.50	
1948	74,950,000	3.00	10.00	18.00	
1948D	52,841,000	4.30	9.00	16.00	
1948S	35,520,000	2.80	6.25	12.50	
1949	30,940,000	17.00	22.00	27.00	
1949D	26,034,000	6.75	11.00	13.50	
1949S	13,510,000	23.00	31.00	34.00	
1950	(51,386)	50,130,114	7.25	11.00	15.50	$36
1950D	46,803,000	3.20	8.00	13.50	
1950S	20,440,000	23.00	27.00	32.00	
1951	(57,500)	103,880,102	2.80	9.00	18.00	32
1951D	56,529,000	3.00	9.00	16.00	
1951S	31,630,000	11.00	13.50	20.00	
1952	(81,980)	99,040,093	2.80	8.00	17.00	22
1952D	122,100,000	2.60	9.00	13.50	
1952S	44,419,500	3.20	11.00	17.00	
1953	(128,800)	53,490,120	2.80	6.25	20.00	18
1953D	136,433,000	2.50	7.25	14.50	
1953S	39,180,000	3.20	14.50	27.00	
1954	(233,300)	114,010,203	2.30	8.00	13.50	11
1954D	106,397,000	2.30	6.25	12.50	
1954S	22,860,000	2.40	7.25	12.50	

Chart continued on next page.

	Mintage	MS-65	MS-66	PF-65
1955 ....(378,200)	12,450,181	$6.25	$15.50	$9.00
1955D	13,959,000	6.25	13.50	
1955S	18,510,000	6.25	12.50	
1956 ....(669,384)	108,640,000	6.25	13.50	5.50
1956D	108,015,100	6.25	12.50	
1957 ....(1,247,952)	160,160,000	6.25	13.50	3.40
1957D	113,354,330	6.25	12.50	
1958 ....(875,652)	31,910,000	6.25	13.50	3.40
1958D	136,564,600	6.25	11.50	
1959 ....(1,149,291)	85,780,000	6.25	15.50	3.40
1959D	164,919,790	6.25	11.50	
1960 ....(1,691,602)	70,390,000	6.25	11.50	3.40
1960D	200,160,400	6.25	11.50	
1961 ....(3,028,244)	93,730,000	6.25	12.50	3.40
1961D	209,146,550	6.25	11.50	
1962 ....(3,218,019)	72,450,000	6.25	11.50	3.40
1962D	334,948,380	6.25	11.50	
1963 ....(3,075,645)	123,650,000	7.25	13.50	3.40
1963D	421,476,530	6.25	11.50	
1964 ....(3,950,762)	929,360,000	6.25	11.50	4.30
1964D	1,357,517,180	6.25	11.50	

Clad Coinage and Silver Proofs (1965 to Date)

*Mintmark on obverse,
starting in 1968.*

	Mintage	MS-65	MS-66	PF-65
1965	1,652,140,570	$1.90	$8.00	
1966	1,382,734,540	0.90	2.60	
1967	2,244,007,320	0.90	2.60	
1968	424,470,400	0.90	4.30	
1968D	480,748,280	1.70	11.00	
1968S	(3,041,506)			$0.90
1969	145,790,000	1.70	22.00	
1969D	563,323,870	1.70	6.25	
1969S	(2,394,631)			0.90
1970	345,570,000	1.30	22.00	
1970D	754,942,100	0.90	2.60	
1970S	(2,632,810)			0.90
1971	162,690,000	0.90	15.50	
1971D	377,914,240	0.90	2.60	
1971S	(3,220,733)			0.90
1972	431,540,000	0.90	8.00	
1972D	330,290,000	0.90	2.60	
1972S	(3,260,996)			0.90
1973	315,670,000	0.90	5.50	
1973D	455,032,426	0.90	4.30	

	Mintage	MS-65	MS-66	PF-65
1973S	(2,760,339)			$0.90
1974	470,248,000	$0.90	$22.00	
1974D	571,083,000	0.90	4.30	
1974S	(2,612,568)			0.90
1975	585,673,900	0.90	7.25	
1975D	313,705,300	0.90	2.60	
1975S	(2,845,450)			0.90
1976	568,760,000	0.90	10.00	
1976D	695,222,774	0.90	2.60	
1976S	(4,149,730)			0.90
1977	796,930,000	0.90	9.00	
1977D	376,607,228	0.90	2.60	
1977S	(3,251,152)			
1978	663,980,000	0.90	2.60	
1978D	282,847,540	0.90	2.60	
1978S	(3,127,781)			0.90
1979	315,440,000	0.90	2.60	
1979D	390,921,184	0.90	2.60	
1979S, Variety 1	(3,677,175)			0.90
1979S, Variety 2 ....*				0.90

* Included in number above.

DIMES

Mintage	MS-65	MS-66	PF-65
1980P 735,170,000	$0.90	$2.60	
1980D 719,354,321	0.90	7.25	
1980S . . . . (3,554,806)			$0.90
1981P 676,650,000	0.90	2.60	
1981D 712,284,143	0.90	2.60	
1981S, Variety 1 (4,063,083)			0.90
1981S, Variety 2 . . . .*			3.40
1982P 519,475,000	12.50	55.00	
1982, No Mmk. . . . .*	125.00	200.00	
1982D 542,713,584	10.00	36.00	
1982S . . . . (3,857,479)			0.90
1983P 647,025,000	5.50	16.00	
1983D 730,129,224	5.50	16.00	
1983S . . . . (3,279,126)			0.90
1984P 856,669,000	0.90	2.60	
1984D 704,803,976	0.90	4.30	
1984S . . . . (3,065,110)			0.90
1985P 705,200,962	0.90	2.60	
1985D 587,979,970	0.90	2.60	
1985S . . . . (3,362,821)			0.90
1986P 682,649,693	0.90	2.60	
1986D 473,326,970	0.90	4.30	
1986S . . . . (3,010,497)			0.90
1987P 762,709,481	0.90	3.40	
1987D 653,203,402	0.90	2.60	
1987S . . . . (4,227,728)			0.90
1988P 1,030,550,000	0.90	2.60	
1988D 962,385,489	0.90	2.60	
1988S . . . . (3,262,948)			0.90
1989P 1,298,400,000	0.90	2.60	
1989D 896,535,597	0.90	2.60	
1989S . . . . (3,220,194)			0.90
1990P 1,034,340,000	0.90	2.60	
1990D 839,995,824	0.90	2.60	
1990S . . . . (3,299,559)			0.90
1991P 927,220,000	0.90	2.60	
1991D 601,241,114	0.90	2.60	
1991S . . . . (2,867,787)			0.90
1992P 593,500,000	0.90	2.60	
1992D 616,273,932	0.90	2.60	
1992S . . . . (2,858,981)			0.90
1992S, Silver . . . (1,317,579)			3.40
1993P 766,180,000	0.90	2.60	
1993D 750,110,166	0.90	2.60	
1993S . . . . (2,633,439)			2.60
1993S, Silver . . . . . (761,353)			4.30
1994P 1,189,000,000	0.90	2.60	
1994D 1,303,268,110	0.90	2.60	
1994S . . . . (2,484,594)			1.70
1994S, Silver . . . . . (785,329)			3.40

Mintage	MS-65	MS-66	PF-65
1995P 1,125,500,000	$0.90	$2.60	
1995D 1,274,890,000	0.90	2.60	
1995S . . . . (2,117,496)			$3.40
1995S, Silver . . . . (679,985)			6.25
1996P 1,421,163,000	0.90	2.60	
1996D 1,400,300,000	0.90	2.60	
1996W 1,457,000	10.00	13.50	
1996S . . . . (1,750,244)			0.90
1996S, Silver . . . . (775,021)			6.25
1997P 991,640,000	0.90	2.60	
1997D 979,810,000	0.90	2.60	
1997S . . . . (2,055,000)			2.60
1997S, Silver . . . . (741,678)			6.25
1998P 1,163,000,000	0.90	3.40	
1998D 1,172,250,000	0.90	2.60	
1998S . . . . (2,086,507)			1.30
1998S, Silver . . . . (878,792)			3.40
1999P 2,164,000,000	0.90	2.60	
1999D 1,397,750,000	0.90	2.60	
1999S . . . . (2,543,401)			0.90
1999S, Silver . . . . (804,565)			3.40
2000P 1,842,500,000	0.90	2.60	
2000D 1,818,700,000	0.90	2.60	
2000S . . . . (3,082,572)			0.90
2000S, Silver . . . . (965,421)			3.40
2001P 1,369,590,000	0.90	2.60	
2001D 1,412,800,000	0.90	2.60	
2001S . . . . (2,294,909)			0.90
2001S, Silver . . . . (889,697)			3.40
2002P 1,187,500,000	0.90	2.60	
2002D 1,379,500,000	0.90	2.60	
2002S . . . . (2,319,766)			0.90
2002S, Silver . . . . (892,229)			3.40
2003P 1,085,500,000	0.90	2.60	
2003D 986,500,000	0.90	2.60	
2003S . . . . (2,172,684)			0.90
2003S, Silver . . . (1,125,755)			3.40
2004P 1,328,000,000	0.90	2.60	
2004D 1,159,500,000	0.90	2.60	
2004S . . . . (1,789,488)			1.70
2004S, Silver . . . (1,175,934)			3.40
2005P 1,412,000,000	0.90	2.60	
2005D 1,423,500,000	0.90	2.60	
2005S . . . . (2,275,000)			0.90
2005S, Silver . . . (1,069,679)			3.40
2006P 1,381,000,000	0.90	2.60	
2006D 1,447,000,000	0.90	2.60	
2006S . . . . (2,000,428)			1.70
2006S, Silver . . . (1,054,008)			3.40
2007P 1,047,500,000	0.90	2.60	

* Included in number above.

Chart continued on next page.

	Mintage	MS-65	MS-66	PF-65
2007D	1,042,000,000	$0.90	$2.60	
2007S	(1,702,116)			$1.70
2007S, Silver	(875,050)			3.40
2008P	391,000,000	0.90	5.50	
2008D	624,500,000	0.90	2.60	
2008S	(1,405,674)			1.70
2008S, Silver	(763,887)			3.40
2009P	96,500,000	0.90	2.60	
2009D	49,500,000	0.90	2.60	
2009S	(1,482,502)			1.70
2009S, Silver	(697,365)			3.40
2010P	557,000,000	0.90	2.60	
2010D	562,000,000	0.90	2.60	
2010S	(1,103,815)			3.40
2010S, Silver	(585,401)			4.30
2011P	748,000,000	0.90	2.60	
2011D	754,000,000	0.90	2.60	
2011S	(1,098,835)			3.40
2011S, Silver	(574,175)			4.30
2012P	808,000,000	0.90	2.60	
2012D	868,000,000	0.90	2.60	

	Mintage	MS-65	MS-66	PF-65
2012S	(843,705)			$3.40
2012S, Silver	(445,612)			5.50
2013P	1,086,500,000	$0.90	$2.60	
2013D	1,025,500,000	0.90	2.60	
2013S	(856,953)			3.40
2013S, Silver	(467,691)			4.30
2014P	1,125,500,000	0.90	2.60	
2014D	1,177,000,000	0.90	2.60	
2014S	(783,256)			3.40
2014S, Silver	(472,107)			4.30
2015P	1,497,510,000	0.90	2.60	
2015P, Rev Pf, Silver (a)	(74,430)			15.50
2015D	1,543,500,000	0.90	2.60	
2015S	(711,872)			3.40
2015S, Silver	(387,310)			4.30
2015W, Silver (a)	(74,430)			7.25
2016P	1,517,000,000	0.90	2.60	
2016D	1,437,000,000	0.90	2.60	
2016S	(641,775)			3.40
2016S, Silver	(419,496)			4.30

a. Included in March of Dimes commemorative Proof set.

	Mintage	OGP*	MS-69	MS-70
2016W, Gold (a)	125,000	$320	$350	$470

* OGP = Coin in original government packaging. a. In 2016 the Mint issued a centennial version of the Winged Liberty Head ("Mercury") dime in gold.

	Mintage	MS-65	MS-66	PF-65
2017P	1,437,500,000	$0.90	$2.60	
2017D	1,290,500,000	0.90	2.60	
2017S	(621,390)			$3.40
2017S, Silver	(406,986)			4.30
2018P	1,193,000,000	0.90	2.60	
2018D	1,006,000,000	0.90	2.60	
2018S	(568,804)			3.40
2018S, Silver	(381,748)			4.30
2019P	1,147,500,000	0.90	2.60	
2019D	1,001,500,000	0.90	2.60	
2019S	(649,050)			3.40
2019S, Silver	(460,925)			4.30
2020P	1,349,250,000	0.90	2.60	
2020D	1,481,000,000	0.90	2.60	
2020S	(511,148)			3.40
2020S, Silver	(363,179)			4.30
2021P	1,349,250,000	0.90	2.60	
2021D	1,481,000,000	0.90	2.60	

	Mintage	MS-65	MS-66	PF-65
2021S	(868,644)			$3.40
2021S, Silver	(355,778)			4.30
2022P	1,583,000,000	$0.90	$2.60	
2022D	1,515,000,000	0.90	2.60	
2022S	(699,097)			3.40
2022S, Silver	(299,096)			5.50
2023P	1,410,500,000	0.90	2.60	
2023D	1,295,000,000	0.90	2.60	
2023S	(593,245)			3.40
2023S, Silver	(242,012)			4.30
2024P		0.90	2.60	
2024D		0.90	2.60	
2024S				3.40
2024S, Silver				4.30
2025P		0.90	2.60	
2025D		0.90	2.60	
2025S				3.40
2025S, Silver				4.30

LIBERTY SEATED (1875–1878)

The twenty-cent piece was a short-lived coin authorized by the Act of March 3, 1875. The edge of the coin is plain. Most of the 1876-CC coins were melted at the Mint and never released. The mintmark is on the reverse below the eagle.

G-4 Good: LIBERTY on shield obliterated. Letters and date legible.
VG-8 Very Good: One or two letters in LIBERTY barely visible. Other details bold.
F-12 Fine: Some letters of LIBERTY possibly visible.
VF-20 Very Fine: LIBERTY readable, but partly weak.
EF-40 Extremely Fine: LIBERTY mostly sharp. Only slight wear on high points of coin.
AU-50 About Uncirculated: Slight trace of wear on breast, head, and knees.
MS-60 Uncirculated: No trace of wear. Light blemishes.
MS-63 Choice Uncirculated: Some distracting blemishes in prime focal areas. Some impairment of luster possible.
PF-63 Choice Proof: Reflective surfaces with only a few blemishes in secondary focal places. No major flaws.

	Mintage	G-4	VG-8	F-12	VF-20	EF-40	AU-50	MS-60	MS-63	PF-63
1875 . . . . (1,200)	38,500	$155	$170	$195	$225	$315	$435	$700	$1,300	$2,250
1875CC	133,290	170	205	315	370	650	800	1,600	2,700	
1875S	1,155,000	90	105	135	160	195	275	625	925	
1876 . . . . (1,150)	14,750	180	240	295	360	435	525	1,000	1,500	2,350
1876CC	10,000	—	—	—	—	126,000	148,500	193,500	288,000	
1877 . . . . . . (510)					2,750	3,400				6,250
1878 . . . . . . (600)					1,750	1,950				3,100

Authorized in 1792, this denomination was not issued until four years later. The first type weighed 104 grains, the standard until modified to 103-1/8 grains by the Act of January 18, 1837. As with the dime and half dime, the weight was reduced and arrows placed at the date in 1853. Rays were placed in the field of the reverse during that year only.

DRAPED BUST (1796–1807)

AG-3 About Good: Details clear enough to identify.
G-4 Good: Date readable. Bust outlined, but no detail.
VG-8 Very Good: All but deepest drapery folds worn smooth. Hairlines nearly gone and curls lacking in detail.
F-12 Fine: All drapery lines visible. Hair partly worn.
VF-20 Very Fine: Only left side of drapery indistinct.
EF-40 Extremely Fine: Hair well outlined and detailed.
AU-50 About Uncirculated: Slight trace of wear on shoulder and highest waves of hair.
MS-60 Uncirculated: No trace of wear. Light blemishes.
MS-63 Choice Uncirculated: Some distracting marks or blemishes in focal areas. Impaired luster possible.

Small Eagle Reverse (1796)

	Mintage	G-4	VG-8	F-12	VF-20	EF-40	AU-50	MS-60	MS-63
1796	6,146	$9,750	$17,000	$24,000	$31,500	$48,000	$51,500	$83,000	$148,500

Heraldic Eagle Reverse (1804–1807)

	Mintage	G-4	VG-8	F-12	VF-20	EF-40	AU-50	MS-60	MS-63
1804	6,738	$2,800	$4,200	$6,250	$8,750	$23,500	$42,000	$83,000	$139,500
1805	121,394	285	390	575	1,250	2,600	4,100	8,500	12,000
1806, 6 Over 5	*	370	550	875	1,300	3,000	5,750	10,500	22,500
1806	206,124	285	390	575	1,100	2,300	3,700	8,500	12,000
1807	220,643	285	390	575	1,100	2,300	3,700	8,500	12,000

* Included in number below.

CAPPED BUST (1815–1838)
Variety 1 – Large Diameter (1815–1828)

AG-3 About Good: Details clear enough to identify.
G-4 Good: Date, letters, stars legible. Hair under Liberty's headband smooth. Cap lines worn smooth.
VG-8 Very Good: Rim well defined. Main details visible. Full LIBERTY on cap. Hair above eye nearly smooth.
F-12 Fine: All hair lines visible, but only partial detail visible in drapery. Shoulder clasp distinct.
VF-20 Very Fine: All details visible, but some wear evident. Clasp and ear sharp.
EF-40 Extremely Fine: All details distinct. Hair well outlined.
AU-50 About Uncirculated: Slight trace of wear on tips of curls and above the eye, and on the wing and claw tips.
MS-60 Uncirculated: No trace of wear. Light blemishes.
MS-63 Choice Uncirculated: Some distracting marks or blemishes in focal areas. Impaired luster possible.

QUARTER DOLLARS

	Mintage	G-4	VG-8	F-12	VF-20	EF-40	AU-50	MS-60	MS-63
1815	89,235	$180	$275	$370	$550	$1,750	$2,050	$2,900	$4,650
1818, 8 Over 5	*	105	145	240	370	975	1,550	2,900	4,650
1818	361,174	105	145	240	370	975	1,550	2,900	4,650
1819	144,000	105	145	240	370	975	1,550	3,250	7,250
1820	127,444	105	145	240	370	975	1,550	3,250	8,000
1821	216,851	105	145	240	370	975	1,550	2,900	4,650
1822	64,080	160	255	415	725	1,400	2,300	5,000	8,000
1822, 25 Over 50 C.	*	4,100	6,250	13,000	17,500	28,000	36,000	46,500	69,000
1823, 3 Over 2	17,800	36,000	41,000	55,000	64,500	73,500	94,500	207,000	—
1824, 4 Over 2	**	415	675	1,000	1,400	3,000	5,000	19,000	42,000
1825	168,000	135	170	320	460	1,100	1,850	3,700	5,250
1827, Original (Curl-Base 2 in 25 C.) **(a)**	*Fewer than 10 known*	—	—	—	—	—	—	—	—
1827, Restrike (Square-Base 2 in 25 C.) **(a)**	*10–12 est. known*	—	—	—	—	—	—	—	—
1828	102,000	105	145	240	370	975	1,550	2,900	4,650
1828, 25 Over 50 C.	*	825	1,150	1,850	2,400	5,750	8,500	14,000	46,500

* Included in regular mintage. ** Included in 1825 mintage. **a.** The 7 is punched over a 3, which is punched over an earlier 2.

Variety 2 – Reduced Diameter (1831–1838), Motto Removed

G-4 Good: Bust of Liberty well defined. Hair under headband smooth. Date, letters, stars legible. Scant rims.
VG-8 Very Good: Details apparent but worn on high spots. Rims strong. Full LIBERTY.
F-12 Fine: All hair lines visible. Drapery partly worn. Shoulder clasp distinct.
VF-20 Very Fine: Only top spots worn. Clasp sharp. Ear distinct.
EF-40 Extremely Fine: Hair details and clasp bold and clear.

AU-50 About Uncirculated: Slight trace of wear on hair around forehead, on cheek, and at top and bottom tips of eagle's wings and left claw.
MS-60 Uncirculated: No trace of wear. Light blemishes.
MS-63 Choice Uncirculated: Some distracting contact marks or blemishes in prime focal areas. Impaired luster possible.

	Mintage	G-4	VG-8	F-12	VF-20	EF-40	AU-50	MS-60	MS-63
1831	398,000	$70	$85	$100	$125	$285	$525	$1,500	$2,800
1832	320,000	70	85	100	125	285	525	1,500	2,800
1833	156,000	70	85	100	135	345	550	1,850	3,350
1834	286,000	70	85	100	125	285	525	1,500	2,800
1835	1,952,000	70	85	100	125	285	525	1,500	2,800
1836	472,000	70	85	100	125	285	525	1,650	4,100
1837	252,400	70	85	100	125	285	525	1,500	2,800
1838	366,000	70	85	100	125	285	525	1,500	2,800

LIBERTY SEATED (1838–1891)

G-4 Good: Scant rim. LIBERTY on shield worn off. Date and letters legible.
VG-8 Very Good: Rim fairly defined, at least three letters in LIBERTY evident.
F-12 Fine: LIBERTY complete, but partly weak.
VF-20 Very Fine: LIBERTY strong.
EF-40 Extremely Fine: Complete LIBERTY and edges of scroll. Shoulder clasp clear on Liberty's gown.
AU-50 About Uncirculated: Slight wear on Liberty's knees and breast and on eagle's neck, wing tips, and claws.
MS-60 Uncirculated: No trace of wear. Light blemishes.
MS-63 Choice Uncirculated: Some distracting marks or blemishes in focal areas. Impaired luster possible.

Variety 1 – No Motto Above Eagle (1838–1853)

Small Date

Mintmark location is on reverse, below eagle. **Large Date**

	Mintage	G-4	VG-8	F-12	VF-20	EF-40	AU-50	MS-60	MS-63
1838	466,000	$25	$38	$70	$190	$415	$825	$1,400	$3,700
1839	491,146	25	38	70	190	415	825	1,400	3,700
1840	188,127	20	22	45	115	255	460	1,400	4,100
1840O	425,200	27	38	70	135	370	550	1,250	3,700
1841	120,000	45	70	90	180	350	600	975	1,350
1841O	452,000	29	45	90	180	260	360	725	1,350
1842, Large Date	88,000	45	60	100	180	300	550	1,100	3,500
1842O, Small Date	*	460	925	1,200	2,250	6,250	9,000	31,500	53,500
1842O, Large Date	769,000	34	38	49	90	200	415	1,300	2,800
1843	645,600	20	22	29	55	155	255	500	1,100
1843O	968,000	34	55	110	260	725	1,200	2,050	4,650
1844	421,200	22	29	45	80	160	260	700	1,650
1844O	740,000	36	45	55	80	180	320	1,000	1,200
1845	922,000	20	22	29	45	110	180	460	775
1846	510,000	36	55	70	90	200	315	725	1,500
1847	734,000	20	22	29	34	80	180	500	1,300
1847O	368,000	75	110	225	415	700	1,200	5,750	11,500
1848	146,000	36	55	75	110	275	390	925	3,700
1849	340,000	20	22	29	55	80	225	725	1,100
1849O	(a)	1,050	1,550	2,250	2,600	5,500	6,000	14,000	23,500
1850	190,800	22	36	70	90	180	460	1,300	2,300
1850O	412,000	50	95	125	170	500	675	1,500	3,700
1851	160,000	80	135	240	350	485	725	925	1,850
1851O	88,000	345	500	675	1,000	2,250	3,000	8,500	30,000
1852	177,060	45	70	95	185	370	550	875	1,400
1852O	96,000	255	370	550	1,100	1,650	5,000	8,000	23,500
1853, Recut Date, No Arrows or Rays	44,200	975	1,400	2,050	2,550	3,150	3,650	5,250	5,750

* Included in number below. **a.** Mintage for 1849-O included with 1850-O.

Variety 2 – Arrows at Date, Rays Around Eagle (1853)

1853, 3 Over 4

	Mintage	G-4	VG-8	F-12	VF-20	EF-40	AU-50	MS-60	MS-63
1853	15,210,020	$23	$29	$36	$65	$155	$305	$825	$1,300
1853, 3 Over 4	*	45	70	135	240	460	700	1,650	3,350
1853O	1,332,000	34	45	70	110	300	725	3,250	7,500

* Included in number above.

Variety 3 – Arrows at Date, No Rays (1854–1855)

	Mintage	G-4	VG-8	F-12	VF-20	EF-40	AU-50	MS-60	MS-63
1854	12,380,000	$20	$22	$27	$29	$75	$180	$525	$875
1854O	1,484,000	34	38	45	60	90	225	725	1,300
1855	2,857,000	20	22	27	29	75	180	525	875
1855O	176,000	110	160	275	550	1,400	2,300	5,250	12,000
1855S	396,400	135	200	320	500	825	1,300	2,800	7,000

Variety 1 Resumed, With Weight Standard of Variety 2 (1856–1865)

	Mintage	G-4	VG-8	F-12	VF-20	EF-40	AU-50	MS-60	MS-63	PF-63
1856	7,264,000	$20	$22	$29	$34	$80	$170	$305	$500	
1856O	968,000	34	40	60	90	180	415	925	1,450	
1856S	286,000	285	405	550	700	1,500	2,800	7,000	14,000	
1857	9,644,000	20	22	29	34	80	170	305	500	
1857O	1,180,000	34	43	70	110	200	370	925	1,850	
1857S	82,000	240	370	460	600	925	1,600	3,550	7,000	
1858 . . . . . . *(300)*	7,368,000	20	22	29	34	80	170	305	500	$1,200
1858O	520,000	34	40	60	90	200	460	3,250	7,500	
1858S	121,000	200	315	460	775	2,050	3,550	17,000	—	
1859 . . . . . *(800)*	1,343,200	20	22	29	34	80	170	320	650	975
1859O	260,000	40	60	75	115	225	825	2,050	5,750	
1859S	80,000	320	440	700	1,000	3,150	8,250	—	—	
1860 . . . . *(1,000)*	804,400	20	22	29	34	85	180	385	725	975
1860O	388,000	34	40	60	75	180	345	825	1,500	
1860S	56,000	750	1,200	2,250	4,200	6,750	12,000	32,500	—	
1861 . . . . *(1,000)*	4,853,600	20	22	29	34	80	170	335	500	875
1861S	96,000	500	700	925	1,850	3,500	7,500	—	—	
1862 . . . . . *(550)*	932,000	23	27	36	55	100	180	425	675	875
1862S	67,000	135	225	320	460	1,000	1,850	3,250	6,250	
1863 . . . . . *(460)*	191,600	27	36	45	85	370	500	825	1,300	875
1864 . . . . . *(470)*	93,600	150	200	255	350	550	650	1,300	2,400	875
1864S	20,000	775	925	1,100	1,650	3,950	5,750	11,500	16,500	
1865 . . . . . . *(500)*	58,800	70	90	160	285	390	650	1,350	2,250	875
1865S	41,000	200	275	415	650	925	1,400	4,400	8,500	

Variety 4 – Motto Above Eagle (1866–1873)

	Mintage	G-4	VG-8	F-12	VF-20	EF-40	AU-50	MS-60	MS-63	PF-63
1866 . . . . . . *(725)*	16,800	$550	$775	$925	$1,050	$1,200	$1,400	$1,800	$2,100	$750
1866S	28,000	415	700	1,050	1,200	1,850	2,300	4,650	12,000	

Chart continued on next page.

	Mintage	G-4	VG-8	F-12	VF-20	EF-40	AU-50	MS-60	MS-63	PF-63
1867 . . . . (625) 20,000		$370	$550	$725	$925	$1,250	$1,550	$2,400	$4,200	$650
1867S 48,000		460	725	925	1,150	2,250	6,750	8,500	11,500	
1868 . . . . (600) . . . 29,400		180	255	320	370	575	775	1,400	2,800	625
1868S 96,000		90	135	225	550	650	1,400	3,700	6,750	
1869 . . . . (600) . . . 16,000		390	500	650	775	950	1,250	1,650	3,700	625
1869S 76,000		140	225	390	550	925	1,500	3,900	6,250	
1870 . . . . . . (1,000) . . . 86,400		45	70	110	180	300	500	725	1,850	625
1870CC 8,340		7,500	11,500	17,000	21,500	44,500	117,000	—	—	
1871 . . . . (960) . . . 118,200		36	55	75	110	225	330	550	1,200	625
1871CC 10,890		8,000	12,000	17,000	28,000	44,500	60,500	103,500	171,000	
1871S 30,900		650	975	1,500	1,850	3,000	3,700	6,250	8,500	
1872 . . . . (950) . . . 182,000		45	70	120	160	300	415	1,100	1,850	625
1872CC 22,850		1,650	2,100	3,700	8,500	12,500	17,000	53,500	—	
1872S 83,000		1,650	1,850	2,250	3,350	5,750	8,500	14,000	21,000	
1873 . . . . (600) . . . 212,000		70	90	135	200	275	415	925	1,700	625
1873CC 4,000		—	—	—	55,000	64,500	73,500	135,000	360,000	

Variety 5 – Arrows at Date (1873–1874)

	Mintage	G-4	VG-8	F-12	VF-20	EF-40	AU-50	MS-60	MS-63	PF-63
1873 . . . . (500) . . 1,271,200		$20	$22	$32	$65	$145	$360	$625	$1,100	$1,300
1873CC 12,462		4,650	8,000	11,000	15,000	22,500	50,500	87,500	135,000	
1873S 156,000		70	90	125	180	320	485	1,400	3,250	
1874 . . . . (700) . . . 471,200		20	22	32	65	145	360	625	1,100	1,300
1874S 392,000		20	22	32	65	145	360	625	1,100	

Variety 4 Resumed, With Weight Standard of Variety 5 (1875–1891)

1877-S, S Over Horizontal S

	Mintage	G-4	VG-8	F-12	VF-20	EF-40	AU-50	MS-60	MS-63	PF-63
1875 . . . . . . (700) 4,292,800		$20	$22	$23	$29	$50	$110	$200	$385	$575
1875CC 140,000		180	275	415	650	1,200	1,750	3,900	6,250	
1875S 680,000		22	32	45	75	135	200	485	600	
1876 . . . . (1,150) . . . 17,816,000		20	22	23	29	50	110	200	385	575
1876CC 4,944,000		40	60	80	100	145	215	525	875	
1876S 8,596,000		20	22	27	29	50	110	200	385	
1877 . . . . . . (510) . . . 10,911,200		20	22	23	29	50	110	200	385	575
1877CC 4,192,000		40	60	80	100	135	240	425	1,100	
1877S 8,996,000		20	22	23	29	50	110	200	385	

	Mintage	G-4	VG-8	F-12	VF-20	EF-40	AU-50	MS-60	MS-63	PF-63
1877S, S Over Horizontal S . . . . .*		$22	$32	$55	$135	$225	$415	$825	$1,200	
1878 . . . . (800). . 2,260,000		20	22	23	29	50	110	200	385	$575
1878CC 996,000		40	50	60	90	190	275	650	1,050	
1878S 140,000		320	415	550	925	1,500	2,300	3,900	5,250	
1879 . . . . . . (1,100). 13,600		110	145	200	275	370	415	500	650	575
1880 . . . . . . (1,355). 13,600		110	145	200	295	390	435	525	650	575
1881 . . . . (975). 12,000		110	145	200	275	415	460	575	775	575
1882 . . . . . . (1,100). 15,200		110	145	200	275	370	415	500	650	575
1883 . . . . . . (1,039). 14,400		110	145	200	275	370	415	500	650	575
1884 . . . . (875). 8,000		160	180	255	275	370	415	500	650	575
1885 . . . . (930). 13,600		110	135	180	275	370	415	500	675	575
1886 . . . . (886). 5,000		240	315	385	460	675	725	1,000	1,400	575
1887 . . . . (710). 10,000		135	180	225	300	435	500	700	875	575
1888 . . . . (832). 10,001		160	200	240	305	405	485	725	1,050	575
1888S 1,216,000		20	22	23	29	50	145	275	550	
1889 . . . . (711). 12,000		110	145	200	255	300	370	575	875	575
1890 . . . . (590). 80,000		90	110	135	180	200	255	495	600	575
1891 . . . . (600). . 3,920,000		20	22	23	29	50	110	200	385	575
1891O 68,000		275	550	875	1,300	2,050	2,800	6,250	10,500	
1891S 2,216,000		20	22	23	29	50	135	275	415	

* Included in 1877-S regular mintage (previous page).

BARBER (1892–1916)

Like other silver coins of this type, the quarter dollars minted from 1892 to 1916 were designed by U.S. Mint chief engraver Charles E. Barber. His initial B is found at the truncation of the neck of Liberty.

G-4 Good: Date and legends legible. LIBERTY worn off headband.

VG-8 Very Good: Some letters in LIBERTY legible.

F-12 Fine: LIBERTY completely legible but not sharp.

VF-20 Very Fine: All letters in LIBERTY evenly plain.

EF-40 Extremely Fine: LIBERTY bold, its ribbon distinct.

AU-50 About Uncirculated: Slight trace of wear above forehead, on cheek, and on eagle's head, wings, and tail.

MS-60 Uncirculated: No trace of wear. Light blemishes.

MS-63 Choice Uncirculated: Some distracting marks or blemishes in focal areas. Impaired luster possible.

PF-63 Choice Proof: Reflective surfaces with only a few blemishes in secondary focal places. No major flaws.

	Mintage	G-4	VG-8	F-12	VF-20	EF-40	AU-50	MS-60	MS-63	PF-63
1892 . . . . . . (1,245). . 8,236,000		$8.25	$9.00	$12.50	$20	$40	$95	$180	$245	$460
1892O 2,460,000		11.00	15.50	32.00	45	70	135	245	370	
1892S 964,079		22.00	43.00	70.00	105	165	345	500	775	
1893 . . . . (792). . 5,444,023		8.25	9.00	12.50	25	55	110	200	385	460
1893O 3,396,000		9.00	11.50	25.00	43	85	135	225	370	
1893S 1,454,535		14.50	27.00	55.00	90	135	250	345	825	
1894 . . . . (972). . 3,432,000		9.00	11.50	22.00	34	65	105	180	320	460
1894O 2,852,000		11.50	20.00	50.00	90	140	200	350	575	
1894S 2,648,821		9.25	10.00	25.00	50	110	160	205	435	
1895 . . . . (880). . 4,440,000		9.25	10.00	21.00	27	55	95	200	320	460
1895O 2,816,000		10.00	14.50	32.00	55	100	160	300	725	
1895S 1,764,681		14.50	27.00	60.00	90	130	200	300	725	
1896 . . . . (762). . 3,874,000		8.25	9.00	12.50	20	40	95	180	245	460
1896O 1,484,000		45.00	70.00	145.00	225	460	725	875	1,550	

Chart continued on next page.

	Mintage	G-4	VG-8	F-12	VF-20	EF-40	AU-50	MS-60	MS-63	PF-63
1896S	188,039	$485.00	$1,000.00	$1,750.00	$2,800	$3,900	$5,750	$11,500	$14,500	
1897	(731) . .8,140,000	8.25	10.00	12.50	20	40	95	180	265	$460
1897O	1,414,800	32.00	65.00	160.00	295	460	700	1,200	1,850	
1897S	542,229	80.00	115.00	225.00	460	600	900	1,300	2,300	
1898	(735) 11,100,000	8.25	9.00	12.50	20	40	95	180	245	460
1898O	1,868,000	11.00	22.00	65.00	110	255	370	675	925	
1898S	1,020,592	10.00	16.00	36.00	70	160	330	975	2,050	
1899	(846) 12,624,000	8.25	9.00	12.50	20	40	95	200	275	460
1899O	2,644,000	12.50	20.00	40.00	75	125	180	390	575	
1899S	708,000	25.00	50.00	95.00	135	180	300	1,000	1,850	
1900	(912) 10,016,000	8.25	9.00	12.50	24	60	110	215	330	460
1900O	3,416,000	11.00	21.00	60.00	85	120	300	525	650	
1900S	1,858,585	8.25	12.50	18.00	36	85	200	500	1,050	
1901	(813) . .8,892,000	8.25	9.00	12.50	20	40	95	180	275	460
1901O	1,612,000	40.00	70.00	155.00	305	625	975	1,500	2,050	
1901S	72,664	3,350.00	8,000.00	12,500.00	17,500	24,000	26,500	41,000	48,000	
1902	(777) 12,196,967	8.25	9.00	12.50	20	40	95	180	265	460
1902O	4,748,000	8.25	13.50	27.00	60	130	215	500	750	
1902S	1,524,612	10.00	16.00	29.00	65	110	200	435	725	
1903	(755) . .9,759,309	8.25	9.00	12.50	20	40	95	180	345	460
1903O	3,500,000	8.25	13.50	20.00	45	90	170	370	725	
1903S	1,036,000	11.00	17.00	31.00	65	105	190	460	875	
1904	(670) . .9,588,143	8.25	9.00	12.50	20	40	95	190	370	460
1904O	2,456,000	22.00	40.00	75.00	135	190	370	725	900	
1905	(727) . .4,967,523	13.50	20.00	34.00	45	50	100	180	320	460
1905O	1,230,000	32.00	50.00	100.00	170	240	300	725	1,100	
1905S	1,884,000	18.00	27.00	60.00	80	105	160	460	975	
1906	(675) . .3,655,760	8.25	9.00	12.50	20	40	95	180	245	460
1906D	3,280,000	8.25	9.00	12.50	20	40	95	180	280	
1906O	2,056,000	8.25	12.50	27.00	41	80	135	195	370	
1907	(575) . .7,132,000	8.25	9.00	12.50	20	40	95	180	245	460
1907D	2,484,000	8.25	9.00	18.00	34	50	145	290	550	
1907O	4,560,000	8.25	9.00	12.50	27	45	100	180	355	
1907S	1,360,000	8.25	18.00	40.00	80	240	355	725	1,500	
1908	(545) . .4,232,000	8.25	9.00	12.50	20	40	95	180	245	460
1908D	5,788,000	8.25	9.00	12.50	20	40	95	180	245	
1908O	6,244,000	8.25	9.00	12.50	20	40	95	180	275	
1908S	784,000	34.00	65.00	110.00	150	315	500	1,000	1,400	
1909	(650) . .9,268,000	8.25	9.00	12.50	20	40	95	180	245	460
1909D	5,114,000	8.25	9.00	12.50	20	40	95	180	245	
1909O	712,000	49.00	145.00	425.00	725	2,050	3,000	3,900	4,550	
1909S	1,348,000	8.25	12.50	25.00	38	65	160	275	600	
1910	(551) . .2,244,000	8.25	9.00	12.50	20	40	95	180	245	460
1910D	1,500,000	9.25	12.50	32.00	50	90	180	320	550	
1911	(543) . .3,720,000	8.25	9.00	12.50	20	40	95	180	245	460
1911D	933,600	16.00	32.00	115.00	225	345	485	675	875	
1911S	988,000	8.25	14.50	29.00	55	135	215	370	500	
1912	(700) . .4,400,000	8.25	9.00	12.50	20	40	95	180	245	460
1912S	708,000	13.50	18.00	45.00	70	90	180	370	650	
1913	(613) . . 484,000	27.00	47.00	90.00	145	305	405	575	700	460
1913D	1,450,800	9.25	10.00	25.00	39	65	120	275	460	
1913S	40,000	1,000.00	1,800.00	3,650.00	5,750	8,500	9,750	12,000	15,500	

	Mintage	G-4	VG-8	F-12	VF-20	EF-40	AU-50	MS-60	MS-63	PF-63
1914 . . . . . .(380). . . .	6,244,230	$8.25	$9.00	$12.50	$20	$40	$95	$180	$245	$550
1914D	3,046,000	8.25	9.00	12.50	20	40	95	180	245	
1914S	264,000	70.00	125.00	275.00	435	775	1,050	1,600	2,400	
1915 . . . . . .(450). . . .	3,480,000	8.25	9.00	12.50	20	40	95	180	245	460
1915D	3,694,000	8.25	9.00	12.50	20	40	95	180	245	
1915S	704,000	20.00	31.00	45.00	65	75	145	205	350	
1916	1,788,000	8.25	9.00	12.50	20	40	95	180	245	
1916D	6,540,800	8.25	9.00	12.50	20	40	95	180	245	

STANDING LIBERTY (1916–1930)

This design is by Hermon A. MacNeil, whose initial M is above and to the right of the date. Liberty bears a shield of protection in her left arm, while the right hand holds the olive branch of peace. There was a modification in 1917. The reverse had a new arrangement of stars and the eagle was higher. After 1924 the date was "recessed," thereby giving it greater protection from the effects of circulation. A centennial gold issue was struck in 2016.

G-4 Good: Date and lettering legible. Top of date worn. Liberty's right leg and toes worn off. Much wear evident on left leg and drapery lines.

VG-8 Very Good: Distinct date. Toes faintly visible. Drapery lines visible above Liberty's left leg.

F-12 Fine: High curve of right leg flat from thigh to ankle. Only slight wear evident on left leg. Drapery lines over right thigh seen only at sides of leg.

VF-20 Very Fine: Garment line across right leg worn, but visible at sides.

EF-40 Extremely Fine: Flattened only at high spots. Liberty's toes are sharp. Drapery lines across right leg evident.

AU-50 About Uncirculated: Slight trace of wear on head, kneecap, shield's center, and highest point on eagle's body.

MS-60 Uncirculated: No trace of wear, but contact marks, surface spots, or faded luster possible.

MS-63 Choice Uncirculated: No trace of wear. Light blemishes. Attractive mint luster.

Variety 1 – No Stars Below Eagle (1916–1917)

Mintmark location is on obverse, to left of date.

	Mintage	VG-8	F-12	VF-20	EF-40	AU-50	MS-60	MS-63	MS-65
1916	52,000	$4,300	$5,000	$5,750	$7,500	$8,500	$10,500	$13,500	$16,500
1917, Variety 1	8,740,000	34	45	70	105	125	180	265	525
1917D, Variety 1 . . .	1,509,200	50	65	80	110	170	225	315	600
1917S, Variety 1 . . .	1,952,000	55	75	110	135	200	255	315	825

Variety 2 – Stars Below Eagle (1917–1930)
Pedestal Date (1917–1924)

1918-S, 8 Over 7

See next page for chart.

	Mintage	VG-8	F-12	VF-20	EF-40	AU-50	MS-60	MS-63	MS-65
1917, Variety 2	13,880,000	$32.00	$38	$45	$70	$95	$145	$215	$440
1917D, Variety 2	6,224,400	48.00	70	100	110	150	195	265	975
1917S, Variety 2	5,552,000	47.00	70	85	115	145	200	295	925
1918	14,240,000	16.00	20	24	34	65	130	215	460
1918D	7,380,000	29.00	50	70	100	135	200	290	1,100
1918S, Normal Date . . .	11,072,000	13.50	21	26	70	110	180	305	1,200
1918S, 8 Over 7	*1,850,000	2,350	2,900	5,250	7,500	15,000	20,500	69,000
1919	11,324,000	36.00	43	50	60	85	160	240	460
1919D	1,944,000	100.00	160	315	485	700	1,450	2,400	4,200
1919S	1,836,000	90.00	145	300	500	725	1,750	2,400	7,500
1920	27,860,000	13.50	16	25	36	70	140	215	380
1920D	3,586,400	90.00	110	135	170	245	485	850	1,650
1920S	6,380,000	16.00	19	24	55	150	320	800	2,250
1921	1,916,000	135.00	245	385	550	750	1,200	1,600	2,000
1923	9,716,000	13.50	22	27	38	70	140	215	360
1923S	1,360,000	330.00	460	600	1,100	1,450	2,150	2,900	3,250
1924	10,920,000	13.50	16	24	32	75	140	215	360
1924D	3,112,000	45.00	70	95	140	165	200	275	375
1924S	2,860,000	22.00	31	50	110	200	370	750	1,700

* Included in number above.

Recessed Date (1925–1930)

	Mintage	VG-8	F-12	VF-20	EF-40	AU-50	MS-60	MS-63	MS-65
1925	12,280,000	$6.75	$8.00	$11	$27	$65	$130	$195	$360
1926	11,316,000	6.75	8.00	11	27	65	130	195	360
1926D	1,716,000	11.50	18.00	32	70	95	140	215	360
1926S	2,700,000	6.75	14.50	38	100	180	405	975	2,150
1927	11,912,000	6.75	8.00	11	27	65	130	195	395
1927D	976,000	15.50	22.00	55	125	190	260	305	460
1927S	396,000	60.00	105.00	215	725	1,950	5,250	9,000	13,500
1928	6,336,000	6.75	8.00	11	27	65	130	195	360
1928D	1,627,600	6.75	8.00	11	27	65	130	195	360
1928S	2,644,000	6.75	8.00	11	27	65	130	195	360
1929	11,140,000	6.75	8.00	11	27	65	130	195	360
1929D	1,358,000	6.75	8.00	11	27	65	130	195	360
1929S	1,764,000	6.75	8.00	11	27	65	140	215	360
1930	5,632,000	6.75	8.00	11	27	65	130	195	360
1930S	1,556,000	6.75	8.00	11	27	65	130	195	360

WASHINGTON (1932 TO DATE)

This type was intended to be a commemorative issue marking the 200th anniversary of President Washington's birth. John Flanagan, a New York sculptor, was the designer. The initials JF are found at the base of the neck. The mintmark is on the reverse below the wreath for coins from 1932 to 1964. Starting in 1968, the mintmark was moved to the obverse at the right of the ribbon.

F-12 Fine: Hair lines about Washington's ear visible. Tiny feathers on eagle's breast faintly visible.
VF-20 Very Fine: Most hair details visible. Wing feathers clear.
EF-40 Extremely Fine: Hair lines sharp. Wear spots confined to top of eagle's legs and center of breast.
MS-60 Uncirculated: No trace of wear, but many contact marks, surface spotting, or faded luster possible.
MS-63 Choice Uncirculated: No trace of wear. Light blemishes. Attractive mint luster.
MS-64 Uncirculated: A few scattered contact marks. Good eye appeal and attractive luster.
MS-65 Gem Uncirculated: Only light, scattered, non-distracting marks. Strong luster, good eye appeal.
PF-65 Gem Proof: Hardly any blemishes, and no flaws.

Silver Coinage (1932–1964)

	Mintage	F-12	VF-20	EF-40	AU-50	MS-60	MS-63	MS-65	PF-63
1932	5,404,000	$6.25	$7.00	$7.50	$11.00	$22.00	$38	$190	
1932D	436,800	70.00	95.00	150.00	215.00	725.00	1,100	6,750	
1932S	408,000	65.00	70.00	80.00	110.00	285.00	360	1,700	
1934	31,912,052	6.25	6.75	7.00	8.00	18.00	27	47	
1934D	3,527,200	8.00	13.50	22.00	70.00	135.00	215	320	
1935	32,484,000	6.25	6.50	7.75	9.00	13.50	22	40	
1935D	5,780,000	7.25	11.50	25.00	85.00	155.00	200	220	
1935S	5,660,000	6.50	7.75	12.50	25.00	50.00	65	110	
1936 (3,837)	41,300,000	6.25	7.00	8.75	11.00	18.00	22	60	$370
1936D	5,374,000	7.25	20.00	45.00	110.00	355.00	430	625	
1936S	3,828,000	6.25	8.00	12.50	34.00	65.00	75	150	
1937 (5,542)	19,696,000	6.25	8.50	13.50	20.00	27.00	29	60	115
1937D	7,189,600	6.25	8.00	15.50	22.00	50.00	65	90	
1937S	1,652,000	7.25	12.50	22.00	65.00	110.00	140	190	
1938 (8,045)	9,472,000	6.25	7.50	16.00	32.00	65.00	70	80	70
1938S	2,832,000	6.25	7.25	19.00	36.00	55.00	70	110	
1939 (8,795)	33,540,000	6.25	6.50	7.00	8.00	16.00	20	39	85
1939D	7,092,000	6.25	7.00	9.00	15.50	30.00	38	55	
1939S	2,628,000	6.25	8.50	18.00	40.00	65.00	120	145	

	Mintage	VF-20	EF-40	AU-50	MS-60	MS-63	MS-65	PF-63
1940 (11,246)	35,704,000	$6.75	$8.50	$10.00	$22.00	$22.00	$31	$55
1940D	2,797,600	11.00	27.00	60.00	90.00	110.00	160	
1940S	8,244,000	6.75	9.00	13.50	24.00	34.00	43	
1941 (15,287)	79,032,000	5.75	5.75	5.75	7.25	11.00	29	50
1941D	16,714,800	5.75	6.25	10.00	32.00	39.00	50	
1941S	16,080,000	5.75	6.50	8.00	27.00	32.00	43	
1942 (21,123)	102,096,000	5.75	5.75	6.00	7.50	9.50	20	50
1942D	17,487,200	5.75	5.75	5.75	14.50	16.00	29	
1942S	19,384,000	7.00	8.50	14.50	40.00	50.00	70	
1943	99,700,000	5.75	5.75	5.75	6.75	8.50	31	
1943D	16,095,600	5.75	8.00	11.50	21.00	31.00	40	
1943S	21,700,000	5.75	6.50	10.00	27.00	32.00	70	
1944	104,956,000	5.75	5.75	5.75	6.75	8.50	20	
1944D	14,600,800	5.75	5.75	5.75	9.25	13.50	28	
1944S	12,560,000	5.75	5.75	6.00	10.50	15.00	22	
1945	74,372,000	5.75	5.75	5.75	6.50	7.25	27	
1945D	12,341,600	5.75	5.75	5.75	6.75	18.00	23	
1945S	17,004,001	5.75	5.75	5.75	6.75	11.50	22	
1946	53,436,000	5.75	5.75	6.00	7.50	9.50	25	
1946D	9,072,800	5.75	5.75	6.00	7.50	10.50	23	
1946S	4,204,000	5.75	5.75	6.00	7.50	10.50	22	
1947	22,556,000	5.75	5.75	5.75	6.75	13.50	22	

Chart continued on next page.

	Mintage	VF-20	EF-40	AU-50	MS-60	MS-63	MS-65	PF-63
1947D	15,338,400	$5.75	$5.75	$5.75	$6.25	$11.50	$25.00	
1947S	5,532,000	5.75	5.75	5.75	6.25	11.00	18.00	
1948	35,196,000	5.75	5.75	5.75	6.25	8.00	16.00	
1948D	16,766,800	5.75	5.75	5.75	7.00	12.50	23.00	
1948S	15,960,000	5.75	5.75	5.75	6.25	8.50	30.00	
1949	9,312,000	6.00	7.50	11.50	25.00	31.00	40.00	
1949D	10,068,400	5.75	7.50	9.25	15.00	23.00	29.00	
1950 (51,386)	24,920,126	5.75	5.75	5.75	7.50	11.00	23.00	$32.00
1950D	21,075,600	5.75	5.75	5.75	6.25	13.50	27.00	
1950D, D Over S	*	60.00	80.00	110.00	170.00	550.00	1,650.00	
1950S	10,284,004	5.75	5.75	5.75	6.25	10.00	24.00	
1950S, S Over D	*	80.00	150.00	200.00	260.00	320.00	875.00	
1951 (57,500)	43,448,102	5.75	5.75	5.75	6.25	7.25	16.00	27.00
1951D	35,354,800	5.75	5.75	5.75	6.25	7.25	20.00	
1951S	9,048,000	5.75	5.75	5.75	6.25	15.50	25.00	
1952 (81,980)	38,780,093	5.75	5.75	5.75	6.25	9.00	22.00	25.00
1952D	49,795,200	5.75	5.75	5.75	6.25	7.25	23.00	
1952S	13,707,800	5.75	5.75	5.75	7.25	13.50	27.00	
1953 (128,800)	18,536,120	5.75	5.75	5.75	6.25	8.00	16.00	14.50
1953D	56,112,400	5.75	5.75	5.75	6.25	9.00	22.00	
1953S	14,016,000	5.75	5.75	5.75	6.25	7.25	20.00	
1954 (233,300)	54,412,203	5.75	5.75	5.75	5.75	5.75	11.00	7.75
1954D	42,305,500	5.75	5.75	5.75	5.75	7.25	16.00	
1954S	11,834,722	5.75	5.75	5.75	6.00	7.75	13.50	
1955 (378,200)	18,180,181	5.75	5.75	5.75	5.75	5.75	20.00	7.75
1955D	3,182,400	5.75	5.75	5.75	5.75	5.75	22.00	
1956 (669,384)	44,144,000	5.75	5.75	5.75	5.75	5.75	11.00	6.00
1956D	32,334,500	5.75	5.75	5.75	5.75	5.75	13.50	
1957 (1,247,952)	46,532,000	5.75	5.75	5.75	5.75	5.75	11.00	6.00
1957D	77,924,160	5.75	5.75	5.75	5.75	5.75	20.00	
1958 (875,652)	6,360,000	5.75	5.75	5.75	5.75	5.75	11.00	6.00
1958D	78,124,900	5.75	5.75	5.75	5.75	5.75	20.00	
1959 (1,149,291)	24,384,000	5.75	5.75	5.75	5.75	5.75	11.00	5.25
1959D	62,054,232	5.75	5.75	5.75	5.75	5.75	12.50	
1960 (1,691,602)	29,164,000	5.75	5.75	5.75	5.75	5.75	11.00	5.50
1960D	63,000,324	5.75	5.75	5.75	5.75	5.75	14.50	
1961 (3,028,244)	37,036,000	5.75	5.75	5.75	5.75	5.75	16.00	5.50
1961D	83,656,928	5.75	5.75	5.75	5.75	5.75	20.00	
1962 (3,218,019)	36,156,000	5.75	5.75	5.75	5.75	5.75	20.00	5.50
1962D	127,554,756	5.75	5.75	5.75	5.75	5.75	14.50	
1963 (3,075,645)	74,316,000	5.75	5.75	5.75	5.75	5.75	18.00	5.50
1963D	135,288,184	5.75	5.75	5.75	5.75	5.75	18.00	
1964 (3,950,762)	560,390,585	5.75	5.75	5.75	5.75	5.75	14.50	5.50
1964D	704,135,528	5.75	5.75	5.75	5.75	5.75	16.00	

* Included in number above.

Clad Coinage and Silver Proofs (1965 to Date)

	Mintage	MS-63	MS-65	PF-65		Mintage	MS-63	MS-65	PF-65
1965	1,819,717,540	$2.60	$4.30		1968D	101,534,000	$0.90	$3.40	
1966	821,101,500	0.90	6.25		1968S	(3,041,506)			$4.30
1967	1,524,031,848	3.40	7.25		1969	176,212,000	0.90	11.00	
1968	220,731,500	0.90	5.50		1969D	114,372,000	1.70	5.50	

	Mintage	MS-63	MS-65	PF-65
1969S	(2,934,631)			$4.30
1970	136,420,000	$0.90	$8.00	
1970D	417,341,364	0.90	3.40	
1970S	(2,632,810)			4.30
1971	109,284,000	0.90	4.30	
1971D	258,634,428	0.90	4.30	
1971S	(3,220,733)			4.30
1972	215,048,000	0.90	3.40	

	Mintage	MS-63	MS-65	PF-65
1972D	311,067,732	$0.90	$6.25	
1972S	(3,260,996)			$6.25
1973	346,924,000	0.90	3.40	
1973D	232,977,400	0.90	2.60	
1973S	(2,760,339)			4.30
1974	801,456,000	0.40	2.60	
1974D	353,160,300	0.40	2.60	
1974S	(2,612,568)			4.30

Bicentennial (1776–1976)

	Mintage	MS-63	MS-65	PF-65
1776–1976, Copper-Nickel Clad	809,784,016	$0.40	$2.60	
1776–1976D, Copper-Nickel Clad	860,118,839	0.40	2.60	
1776–1976S, Copper-Nickel Clad	(7,059,099)			$2.20
1776–1976S, Silver Clad	11,000,000	2.00	2.20	
1776–1976S, Silver Clad	(4,000,000)			5.50

Note: Mintage figures for 1976-S silver clad coins are approximate; many were melted in 1982.

Eagle Reverse Resumed (1977–1998)
(Dies Slightly Modified to Lower Relief)

	Mintage	MS-63	MS-65	PF-65
1977	468,556,000	$0.40	$2.60	
1977D	256,524,978	0.40	2.60	
1977S	(3,251,152)			$3.00
1978	521,452,000	0.40	2.60	
1978D	287,373,152	0.40	2.60	
1978S	(3,127,781)			3.00
1979	515,708,000	0.40	2.60	
1979D	489,789,780	0.40	2.60	
1979S	(3,677,175)			
Variety 1				3.00
Variety 2				3.20
1980P	635,832,000	0.40	2.60	
1980D	518,327,487	0.40	2.60	
1980S	(3,554,806)			3.00
1981P	601,716,000	0.40	2.60	
1981D	575,722,833	0.40	2.60	
1981S	(4,063,083)			
Variety 1				3.00
Variety 2				4.30
1982P	500,931,000	3.40	25.00	
1982D	480,042,788	3.40	18.00	
1982S	(3,857,479)			3.20
1983P	673,535,000	12.50	36.00	

	Mintage	MS-63	MS-65	PF-65
1983D	617,806,446	$6.75	$22.00	
1983S	(3,279,126)			$3.20
1984P	676,545,000	0.40	2.60	
1984D	546,483,064	0.40	2.60	
1984S	(3,065,110)			3.20
1985P	775,818,962	0.40	2.60	
1985D	519,962,888	0.40	2.60	
1985S	(3,362,821)			3.20
1986P	551,199,333	0.40	2.60	
1986D	504,298,660	0.40	2.60	
1986S	(3,010,497)			3.00
1987P	582,499,481	0.40	2.60	
1987D	655,594,696	0.40	2.60	
1987S	(4,227,728)			3.00
1988P	562,052,000	0.40	2.60	
1988D	596,810,688	0.40	2.60	
1988S	(3,262,948)			3.00
1989P	512,868,000	0.40	7.25	
1989D	896,535,597	0.40	2.60	
1989S	(3,220,194)			3.00
1990P	613,792,000	0.40	2.60	
1990D	927,638,181	0.40	1.70	
1990S	(3,299,559)			2.20

Chart continued on next page.

	Mintage	MS-63	MS-65	PF-65
1991P	570,968,000	$0.40	$2.60	
1991D	630,966,693	0.40	2.60	
1991S	(2,867,787)			$2.20
1992P	384,764,000	0.40	2.60	
1992D	389,777,107	0.40	2.60	
1992S	(2,858,981)			2.20
1992S, Silver	(1,317,579)			6.00
1993P	639,276,000	0.40	2.60	
1993D	645,476,128	0.40	2.60	
1993S	(2,633,439)			2.20
1993S, Silver	(761,353)			6.00
1994P	825,600,000	0.40	2.60	
1994D	880,034,110	0.40	2.60	
1994S	(2,484,594)			2.20
1994S, Silver	(785,329)			6.00
1995P	1,004,336,000	0.40	2.60	

	Mintage	MS-63	MS-65	PF-65
1995D	1,103,216,000	$0.40	$2.60	
1995S	(2,117,496)			$2.20
1995S, Silver	(679,985)			6.00
1996P	925,040,000	0.40	1.70	
1996D	906,868,000	0.40	1.70	
1996S	(1,750,244)			2.20
1996S, Silver	(775,021)			6.00
1997P	595,740,000	0.40	1.70	
1997D	599,680,000	0.40	1.70	
1997S	(2,055,000)			2.20
1997S, Silver	(741,678)			6.00
1998P	896,268,000	0.40	1.70	
1998D	821,000,000	0.40	1.70	
1998S	(2,086,507)			2.20
1998S, Silver	(878,792)			6.00

State Quarters (1999–2008)

The United States Mint 50 State Quarters Program, which began in 1999, produced a series of 50 quarter dollar coins with special designs honoring each state. Five different designs were issued each year during the period 1999 through 2008. States were commemorated in the order of their entrance into statehood.

These are all legal-tender coins of standard weight and composition. The obverse side depicting President George Washington was modified to include some of the wording previously used on the reverse. The modification was authorized by special legislation, and carried out by Mint sculptor-engraver William Cousins, whose initials were added to the truncation of Washington's neck adjacent to those of the original designer, John Flanagan.

Each state theme was proposed, and the design approved, by the governor of the state. Final designs were created by Mint personnel.

Circulation coins were made at the Philadelphia and Denver mints. Proof coins were made in San Francisco. Both copper-nickel and silver Proof coins were made each year.

	Mintage	MS-65	MS-66	PF-68
Delaware				
1999P	373,400,000	$0.40	$2.60	
1999D	401,424,000	0.40	2.60	
1999S	(3,713,359)			$2.60
1999S, Silver	(804,565)			13.50
Pennsylvania				
1999P	349,000,000	0.40	2.60	
1999D	358,332,000	0.40	2.60	
1999S	(3,713,359)			2.60
1999S, Silver	(804,565)			6.00

	Mintage	MS-65	MS-66	PF-68
New Jersey				
1999P	363,200,000	$0.40	$2.60	
1999D	299,028,000	0.40	2.60	
1999S	(3,713,359)			$2.60
1999S, Silver	(804,565)			6.00
Georgia				
1999P	451,188,000	0.40	2.60	
1999D	488,744,000	0.40	2.60	
1999S	(3,713,359)			2.60
1999S, Silver	(804,565)			6.00

	Mintage	MS-65	MS-66	PF-68
Connecticut				
1999P	688,744,000	$0.40	$2.60	
1999D	657,880,000	0.40	2.60	

	Mintage	MS-65	MS-66	PF-68
Connecticut				
1999S	(3,713,359)			$2.60
1999S, Silver . . .	(804,565)			6.00

	Mintage	MS-65	MS-66	PF-68
Massachusetts				
2000P	628,600,000	$0.40	$2.60	
2000D	535,184,000	0.40	2.60	
2000S	(4,020,172)			$2.60
2000S, Silver . . .	(965,421)			6.00
Maryland				
2000P	678,200,000	0.40	2.60	
2000D	556,532,000	0.40	2.60	
2000S	(4,020,172)			2.60
2000S, Silver . . .	(965,421)			6.00
South Carolina				
2000P	742,576,000	0.40	2.60	
2000D	566,208,000	0.40	2.60	

	Mintage	MS-65	MS-66	PF-68
South Carolina				
2000S	(4,020,172)			$2.60
2000S, Silver . . .	(965,421)			6.00
New Hampshire				
2000P	673,040,000	$0.40	$2.60	
2000D	495,976,000	0.40	2.60	
2000S	(4,020,172)			2.60
2000S, Silver . . .	(965,421)			6.00
Virginia				
2000P	943,000,000	$0.40	$2.60	
2000D	651,616,000	0.40	2.60	
2000S	(4,020,172)			2.60
2000S, Silver . . .	(965,421)			6.00

	Mintage	MS-65	MS-66	PF-68
New York				
2001P	655,400,000	$0.40	$2.60	
2001D	619,640,000	0.40	2.60	
2001S	(3,094,140)			$2.60
2001S, Silver . . .	(889,697)			6.00
North Carolina				
2001P	627,600,000	0.40	2.60	
2001D	427,876,000	0.40	2.60	
2001S	(3,094,140)			2.60
2001S, Silver . . .	(889,697)			6.00
Rhode Island				
2001P	423,000,000	0.40	2.60	
2001D	447,100,000	0.40	2.60	

	Mintage	MS-65	MS-66	PF-68
Rhode Island				
2001S	(3,094,140)			$2.60
2001S, Silver . . .	(889,697)			6.00
Vermont				
2001P	423,400,000	$0.40	$2.60	
2001D	459,404,000	0.40	2.60	
2001S	(3,094,140)			2.60
2001S, Silver . . .	(889,697)			6.00
Kentucky				
2001P	353,000,000	0.40	2.60	
2001D	370,564,000	0.40	2.60	
2001S	(3,094,140)			2.60
2001S, Silver . . .	(889,697)			6.00

APPROXIMATE VALUES, 2002–2008. *P- and D-Mint Circulation Strikes.* REGULAR FINISH: MS-65, all years, either mint—$0.40. • MS-66, most years, either mint—$2.60 (*exceptions*: 2008-D, NM, $15 • 2007-P, ID, WY, and AZ, $10 • 2003, 2006, and 2008, all states, either mint, $5–$6). SATIN FINISH: MS-65, most years, either mint—$1.70 (*exception*: 2007-P, WY, $11). • MS-66, most years, either mint—$2.60 (*exceptions*—2007-P, WY, $45 • 2007-P, UT, $11). *S-Mint Proofs (PF-68, All Years).* CLAD: $2.60. SILVER: $6.

	Mintage		Mintage		Mintage		Mintage
Ohio		**Arkansas**		**Kansas**		**Washington**	
2002P	217,200,000	2003S	(3,408,516)	2005P	263,400,000	2007S	(2,374,778)
2002D	414,832,000	2003S, Silver	(1,125,755)	2005D	300,000,000	2007S, Silver	(1,313,481)
2002S	(3,084,245)	**Michigan**		2005S	(3,262,960)	**Idaho**	
2002S, Silver	(892,229)	2004P	233,800,000	2005S, Silver	(1,678,649)	2007P	294,600,000
Louisiana		2004D	225,800,000	**West Virginia**		2007D	286,800,000
2002P	362,000,000	2004S	(2,740,684)	2005P	365,400,000	2007S	(2,374,778)
2002D	402,204,000	2004S, Silver	(1,769,786)	2005D	356,200,000	2007S, Silver	(1,313,481)
2002S	(3,084,245)	**Florida**		2005S	(3,262,960)	**Wyoming**	
2002S, Silver	(892,229)	2004P	240,200,000	2005S, Silver	(1,678,649)	2007P	243,600,000
Indiana		2004D	241,600,000	**Nevada**		2007D	320,800,000
2002P	362,600,000	2004S	(2,740,684)	2006P	277,000,000	2007S	(2,374,778)
2002D	327,200,000	2004S, Silver	(1,769,786)	2006D	312,800,000	2007S, Silver	(1,313,481)
2002S	(3,084,245)	**Texas**		2006S	(2,882,428)	**Utah**	
2002S, Silver	(892,229)	2004P	278,800,000	2006S, Silver	(1,585,008)	2007P	255,000,000
Mississippi		2004D	263,000,000	**Nebraska**		2007D	253,200,000
2002P	290,000,000	2004S	(2,740,684)	2006P	318,000,000	2007S	(2,374,778)
2002D	289,600,000	2004S, Silver	(1,769,786)	2006D	273,000,000	2007S, Silver	(1,313,481)
2002S	(3,084,245)	**Iowa**		2006S	(2,882,428)	**Oklahoma**	
2002S, Silver	(892,229)	2004P	213,800,000	2006S, Silver	(1,585,008)	2008P	222,000,000
Illinois		2004D	251,400,000	**Colorado**		2008D	194,600,000
2003P	225,800,000	2004S	(2,740,684)	2006P	274,800,000	2008S	(2,078,112)
2003D	237,400,000	2004S, Silver	(1,769,786)	2006D	294,200,000	2008S, Silver	(1,192,908)
2003S	(3,408,516)	**Wisconsin**		2006S	(2,882,428)	**New Mexico**	
2003S, Silver	(1,125,755)	2004P	226,400,000	2006S, Silver	(1,585,008)	2008P	244,200,000
Alabama		2004D	226,800,000	**North Dakota**		2008D	244,400,000
2003P	225,000,000	2004S	(2,740,684)	2006P	305,800,000	2008S	(2,078,112)
2003D	232,400,000	2004S, Silver	(1,769,786)	2006D	359,000,000	2008S, Silver	(1,192,908)
2003S	(3,408,516)	**California**		2006S	(2,882,428)	**Arizona**	
2003S, Silver	(1,125,755)	2005P	257,200,000	2006S, Silver	(1,585,008)	2008P	244,600,000
Maine		2005D	263,200,000	**South Dakota**		2008D	265,000,000
2003P	217,400,000	2005S	(3,262,960)	2006P	245,000,000	2008S	(2,078,112)
2003D	231,400,000	2005S, Silver	(1,678,649)	2006D	265,800,000	2008S, Silver	(1,192,908)
2003S	(3,408,516)	**Minnesota**		2006S	(2,882,428)	**Alaska**	
2003S, Silver	(1,125,755)	2005P	239,600,000	2006S, Silver	(1,585,008)	2008P	251,800,000
Missouri		2005D	248,400,000	**Montana**		2008D	254,000,000
2003P	225,000,000	2005S	(3,262,960)	2007P	257,000,000	2008S	(2,078,112)
2003D	228,200,000	2005S, Silver	(1,678,649)	2007D	256,240,000	2008S, Silver	(1,192,908)
2003S	(3,408,516)	**Oregon**		2007S	(2,374,778)	**Hawaii**	
2003S, Silver	(1,125,755)	2005P	316,200,000	2007S, Silver	(1,313,481)	2008P	254,000,000
Arkansas		2005D	404,000,000	**Washington**		2008D	263,600,000
2003P	228,000,000	2005S	(3,262,960)	2007P	265,200,000	2008S	(2,078,112)
2003D	229,800,000	2005S, Silver	(1,678,649)	2007D	280,000,000	2008S, Silver	(1,192,908)

Some State quarters were accidentally made with misaligned dies and are valued higher than ordinary pieces. Normal United States coins have dies oriented in "coin alignment," such that the reverse appears upside down when the coin is rotated from right to left. Values for the rotated-die quarters vary according to the amount of shifting. The most valuable are those that are shifted 180 degrees, so that both sides appear upright when the coin is turned over (called *medal alignment*).

Manufacturing varieties showing die doubling or other minor, unintentional characteristics are of interest to collectors and are often worth premium prices.

District of Columbia and U.S. Territories Quarters (2009)

At the ending of the U.S. Mint 50 State Quarters Program a new series of quarter-dollar reverse designs was authorized to recognize the District of Columbia and the five U.S. territories: the Commonwealth of Puerto Rico, Guam, American Samoa, the U.S. Virgin Islands, and the Commonwealth of the Northern Mariana Islands. Each of these coins, issued sequentially during 2009, has the portrait of George Washington, as in the past, and is made of the same weight and composition. Each coin commemorates the history, geography, or traditions of the place it represents.

	Mintage	MS-65	MS-66	PF-68
District of Columbia				
2009P	83,600,000	$0.40	$1.70	
2009D	88,800,000	0.40	1.70	
2009S	(2,113,478)			$2.60
2009S, Silver	(996,548)			6.00
Puerto Rico				
2009P	53,200,000	0.40	1.70	
2009D	86,000,000	0.40	1.70	
2009S	(2,113,478)			2.60
2009S, Silver	(996,548)			6.00
Guam				
2009P	45,000,000	0.40	1.70	
2009D	42,600,000	0.40	1.70	
2009S	(2,113,478)			2.60
2009S, Silver	(996,548)			6.00

	Mintage	MS-65	MS-66	PF-68
American Samoa				
2009P	42,600,000	$0.40	$1.70	
2009D	39,600,000	0.40	1.70	
2009S	(2,113,478)			$2.60
2009S, Silver	(996,548)			
U.S. Virgin Islands		0.40	1.70	
2009P	41,000,000	0.40	1.70	
2009D	41,000,000			2.60
2009S	(2,113,478)			6.00
2009S, Silver	(996,548)			
Northern Mariana Islands		0.40	1.70	
2009P	35,200,000	0.40	1.70	
2009D	37,600,000			2.60
2009S	(2,113,478)			6.00
2009S, Silver	(996,548)			6.00

America the Beautiful Quarters Program (2010–2021)

Following up on the popularity of the 50 State Quarters Program, Congress authorized the production of new circulating commemorative quarters from 2010 to 2021. The coins honor a site of "natural or historic significance" from each of the 50 states, five U.S. territories, and the District of Columbia. They continue to bear George Washington's portrait on the obverse.

Five designs were released each year from 2010 through 2020, in the order the coins' featured locations were designated national parks or national sites. The 56th and final coin of the series was issued in early 2021. The West Point Mint produced circulation strikes in 2019 and 2020 as part of an effort to stimulate public interest in coin collecting.

In addition to the circulating quarters, a series of five-ounce silver bullion pieces were coined each year with designs nearly identical to those of the America the Beautiful quarters, with two main exceptions: the size, which is three inches in diameter; and the edge, which is marked .999 FINE SILVER 5.0 OUNCE, rather than reeded as on the standard quarters.

APPROXIMATE VALUES, 2010–2021. *P-, D-, and S-Mint Circulation Strikes (MS-65 and MS-66, respectively).* REGULAR FINISH: *All years, P or D*—$0.40, $1.70. SATIN FINISH: *2010 only, P or D*—$2.60, $3. ENHANCED UNC.: *2017-S only*—$2.60, $3. *W-Mint Circulation Strikes (MS-65 and MS-66, respectively). 2019 only*—Lowell, Am. Memorial, and San Antonio, $70, $110 • War in the Pacific, $13.50, $22 • Frank Church, $32, $70. *2020 only (with V-75 privy mark)*—Am. Samoa, $12.50, $23 • Weir Farm, $14.50, $18 • Salt River Bay, $13.50, $36 • Marsh-Bill.-R'feller and Tall. Prairie, $36, $90. *S-Mint Proofs (PF-68, All Years).* CLAD. $2.60. SILVER. $6.

Mintage	Mintage	Mintage	Mintage
Hot Springs Nat'l Park (AR)	**Glacier Nat'l Park (MT)**	**Hawai'i Volcanoes**	**Ft. McHenry Nat'l Mon.**
2010P 35,600,000	2011S, Silver. . . . (722,076)	**National Park (HI)**	**and Historic Shrine (MD)**
2010D 34,000,000	**Olympic Nat'l Park (WA)**	2012P 46,200,000	2013S 1,313,680
2010S . . . . (1,402,889)	2011P 30,400,000	2012D 78,600,000	2013S, Silver. . . . (946,380)
2010S, Silver. . . . (859,417)	2011D 30,600,000	2012S 1,409,120	2013S, Silver. . . . (467,691)
Yellowstone National	2011S . . . . (1,268,231)	2012S, Silver. . . . (962,447)	**Mount Rushmore National**
Park (WY)	2011S, Silver. . . . (722,076)	2012S, Silver. . . . (608,060)	**Memorial (SD)**
2010P 33,600,000	**Vicksburg National**	**Denali National Park and**	2013P 231,800,000
2010D 34,800,000	**Military Park (MS)**	**Preserve (AK)**	2013D 272,400,000
2010S . . . . (1,404,259)	2011P 30,800,000	2012P 135,400,000	2013S 1,373,260
2010S, Silver. . . . (859,417)	2011D 33,400,000	2012D 166,600,000	2013S, Silver. . . . (958,853)
Yosemite Nat'l Park (CA)	2011S . . . . (1,268,623)	2012S 1,409,220	**Great Smoky Mountains**
2010P 35,200,000	2011S, Silver. . . . (722,076)	2012S, Silver. . . . (959,602)	**National Park (TN)**
2010D 34,800,000	**Chickasaw National**	2012S, Silver. . . . (608,060)	2014P 73,200,000
2010S . . . . (1,401,522)	**Recreation Area (OK)**	**White Mountain National**	2014D 99,400,000
2010S, Silver. . . . (859,417)	2011P 73,800,000	**Forest (NH)**	2014S 1,360,780
Grand Canyon National	2011D 69,400,000	2013P 68,800,000	2014S, Silver. . . . (884,381)
Park (AZ)	2011S . . . . (1,266,825)	2013D 107,600,000	**Shenandoah Nat'l Park (VA)**
2010P 34,800,000	2011S, Silver. . . . (722,076)	2013S 1,606,900	2014P 112,800,000
2010D 35,400,000	**El Yunque Nat'l Forest (PR)**	2013S, Silver. . . . (989,803)	2014D 197,800,000
2010S . . . . (1,401,462)	2012P 25,800,000	2013S, Silver. . . . (467,691)	2014S 1,266,720
2010S, Silver. . . . (859,417)	2012D 25,000,000	**Perry's Victory and Int'l**	2014S, Silver. . . . (847,191)
Mount Hood National	2012S 1,680,140	**Peace Memorial (OH)**	**Arches National Park (UT)**
Forest (OR)	2012S . . . . (1,012,094)	2013P 107,800,000	2014P 214,200,000
2010P 34,400,000	2012S, Silver. . . . (608,060)	2013D 131,600,000	2014D 251,400,000
2010D 34,400,000	**Chaco Culture National**	2013S 1,425,860	2014S 1,235,940
2010S . . . . (1,398,106)	**Historical Park (NM)**	2013S, Silver. . . . (947,815)	2014S . . . . (845,699)
2010S, Silver. . . . (859,417)	2012P 22,000,000	**Great Basin Nat'l Park (NV)**	2014S, Silver. . . . (591,358)
Gettysburg National	2012D 22,000,000	2013P 122,400,000	**Great Sand Dunes**
Military Park (PA)	2012S 1,389,020	2013D 141,400,000	**National Park (CO)**
2011P 30,800,000	2012S . . . . (961,464)	2013S 1,316,500	2014P 159,600,000
2011D 30,400,000	2012S, Silver. . . . (608,060)	2013S . . . . (945,777)	2014D 171,800,000
2011S . . . . (1,273,068)	**Acadia National Park (ME)**	2013S, Silver. . . . (467,691)	2014S 1,176,760
2011S, Silver. . . . (722,076)	2012P 24,800,000	**Ft. McHenry Nat'l Mon.**	2014S . . . . (843,959)
Glacier Nat'l Park (MT)	2012D 21,606,000	**and Historic Shrine (MD)**	2014S, Silver. . . . (591,358)
2011P 30,400,000	2012S 1,409,120	2013P 120,000,000	
2011D 31,200,000	2012S . . . . (962,038)	2013D 151,400,000	
2011S . . . . (1,269,422)	2012S, Silver. . . . (608,060)		

	Mintage
Everglades Nat'l Park (FL)	
2014P	157,601,200
2014D	142,400,000
2014S	1,180,900
2014S	(857,805)
2014S, Silver	(591,358)
Homestead National	
Mon. of America (NE)	
2015P	214,400,000
2015D	248,600,000
2015S	1,153,840
2015S	(831,503)
2015S, Silver	(490,829)
Kisatchie Nat'l Forest (LA)	
2015P	397,200,000
2015D	379,600,000
2015S	1,099,380
2015S	(762,407)
2015S, Silver	(490,829)

	Mintage
Blue Ridge Parkway (NC)	
2015P	325,616,000
2015D	505,200,000
2015S	1,096,620
2015S	(762,407)
2015S, Silver	(490,829)
Bombay Hook National	
Wildlife Refuge (DE)	
2015P	275,000,000
2015D	206,400,000
2015S	1,013,920
2015S	(762,407)
2015S, Silver	(490,829)
Saratoga National	
Historical Park (NY)	
2015P	223,000,000
2015D	215,800,000
2015S	1,045,500
2015S	(791,347)

	Mintage
Saratoga National	
Historical Park (NY)	
2015S, Silver	(490,829)
Shawnee Nat'l Forest (IL)	
2016P	155,600,000
2016D	151,800,000
2016S	1,081,914
2016S	(732,039)
2016S, Silver	(515,205)
Cumberland Gap National	
Historical Park (KY)	
2016P	215,400,000
2016D	223,200,000
2016S	1,036,093
2016S	(701,831)
2016S, Silver	(515,205)
Harpers Ferry National	
Historical Park (WV)	
2016P	434,630,000

	Mintage
Harpers Ferry National	
Historical Park (WV)	
2016D	424,000,000
2016S	1,050,185
2016S	(701,203)
2016S, Silver	(515,205)
Theodore Roosevelt	
National Park (ND)	
2016P	231,600,000
2016D	223,200,000
2016S	1,073,092
2016S	(716,236)
2016S, Silver	(515,205)
Ft. Moultrie at Ft. Sumter	
Nat'l Monument (SC)	
2016P	154,400,000
2016D	142,200,000
2016S	979,566
2016S	(703,742)
2016S, Silver	(515,205)

	Mintage	OGP*	MS-69	MS-70
2016W, Gold **(a)**	100,000	$725	$725	$750

* OGP = Coin in original government packaging. **a.** In 2016 the Mint issued a centennial version of the Standing Liberty quarter in gold.

Mintage	Mintage	Mintage	Mintage
Effigy Mounds National Monument (IA)	**Pictured Rocks National Lakeshore (MI)**	**American Memorial Park (N. Mariana Islands)**	**Weir Farm National Historic Site (CT)**
2017P 271,200,000	2018P 186,714,000	2019P 142,800,000	2020P 125,600,000
2017D 210,800,000	2018D 182,600,000	2019D 182,600,000	2020D 155,000,000
2017S *945,853*	2018S 931,220	2019S *904,880*	2020S *945,820*
2017S . . . . *(692,129)*	2018S . . . . *(653,176)*	2019S . . . . *(749,279)*	2020S . . . . *(544,309)*
2017S, Silver . . . *(496,618)*	2018S, Silver . . . *(461,048)*	2019S, Silver . . . *(539,710)*	2020S, Silver . . . *(427,256)*
Frederick Douglass National Historic Site (DC)	**Apostle Islands National Lakeshore (WI)**	2019W 2,000,000	2020W (a) 2,000,000
2017P 184,800,000	2018P 223,200,000	**War in the Pacific Nat'l Historical Park (Guam)**	**Salt River Bay National Historical Park and Ecological Preserve (USVI)**
2017D 185,800,000	2018D 216,600,000	2019P 116,600,000	2020P 580,200,000
2017S *950,503*	2018S 889,080	2019D 114,400,000	2020D 515,000,000
2017S . . . . *(657,587)*	2018S, Silver . . . *(618,988)*	2019S *924,380*	2020S *930,960*
2017S, Silver . . . *(496,618)*	**Voyageurs Nat'l Park (MN)**	2019S . . . . *(749,283)*	2020S . . . . *(544,287)*
Ozark National Scenic Riverways (MO)	2018P 237,400,000	2019S, Silver . . . *(539,710)*	2020S, Silver . . . *(427,256)*
2017P 203,000,000	2018D 197,800,000	2019W 2,000,000	2020W (a) 2,000,000
2017D 200,000,000	2018S 867,400	**San Antonio Missions Nat'l Historical Park (TX)**	**Marsh-Billings-Rockefeller Nat'l Historical Park (VT)**
2017S *921,747*	2018S, Silver . . . *(461,048)*	2019P 142,800,000	2020P 304,600,000
2017S . . . . *(657,587)*	**Cumberland Island National Seashore (GA)**	2019D 129,400,000	2020D 345,800,000
2017S . . . . *(496,618)*	2018P, ... 138,000,000	2019S *931,580*	2020S *928,940*
Ellis Island (Statue of Liberty National Monument, NJ)	2018D 151,600,000	2019S . . . . *(749,258)*	2020S . . . . *(544,249)*
2017P 234,000,000	2018S 880,940	2019S, Silver . . . *(539,710)*	2020S, Silver . . . *(427,256)*
2017D 254,000,000	2018S . . . . *(618,725)*	2019W 2,000,000	2020W (a) 2,000,000
2017S *973,147*	2018S, Silver . . . *(461,048)*	**Frank Church River of No Return Wilderness (ID)**	**Tallgrass Prairie National Preserve (KS)**
2017S . . . . *(657,587)*	**Block Island National Wildlife Refuge (RI)**	2019P 223,400,000	2020P 101,200,000
2017S, Silver . . . *(496,618)*	2018P 159,600,000	2019D 251,600,000	2020D 142,400,000
George Rogers Clark Nat'l Historical Park (IN)	2018D 159,600,000	2019S *901,920*	2020S *931,060*
2017P 191,600,000	2018S 854,940	2019S . . . . *(768,340)*	2020S . . . . *(561,030)*
2017D 180,800,000	2018S, Silver . . . *(636,372)*	2019S, Silver . . . *(539,710)*	2020S, Silver . . . *(427,256)*
2017S *933,150*	2018S, Silver . . . *(461,048)*	2019W 2,000,000	2020W (a) 2,000,000
2017S, Silver . . . *(675,757)*	**Lowell National Historical Park (MA)**	**Nat'l Park of American Samoa (American Samoa)**	**Tuskegee Airmen National Historic Site (AL)**
2017S, Silver . . . *(496,618)*	2019P 165,800,000	2020P 286,000,000	2021P 160,400,000
	2019D 182,200,000	2020D 212,200,000	2021D 304,000,000
	2019S *909,080*	2020S *939,760*	2021S *305,680*
	2019S . . . . *(821,610)*	2020S . . . . *(573,615)*	2021S . . . . *(528,201)*
	2019S, Silver . . . *(539,710)*	2020S, Silver . . . *(427,256)*	2021S, Silver . . . *(350,323)*
	2019W 2,000,000	2020W (a) 2,000,000	

a. The 2020-W quarters have a "V75" privy mark on the obverse commemorating the 75th anniversary of the end of World War II.

Crossing the Delaware (2021)

The America's Beautiful National Parks Quarter Dollar Coin Act of 2008 specified what would happen to the coin after that program ended in 2021: "The reverse of the quarter dollar shall contain an image of General Washington crossing the Delaware River prior to the Battle of Trenton," and the obverse would "revert to the same design" containing an image of President Washington" that was used before the State quarters program started in 1999.

	Mintage	MS-65	MS-66	PF-68
2021P	998,800,000	$0.40	$1.70	
2021D	1,169,400,000	0.40	1.70	

	Mintage	MS-65	MS-66	PF-68
2021S	*(512,729)*			$2.60
2021S, Silver	*(350,323)*			6.00

American Women (2022–2025)

The Circulating Collectible Coin Redesign Act of 2020, signed into law January 13, 2021, brought wide-ranging changes involving all of America's circulating coins. In particular, it scheduled the quarter dollar as the venue for several new educational coin programs, including the American Women Quarters program.

Scan to learn more about the program honorees.

From 2022 to 2025, the quarter commemorates prominent American women and the ratification of the Nineteenth Amendment granting women the right to vote. Five coins are being issued per year, each featuring a new reverse design honoring a woman selected from fields and accomplishments such as "suffrage, civil rights, abolition, government, humanities, science, space, and arts."

Common obverse design by Laura Gardin Fraser.

	Mintage	MS-65	MS-66	PF-68
2022P, Maya Angelou	237,600,000	$0.30	$3.40	
2022D, Maya Angelou	258,200,000	0.30	3.40	
2022S, Maya Angelou **(a)**	*(699,097)*	303,520	2.60	5.50	$3.40
2022S, Maya Angelou, Silver	*(356,823)*			8.50

Uncirculated strikes were made at the San Francisco Mint starting in 2012. Not intended for circulation, they were sold to collectors in rolls and bags at a premium above face value.

	Mintage	MS-65	MS-66	PF-68
2022P, Dr. Sally Ride	275,200,000	$0.30	$3.40	
2022D, Dr. Sally Ride	278,000,000	0.30	3.40	
2022S, Dr. Sally Ride (a)	(699,097) 304,120	2.60	5.50	$3.40
2022S, Dr. Sally Ride, Silver	(356,823)			8.50
2022P, Wilma Mankiller	310,000,000	0.30	3.40	
2022D, Wilma Mankiller	296,800,000	0.30	3.40	
2022S, Wilma Mankiller (a)	(699,097) 304,640	2.60	5.50	3.40
2022S, Wilma Mankiller, Silver	(356,823)			8.50
2022P, Nina Otero-Warren	225,000,000	0.30	3.40	
2022D, Nina Otero-Warren	219,200,000	0.30	3.40	
2022S, Nina Otero-Warren (a)	(699,097) 305,560	2.60	5.50	3.40
2022S, Nina Otero-Warren, Silver	(356,823)			8.50
2022P, Anna May Wong	226,800,000	0.30	3.40	
2022D, Anna May Wong	240,800,000	0.30	3.40	
2022S, Anna May Wong (a)	(699,097) 304,680	2.60	5.50	3.40
2022S, Anna May Wong, Silver	(356,823)			8.50

a. Uncirculated strikes were made at the San Francisco Mint starting in 2012. Not intended for circulation, they were sold to collectors in rolls and bags at a premium above face value.

	Mintage	MS-65	MS-66	PF-68
2023P, Bessie Coleman	302,000,000	$0.30	$3.40	
2023D, Bessie Coleman	317,200,000	0.30	3.40	
2023S, Bessie Coleman (a)	(593,245) 500,360	2.60	5.50	$3.40
2023S, Bessie Coleman, Silver	(269,709)			8.50
2023P, Edith Kanaka'ole	372,800,000	0.30	3.40	
2023D, Edith Kanaka'ole	368,600,000	0.30	3.40	
2023S, Edith Kanaka'ole (a)	(593,245) 503,400	2.60	5.50	3.40
2023S, Edith Kanaka'ole, Silver	(269,709)			8.50
2023P, Eleanor Roosevelt	284,000,000	0.30	3.40	
2023D, Eleanor Roosevelt	271,800,000	0.30	3.40	
2023S, Eleanor Roosevelt (a)	(593,245) 507,120	2.60	5.50	3.40
2023S, Eleanor Roosevelt, Silver	(269,709)			8.50
2023P, Jovita Idar	190,600,000	0.30	3.40	
2023D, Jovita Idar	188,000,000	0.30	3.40	
2023S, Jovita Idar (a)	(593,245) 503,840	2.60	5.50	3.40
2023S, Jovita Idar, Silver	(269,709)			8.50
2023P, Maria Tallchief	185,800,000	0.30	3.40	

a. Uncirculated strikes were made at the San Francisco Mint starting in 2012. Not intended for circulation, they were sold to collectors in rolls and bags at a premium above face value.

	Mintage	MS-65	MS-66	PF-68
2023D, Maria Tallchief	184,800,000	$0.30	$3.40	
2023S, Maria Tallchief **(a)**	(593,245) 502,200	2.60	5.50	$3.40
2023S, Maria Tallchief, Silver	(269,709)			8.50

a. Uncirculated strikes were made at the San Francisco Mint starting in 2012. Not intended for circulation, they were sold to collectors in rolls and bags at a premium above face value.

	Mintage	MS-65	MS-66	PF-68
2024P, Rev. Dr. Pauli Murray		$0.30	$3.40	
2024D, Rev. Dr. Pauli Murray		0.30	3.40	
2024S, Rev. Dr. Pauli Murray **(a)**		2.60	5.50	$3.40
2024S, Rev. Dr. Pauli Murray, Silver				8.50
2024P, Patsy Takemoto Mink		0.30	3.40	
2024D, Patsy Takemoto Mink		0.30	3.40	
2024S, Patsy Takemoto Mink **(a)**		2.60	5.50	3.40
2024S, Patsy Takemoto Mink, Silver				8.50
2024P, Dr. Mary Edwards Walker		0.30	3.40	
2024D, Dr. Mary Edwards Walker		0.30	3.40	
2024S, Dr. Mary Edwards Walker **(a)**		2.60	5.50	3.40
2024S, Dr. Mary Edwards Walker, Silver				8.50
2024P, Celia Cruz		0.30	3.40	
2024D, Celia Cruz		0.30	3.40	
2024S, Celia Cruz **(a)**		2.60	5.50	3.40
2024S, Celia Cruz, Silver				8.50
2024P, Zitkala-Ša		0.30	3.40	
2024D, Zitkala-Ša		0.30	3.40	
2024S, Zitkala-Ša **(a)**		2.60	5.50	3.40
2024S, Zitkala-Ša, Silver				8.50

a. Uncirculated strikes were made at the San Francisco Mint starting in 2012. Not intended for circulation, they were sold to collectors in rolls and bags at a premium above face value.

	Mintage	MS-65	MS-66	PF-68
2025P, Ida B. Wells		$0.30	$3.40	
2025D, Ida B. Wells		0.30	3.40	
2025S, Ida B. Wells **(a)**		2.60	5.50	$3.40
2025S, Ida B. Wells, Silver				8.50
2025P, Juliette Gordon Low		0.30	3.40	
2025D, Juliette Gordon Low		0.30	3.40	
2025S, Juliette Gordon Low **(a)**		2.60	5.50	3.40
2025S, Juliette Gordon Low, Silver				8.50

a. Uncirculated strikes were made at the San Francisco Mint starting in 2012. Not intended for circulation, they were sold to collectors in rolls and bags at a premium above face value.

	Mintage	MS-65	MS-66	PF-68
2025P, Dr. Vera Rubin		$0.30	$3.40	
2025D, Dr. Vera Rubin		0.30	3.40	
2025S, Dr. Vera Rubin (a)		2.60	5.50	$3.40
2025S, Dr. Vera Rubin, Silver			8.50	
2025P, Stacey Park Milburn		0.30	3.40	
2025D, Stacey Park Milburn		0.30	3.40	
2025S, Stacey Park Milburn (a)		2.60	5.50	3.40
2025S, Stacey Park Milburn, Silver			8.50	
2025P, Althea Gibson		0.30	3.40	
2025D, Althea Gibson		0.30	3.40	
2025S, Althea Gibson (a)		2.60	5.50	3.40
2025S, Althea Gibson, Silver			8.50	

a. Uncirculated strikes were made at the San Francisco Mint starting in 2012. Not intended for circulation, they were sold to collectors in rolls and bags at a premium above face value.

The half dollar, authorized by the Act of April 2, 1792, was not minted until December 1794. The weight of the half dollar was 208 grains and its fineness .8924 when first issued. This standard was not changed until 1837 when the Act of January 18, 1837, specified 206-1/4 grains, .900 fine. This fineness continued in use until 1965.

Arrows at the date in 1853 indicate the reduction of weight to 192 grains. During that year only, rays were added to the reverse. Arrows remained in 1854 and 1855. In 1873 the weight was raised by .9 grains and arrows were again placed at the date.

FLOWING HAIR (1794–1795)

AG-3 About Good: Clear enough to identify.
G-4 Good: Date and letters sufficient to be legible. Main devices outlined, but lacking in detail.
VG-8 Very Good: Major details discernible. Letters well formed but worn.
F-12 Fine: Hair ends distinguishable. Top hair lines visible, but otherwise worn smooth.
VF-20 Very Fine: Some detail visible in hair in center; other details more bold.
EF-40 Extremely Fine: Hair above head and down neck detailed, with slight wear.
AU-50 About Uncirculated: All hair visible; slight wear on bust of Liberty and on top edges of eagle's wings, head, and breast.

1795, 2 Leaves Under Each Wing

1795, 3 Leaves Under Each Wing

	Mintage	AG-3	G-4	VG-8	F-12	VF-20	EF-40	AU-50
1794	23,464	$2,050	$2,600	$3,550	$6,000	$10,000	$24,000	$53,500
1795	299,680	725	1,200	1,650	2,150	3,000	5,250	10,500
1795, Recut Date	*	725	1,200	1,650	2,150	3,500	9,750	16,000
1795, 3 Leaves Under Each Wing	*	1,200	1,500	1,950	3,700	5,750	15,500	28,000

* Included in number above.

DRAPED BUST (1796–1807)

AG-3 About Good: Clear enough to identify.
G-4 Good: Date and letters sufficiently clear to be legible. Main devices outlined, but lacking in detail.
VG-8 Very Good: Major details discernible. Letters well formed but worn.
F-12 Fine: Hair ends distinguishable. Top hair lines visible, but otherwise worn smooth.
VF-20 Very Fine: Right side of drapery slightly worn. Left side to curls smooth.
EF-40 Extremely Fine: All lines in drapery on bust distinctly visible around to hair curls.
AU-50 About Uncirculated: Slight trace of wear on cheek, hair, and shoulder.

Small Eagle Reverse (1796–1797)

1796, 16 Stars

1797, 15 Stars

See next page for chart.

	Mintage	AG-3	G-4	VG-8	F-12	VF-20	EF-40	AU-50
1796 and 1797, All kinds........3,918								
1796, 15 Stars		$22,500	$26,000	$31,500	$36,500	$44,500	$79,000	$112,500
1796, 16 Stars		22,500	26,000	31,500	36,500	44,500	79,000	112,500
1797, 15 Stars		22,500	26,000	31,500	36,500	44,500	79,000	112,500

Heraldic Eagle Reverse (1801–1807)

1805, 5 Over 4

1806, 6 Over 5

	Mintage	G-4	VG-8	F-12	VF-20	EF-40	AU-50	MS-60
1801 30,289		$725	$1,200	$1,700	$2,050	$4,950	$9,000	$64,500
1802 29,890		1,300	1,650	2,250	3,350	5,750	12,000	60,500
1803 188,234		260	330	405	700	1,650	2,700	15,000
1805, 5 Over 4 211,722		370	650	1,000	1,500	2,800	5,250	28,000
1805, Normal Date ....*		205	330	440	725	1,550	2,700	17,000
1806, All kinds..............839,576								
1806, Normal Date		220	280	440	660	1,400	2,000	—
1806, 6 Over 5		225	310	415	650	1,500	2,600	9,500
1806, 6 Over Inverted 6...........		255	320	650	1,050	3,250	6,250	23,500
1807 301,076		200	260	405	600	1,250	1,650	5,750

* Included in number above.

CAPPED BUST, LETTERED EDGE (1807–1836)

John Reich designed this capped-head concept of Liberty. Reich's design of Liberty facing left was used on all U.S. silver denominations for the next 30 years.

G-4 Good: Date and letters legible. Bust worn smooth with outline distinct.

VG-8 Very Good: LIBERTY faint. Legends distinguishable. Clasp at shoulder visible; curl above it nearly smooth.

F-12 Fine: Clasp and adjacent curl clearly outlined with slight details.

VF-20 Very Fine: Clasp at shoulder clear. Wear visible on highest point of curl. Hair over brow distinguishable.

EF-40 Extremely Fine: Clasp and adjacent curl fairly sharp. Brow and hair above distinct. Curls well defined

AU-50 About Uncirculated: Trace of wear on hair over eye and over ear.

MS-60 Uncirculated: No trace of wear. Light blemishes. Possible slide marks from storage handling.

MS-63 Choice Uncirculated: Some distracting contact marks or blemishes in prime focal areas. Impaired luster possible.

First Style (1807–1808)

	Mintage	G-4	VG-8	F-12	VF-20	EF-40	AU-50	MS-60	MS-63
1807	750,500	$115	$200	$370	$500	$925	$1,850	$5,750	$9,000
1808, 8 Over 7	*	80	120	190	265	600	1,100	4,100	9,500
1808	1,368,600	60	80	110	200	370	975	3,150	5,000

* Included in number below.

Remodeled Portrait and Eagle (1809–1836)

	Mintage	G-4	VG-8	F-12	VF-20	EF-40	AU-50	MS-60	MS-63
1809	1,405,810	$80	$110	$160	$215	$425	$825	$2,050	$4,100
1810	1,276,276	60	80	115	180	390	600	2,050	4,200
1811	1,203,644	60	80	100	200	350	700	1,600	3,250

1812, 2 Over 1	1813, 50 C. Over UNI	1814, 4 Over 3

	Mintage	G-4	VG-8	F-12	VF-20	EF-40	AU-50	MS-60	MS-63
1812, 2 Over 1	1,628,059	$90	$110	$160	$225	$390	$1,000	$3,000	$7,000
1812	*	60	80	95	135	370	525	1,400	2,250
1813	1,241,903	70	90	110	160	385	675	1,750	3,000
1813, 50 C. Over UNI	*	90	125	200	350	650	1,200	2,600	6,500
1814, 4 Over 3	1,039,075	120	165	255	370	775	1,350	3,700	9,000
1814	*	80	105	130	190	525	750	1,650	3,550

* Included in number above.

1817, 7 Over 3	1817, 7 Over 4	1817, "Punctuated" Date

	Mintage	G-4	VG-8	F-12	VF-20	EF-40	AU-50	MS-60	MS-63
1815, 5 Over 2	47,150	$1,650	$2,250	$2,700	$3,250	$5,250	$6,750	$15,500	$31,500
1817, All kinds	1,215,567								
1817, 7 Over 3		135	200	370	485	925	2,050	3,900	12,000
1817, 7 Over 4 *(8 known)*		83,000	112,500	153,000	247,500	315,000	378,000	—	—
1817, Dated 181.7		90	135	180	225	600	2,100	8,500	20,500
1817		80	100	115	180	340	750	1,850	4,650

1818, 2nd 8 Over 7

1819, 9 Over 8

1820, 20 Over 19

	Mintage	G-4	VG-8	F-12	VF-20	EF-40	AU-50	MS-60	MS-63
1818, 2nd 8 Over 7 . . . . *		$70	$95	$110	$165	$460	$1,000	$2,650	$5,250
1818	1,960,322	65	85	100	140	315	625	1,500	2,900
1819, 9 Over 8 . . . . *		55	70	95	160	320	525	1,850	5,250
1819	2,208,000	47	65	95	145	260	460	1,650	3,650
1820, 20 Over 19 . . . . *		77	105	125	200	600	900	3,200	—
1820	751,122	60	85	110	160	390	675	2,600	6,750
1821	1,305,797	55	65	75	120	255	370	1,050	2,900
1822	1,559,573	47	65	75	120	275	350	1,100	1,600
1823	1,694,200	47	65	75	110	225	425	1,100	2,400

* Included in number below.

"Various Dates"
*Probably 4 Over
2 Over 0.*

1824, 4 Over 1

**1828, Curl Base,
Knob 2**

**1828, Square
Base 2**

	Mintage	G-4	VG-8	F-12	VF-20	EF-40	AU-50	MS-60	MS-63
1824, All kinds.	3,504,954								
1824, 4 Over Various Dates		$55	$70	$95	$125	$345	$925	$2,550	$4,550
1824, 4 Over 1		70	95	110	135	275	460	2,250	5,250
1824		47	55	65	75	145	235	925	1,650
1825	2,943,166	47	55	65	75	145	235	725	1,300
1826	4,004,180	47	55	65	75	145	235	725	1,400
1827, 7 Over 6	5,493,400	75	95	110	140	320	500	1,500	3,100
1827 . . . . *		47	55	65	75	145	260	825	1,850
1828, All kinds.	3,075,200								
1828, Curl-Base 2, No Knob		47	55	65	75	145	255	925	1,850
1828, Curl-Base 2, With Knob		55	70	90	130	260	550	1,850	3,250
1828, Square-Base 2		47	55	65	75	145	275	775	1,300
1829, 9 Over 7 . . . . **		55	70	95	125	260	525	1,300	3,050
1829	3,712,156	47	55	65	75	145	235	725	1,300
1830	4,764,800	47	55	65	75	145	235	725	1,300
1831	5,873,660	47	55	65	75	145	235	725	1,300
1832	4,797,000	47	55	65	75	145	235	725	1,300
1833	5,206,000	47	55	65	75	145	235	725	1,300
1834	6,412,004	47	55	65	75	145	235	725	1,300
1835	5,352,006	47	55	65	75	145	235	725	1,300
1836	6,545,000	47	55	65	75	145	235	725	1,300
1836, 50 Over 00 . . . . *		90	110	160	255	345	600	2,050	3,900

* Included in number above. ** Included in number below.

CAPPED BUST, REEDED EDGE (1836–1839)

G-4 Good: LIBERTY barely discernible on headband.
VG-8 Very Good: Some letters in LIBERTY clear.
F-12 Fine: LIBERTY complete but faint.
VF-20 Very Fine: LIBERTY sharp. Shoulder clasp clear.
EF-40 Extremely Fine: LIBERTY sharp and strong. Hair details visible.
AU-50 About Uncirculated: Slight trace of wear on cap, cheek, and hair above forehead, and on eagle's claws, wing tops, and head.
MS-60 Uncirculated: No trace of wear. Light blemishes.
MS-63 Choice Uncirculated: Some distracting marks or blemishes in focal areas. Impaired luster possible.

Reverse 50 CENTS (1836–1837)

	Mintage	G-4	VG-8	F-12	VF-20	EF-40	AU-50	MS-60	MS-63
1836	1,200+	$800	$1,000	$1,500	$1,850	$2,800	$3,150	$8,000	$15,500
1837	3,629,820	50	60	80	110	200	395	900	2,250

Reverse HALF DOL. (1838–1839)

On half dollars of 1838 and 1839, the mintmark appears on the obverse; on those thereafter, through 1915, it is on the reverse.

	Mintage	G-4	VG-8	F-12	VF-20	EF-40	AU-50	MS-60	MS-63
1838	3,546,000	$50	$60	$80	$110	$200	$395	$900	$2,250
1838O, Proof only	(20)					275,000	300,000	375,000	
1839	1,392,976	50	60	80	115	215	460	1,300	3,150
1839O	116,000	525	675	1,050	1,400	2,050	2,800	7,500	13,000

LIBERTY SEATED (1839–1891)

G-4 Good: Scant rim. LIBERTY on shield worn off. Date and letters legible.
VG-8 Very Good: Rim fairly defined. Some letters in LIBERTY evident.
F-12 Fine: LIBERTY complete, but weak.
VF-20 Very Fine: LIBERTY mostly sharp.
EF-40 Extremely Fine: LIBERTY entirely sharp. Scroll edges and clasp distinct.
AU-50 About Uncirculated: Slight wear on Liberty's breast and knees; eagle's head, claws, and wing tops.
MS-60 Uncirculated: No trace of wear. Light blemishes.
MS-63 Choice Uncirculated: Some distracting blemishes in prime focal areas. Impaired luster possible.
PF-63 Choice Proof: Reflective surfaces with only a few blemishes in secondary focal places. No major flaws.

Variety 1 – No Motto Above Eagle (1839–1853)

1842, Small Date

1842, Medium Date

No Drapery From Elbow

Drapery From Elbow (Starting 1839)

	Mintage	G-4	VG-8	F-12	VF-20	EF-40	AU-50	MS-60	MS-63
1839, No Drapery From Elbow......*		$275	$330	$440	$800	$1,850	$3,050	$7,500	$19,500
1839, Drapery.........	1,972,400	40	60	70	110	305	550	1,650	3,700
1840...............	1,435,008	65	85	100	135	275	370	725	1,500
1840O.................	855,100	40	50	70	125	225	345	1,650	4,200
1841...............	310,000	50	70	85	135	275	500	1,100	2,150
1841O.................	401,000	50	70	85	115	320	600	1,100	2,650
1842, Small Date.......	2,012,764	60	80	100	125	200	435	1,300	2,650
1842, Medium Date............**		40	55	70	90	155	320	825	1,650
1842O, Small Date	957,000	42	50	68	100	290	650	2,000	4,200
1842O, Medium Date...........**		38	45	60	90	265	600	1,850	3,900
1843...............	3,844,000	36	42	50	65	135	250	700	1,600
1843O...............	2,268,000	45	55	65	70	160	330	1,100	2,600
1844...............	1,766,000	36	42	60	100	180	315	650	1,500
1844O...............	2,005,000	36	42	70	120	245	390	1,300	2,800
1845...............	589,000	45	60	80	125	330	550	1,100	3,250
1845O...............	2,094,000	36	55	65	90	145	345	725	2,500
1846...............	2,210,000	36	42	50	65	135	330	750	1,600
1846, 6 Over Horizontal 6 ....**		225	330	600	925	1,600	2,400	4,650	7,250
1846O...............	2,304,000	36	55	85	115	215	370	1,500	3,700
1847...............	1,156,000	40	55	70	100	170	275	600	1,650
1847O...............	2,584,000	36	42	50	70	135	370	1,050	3,700
1848...............	580,000	36	42	90	145	255	500	925	2,250
1848O...............	3,180,000	36	42	60	110	215	405	1,150	1,850
1849...............	1,252,000	36	55	60	90	135	300	825	2,050
1849O...............	2,310,000	40	50	65	100	285	600	1,200	2,600
1850...............	227,000	320	415	500	600	725	975	1,600	3,350
1850O...............	2,456,000	36	42	50	80	160	275	725	1,500
1851...............	200,750	650	700	825	1,000	1,600	1,850	2,800	3,550
1851O...............	402,000	50	75	110	135	390	675	1,100	2,600
1852...............	77,130	370	460	550	825	1,400	1,750	2,600	3,700
1852O...............	144,000	330	425	550	700	1,000	1,650	3,350	10,500
1853O *(4 known)*........	126,000	144,000	207,000	306,000	540,000	—	—	—	—

* Included in number below.   **Included in number above.

Variety 2 – Arrows at Date, Rays Around Eagle (1853)

	Mintage	G-4	VG-8	F-12	VF-20	EF-40	AU-50	MS-60	MS-63
1853	3,532,708	$45	$65	$90	$115	$260	$495	$1,150	$3,000
18530	1,328,000	45	65	90	115	330	700	2,300	5,250

Variety 3 – Arrows at Date, No Rays (1854–1855)

	Mintage	G-4	VG-8	F-12	VF-20	EF-40	AU-50	MS-60	MS-63
1854	2,982,000	$36	$42	$50	$70	$120	$195	$415	$925
18540	5,240,000	36	42	50	70	120	195	415	925
1855, Over 1854	*	70	110	160	275	395	725	1,600	3,000
1855	759,500	36	42	50	70	135	300	775	1,500
18550	3,688,000	36	42	50	70	120	195	415	1,000
1855S	129,950	370	875	1,000	1,300	2,800	4,650	28,000	46,500

* Included in number below.

Variety 1 Resumed, With Weight Standard of Variety 2 (1856–1866)

	Mintage	G-4	VG-8	F-12	VF-20	EF-40	AU-50	MS-60	MS-63	PF-63
1856	938,000	$36	$42	$50	$65	$110	$215	$460	$1,050	
18560	2,658,000	36	45	55	80	145	260	500	1,300	
1856S	211,000	115	180	320	435	900	1,550	4,200	8,250	
1857	1,988,000	36	42	50	65	110	215	405	875	
18570	818,000	36	42	50	80	180	370	1,300	3,250	
1857S	158,000	145	180	275	370	925	1,500	2,800	7,250	
1858 . . . . . . (300+). . .	4,225,700	36	42	50	65	110	215	405	875	$1,400
18580	7,294,000	36	42	50	65	110	215	500	1,400	
1858S	476,000	40	65	90	160	255	460	1,500	3,500	
1859 . . . . . . (800).	747,200	36	42	50	65	110	215	405	875	1,400
18590	2,834,000	36	50	55	70	120	245	500	1,500	
1859S	566,000	45	60	70	125	200	460	1,050	2,800	
1860 . . . . (1,000). . . .	302,700	36	42	50	65	125	255	485	875	1,200
18600	1,290,000	36	42	50	80	140	255	550	925	
1860S	472,000	45	70	90	110	225	370	1,300	3,900	
1861 . . . . (1,000). . . .	2,887,400	40	43	55	80	180	305	550	1,100	1,200
18610	2,532,633	60	90	125	180	415	600	1,350	2,800	
1861S	939,500	40	50	70	90	300	550	925	2,600	
1862 . . . . . (550).	253,000	55	75	110	160	275	460	850	1,400	1,200
1862S	1,352,000	45	60	65	110	180	320	975	1,950	
1863 . . . . . (460).	503,200	50	75	110	180	275	500	700	1,100	1,200
1863S	916,000	45	65	85	125	225	370	1,000	1,600	
1864 . . . . . (470).	379,100	45	80	110	255	390	650	1,250	1,750	1,200
1864S	658,000	70	100	150	180	415	725	1,850	4,650	
1865 . . . . . (500).	511,400	80	95	115	200	500	925	1,750	2,200	1,200
1865S	675,000	90	115	145	190	435	650	1,850	3,250	
1866S, No Motto	60,000	500	600	700	850	1,400	2,050	7,500	12,000	

Variety 4 – Motto Above Eagle (1866–1873)

	Mintage	G-4	VG-8	F-12	VF-20	EF-40	AU-50	MS-60	MS-63	PF-63
1866 . . . . . (725) 744,900		$45	$55	$60	$80	$145	$225	$550	$1,550	$900
1866S 994,000		50	60	75	125	190	320	1,000	2,250	
1867 . . . . . (625) 449,300		55	70	110	170	255	440	825	1,500	950
1867S 1,196,000		45	55	75	110	180	415	1,400	2,650	
1868 . . . . . (600) 417,600		60	75	90	145	225	415	725	1,500	950
1868S 1,160,000		38	50	75	130	225	315	1,100	2,800	
1869 . . . . . (600) 795,300		45	55	65	70	150	285	650	1,250	1,100
1869S 656,000		50	60	70	80	180	370	925	2,300	
1870 . . . . (1,000) 633,900		36	45	55	70	145	275	550	1,200	1,150
1870CC 54,617	1,100	2,250	3,250	4,200	7,500	19,000	57,000	144,000	
1870S 1,004,000		55	70	90	135	390	600	2,050	3,550	
1871 . . . . . (960) 1,203,600		36	42	50	65	110	200	550	1,000	950
1871CC 153,950		525	725	1,000	1,650	3,000	4,950	24,000	60,000	
1871S 2,178,000		36	42	50	65	135	200	725	1,750	
1872 . . . . . (950) 880,600		36	42	50	65	125	200	600	1,000	925
1872CC 257,000		275	460	650	1,000	1,850	3,250	19,000	44,500	
1872S 580,000		36	45	75	135	225	460	1,500	2,900	
1873 . . . . . (600) 801,200		36	45	55	100	150	305	825	1,650	900
1873CC 122,500		275	460	825	1,500	2,600	4,650	9,750	25,000	

Variety 5 – Arrows at Date (1873–1874)

	Mintage	G-4	VG-8	F-12	VF-20	EF-40	AU-50	MS-60	MS-63	PF-63
1873 . . . . . . (550) 1,815,200		$36	$43	$55	$70	$215	$350	$725	$1,600	$1,500
1873CC 214,560		190	370	460	725	1,500	2,450	7,000	14,000	
1873S 228,000		55	110	160	180	460	600	2,400	6,750	
1874 . . . . . . (700) 2,359,600		36	43	55	70	215	350	725	1,600	1,500
1874CC 59,000		875	1,400	2,250	3,150	4,650	6,250	12,500	24,000	
1874S 394,000		70	135	160	180	275	525	1,250	2,150	

Variety 4 Resumed, With Weight Standard of Variety 5 (1875–1891)

	Mintage	G-4	VG-8	F-12	VF-20	EF-40	AU-50	MS-60	MS-63	PF-63
1875 . . . . . .(700). . . .	6,026,800	$36	$42	$50	$65	$90	$150	$320	$575	$900
1875CC	1,008,000	70	110	200	315	650	925	1,650	3,050	
1875S	3,200,000	36	42	50	65	90	150	320	575	
1876 . . . . (1,150). . . .	8,418,000	36	42	50	65	90	150	320	575	900
1876CC	1,956,000	70	90	165	225	550	825	1,450	2,800	
1876S	4,528,000	36	42	50	65	90	150	370	775	
1877 . . . . .(510). . . .	8,304,000	36	42	50	65	90	150	320	575	900
1877CC	1,420,000	70	90	145	275	415	600	1,150	2,100	
1877S	5,356,000	36	42	50	65	90	150	320	575	
1878 . . . . . .(800). . . .	1,377,600	45	70	90	95	145	200	370	925	900
1878CC	62,000	1,150	1,500	1,950	2,400	3,350	4,300	9,500	16,000	
1878S	12,000	24,000	35,500	41,000	46,500	58,000	62,500	78,000	105,500	
1879 . . . . (1,100).	4,800	295	370	460	550	675	800	1,000	1,350	900
1880 . . . . (1,355).	8,400	225	370	435	500	675	750	1,000	1,500	900
1881 . . . . . .(975).	10,000	225	255	345	415	600	700	875	1,300	900
1882 . . . . (1,100).	4,400	225	255	345	415	600	700	875	1,200	900
1883 . . . . (1,039).	8,000	260	295	405	460	650	750	1,000	1,750	900
1884 . . . . .(875).	4,400	275	330	460	600	825	925	1,150	1,600	900
1885 . . . . . .(930).	5,200	255	275	345	415	600	700	875	1,500	900
1886 . . . . . .(886).	5,000	275	345	370	415	600	725	925	1,400	900
1887 . . . . . .(710).	5,000	345	390	435	485	600	700	875	1,500	900
1888 . . . . . .(832).	12,001	200	255	320	390	600	700	875	1,200	900
1889 . . . . .(711).	12,000	180	255	320	390	650	725	925	1,750	925
1890 . . . . .(590).	12,000	190	255	320	390	525	700	975	1,250	900
1891 . . . . . .(600).	200,000	40	60	100	110	160	255	390	925	900

BARBER (1892–1915)

Like the dime and quarter dollar, this type was designed by U.S. Mint chief engraver Charles E. Barber, whose initial B is on the truncation of the neck.

G-4 Good: Date and legends legible. LIBERTY worn off headband.
VG-8 Very Good: Some letters legible in LIBERTY.
F-12 Fine: LIBERTY nearly completely legible, but worn.
VF-20 Very Fine: All letters in LIBERTY evenly plain.
EF-40 Extremely Fine: LIBERTY bold, and its ribbon distinct.
AU-50 About Uncirculated: Slight trace of wear above forehead, leaf tips, and cheek, and on eagle's head, tail, and wing tips.
MS-60 Uncirculated: No trace of wear. Light blemishes.
MS-63 Choice Uncirculated: Some distracting contact marks or blemishes in prime focal areas. Impaired luster possible.
PF-63 Choice Proof: Reflective surfaces with only a few blemishes in secondary focal places. No major flaws.

Mintmark location on reverse, below eagle.

	Mintage	G-4	VG-8	F-12	VF-20	EF-40	AU-50	MS-60	MS-63	PF-63
1892 . . . . (1,245).	934,000	$45	$55	$65	$125	$165	$260	$435	$650	$750
18920	390,000	200	425	460	550	700	775	950	1,500	

Chart continued on next page.

	Mintage	G-4	VG-8	F-12	VF-20	EF-40	AU-50	MS-60	MS-63	PF-63
1892S	1,029,028	$210.00	$260	$320	$460	$575	$725	$1,100	$1,850	
1893 . . . . . . (792)	1,826,000	21.00	28	60	125	165	285	485	725	$750
1893O	1,389,000	32.00	60	105	180	300	405	625	900	
1893S	740,000	110.00	275	500	700	1,100	1,450	2,100	3,550	
1894 . . . . . . (972)	1,148,000	28.00	38	80	145	180	290	485	725	750
1894O	2,138,000	23.00	32	70	125	175	285	485	875	
1894S	4,048,690	16.00	27	65	125	215	330	525	1,150	
1895 . . . . . . (880)	1,834,338	16.00	25	49	125	165	265	485	750	750
1895O	1,766,000	29.00	50	110	135	175	290	600	1,200	
1895S	1,108,086	36.00	85	160	215	295	370	700	1,300	
1896 . . . . . . (762)	950,000	31.00	38	65	125	165	330	550	925	750
1896O	924,000	34.00	80	180	390	1,550	2,800	6,250	11,500	
1896S	1,140,948	75.00	125	240	485	975	1,250	1,950	2,400	
1897 . . . . . . (731)	2,480,000	16.00	22	45	120	165	265	485	825	750
1897O	632,000	110.00	165	320	650	925	1,150	2,150	3,150	
1897S	933,900	110.00	160	260	415	1,000	1,400	2,250	2,550	
1898 . . . . . . (735)	2,956,000	15.50	20	45	110	150	240	435	675	750
1898O	874,000	26.00	70	155	370	500	625	1,250	1,950	
1898S	2,358,550	20.00	32	65	125	275	440	1,250	1,550	
1899 . . . . . . (846)	5,538,000	15.50	18	40	110	150	240	435	650	750
1899O	1,724,000	16.00	29	65	125	175	285	825	1,450	
1899S	1,686,411	16.00	30	65	125	180	320	725	1,750	
1900 . . . . . . (912)	4,762,000	15.50	18	40	125	165	265	485	725	750
1900O	2,744,000	21.00	40	70	140	295	435	1,650	3,550	
1900S	2,560,322	15.50	22	47	125	180	265	700	1,550	
1901 . . . . . . (813)	4,268,000	13.50	16	40	110	150	240	435	650	750
1901O	1,124,000	16.00	31	90	215	975	1,250	1,650	3,250	
1901S	847,044	55.00	90	240	385	1,150	1,750	3,250	5,500	
1902 . . . . . . (777)	4,922,000	13.50	18	40	110	150	240	435	650	750
1902O	2,526,000	15.50	22	45	125	175	330	725	1,500	
1902S	1,460,670	16.00	27	80	180	330	460	1,150	2,150	
1903 . . . . . . (755)	2,278,000	15.50	21	49	125	165	265	500	875	750
1903O	2,100,000	15.50	23	43	125	165	335	675	1,100	
1903S	1,920,772	15.50	26	60	150	275	460	925	1,650	
1904 . . . . . . (670)	2,992,000	13.50	16	40	110	150	240	435	650	750
1904O	1,117,600	22.00	36	90	200	460	825	1,500	3,050	
1904S	553,038	45.00	110	320	725	1,550	5,000	9,500	14,000	
1905 . . . . . . (727)	662,000	16.00	32	70	130	165	345	550	975	750
1905O	505,000	18.00	39	120	180	295	550	925	1,400	
1905S	2,494,000	16.00	21	55	125	175	330	600	1,000	
1906 . . . . . . (675)	2,638,000	13.50	16	40	110	150	240	435	650	750
1906D	4,028,000	13.50	16	41	110	150	240	435	650	
1906O	2,446,000	15.50	18	43	110	165	320	700	1,200	
1906S	1,740,154	16.00	23	65	125	165	320	675	1,100	
1907 . . . . . . (575)	2,598,000	13.50	18	40	110	150	240	435	650	750
1907D	3,856,000	15.50	16	40	110	150	240	435	700	
1907O	3,946,600	16.00	23	45	110	150	240	435	700	
1907S	1,250,000	16.00	23	65	135	300	650	2,050	3,350	
1908 . . . . . . (545)	1,354,000	13.50	18	40	110	150	240	435	650	750
1908D	3,280,000	13.50	16	40	110	150	240	435	650	
1908O	5,360,000	13.50	18	40	110	160	240	460	675	
1908S	1,644,828	16.00	30	55	125	350	500	925	1,300	

	Mintage	G-4	VG-8	F-12	VF-20	EF-40	AU-50	MS-60	MS-63	PF-63
1909 . . . . . . (650). . . .	2,368,000	$13.50	$18	$40	$110	$150	$240	$435	$650	$750
1909O	925,400	15.50	20	60	135	370	500	825	1,200	
1909S	1,764,000	15.50	19	40	110	255	370	550	925	
1910 . . . . . . (551).	418,000	16.00	35	65	125	250	315	490	925	750
1910S	1,948,000	15.50	21	45	115	225	370	625	1,250	
1911 . . . . . . (543). . . .	1,406,000	15.50	18	40	110	150	240	435	650	750
1911D	695,080	15.50	19	45	125	165	260	445	650	
1911S	1,272,000	15.50	18	45	125	180	370	875	1,350	
1912 . . . . . . (700). . . .	1,550,000	13.50	18	40	110	150	240	435	650	750
1912D	2,300,800	13.50	18	40	110	150	240	435	650	
1912S	1,370,000	15.50	18	45	120	170	290	525	750	
1913 . . . . . . (627).	188,000	50.00	80	155	305	650	1,100	1,650	2,050	750
1913D	534,000	15.50	18	45	125	170	265	485	800	
1913S	604,000	16.00	27	70	125	275	375	825	1,350	
1914 . . . . . . (380).	124,230	80.00	120	240	385	750	925	1,550	2,150	750
1914S	992,000	15.50	16	45	110	165	345	550	975	
1915 . . . . . . (450).	138,000	65.00	100	200	320	525	825	1,150	2,150	750
1915D	1,170,400	13.50	18	40	110	150	240	435	650	
1915S	1,604,000	13.50	18	40	110	150	240	435	650	

LIBERTY WALKING (1916–1947)

This type was designed by American sculptor Adolph A. Weinman, whose monogram, AW, appears under the tip of the tail feathers. On the 1916 coins and some of the 1917 coins, the mintmark is located on the obverse below the motto. A centennial gold issue was struck in 2016.

G-4 Good: Rims defined. Motto IN GOD WE TRUST legible.
VG-8 Very Good: Motto distinct. About half of skirt lines at left clear.
F-12 Fine: All skirt lines evident, but worn in spots. Clear details in sandal below motto.
VF-20 Very Fine: Skirt lines sharp, including leg area. Little wear on breast and right arm.
EF-40 Extremely Fine: All skirt lines bold.
AU-50 About Uncirculated: Slight trace of wear on Liberty's head, knee, and breast tips and on eagle's claws and head.
MS-60 Uncirculated: No trace of wear. Light blemishes.
MS-63 Choice Uncirculated: Some distracting contact marks or blemishes in prime focal areas. Impaired luster possible.
PF-63 Choice Proof: Reflective surfaces with only a few blemishes in secondary focal places. No major flaws.
PF-65 Gem Proof: Brilliant surfaces with no noticeable blemishes or flaws. A few scattered, barely noticeable marks or hairlines possible.

Mintmark Locations

1916–1917   *1917–1947*

Coin dealers often pay more than the Mint State prices shown for choice Uncirculated examples that are well struck.

	Mintage	VG-8	F-12	VF-20	EF-40	AU-50	MS-60	MS-63	MS-65
1916	608,000	$40.00	$70.00	$120.00	$170	$275	$600	$850	$1,750
1916D, Obverse Mintmark. . . .	1,014,400	45.00	70.00	110.00	180	275	550	750	1,550
1916S, Obverse Mintmark	508,000	115.00	240.00	405.00	650	1,000	2,050	2,800	6,000
1917	12,292,000	13.50	14.00	16.50	29	70	170	295	725

Chart continued on next page.

	Mintage	VG-8	F-12	VF-20	EF-40	AU-50	MS-60	MS-63	MS-65
1917D, Obverse Mintmark	765,400	$36.00	$70.00	$110.00	$240.00	$370	$725	$1,150	$3,700
1917D, Reverse Mintmark	1,940,000	20.00	40.00	90.00	205.00	415	1,000	1,650	7,750
1917S, Obverse Mintmark	952,000	40.00	120.00	320.00	825.00	1,400	3,450	4,650	15,000
1917S, Reverse Mintmark	5,554,000	20.00	32.00	60.00	160.00	260	725	1,300	7,500
1918	6,634,000	14.50	20.00	60.00	110.00	225	575	925	2,700
1918D	3,853,040	23.00	50.00	125.00	255.00	460	1,250	1,850	19,000
1918S	10,282,000	14.50	18.00	32.00	90.00	215	550	1,250	10,000
1919	962,000	36.00	70.00	225.00	500.00	925	2,200	2,700	7,000
1919D	1,165,000	70.00	160.00	295.00	1,050.00	1,750	4,650	6,750	108,000
1919S	1,552,000	27.00	80.00	285.00	825.00	1,850	5,750	7,500	16,000
1920	6,372,000	13.50	17.50	29.00	65.00	180	485	825	2,300
1920D	1,551,000	27.00	70.00	255.00	650.00	1,350	3,150	5,750	19,000
1920S	4,624,000	18.00	27.00	90.00	200.00	550	1,200	2,500	12,000
1921	246,000	155.00	370.00	725.00	1,950.00	3,350	6,250	7,500	23,500
1921D	208,000	320.00	550.00	1,050.00	3,350.00	4,450	7,500	9,750	30,500
1921S	548,000	85.00	275.00	700.00	3,000.00	8,250	20,500	30,000	72,000
1923S	2,178,000	22.00	40.00	180.00	825.00	1,550	3,050	3,700	12,000
1927S	2,392,000	16.00	20.00	45.00	315.00	700	1,400	2,150	5,000
1928S	1,940,000	16.50	26.00	70.00	255.00	825	1,950	2,800	5,250
1929D	1,001,200	13.00	18.00	30.00	75.00	180	485	825	1,650
1929S	1,902,000	14.50	21.00	30.00	110.00	240	500	975	2,250
1933S	1,786,000	13.50	17.50	25.00	65.00	200	600	1,100	2,400
1934	6,964,000	12.00	12.50	13.00	15.50	20	70	105	260
1934D	2,361,000	12.00	13.00	15.50	31.00	70	135	240	725
1934S	3,652,000	12.00	12.50	14.00	32.00	70	275	700	1,500
1935	9,162,000	12.00	12.50	13.00	16.50	21	50	70	215
1935D	3,003,800	12.00	12.50	13.50	22.00	55	125	265	925
1935S	3,854,000	12.00	12.50	14.50	32.00	90	275	485	1,150

	Mintage	VG-8	F-12	VF-20	EF-40	AU-50	MS-60	MS-63	MS-65	PF-63	PF-65
1936 .... (3,901)	12,614,000	$12.50	$13.00	$13.50	$16.50	$19.00	$47	$75	$170	$1,490	$2,300
1936D	4,252,400	12.50	12.50	13.00	16.00	29.00	80	125	330		
1936S	3,884,000	12.50	12.50	13.50	25.00	60.00	145	215	525		
1937 .... (5,728)	9,522,000	12.50	12.50	12.50	14.50	17.00	50	80	170	460	600
1937D	1,676,000	12.00	13.00	14.50	32.00	70.00	190	260	485		
1937S	2,090,000	12.00	12.50	13.00	22.00	49.00	145	215	525		
1938 .... (8,152)	4,110,000	12.00	12.50	13.50	17.50	27.00	65	130	265	430	525
1938D	491,600	36.00	60.00	70.00	110.00	155.00	460	575	975		
1939 .... (8,808)	6,812,000	12.50	12.50	12.50	14.50	22.00	45	70	150	420	480
1939D	4,267,800	12.50	12.50	13.00	15.50	19.00	45	70	160		
1939S	2,552,000	12.50	12.50	13.00	20.00	55.00	100	145	215		
1940 ... (11,279)	9,156,000	12.00	12.00	12.00	13.00	15.50	28	46	115	330	350
1940S	4,550,000	12.00	12.00	13.00	14.50	27.00	38	70	280		
1941 ... (15,412)	24,192,000	12.00	12.00	12.00	13.00	14.50	25	41	70	260	305
1941D	11,248,400	12.00	12.00	12.00	13.00	15.00	29	60	105		
1941S	8,098,000	12.00	12.00	12.00	14.50	21.00	60	90	310		
1942 ... (21,120)	47,818,000	12.00	12.00	12.00	13.00	14.50	25	41	70	260	305

	Mintage	F-12	VF-20	EF-40	AU-50	MS-60	MS-63	MS-65
1942D	10,973,800	$12.00	$12.00	$13.00	$15.00	$26	$46	$105
1942S	12,708,000	12.00	12.00	13.50	18.00	32	60	170
1943	53,190,000	12.00	12.00	13.00	14.50	25	41	70
1943D	11,346,000	12.00	12.00	13.00	16.00	34	55	120
1943S	13,450,000	12.00	12.00	13.00	18.00	36	60	125
1944	28,206,000	12.00	12.00	13.00	14.50	25	41	70
1944D	9,769,000	12.00	12.00	13.00	16.00	31	46	75
1944S	8,904,000	12.00	12.00	13.50	20.00	36	55	160
1945	31,502,000	12.00	12.00	13.00	14.50	25	41	70
1945D	9,966,800	12.00	12.00	13.00	15.50	25	41	70
1945S	10,156,000	12.00	12.00	13.50	20.00	36	49	75
1946	12,118,000	12.00	12.00	13.00	14.50	25	41	70
1946D	2,151,000	13.00	14.00	17.00	20.00	27	43	75
1946S	3,724,000	12.00	13.00	15.50	27.00	40	47	80
1947	4,094,000	12.50	13.00	14.50	21.00	34	50	75
1947D	3,900,600	12.50	13.00	14.00	20.00	34	55	70

FRANKLIN (1948–1963)

The Benjamin Franklin half dollar and the Roosevelt dime were both designed by U.S. Mint chief engraver John R. Sinnock. His initials appear below the shoulder.

VF-20 Very Fine: At least half of the lower and upper incused lines on rim of Liberty Bell on reverse visible.
EF-40 Extremely Fine: Wear spots at top of end of Franklin's curls and hair at back of ears. Wear evident at top and on lettering of Liberty Bell.
MS-60 Uncirculated: No trace of wear. Light blemishes.
MS-63 Choice Uncirculated: Some distracting contact marks or blemishes in prime focal areas. Impaired luster possible.
MS-65 Gem Uncirculated: Only light, scattered contact marks that are not distracting. Strong luster, good eye appeal.
PF-63 Choice Proof: Reflective surfaces with only a few blemishes in secondary focal places. No major flaws.
PF-65 Gem Proof: Brilliant surfaces with no noticeable blemishes or flaws. A few scattered, barely noticeable marks or hairlines possible.

Coin dealers usually pay more than the Mint State prices shown for well-struck Uncirculated halves with full bell lines.

Mintmark Location

	Mintage	AU-50	MS-60	MS-63	MS-65	MS-66	PF-63	PF-65
1948	3,006,814	$13.00	$15.50	$19.50	$55	$150		
1948D	4,028,600	13.00	15.50	16.00	55	135		
1949	5,614,000	12.50	22.00	27.00	55	160		
1949D	4,120,600	20.00	33.00	36.00	125	550		
1949S	3,744,000	27.00	48.00	55.00	60	105		
1950 . . . . . (51,386)	7,742,123	12.50	22.00	23.00	70	205	$265	$350
1950D	8,031,600	12.50	19.00	22.00	105	415		
1951 . . . . . (57,500) . . .	16,802,102	12.50	13.00	15.50	55	135	180	210
1951D	9,475,200	16.00	23.00	25.00	65	215		

Chart continued on next page.

	Mintage	AU-50	MS-60	MS-63	MS-65	MS-66	PF-63	PF-65
1951S 13,696,000		$12.50	$15.50	$18.00	$32.00	$110.00		
1952 . . . . . (81,980). . . 21,192,093		12.50	13.00	15.50	45.00	115.00	$90.00	$115
1952D 25,395,600		12.50	13.00	15.50	70.00	180.00		
1952S 5,526,000		29.00	38.00	43.00	65.00	100.00		
1953 . . . . (128,800). . . . 2,668,120		12.50	13.00	15.50	43.00	125.00	60.00	70
1953D 20,900,400		12.50	13.00	15.50	50.00	180.00		
1953S 4,148,000		15.50	21.00	22.00	33.00	105.00		
1954 . . . . (233,300). . . 13,188,202		12.50	13.00	15.50	25.00	145.00	38.00	45
1954D 25,445,580		12.50	13.00	15.50	32.00	160.00		
1954S 4,993,400		12.50	13.00	15.50	24.00	50.00		
1955 . . . . (378,200). . . . 2,498,181		12.50	13.00	15.50	32.00	80.00	34.00	41
1956 . . . . (669,384). . . . 4,032,000		12.50	13.00	15.50	22.00	43.00	18.00	27
1957 . . . (1,247,952). . . . 5,114,000		12.50	13.00	15.50	22.00	43.00	17.00	21
1957D 19,966,850		12.50	13.00	15.50	23.00	70.00		
1958 . . . . (875,652). . . . 4,042,000		12.50	13.00	15.50	22.00	43.00	21.00	23
1958D 23,962,412		12.50	13.00	15.50	22.00	43.00		
1959 . . . (1,149,291). . . . 6,200,000		12.50	13.00	15.50	25.00	205.00	15.50	18
1959D 13,053,750		12.50	13.00	15.50	27.00	200.00		
1960 . . . (1,691,602). . . . 6,024,000		12.50	13.00	15.50	36.00	205.00	15.50	18
1960D 18,215,812		12.50	13.00	15.50	41.00	215.00		
1961 . . . (3,028,244). . . . 8,290,000		12.50	13.00	15.50	23.00	200.00	15.50	18
1961D 20,276,442		12.50	13.00	15.50	40.00	190.00		
1962 . . . (3,218,019). . . . 9,714,000		13.00	13.50	15.50	31.00	180.00	15.50	18
1962D 35,473,281		13.00	13.50	15.50	27.00	295.00		
1963 . . . (3,075,645). . . 22,164,000		12.50	13.00	15.00	22.00	190.00	15.50	18
1963D 67,069,292		12.50	13.00	15.00	22.00	150.00		

KENNEDY (1964 TO DATE)

Gilroy Roberts, chief engraver of the U.S. Mint from 1948 to 1964, designed the obverse of this coin, a tribute to President John F. Kennedy, who was assassinated in November 1963. Roberts's stylized initials are on the truncation of the bust of Kennedy. The reverse, which uses as its motif the eagle from the Seal of the President of the United States, is the work of assistant engraver Frank Gasparro. The Kennedy half dollar was minted in 90% silver in its first year of issue, 1964. From 1965 to 1970 its fineness was reduced to 40% silver. Since 1971 the coin has been struck in copper-nickel (except for certain silver Proofs, 1992 to date). Dates after 2001 have not been released into general circulation, instead being made available in 20-coin rolls, 200-coin bags, and coin sets sold by the Mint. In 2014 a .999 fine gold version was made for collectors, dual-dated 1964–2014 to mark the coin's 50th anniversary.

In the early 1970's an open contest was held to select a new reverse design for the Kennedy half dollar, to celebrate the nation's bicentennial. Seth G. Huntington's winning entry featured a view of Independence Hall in Philadelphia. The Bicentennial half dollars bear the dual date 1776–1976.

HALF DOLLARS

Mintmark Location (1964)

Mintmark Location (1968 to Date)

Silver Coinage (1964)

	Mintage		MS-63	MS-65	MS-66	PF-66	PF-67
1964 . . . . (3,950,762)	273,304,004	$12.50	$19	$45	$16	$22
1964D	156,205,446	12.50	22	45		

Silver Clad Coinage (1965–1970)

	Mintage	MS-63	MS-65	PF-66
1965	65,879,366	$4.60	$18.00	
1966	108,984,932	4.60	18.00	
1967	295,046,978	4.60	18.00	
1968D	246,951,930	4.60	18.00	
1968S . . . . (3,041,506)				$9.50

	Mintage	MS-63	MS-65	PF-66
1969D	129,881,800	$4.60	$18.00	
1969S . . . . (2,934,631)				$9.50
1970D	2,150,000	12.00	32.00	
1970S . . . . (2,632,810)				9.50

Clad Coinage and Silver Proofs (1971 to Date)

	Mintage	MS-63	MS-65	PF-66
1971	155,164,000	$0.90	$18.00	
1971D	302,097,424	0.90	5.50	
1971S . . . . (3,220,733)				$5.50
1972	153,180,000	0.90	9.00	
1972D	141,890,000	0.90	5.50	
1972S . . . . (3,260,996)				5.50

	Mintage	MS-63	MS-65	PF-66
1973	64,964,000	$0.90	$13.50	
1973D	83,171,400	0.90	5.50	
1973S . . . . (2,760,339)				$5.50
1974	201,596,000	0.90	5.50	
1974D	79,066,300	0.90	5.50	
1974S . . . . (2,612,568)				5.50

Bicentennial (1776–1976)

	Mintage	MS-63	MS-65	PF-66	PF-67
1776–1976, Clad	234,308,000	$0.90	$9.00		
1776–1976D, Clad	287,565,248	0.90	18.00		
1776–1976S, Clad . . . . (7,059,099)				$7.25	$8.00
1776–1976S, Silver	11,000,000	4.60	13.50	9.50	
1776–1976S, Silver . . . . (4,000,000)					12.50

Note: Mintage figures for 1976-S silver coins are approximate; many were melted in 1982.

Eagle Reverse Resumed (1977 to Date)

	Mintage	MS-65	PF-66	PF-67
1977	43,598,000	$5.50		
1977D	31,449,106	5.50		
1977S	(3,251,152)		$7.25	$8.00
1978	14,350,000	5.50		
1978D	13,765,799	5.50		
1978S	(3,127,781)		7.25	8.00
1979	68,312,000	5.50		
1979D	15,815,422	5.50		
1979S	(3,677,175)			
Variety 1			7.25	8.00
Variety 2			11.50	14.50
1980P	44,134,000	7.25		
1980D	33,456,449	13.50		
1980S	(3,554,806)		5.50	6.25
1981P	29,544,000	8.00		
1981D	27,839,533	5.50		
1981S	(4,063,083)			
Variety 1			5.50	6.25
Variety 2			16.00	20.00
1982P	10,819,000	40.00		
1982D	13,140,102	9.00		
1982S	(3,857,479)		5.50	6.25
1983P	34,139,000	13.50		
1983D	32,472,244	13.50		
1983S	(3,279,126)		5.50	6.25
1984P	26,029,000	5.50		
1984D	26,262,158	5.50		
1984S	(3,065,110)		5.50	6.25
1985P	18,706,962	5.50		
1985D	19,814,034	5.50		
1985S	(3,362,821)		5.50	6.25
1986P	13,107,633	5.50		
1986D	15,336,145	5.50		
1986S	(3,010,497)		5.50	6.25
1987P (a)	2,890,758	5.50		
1987D (a)	2,890,758	5.50		
1987S	(4,227,728)		5.50	6.25
1988P	13,626,000	5.50		
1988D	12,000,096	5.50		
1988S	(3,262,948)		5.50	6.25
1989P	24,542,000	5.50		
1989D	23,000,216	5.50		
1989S	(3,220,194)		5.50	6.25
1990P	22,278,000	5.50		
1990D	20,096,242	5.50		
1990S	(3,299,559)		5.50	6.25
1991P	14,874,000	5.50		
1991D	15,054,678	5.50		
1991S	(2,867,787)		5.50	6.25
1992P	17,628,000	5.50		
1992D	17,000,106	$5.50		
1992S	(2,858,981)		$5.50	$6.25
1992S, Silver	(1,317,579)		14.50	15.50
1993P	15,510,000	5.50		
1993D	15,000,006	5.50		
1993S	(2,633,439)		5.50	6.25
1993S, Silver	(761,353)		14.50	15.50
1994P	23,718,000	5.50		
1994D	23,828,110	5.50		
1994S	(2,484,594)		5.50	6.25
1994S, Silver	(785,329)		14.50	15.50
1995P	26,496,000	5.50		
1995D	26,288,000	5.50		
1995S	(2,117,496)		5.50	6.25
1995S, Silver	(679,985)		25.00	27.00
1996P	24,442,000	5.50		
1996D	24,744,000	5.50		
1996S	(1,750,244)		5.50	6.25
1996S, Silver	(775,021)		14.50	15.50
1997P	20,882,000	5.50		
1997D	19,876,000	5.50		
1997S	(2,055,000)		5.50	6.25
1997S, Silver	(741,678)		14.50	15.50
1998P	15,646,000	5.50		
1998D	15,064,000	5.50		
1998S	(2,086,507)		5.50	6.25
1998S, Silver	(878,792)		14.50	15.50
1998S, Silver, Matte Finish	(62,000)		55.00	60.00
1999P	8,900,000	5.50		
1999D	10,682,000	5.50		
1999S	(2,543,401)		5.50	6.25
1999S, Silver	(804,565)		14.50	15.50
2000P	22,600,000	5.50		
2000D	19,466,000	5.50		
2000S	(3,082,483)		5.50	6.25
2000S, Silver	(965,421)		14.50	15.50
2001P	21,200,000	5.50		
2001D	19,504,000	5.50		
2001S	(2,294,909)		5.50	6.25
2001S, Silver	(889,697)		14.50	15.50
2002P (a)	3,100,000	5.50		
2002D (a)	2,500,000	5.50		
2002S	(2,319,766)		5.50	6.25
2002S, Silver	(892,229)		14.50	15.50
2003P (a)	2,500,000	5.50		
2003D (a)	2,500,000	5.50		
2003S	(2,172,684)		5.50	6.25
2003S, Silver	(1,125,755)		14.50	15.50
2004P (a)	2,900,000	5.50		

a. Not issued for circulation.

	Mintage	MS-65	PF-66	PF-67
2004D **(a)**	2,900,000	$5.50		
2004S	(1,789,488)		$5.50	$6.25
2004S, Silver	(1,175,934)		14.50	15.50
2005P **(a)**	3,800,000	5.50		
2005D **(a)**	3,500,000	5.50		
2005S	(2,275,000)		5.50	6.25
2005S, Silver	(1,069,679)		14.50	15.50
2006P **(a)**	2,400,000	5.50		
2006D **(a)**	2,000,000	5.50		
2006S	(2,000,428)		5.50	6.25
2006S, Silver	(1,054,008)		14.50	15.50
2007P **(a)**	2,400,000	5.50		
2007D **(a)**	2,400,000	5.50		
2007S	(1,702,116)		5.50	6.25
2007S, Silver	(875,050)		14.50	15.50
2008P **(a)**	1,700,000	5.50		
2008D **(a)**	1,700,000	5.50		
2008S	(1,405,674)		5.50	6.25
2008S, Silver	(763,887)		14.50	15.50
2009P **(a)**	1,900,000	5.50		
2009D **(a)**	1,900,000	5.50		
2009S	(1,482,502)		5.50	6.25
2009S, Silver	(697,365)		14.50	15.50
2010P **(a)**	1,800,000	5.50		
2010D **(a)**	1,700,000	5.50		
2010S	(1,103,815)		5.50	6.25
2010S, Silver	(585,401)		14.50	15.50
2011P **(a)**	1,750,000	5.50		
2011D **(a)**	1,700,000	5.50		
2011S	(1,098,835)		5.50	6.25
2011S, Silver	(574,175)		14.50	15.50
2012P **(a)**	1,800,000	5.50		

	Mintage	MS-65	PF-66	PF-67
2012D **(a)**	1,700,000	$5.50		
2012S	(843,705)		$5.50	$6.25
2012S, Silver	(445,612)		65.00	70.00
2013P **(a)**	5,000,000	5.50		
2013D **(a)**	4,600,000	5.50		
2013S	(854,785)		5.50	6.25
2013S, Silver	(467,691)		14.50	15.50
2014P **(a)**	2,500,000	5.50		
2014P, High Relief **(b)**	197,608	16.00		
2014P, Silver **(c)**	(219,173)		11.50	12.50
2014D **(a)**	2,100,000	5.50		
2014D, High Relief **(b)**	197,608	7.25		
2014D, Silver **(c)**	219,173	13.00		
2014S, Silver Enh Unc **(c)**	219,173	12.50		
2014S	(777,357)		5.50	6.25
2014S, Silver	(472,107)		14.50	15.50
2014W, Reverse Proof, Silver **(c)**	(219,173)		29.00	31.00
2014W, 50th Anniversary, Gold **(d)**	(73,722)		1,350.00	1,500.00
2015P **(a)**	2,300,000	5.50		
2015D **(a)**	2,300,000	5.50		
2015S	(662,854)		5.50	6.25
2015S, Silver	(387,310)		14.50	15.50
2016P **(a)**	2,100,000	5.50		
2016D **(a)**	2,100,000	5.50		
2016S	(641,775)		5.50	6.25
2016S, Silver	(419,496)		14.50	15.50

a. Not issued for circulation. **b.** To celebrate the 50th anniversary of the Kennedy half dollar, the U.S. Mint issued an Uncirculated two-coin set featuring a Kennedy half dollar from Philadelphia and one from Denver. **c.** Featured in the 2014 half dollar silver-coin collection released by the U.S. Mint to commemorate the 50th anniversary of the Kennedy half dollar. **d.** First gold half dollar offered by the U.S. Mint. It commemorates the 50th anniversary of the first release of the Kennedy half dollar in 1964.

	Mintage	OGP*	MS-69	MS-70
2016W, Gold **(a)**	70,000	$1,450	$1,450	$1,550

* OGP = Coin in original government packaging. **a.** In 2016 the Mint issued a centennial version of the Liberty Walking half dollar in gold.

	Mintage	MS-65	PF-66	PF-67
2017P **(a)**	1,800,000	$5.50		
2017D **(a)**	2,900,000	5.50		
2017S	(621,390)		$5.50	$6.25
2017S, Silver	(406,986)		14.50	15.50
2018P **(a)**	4,800,000	5.50		
2018D **(a)**	6,100,000	5.50		
2018S	(567,856)		5.50	6.25
2018S, Silver	(381,748)		14.50	15.50
2019P **(a)**	1,700,000	5.50		
2019D **(a)**	1,700,000	5.50		
2019S	(642,309)		5.50	6.25
2019S, Silver	(460,925)		14.50	15.50
2019S, Enhanced RevPf **(b)**	(99,998)		18.00	20.00
2020P **(a)**	2,300,000	5.50		
2020D **(a)**	3,400,000	5.50		
2020S	(510,726)		22.00	25.00
2020S, Silver	(363,244)		50.00	55.00
2021P	5,400,000	5.50		
2021D	7,700,000	$5.50		
2021S	(868,644)		$5.50	$6.25
2021S, Silver	(355,778)		60.00	65.00
2022P	4,800,000	5.50		
2022D	4,900,000	5.50		
2022S	(699,097)		16.00	20.00
2022S, Silver	(299,096)		50.00	55.00
2023P	30,200,000	5.50		
2023D	27,800,000	5.50		
2023S	(593,245)		16.00	20.00
2023S, Silver	(244,012)		43.00	50.00
2024P **(a)**		5.50		
2024D **(a)**		5.50		
2024S			16.00	20.00
2024S, Silver			43.00	50.00
2025P **(a)**		5.50		
2025D **(a)**		5.50		
2025S			16.00	20.00
2025S, Silver			43.00	50.00

a. Not issued for circulation. **b.** In 2019, an Enhanced Reverse Proof half dollar from the San Francisco Mint was included in the Apollo 11 50th Anniversary Half Dollar Set.

The silver dollar was authorized by Congress April 2, 1792. Its weight was specified at 416 grains and its fineness at .8924. The first issues appeared in 1794, and until 1804 all silver dollars had the value stamped on the edge: HUNDRED CENTS, ONE DOLLAR OR UNIT. After a lapse in coinage of the silver dollar during the period 1804 to 1835, coins were made with either plain (1836 only) or reeded edges and the value was placed on the reverse side.

Mintages shown here are as reported by the Mint for calendar years and do not necessarily refer to the dates on the coins.

The weight was changed by the law of January 18, 1837, to 412-1/2 grains, fineness .900. The coinage was discontinued by the Act of February 12, 1873, and reauthorized by the Act of February 28, 1878. The silver dollar was again discontinued after 1935, and since then copper-nickel and other base-metal pieces have been coined for circulation. (See also "$1 American Silver Eagle Coins" starting on page 254.)

FLOWING HAIR (1794–1795)

AG-3 About Good: Clear enough to identify.
G-4 Good: Date and letters legible. Main devices outlined, but lacking in detail.
VG-8 Very Good: Major details discernible. Letters well formed but worn.
F-12 Fine: Hair ends distinguishable. Top hair lines visible, but otherwise worn smooth.
VF-20 Very Fine: Some detail visible in hair in center. Other details more bold.
EF-40 Extremely Fine: Hair well defined but with some wear.
AU-50 About Uncirculated: Slight trace of wear on tips of highest curls; breast feathers usually weak.
MS-60 Uncirculated: No trace of wear. Light blemishes.

	Mintage	AG-3	G-4	VG-8	F-12	VF-20	EF-40	AU-50	MS-60
1794	1,758	$39,000	$50,500	$83,000	$99,000	$144,000	$279,000	$450,000	$855,000
1795	160,295	1,700	2,250	3,000	4,300	6,000	11,000	17,000	48,000

DRAPED BUST (1795–1804)
Small Eagle Reverse (1795–1798)

AG-3 About Good: Clear enough to identify.
G-4 Good: Bust outlined, no detail. Date legible, some leaves evident.
VG-8 Very Good: Drapery worn except deepest folds. Hair lines smooth.
F-12 Fine: All drapery lines distinguishable. Some detail visible in hair lines near cheek and neck.
VF-20 Very Fine: Left side of drapery worn smooth.
EF-40 Extremely Fine: Drapery distinctly visible. Hair well outlined and detailed.
AU-50 About Uncirculated: Slight trace of wear on the bust shoulder and hair to left of forehead, as well as on eagle's breast and top edges of wings.
MS-60 Uncirculated: No trace of wear. Light blemishes.

Mintage	AG-3	G-4	VG-8	F-12	VF-20	EF-40	AU-50	MS-60
1795, Bust Type. . *42,738*	$1,400	$1,850	$2,250	$3,000	$3,700	$6,250	$9,750	$39,000
1796 79,920	1,400	1,850	2,250	3,000	3,700	7,000	11,500	99,000
1797 7,776	1,400	1,850	2,250	3,000	3,700	6,250	9,750	39,000
1798 327,536	725	925	1,150	1,600	2,050	3,000	4,950	17,500

Heraldic Eagle Reverse (1798–1804)

G-4 Good: Letters and date legible. E PLURIBUS UNUM illegible.

VG-8 Very Good: Motto partially legible. Only deepest drapery details visible. All other lines smooth.

F-12 Fine: All drapery lines distinguishable. Some detail visible in hair lines near cheek and neck.

VF-20 Very Fine: Left side of drapery worn smooth.

EF-40 Extremely Fine: Drapery distinct. Hair well detailed.

AU-50 About Uncirculated: Slight trace of wear on the bust shoulder and hair to left of forehead, as well as on eagle's breast and top edges of wings.

MS-60 Uncirculated: No trace of wear. Light blemishes.

	Mintage	G-4	VG-8	F-12	VF-20	EF-40	AU-50	MS-60
1798, Heraldic Eagle	*	$925	$1,150	$1,600	$2,050	$3,000	$4,950	$17,500
1799	423,515	925	1,150	1,600	2,050	3,000	4,950	17,500
1800	220,920	950	1,200	1,650	2,150	3,200	5,250	19,000
1801	54,454	1,000	1,300	1,900	2,150	3,950	5,500	18,500
1802	41,650	1,000	1,300	1,900	2,450	3,650	5,500	17,500
1803	85,634	1,000	1,300	1,750	2,050	3,350	5,750	24,000
1804, Class I, First Rev (0 Above Cloud) **(a)** *(8 known)*				PF-60: $2,250,000				
1804, Class II, Second Rev (0 Above Space Between Clouds, Plain Edge) **(b)** . . .				*(unique, in Smithsonian collection)*				
1804, Class III, Second Rev (0 Above Space Between Clouds, Lettered Edge) **(a)** *(6 known)*				PF-58: $1,296,000				

* Included in number above. **a.** Numerous counterfeits exist. **b.** Electrotype copies exist, made at the Mint from their specimen.

GOBRECHT (1836–1839)

Silver dollars of 1836, 1838, and 1839 were mostly made as patterns and restrikes, but some dated 1836 were made for general circulation.

	AU-50	PF-60	PF-63	PF-65
1836, C. GOBRECHT F. on base. Reverse eagle flying upward amid stars. Plain edge. Although scarce, this is the most common variety and was issued for circulation as regular coinage....................	$12,000	$19,500	$29,000	$66,500
1838, Similar obverse, designer's name omitted, stars added around border. Reverse eagle flying left in plain field. Reeded edge...............	23,500	28,000	42,000	78,000
1839, Obverse as above. Reverse eagle in plain field. Reeded edge. Issued for circulation as regular coinage............................	23,500	29,000	42,000	78,000

LIBERTY SEATED (1840–1873)

Starting again in 1840, silver dollars were issued for general circulation, continuing to about 1850, after which their main use was in the export trade to China. The seated figure of Liberty was adopted for the obverse, and a heraldic eagle for the reverse.

VG-8 Very Good: Any three letters of LIBERTY at least two-thirds complete.
F-12 Fine: All seven letters of LIBERTY visible, though weak.
VF-20 Very Fine: LIBERTY strong, but slight wear visible on its ribbon.
EF-40 Extremely Fine: Horizontal lines of shield complete. Eagle's eye plain.
AU-50 About Uncirculated: Traces of light wear on only the high points of the design. Half of mint luster present.
MS-60 Uncirculated: No trace of wear. Light marks or blemishes.
PF-60 Proof: Several contact marks, hairlines, or light rubs possible on surface. Luster possibly dull and eye appeal lacking.
PF-63 Choice Proof: Reflective surfaces with only a few blemishes in secondary focal places. No major flaws.

No Motto (1840–1865)

Location of mintmark, when present, is on reverse, below eagle.

See next page for chart.   **153**

	Mintage	VG-8	F-12	VF-20	EF-40	AU-50	MS-60	PF-63
1840 61,005		$340	$405	$460	$700	$1,200	$4,200	$22,500
1841 173,000		330	390	480	700	1,100	2,600	69,000
1842 184,618		305	360	405	675	850	2,250	69,000
1843 165,100		305	360	405	600	800	1,800	69,000
1844 20,000		320	375	460	725	1,100	3,950	28,000
1845 24,500		370	460	550	825	1,200	4,200	25,000
1846 110,600		305	360	405	600	800	1,500	19,000
1846O 59,000		315	375	430	700	1,200	5,000	
1847 140,750		305	360	405	600	800	2,000	18,500
1848 15,000		415	500	600	1,200	1,650	4,400	21,000
1849 62,600		320	370	435	725	1,000	2,150	30,000
1850 7,500		550	700	925	1,650	2,550	4,650	17,000
1850O 40,000		320	420	700	1,250	2,300	8,000	
1851 1,300		9,500	11,000	13,000	19,000	25,000	37,000	24,000
1852 1,100		12,000	15,000	20,500	25,000	27,000	34,000	24,000
1853 46,110		500	700	875	1,600	1,950	3,150	39,000
1854 33,140		1,650	2,400	3,150	5,250	6,750	10,500	12,500
1855 26,000		1,400	1,850	2,800	4,650	7,000	8,500	12,000
1856 63,500		825	1,300	1,650	2,600	3,150	6,250	9,500
1857 94,000		725	925	1,400	2,050	2,800	4,200	8,500
1858 . . . . *(300)*.		—	—	—	5,750	6,500	7,500	12,000
1859 . . . . (800). 255,700		460	500	600	875	1,400	3,000	3,800
1859O 360,000		305	360	405	600	800	1,500	
1859S 20,000		525	725	1,150	1,450	3,700	7,250	
1860 . . . . . .(1,330). 217,600		330	405	550	825	1,150	2,250	3,800
1860O 515,000		305	360	405	600	800	1,500	
1861 . . . . . .(1,000). 77,500		1,200	1,650	2,250	3,050	4,100	5,750	3,800
1862 . . . . (550). 11,540		600	925	1,500	2,800	4,200	5,750	3,800
1863 . . . . (460). 27,200		925	1,400	1,750	2,600	3,000	4,300	3,800
1864 . . . . (470). 30,700		650	925	1,500	2,050	3,000	5,500	3,800
1865 . . . . (500). 46,500		550	700	1,200	2,050	2,400	3,700	3,800

With Motto IN GOD WE TRUST (1866–1873)

Motto IN GOD WE TRUST on Reverse (1866–1873)

	Mintage	VG-8	F-12	VF-20	EF-40	AU-50	MS-60	PF-63
1866 . . . . (725). 48,900		$280	$375	$460	$825	$1,100	$2,050	$2,700
1867 . . . . (625). 46,900		460	600	725	1,100	1,500	3,150	2,700
1868 . . . . (600). 162,100		355	425	600	1,200	1,750	3,000	2,700
1869 . . . . (600). 423,700		330	370	500	725	1,000	2,150	2,700

	Mintage	VG-8	F-12	VF-20	EF-40	AU-50	MS-60	PF-63
1870......(1,000)......415,000		$280	$315	$385	$550	$725	$1,850	$2,700
1870CC.................11,758		1,650	2,300	3,000	4,650	6,500	17,000	
1870S.............. *11 known*	180,000	261,000	360,000	472,500	765,000	1,350,000		
1871......(960).....1,073,800		280	315	350	550	725	1,600	2,700
1871CC..................1,376		3,700	5,250	8,000	15,000	19,500	60,000	
1872......(950).....1,105,500		280	315	350	500	650	1,600	3,050
1872CC..................3,150		2,250	2,800	3,550	7,500	11,000	17,000	
1872S...................9,000		675	925	1,300	1,850	3,050	9,500	
1873......(600)......293,000		280	315	350	525	1,000	2,800	2,700
1873CC..................2,300		13,000	15,500	18,000	26,000	46,500	99,000	

TRADE DOLLARS (1873–1885)

This trade dollar was issued for circulation in Asia to compete with dollar-size coins of other countries. It weighed 420 grains compared to 412-1/2 grains, the weight of the regular silver dollar.

VG-8 Very Good: About half of mottoes IN GOD WE TRUST (on Liberty's pedestal) and E PLURIBUS UNUM (on obverse ribbon) visible. Rim on both sides well defined.

F-12 Fine: Mottoes and LIBERTY legible but worn.

EF-40 Extremely Fine: Mottoes and LIBERTY sharp. Only slight wear on rims.

AU-50 About Uncirculated: Slight trace of wear on Liberty's left breast and left knee and on hair above ear, as well as on eagle's head, knee, and wing tips.

MS-60 Uncirculated: No trace of wear. Light blemishes.

MS-63 Choice Uncirculated: Some distracting contact marks or blemishes in prime focal areas. Impaired luster possible.

PF-63 Choice Proof: Reflective surfaces with only a few blemishes in secondary focal places. No major flaws.

1875-S, S Over CC

	Mintage	VG-8	F-12	VF-20	EF-40	AU-50	MS-60	MS-63	PF-63
1873........(600)....396,900		$160	$190	$260	$395	$460	$975	$2,350	$2,250
1873CC.............124,500		550	775	1,100	2,250	3,000	6,500	19,000	
1873S..............703,000		180	240	370	460	550	1,100	2,900	
1874........(700)....987,100		160	200	255	395	460	1,000	2,150	2,250
1874CC............1,373,200		285	360	500	875	1,100	2,050	4,950	
1874S.............2,549,000		155	180	245	320	360	775	1,600	
1875........(700)....218,000		300	370	550	875	1,100	1,850	3,250	2,250
1875CC............1,573,700		275	330	525	725	925	2,250	3,750	
1875S.............4,487,000		155	180	245	320	360	775	1,100	
1875S, S Over CC...........*		410	520	735	1,100	1,450	4,200	11,000	
1876......(1,150)....455,000		170	200	270	345	405	800	1,500	2,250
1876CC..............509,000		485	550	700	1,100	1,500	4,000	12,000	

* Included in number above.

Chart continued on next page.

	Mintage	VG-8	F-12	VF-20	EF-40	AU-50	MS-60	MS-63	PF-63
1876S	5,227,000	$155	$180	$245	$320	$360	$825	$1,350	
1877 . . . . (510)	3,039,200	155	200	245	320	430	850	1,350	$2,600
1877CC	534,000	390	525	675	1,050	1,600	3,550	8,000	
1877S	9,519,000	155	180	245	320	360	775	1,100	
1878 . . . . (900)									2,250
1878CC (a)	97,000	825	1,200	1,850	3,700	5,250	12,000	23,500	
1878S	4,162,000	155	180	245	320	360	775	1,100	
1879 . . . . . . (1,541)					1,250				2,250
1880 . . . . . . (1,987)					1,250				2,250
1881 . . . . (960)					1,250				2,250
1882 . . . . . . (1,097)					1,250				2,250
1883 . . . . (979)					1,250				2,250
1884 (b) . . . . . . (10)									360,000
1885 (b) . . . . (5)									1,215,000

a. 44,148 trade dollars were melted on July 19, 1878. Many of these may have been 1878-CC. **b.** The trade dollars of 1884 and 1885 were unknown to collectors until 1908. None are listed in the Mint director's report, and numismatists believe that they are not a part of the regular Mint issue.

MORGAN (1878–1921)

George T. Morgan, formerly a pupil of William Wyon at the Royal Mint in London, designed the new dollar. His initial M is found at the truncation of the neck, at the last tress. It also appears on the reverse on the left-hand loop of the ribbon.

Sharply struck prooflike coins have a highly reflective surface and usually command substantial premiums.

The 1921 Silver Dollar Coin Anniversary Act authorized the Mint to produce coins celebrating the 2021 centennial of the last Morgan dollar.

VF-20 Very Fine: Two thirds of hair lines from top of forehead to ear visible. Ear well defined. Feathers on eagle's breast worn.

EF-40 Extremely Fine: All hair lines strong and ear bold. Eagle's feathers all plain but with slight wear on breast and wing tips.

AU-50 About Uncirculated: Slight trace of wear on the bust shoulder and hair left of forehead, and on eagle's breast and top edges of wings.

MS-60 Uncirculated: No trace of wear. Full mint luster present, but may be noticeably marred by scuff marks or bag abrasions.

MS-63 Choice Uncirculated: No trace of wear; full mint luster; few noticeable surface marks.

MS-64 Uncirculated: A few scattered contact marks. Good eye appeal and attractive luster.

MS-65 Gem Uncirculated: Only light, scattered contact marks that are not distracting. Strong luster, good eye appeal.

8 Tail Feathers, 1878, Philadelphia Only
Mintmark location on reverse, below wreath.

SILVER AND RELATED DOLLARS

Most Proof Morgan dollars, where indicated in mintage records (quantity shown in parentheses), are valued by coin dealers approximately as follows:
Proof-60 – $1,850; Proof-63 – $2,750; Proof-65 – $4,450.

Most Uncirculated silver dollars have scratches or nicks because of handling of mint bags in shipping and storage. Coin dealers usually pay more than the listed prices for choice sharply struck pieces with full brilliance and without blemishes.

	Mintage	VF-20	EF-40	AU-50	MS-60	MS-63	MS-65
1878, 8 Feathers ....(500).....749,500		$65	$70	$110	$200	$415	$1,800
1878, 7 Feathers ....(250)... 9,759,300		36	38	55	75	165	435
1878, 7 Over 8 Tail Feathers, Strong........ *		36	45	110	200	415	1,800
1878, 7 Over 8 Tail Feathers, Weak .... *		36	38	60	100	135	435
1878CC......................... 2,212,000		130	180	225	300	495	1,550
1878S......................... 9,774,000		36	37	41	70	120	310
1879 .... (1,100).. 14,806,000		32	33	38	65	105	370
1879CC, CC Over CC..............756,000		460	1,700	2,800	5,000	7,000	19,000
1879O..................... 2,887,000		39	42	55	100	375	1,850
1879S......................... 9,110,000		32	33	38	45	70	125
1880 .... (1,355).. 12,600,000		32	33	38	48	75	345
1880CC.........................591,000		190	215	275	500	650	975
1880O..................... 5,305,000		32	33	45	80	485	9,500
1880S......................... 8,900,000		32	33	38	45	55	120
1881 ....(984)... 9,163,000		32	33	38	48	65	330
1881CC.........................296,000		315	330	345	525	625	825
1881O..................... 5,708,000		32	33	38	45	80	725
1881S......................... 12,760,000		32	33	38	45	55	120
1882 .... (1,100).. 11,100,000		32	33	38	48	85	275
1882CC......................... 1,133,000		125	160	195	250	300	440
1882O..................... 6,090,000		32	33	38	50	70	415
1882S......................... 9,250,000		32	33	38	45	75	165
1883 .... (1,039).. 12,290,000		32	33	38	47	80	160
1883CC......................... 1,204,000		125	160	195	250	285	405
1883O..................... 8,725,000		32	33	38	48	65	120
1883S......................... 6,250,000		34	60	160	1,050	2,400	22,500
1884 ....(875).. 14,070,000		32	33	38	45	70	145
1884CC......................... 1,136,000		125	160	195	250	285	405
1884O..................... 9,730,000		32	33	38	45	55	120
1884S......................... 3,200,000		44	85	285	7,250	26,000	180,000
1885 ....(930).. 17,787,000		32	33	38	48	60	130
1885CC.........................228,000		455	485	495	550	700	975
1885O..................... 9,185,000		32	33	38	48	60	130
1885S......................... 1,497,000		36	70	135	275	485	1,450
1886 ....(886).. 19,963,000		32	33	38	48	60	120
1886O..................... 10,710,000		38	70	110	1,000	2,900	108,000
1886S.........................750,000		65	90	160	345	625	1,550
1887 ....(710).. 20,290,000		32	33	38	45	55	130
1887O..................... 11,550,000		34	36	55	80	200	1,600
1887S......................... 1,771,000		34	40	60	125	370	1,250
1888 ....(833).. 19,183,000		32	33	38	45	70	130
1888O..................... 12,150,000		34	36	40	55	70	260
1888S.........................657,000		100	110	180	320	725	1,700
1889 ....(811).. 21,726,000		32	33	38	50	65	200
1889CC.........................350,000		1,550	3,550	7,500	19,500	32,500	216,000
1889O..................... 11,875,000		32	45	100	315	500	2,250

*Included in number above.

Chart continued on next page.

	Mintage	VF-20	EF-40	AU-50	MS-60	MS-63	MS-65
1889S	700,000	$50	$65	$110	$255	$485	$1,450
1890 (590)	16,802,000	32	33	38	50	95	600
1890CC	2,309,041	135	215	300	550	1,100	4,300
1890O	10,701,000	32	33	41	90	180	775
1890S	8,230,373	32	40	44	75	155	625
1891 (650)	8,693,556	32	33	38	60	180	1,800
1891CC	1,618,000	130	215	320	575	825	2,900
1891O	7,954,529	50	75	110	180	425	3,250
1891S	5,296,000	32	33	50	95	300	1,150
1892 (1,245)	1,036,000	38	70	130	355	775	2,300
1892CC	1,352,000	320	550	725	1,400	2,250	5,750
1892O	2,744,000	32	70	115	345	650	2,250
1892S	1,200,000	110	370	1,700	41,000	85,500	198,000
1893 (792)	378,000	320	500	650	1,400	2,050	5,000
1893CC	677,000	725	1,950	3,050	4,450	7,500	92,000
1893O	300,000	425	650	1,100	4,550	7,500	148,500
1893S	100,000	4,950	9,500	22,500	171,000	247,500	567,000
1894 (972)	110,000	725	975	1,400	3,000	4,950	24,500
1894O	1,723,000	38	110	205	1,700	3,550	32,500
1894S	1,260,000	110	225	460	1,000	1,750	4,200
1895 (880)					46,500 (a)	53,000 (a)	68,000 (a)
1895O	450,000	345	650	1,350	11,500	37,000	162,000
1895S	400,000	725	1,300	1,750	4,450	5,750	16,500
1896 (762)	9,976,000	32	33	38	45	55	120
1896O	4,900,000	40	60	110	1,350	4,650	157,500
1896S	5,000,000	115	370	925	2,400	3,250	9,000
1897 (731)	2,822,000	32	33	38	48	125	200
1897O	4,004,000	37	60	90	975	3,050	43,000
1897S	5,825,000	34	36	45	80	180	435
1898 (735)	5,884,000	32	33	38	48	80	145
1898O	4,440,000	32	33	38	48	55	120
1898S	4,102,000	37	60	110	370	825	1,650
1899 (846)	330,000	85	95	135	185	320	650
1899O	12,290,000	32	33	38	45	55	120
1899S	2,562,000	55	100	255	500	900	1,600
1900 (912)	8,830,000	32	33	38	48	65	140
1900O	12,590,000	32	33	38	48	70	130
1900S	3,540,000	36	70	125	320	700	1,000
1901 (813)	6,962,000	70	180	320	3,650	8,250	315,000
1901O	13,320,000	32	33	38	45	65	120
1901S	2,284,000	60	120	245	525	1,100	2,050
1902 (777)	7,994,000	35	38	55	100	215	300
1902O	8,636,000	32	33	38	48	60	135
1902S	1,530,000	120	190	225	435	850	1,750
1903 (755)	4,652,000	36	37	45	65	105	205
1903O	4,450,000	425	435	440	525	675	800
1903S	1,241,000	160	550	1,850	5,500	7,750	12,000
1904 (650)	2,788,000	32	38	55	130	390	1,500
1904O	3,720,000	32	33	38	48	60	130
1904S	2,304,000	115	360	1,150	3,000	4,000	6,250
1921	44,690,000	27	28	29	31	38	110
1921D	20,345,000	27	28	29	50	140	340
1921S	21,695,000	27	28	29	55	125	650

a. Values are for Proofs.

SILVER AND RELATED DOLLARS

PEACE (1921–1935)

Anthony de Francisci, a medalist, designed this dollar. His monogram is located in the field of the coin under the neck of Liberty.

The 1921 Silver Dollar Coin Anniversary Act authorized the Mint to produce coins celebrating the 2021 centennial of the first Peace dollar.

VF-20 Very Fine: Hair over eye well worn. Some strands over ear well defined. Some eagle feathers on top and outside edge of right wing visible.

EF-40 Extremely Fine: Hair lines over brow and ear are strong, though slightly worn. Outside wing feathers at right and those at top visible but faint.

AU-50 About Uncirculated: Slight trace of wear. Most luster present, although marred by contact marks.

MS-60 Uncirculated: No trace of wear. Full mint luster, but possibly noticeably marred by stains, surface marks, or bag abrasions.

MS-63 Choice Uncirculated: Some distracting contact marks or blemishes in prime focal areas. Impaired luster possible.

MS-64 Uncirculated: A few scattered contact marks. Good eye appeal and attractive luster.

MS-65 Gem Uncirculated: Only light, scattered, non-distracting contact marks. Strong luster, good eye appeal.

PF-65 Choice Proof: Satin surfaces, no noticeable blemishes or flaws.

Most Uncirculated silver dollars have scratches or nicks because of handling of mint bags in shipping and storage. Coin dealers usually pay more than the listed prices for choice sharply struck pieces with full brilliance and without blemishes.

Mintmark location on reverse, below ONE.

	Mintage	VF-20	EF-40	AU-50	MS-60	MS-63	MS-64	MS-65
1921	1,006,473	$110	$150	$180	$405	$750	$1,200	$2,250
1922	51,737,000	23	25	28	29	47	55	85
1922D	15,063,000	23	25	32	38	85	165	420
1922S	17,475,000	23	25	32	45	80	200	975
1923	30,800,000	23	25	28	29	47	55	85
1923D	6,811,000	23	25	45	90	200	300	775
1923S	19,020,000	23	25	32	45	75	225	1,700
1924	11,811,000	23	25	28	29	47	55	150
1924S	1,728,000	32	40	70	225	500	975	4,650
1925	10,198,000	23	25	28	29	47	55	95
1925S	1,610,000	31	38	55	110	300	575	15,000
1926	1,939,000	23	27	40	65	110	255	415
1926D	2,348,700	23	27	65	135	345	440	825
1926S	6,980,000	23	25	45	80	160	285	700
1927	848,000	31	40	50	110	235	420	1,250
1927D	1,268,900	33	65	110	265	625	925	2,800
1927S	866,000	33	55	75	275	600	1,000	3,050
1928	360,649	180	200	225	390	700	800	2,900
1928S	1,632,000	32	50	65	165	460	975	9,000
1934	954,057	29	40	50	110	200	310	700
1934D	1,569,500	34	50	60	100	275	485	1,350
1934S	1,011,000	50	110	310	2,600	5,250	5,750	6,750
1935	1,576,000	34	41	55	110	170	260	525
1935S	1,964,000	36	48	100	255	485	725	1,400

EISENHOWER (1971–1978)
Eagle Reverse (1971–1974)

Honoring both President Dwight D. Eisenhower and the first landing of man on the moon, this design is the work of Chief Engraver Frank Gasparro, whose initials are on the truncation of the President's neck and below the eagle. The reverse is an adaptation of the official *Apollo 11* insignia.

Mintmark location is above date.

	Mintage	MS-63	MS-65	PF-68	PF-69
1971, Copper-Nickel Clad	47,799,000	$2.60	$60.00		
1971D, Copper-Nickel Clad	68,587,424	6.25	18.00		
1971S, Silver Clad (4,265,234)	6,868,530	9.75	16.00	$15.00	$27
1972, Copper-Nickel Clad	75,890,000	7.25	55.00		
1972D, Copper-Nickel Clad	92,548,511	4.30	13.50		
1972S, Silver Clad (1,811,631)	2,193,056	9.75	18.00	15.00	22
1973, Copper-Nickel Clad (a)	2,000,056	3.40	36.00		
1973D, Copper-Nickel Clad (a)	2,000,000	6.25	16.00		
1973S, Copper-Nickel Clad (2,760,339)				11.00	20
1973S, Silver Clad (1,013,646)	1,883,140	9.25	13.50	21.00	29
1974, Copper-Nickel Clad	27,366,000	2.60	36.00		
1974D, Copper-Nickel Clad	45,517,000	2.60	16.00		
1974S, Copper-Nickel Clad (2,612,568)				11.00	16
1974S, Silver Clad (1,306,579)	1,900,156	9.25	13.50	15.50	55

a. 1,769,258 of each sold only in sets and not released for circulation. Unissued coins destroyed at mint.

Bicentennial (1776–1976)

| Obverse | Reverse Variety 2 | Reverse Variety 1 |

Variety 1: Design in low relief, bold lettering on reverse.
Variety 2: Sharp design, delicate lettering on reverse.

	Mintage	MS-63	MS-65	PF-68	PF-69
1776–1976, Copper-Nickel Clad, Variety 1	4,019,000	$3.40	$70.00		
1776–1976, Copper-Nickel Clad, Variety 2	113,318,000	2.60	11.00		
1776–1976D, Copper-Nickel Clad, Variety 1	21,048,710	2.60	27.00		
1776–1976D, Copper-Nickel Clad, Variety 2	82,179,564	2.60	13.50		
1776–1976S, Copper-Nickel Clad, Variety 1	(2,845,450)			$11	$16
1776–1976S, Copper-Nickel Clad, Variety 2	(4,149,730)			11	16
1776–1976S, Silver Clad, Variety 1	11,000,000	9.25	16.00		
1776–1976S, Silver Clad, Variety 1	(4,000,000)			21	29

Eagle Reverse Resumed (1977–1978)

	Mintage	MS-63	MS-65	PF-68	PF-69
1977, Copper-Nickel Clad	12,596,000	$2.60	$18		
1977D, Copper-Nickel Clad	32,983,006	2.60	20		
1977S, Copper-Nickel Clad	(3,251,152)			$11	$16
1978, Copper-Nickel Clad	25,702,000	2.60	16		
1978D, Copper-Nickel Clad	33,012,890	2.60	22		
1978S, Copper-Nickel Clad	(3,127,781)			11	16

SUSAN B. ANTHONY (1979–1999)

Filled S   Clear S

	Mintage	MS-63	MS-65	MS-66
1979P, Narrow Rim	360,222,000	$13.50	$18.00	$32
1979P, Wide Rim	*	14.50	22.00	43
1979D	288,015,744	1.70	4.30	16
1979S	109,576,000	2.20	11.00	20

* Included in number above.

	Mintage	MS-65	PF-68	PF-69
1979S, Proof, Variety 1	(3,677,175)		$6.25	$11.00
1979S, Proof, Variety 2	*	22.00		23.00
1980P	27,610,000	$5.50		
1980D	41,628,708	6.25		
1980S	20,422,000	9.00		
1980S, Proof	(3,554,806)		5.50	7.25
1981P	3,000,000	13.50		

	Mintage	MS-65	PF-68	PF-69
1981D	3,250,000	$14.50		
1981S	3,492,000	14.50		
1981S, Proof, Variety 1	(4,063,083)		$5.50	$7.25
1981S, Proof, Variety 2	*		60.00	70.00
1999P	29,592,000	4.30		
1999P, Proof	(750,000)		18.00	22.00
1999D	11,776,000	5.50		

* Included in number above.

SACAGAWEA (2000–2008)

The design of this coin was selected in national competition from among 120 submissions that were considered by a panel appointed by Treasury Secretary Robert Rubin. The adopted motif depicts Sacagawea, a young Native American Shoshone, as rendered by artist Glenna Goodacre. On her back she carries Jean Baptiste, her infant son. The reverse shows an eagle in flight, designed by Mint engraver Thomas D. Rogers Sr.

The composition exemplifies the spirit of Liberty, Peace, and Freedom shown by Sacagawea in her conduct as interpreter and guide to explorers Meriwether Lewis and William Clark during their famed journey westward from St. Louis to the Pacific.

These coins have a distinctive golden color and a plain edge to distinguish them from other denominations or coins of a similar size. The change in composition and appearance was mandated under the United States Dollar Coin Act of 1997.

Several distinctive finishes can be identified on the Sacagawea dollars as a result of the Mint attempting to adjust the dies, blanks, strikes, or finishing to produce coins with minimal spotting and a better surface color. One group of 5,000 pieces dated 2000 with a special finish were presented to sculptor Glenna Goodacre in payment for the obverse design. Unexplained error coins made from mismatched dies (a State quarter obverse combined with a Sacagawea dollar reverse) are extremely rare.

	Mintage	MS-65	PF-68	PF-69
2000P	767,140,000	$2.00		
2000D	518,916,000	2.00		
2000S	(4,097,904)		$5.00	$5.50
2001P	62,468,000	2.00		
2001D	70,939,500	2.00		
2001S	(3,183,740)		8.00	8.50
2002P (a)	3,865,610	2.00		
2002D (a)	3,732,000	2.00		
2002S	(3,211,995)		5.75	6.25
2003P (a)	3,080,000	2.00		
2003D (a)	3,080,000	2.00		
2003S	(3,298,439)		5.75	6.25
2004P (a)	2,660,000	2.00		
2004D (a)	2,660,000	2.00		

	Mintage	MS-65	PF-68	PF-69
2004S	(2,965,422)		$5.00	$5.50
2005P (a)	2,520,000	$2.00		
2005D (a)	2,520,000	2.00		
2005S	(3,344,679)		5.00	5.50
2006P (a)	4,900,000	2.00		
2006D (a)	2,800,000	3.40		
2006S	(3,054,436)		5.50	6.00
2007P (a)	3,640,000	2.00		
2007D (a)	3,920,000	2.00		
2007S	(2,577,166)		5.50	6.00
2008P (a)	1,820,000	2.20		
2008D (a)	1,820,000	2.20		
2008S	(2,169,561)		10.00	10.50

a. Not issued for circulation.

PRESIDENTIAL (2007–2016, 2020)

Four different coins, each bearing the image of a former U.S. president, were issued each year in the order that the presidents served. The size and composition of these coins is the same as that of the Native American dollars that are also made each year. A companion series of ten-dollar gold bullion coins (listed in the Bullion section) honors the spouse of each president.

Presidential Dollars Reverse

Date, Mintmark, and Motto Incused on Edge (Motto Moved to Obverse in 2009)

The 2016 Ronald Reagan issues brought the regular production of Presidential dollars to a close. In 2020, the Mint produced a new coin to honor President George H.W. Bush (d. November 30, 2018), along with a gold bullion coin honoring Barbara Bush, his late wife.

SILVER AND RELATED DOLLARS

	Mintage	MS-65	PF-68
2007P, Washington	176,680,000	$2.20	
2007D, Washington	163,680,000	2.20	
2007S, Washington	(3,965,989)		$5.25
2007P, J. Adams	112,420,000	2.20	
2007D, J. Adams	112,140,000	2.20	
2007S, J. Adams	(3,965,989)		5.25

	Mintage	MS-65	PF-68
2007P, Jefferson	100,800,000	$2.20	
2007D, Jefferson	102,810,000	2.20	
2007S, Jefferson	(3,965,989)		$5.25
2007P, Madison	84,560,000	2.20	
2007D, Madison	87,780,000	2.20	
2007S, Madison	(3,965,989)		5.25

	Mintage	MS-65	PF-68
2008P, Monroe	64,260,000	$2.20	
2008D, Monroe	60,230,000	2.20	
2008S, Monroe	(3,083,940)		$6.25
2008P, J.Q. Adams	57,540,000	2.20	
2008D, J.Q. Adams	57,720,000	2.20	
2008S, J.Q. Adams	(3,083,940)		6.25

	Mintage	MS-65	PF-68
2008P, Jackson	61,180,000	$2.20	
2008D, Jackson	61,070,000	2.20	
2008S, Jackson	(3,083,940)		$6.25
2008P, Van Buren	51,520,000	2.20	
2008D, Van Buren	50,960,000	2.20	
2008S, Van Buren	(3,083,940)		6.25

	Mintage	MS-65	PF-68
2009P, Harrison	43,260,000	$2.20	
2009D, Harrison	55,160,000	2.20	
2009S, Harrison	(2,809,452)		$5.25
2009P, Tyler	43,540,000	2.20	
2009D, Tyler	43,540,000	2.20	
2009S, Tyler	(2,809,452)		5.25

	Mintage	MS-65	PF-68
2009P, Polk	46,620,000	$2.20	
2009D, Polk	41,720,000	2.20	
2009S, Polk	(2,809,452)		$5.25
2009P, Taylor	41,580,000	2.20	
2009D, Taylor	36,680,000	2.20	
2009S, Taylor	(2,809,452)		5.25

Note: Errors have been reported in the Presidential dollar series, including coins minted without edge lettering. Depending on their rarity, dealers may pay a premium for such errors.

	Mintage	MS-65	PF-68
2010P, Fillmore	37,520,000	$2.20	
2010D, Fillmore	36,960,000	2.20	
2010S, Fillmore	(2,224,827)		$6.25
2010P, Pierce	38,220,000	2.20	
2010D, Pierce	38,360,000	2.20	
2010S, Pierce	(2,224,827)		6.25

	Mintage	MS-65	PF-68
2010P, Buchanan	36,820,000	$2.20	
2010D, Buchanan	36,540,000	2.20	
2010S, Buchanan	(2,224,827)		$6.25
2010P, Lincoln	49,000,000	2.20	
2010D, Lincoln	48,020,000	2.20	
2010S, Lincoln	(2,224,827)		8.00

	Mintage	MS-65	PF-68
2011P, A. Johnson	35,560,000	$2.20	
2011D, A. Johnson	37,100,000	2.20	
2011S, A. Johnson	(1,972,863)		$6.25
2011P, Grant	38,080,000	2.20	
2011D, Grant	37,940,000	2.20	
2011S, Grant	(1,972,863)		6.25

	Mintage	MS-65	PF-68
2011P, Hayes	37,660,000	$2.20	
2011D, Hayes	36,820,000	2.20	
2011S, Hayes	(1,972,863)		$6.25
2011P, Garfield	37,100,000	2.20	
2011D, Garfield	37,100,000	2.20	
2011S, Garfield	(1,972,863)		6.25

	Mintage	MS-65	PF-68
2012P, Arthur **(a)**	6,020,000	$2.20	
2012D, Arthur **(a)**	4,060,000	2.20	
2012S, Arthur	(1,438,743)		$15.50
2012P, Cleveland, Variety 1 **(a)**	5,460,000	2.20	
2012D, Cleveland, Variety 1 **(a)**	4,060,000	2.20	
2012S, Cleveland, Variety 1	(1,438,743)		15.50

	Mintage	MS-65	PF-68
2012P, Harrison **(a)**	5,640,001	$2.20	
2012D, Harrison **(a)**	4,200,000	2.20	
2012S, Harrison	(1,438,743)		$15.50
2012P, Cleveland, Variety 2 **(a)**	10,680,000	2.20	
2012D, Cleveland, Variety 2 **(a)**	3,920,000	2.20	
2012S, Cleveland, Variety 2	(1,438,743)		15.50

a. Not issued for circulation.

	Mintage	MS-65	PF-68
2013P, McKinley (a)	4,760,000	$2.20	
2013D, McKinley (a)	3,365,100	2.20	
2013S, McKinley	(1,488,798)		$6.25
2013P, T. Roosevelt (a)	5,310,700	2.20	
2013D, T. Roosevelt (a)	3,920,000	2.20	
2013S, T. Roosevelt	(1,503,943)		6.25

	Mintage	MS-65	PF-68
2013P, Taft (a)	4,760,000	$2.20	
2013D, Taft (a)	3,360,000	2.20	
2013S, Taft	(1,488,798)		$6.25
2013P, Wilson (a)	4,620,000	2.20	
2013D, Wilson (a)	3,360,000	2.20	
2013S, Wilson	(1,488,798)		6.25

a. Not issued for circulation.

	Mintage	MS-65	PF-68
2014P, Harding (a)	6,160,000	$2.20	
2014D, Harding (a)	3,780,000	2.20	
2014S, Harding	(1,373,569)		$7.25
2014P, Coolidge (a)	4,480,000	2.20	
2014D, Coolidge (a)	3,780,000	2.20	
2014S, Coolidge	(1,373,569)		7.25

	Mintage	MS-65	PF-68
2014P, Hoover (a)	4,480,000	$2.20	
2014D, Hoover (a)	3,780,000	2.20	
2014S, Hoover	(1,373,569)		$7.25
2014P, F.D. Roosevelt (a)	4,760,000	2.20	
2014D, F.D. Roosevelt (a)	3,920,000	2.20	
2014S, F.D. Roosevelt	(1,392,619)		7.25

a. Not issued for circulation.

	Mintage	MS-65	PF-68
2015P, Truman (a)	4,900,000	$2.20	
2015P, Truman, RevPf	(16,812)		$31.00
2015D, Truman (a)	3,500,000	2.20	
2015S, Truman	(1,272,232)		7.25
2015P, Eisenhower (a)	4,900,000	2.20	
2015P, Eisenhower, RevPf	(16,744)		31.00
2015D, Eisenhower (a)	3,645,998	2.20	
2015S, Eisenhower	(1,272,232)		7.25

	Mintage	MS-65	PF-68
2015P, Kennedy (a)	6,160,000	$2.20	
2015P, Kennedy, RevPf	(49,051)		$31.00
2015D, Kennedy (a)	5,180,000	2.20	
2015S, Kennedy	(1,272,232)		7.25
2015P, L. Johnson (a)	7,840,000	2.20	
2015P, L. Johnson, RevPf	(23,905)		31.00
2015D, L. Johnson (a)	4,200,000	2.20	
2015S, L.B. Johnson	(1,272,232)		7.25

a. Not issued for circulation.

	Mintage	MS-65	PF-68
2016P, Nixon **(a)**	5,460,000	$2.20	
2016D, Nixon **(a)**	4,340,000	2.20	
2016S, Nixon	(1,196,582)		$6.25
2016P, Ford **(a)**	5,460,000	2.20	
2016P, Ford **(a)**	5,040,000	2.20	
2016S, Ford	(1,196,582)		6.25
2016P, Reagan **(a)**	7,140,000	2.20	

	Mintage	MS-65	PF-68
2016D, Reagan **(a)**	5,880,000	$2.20	
2016S, Reagan	(1,196,582)		$6.25
2016S, Reagan, RevPf	(47,447)		31.00
2020P, G.H.W. Bush **(a)**	*1,672,600*	2.20	
2020D, G.H.W. Bush **(a)**	*2,022,950*	2.20	
2020S, G.H.W. Bush, RevPf	*(11,305)*		55.00

a. Not issued for circulation.

NATIVE AMERICAN (2009 TO DATE)

Obverse

Three Sisters (2009)

Great Law of Peace (2010)

Wampanoag Treaty (2011)

Trade Routes in the 17th Century (2012)

Treaty With the Delawares (2013)

Native Hospitality (2014)

Mohawk Ironworkers (2015)

Code Talkers (2016)

Sequoyah (2017)

Jim Thorpe (2018)

American Indians in Space (2019)

Elizabeth Peratrovich and Alaska's Anti-Discrimination Law (2020)

American Indians in the U.S. Military (2021)

Ely S. Parker (2022)

Maria Tallchief and American Indians in Ballet (2023)

Indian Citizenship Act of 1924 Centennial (2024)

	Mintage	MS-65	PF-68
2009P, Three Sisters	39,200,000	$2.50	
2009D, Three Sisters	35,700,000	2.70	
2009S, Three Sisters	(2,179,867)		$8
2010P, Great Law	32,060,000	2.70	
2010D, Great Law	48,720,000	2.70	
2010S, Great Law	(1,689,216)		8
2011P, Wampanoag	29,400,000	2.70	
2011D, Wampanoag	48,160,000	2.70	
2011S, Wampanoag	(1,673,010)		8
2012P, Trade Routes **(a)**	2,800,000	2.20	
2012D, Trade Routes **(a)**	3,080,000	2.20	
2012S, Trade Routes	(1,189,445)		17
2013P, Treaty, Delawares **(a)**	1,820,000	2.20	
2013D, Treaty, Delawares **(a)**	1,820,000	2.20	
2013S, Treaty, Delawares	(1,222,180)		8
2014P, Native Hospitality **(a)**	3,080,000	2.20	
2014D, Native Hospitality **(a)**	2,800,000	2.20	
2014D, Native Hospitality, Enhanced Uncirculated	50,000	5.50	
2014S, Native Hospitality	(1,144,154)		8
2015P, Mohawk Ironworkers **(a)**	2,800,000	2.20	
2015D, Mohawk Ironworkers **(a)**	2,240,000	2.20	
2015S, Mohawk Ironworkers	(1,050,164)		11
2015W, Mohawk Ironworkers, Enhanced Uncirculated	88,805	2.70	
2016P, Code Talkers **(a)**	2,800,000	2.10	
2016D, Code Talkers **(a)**	2,100,000	2.10	
2016S, Code Talkers, Enh. Unc.	50,737	2.70	
2016S, Code Talkers	(965,033)		11
2017P, Sequoyah **(a)**	1,820,000	2.10	
2017D, Sequoyah **(a)**	1,540,000	2.10	
2017S, Sequoyah	(926,763)	2.70	
2017S, Sequoyah, Enh Unc	210,402		11
2018P, Jim Thorpe **(a)**	1,400,000	2.00	
2018D, Jim Thorpe **(a)**	1,400,000	2.00	
2018S, Jim Thorpe	(849,321)		11

	Mintage	MS-65	PF-68
2018S, Jim Thorpe, RevPf	(199,116)		$22
2019P, Am. Indians / Space **(a)**	1,400,000	$2.00	
2019P, Am. Indians / Space, Enhanced Uncirculated	46,964	2.70	
2019D, Am. Indians /Space **(a)**	1,540,000	2.00	
2019S, Am. Indians in Space	(1,056,828)		10
2020P, E. Peratrovich / Alaska's Anti-Discrimination Law **(a)**	1,400,000	2.00	
2020D, E. Peratrovich / Alaska's Anti-Discrimination Law **(a)**	1,260,000	2.00	
2020S, E. Peratrovich / Alaska's Anti-Discrimination Law	(777,841)		11
2021P, American Indians in the U.S. Military **(a)**	1,260,000	2.00	
2021D, American Indians in the U.S. Military **(a)**	1,260,000	2.00	
2021S, American Indians in the U.S. Military	(868,644)		11
2022P, Ely S. Parker **(a)**	980,000	2.00	
2022D, Ely S. Parker **(a)**	980,000	2.00	
2022S, Ely S. Parker	(699,097)		11
2023P, Maria Tallchief and Am. Indians in Ballet **(a)**	1,120,000	2.00	
2023D, Maria Tallchief and Am. Indians in Ballet **(a)**	1,120,000	2.00	
2023S, Maria Tallchief and Am. Indians in Ballet	(593,245)		10
2024P, Indian Citizenship Act of 1924 Centennial **(a)**		2.00	
2024D, Indian Citizenship Act of 1924 Centennial **(a)**		2.00	
2024S, Indian Citizenship Act of 1924 Centennial			11
2025P, Mary Kawena Pukui **(a)**		2.00	
2025D, Mary Kawena Pukui **(a)**		2.00	
2025S, Mary Kawena Pukui			10

a. Not issued for circulation.

167

AMERICAN INNOVATION (2018–2032)

In 2018, the U.S. Mint inaugurated a new, 15-year coin series: the American Innovation $1 Coin Program. Each of the golden dollars in the program features a reverse design that "symbolizes quintessentially American traits—the willingness to explore, to discover, and to create one's own destiny." Four new designs, in Uncirculated and Proof finishes, are issued each year from 2019 through 2032—one for each state, in the order in which the states ratified the Constitution or were admitted to the Union, and then for the District of Columbia and each of the five U.S. territories (Puerto Rico, Guam, American Samoa, the U.S. Virgin Islands, and the Northern Mariana Islands). Like all dollar coins minted after 2011, they are issued for numismatic sales only; none are distributed for circulation.

Privy Marks

2019 *2020* *2021*

2022 *2023* *2024*

Obverse   **American Innovators (2018)**

Delaware: Classifying the Stars (2019)

Pennsylvania: Polio Vaccine (2019)

New Jersey: Light Bulb (2019)

Georgia: Trustees' Garden (2019)

Connecticut: Gerber Variable Scale (2020)

Massachusetts: Telephone (2020)

Maryland: The Hubble Space Telescope (2020)

South Carolina: Septima Clark (2020)

New Hampshire: Ralph Baer (2021)

Virginia: Chesapeake Bay Bridge-Tunnel (2021)

New York: Erie Canal (2021)

North Carolina: Higher Learning (2021)

Rhode Island: Nautical Innovation (2022) **Vermont: Snowboarding (2022)** **Kentucky: Bluegrass Music (2022)** **Tennessee: Tennessee Valley Authority (2022)**

Ohio: Underground Railroad (2023) **Louisiana: Higgins Boat (2023)** **Indiana: Automobile Industry (2023)** **Mississippi: First Human Lung Transplant (2023)**

Illinois: Steel Plow (2024) **Alabama: *Saturn V* Rocket (2024)** **Maine: Direct Current Defibrillator (2024)** **Missouri: George Washington Carver (2024)**

	Mintage	MS-65	MS-67	PF-68
2018P, Innov. (a)	700,500	$4.30	$22.00	
2018D, Innov. (a)	680,525	3.40	18.00	
2018S, Innov.	(206,886)			$9.00
2018S, Innov., RevPf	(74,720)			11.50
2019P, DE (a)	346,850	3.40	18.00	
2019D, DE (a)	358,450	4.30	22.00	
2019S, DE	(85,839)			5.50
2019S, DE, RevPf	(53,724)			7.25
2019P, PA (a)	317,550	4.30	22.00	
2019D, PA (a)	309,375	4.30	22.00	
2019S, PA	(85,839)			5.50
2019S, PA, RevPf	(36,337)			7.25
2019P, NJ (a)	334,500	4.30	22.00	
2019D, NJ (a)	310,675	4.30	22.00	
2019S, NJ	(85,839)			5.50
2019S, NJ, RevPf	(21,101)			7.25
2019P, GA (a)	399,900	3.40	18.00	
2019D, GA (a)	368,475	3.40	18.00	
2019S, GA	(85,839)			5.50

	Mintage	MS-65	MS-67	PF-68
2019S, GA, RevPf	(46,915)			$7.25
2020P, CT (a)	436,000	$4.30	$22.00	
2020D, CT (a)	435,325	3.40	18.00	
2020S, CT	(107,052)			5.50
2020S, CT, RevPf	(46,556)			7.25
2020P, MA (a)	436,750	6.25	32.00	
2020D, MA (a)	436,425	5.50	27.00	
2020S, MA	(107,052)			5.50
2020S, MA, RevPf	(48,529)			7.25
2020P, MD (a)	434,825	8.00	40.00	
2020D, MD (a)	435,475	7.25	36.00	
2020S, MD	(107,052)			5.50
2020S, MD, RevPf	(49,731)			7.25
2020P, SC (a)	432,850	5.50	27.00	
2020D, SC (a)	397,775	3.40	18.00	
2020S, SC	(107,052)			5.50
2020S, SC, RevPf	(41,083)			7.25
2021P, NH (a)	454,325	3.40	18.00	
2021D, NH (a)	454,450	3.40	18.00	

a. Not issued for circulation.

Chart continued on next page.

	Mintage	MS-65	MS-67	PF-65
2021S, NH . . . . *(88,740)*				$5.50
2021S, NH, RevPf . . . *(49,813)*				7.25
2021P, VA **(a)** 454,975	$3.40	$18.00		
2021D, VA **(a)** 453,850	3.40	18.00		
2021S, VA . . . . *(88,740)*				5.50
2021S, VA, RevPf . . . .*(49,813)*				7.25
2021P, NY **(a)** 453,750	3.40	18.00		
2021D, NY **(a)** 453,825	3.40	18.00		
2021S, NY . . . . *(88,740)*				5.50
2021S, NY, RevPf . . . *(49,813)*				7.25
2021P, NC **(a)** 454,150	3.40	18.00		
2021D, NC **(a)** 454,450	3.40	18.00		
2021S, NC . . . . *(88,740)*				5.50
2021S, NC, RevPf . . . *(49,813)*				7.25
2022P, RI **(a)** 454,150	3.40	18.00		
2022D, RI **(a)** 453,775	3.40	18.00		
2022S, RI . . . .*(82,320)*				5.50
2022S, RI, RevPf . . . .*(49,797)*				7.25
2022P, VT **(a)** 454,275	3.40	18.00		
2022D, VT **(a)** 452,875	3.40	18.00		
2022S, VT . . . . *(82,320)*				5.50
2022S, VT, RevPf . . . .*(49,797)*				7.25
2022P, KY **(a)** 451,900	3.40	18.00		
2022D, KY **(a)** 452,625	3.40	18.00		
2022S, KY . . . . *(82,320)*				5.50
2022S, KY, RevPf . . . .*(49,797)*				7.25
2022P, TN **(a)** 452,325	3.40	18.00		
2022D, TN **(a)** 452,275	3.40	18.00		
2022S, TN . . . .*(82,320)*				5.50
2022S, TN, RevPf . . . *(49,797)*				7.25
2023P, OH **(a)**		3.40	18.00	
2023D, OH **(a)**	$3.40	$18.00		
2023S, OH . . . .*(58,154)*				$5.50
2023S, OH, RevPf . . .*(39,308)*				7.25
2023P, LA **(a)**		3.40	18.00	
2023D, LA **(a)**		3.40	18.00	
2023S, LA . . . .*(58,154)*				5.50
2023S, LA, RevPf . . . .*(39,308)*				7.25
2023P, IN **(a)**		3.40	18.00	
2023D, IN **(a)**		3.40	18.00	
2023S, IN . . . . *(58,154)*				5.50
2023S, IN, RevPf . . . .*(39,308)*				7.25
2023P, MS **(a)**		3.40	18.00	
2023D, MS **(a)**		3.40	18.00	
2023S, MS . . . .*(58,154)*				5.50
2023S, MS, RevPf . . .*(39,308)*				7.25
2024P, IL **(a)**		3.40	18.00	
2024D, IL **(a)**		3.40	18.00	
2024S, IL				5.50
2024S, IL, RevPf				7.25
2024P, AL **(a)**		3.40	18.00	
2024D, AL **(a)**		3.40	18.00	
2024S, AL				5.50
2024S, AL, RevPf.				7.25
2024P, ME **(a)**		3.40	18.00	
2024D, ME **(a)**		3.40	18.00	
2024S, ME.				5.50
2024S, ME, RevPf				7.25
2024P, MO **(a)**		3.40	18.00	
2024D, MO **(a)**		3.40	18.00	
2024S, MO				5.50
2024S, MO, RevPf				7.25

a. Not issued for circulation.

1921 SILVER DOLLAR ANNIVERSARY COINS (2021 TO DATE)

Congress passed the 1921 Silver Dollar Coin Anniversary Act "to mint and issue $1 coins in recognition of the 100th anniversary of completion of coinage of the Morgan dollar and the 100th anniversary of commencement of coinage of the Peace dollar." The resulting products, first minted in 2021, are not precise copies of the older coins, but, in the words of the legislation, "honor" the originals with "renditions" of the designs used on the original Morgan and Peace silver dollars.

The Mint's artists use modern technology and historical Mint assets to create the modern designs.

Some of the first-year-of-issue Morgan anniversary coins were minted in Philadelphia with "CC" and "O" privy marks to represent the historical mintages of Carson City and New Orleans.

In November 2021 the Mint announced plans to produce the coins as recurring products, in various finishes and using multiple Mint facilities. Because of a shortage of silver planchets, none were issued in 2022.

"CC" privy mark

"O" privy mark

	Mintage	OGP*	MS-69	MS-70	PF-69	PF-70
2021-(P), Morgan, No Privy Mark	174,854	$120	$120	$170		
2021-(P), Morgan, CC Privy Mark	173,798	170	190	205		
2021-(P), Morgan, O Privy Mark	173,551	120	120	165		
2021-D, Morgan	174,715	120	120	775		
2021-S, Morgan	174,879	120	120	160		
2023-(P), Morgan	273,727	70	70	100		
2023-S, Morgan, Proof	(378,152)	70			$70	$90
2023-S, Morgan, Reverse Proof	(247,820)	95			90	110
2024-(P), Morgan		90	90	120		
2024-S, Morgan, Proof		70			70	90
2024-S, Morgan, Reverse Proof		95			90	110
2021-(P), Peace	(199,940)	170	170	240		
2023-(P), Peace	(273,969)	70	70	100		
2023-S, Peace, Proof	(343,868)	70			70	110
2023-S, Peace, Reverse Proof	(247,820)	95			90	110
2024-(P), Peace		90	90	120		
2024-S, Peace, Proof		70			70	110
2024-S, Peace, Reverse Proof		95			90	110
Two-Coin Set. 2023-S Morgan and Peace Reverse Proof silver dollars		190				
Two-Coin Set. 2024-S Morgan and Peace Reverse Proof silver dollars		200				

* OGP = Coins in original government packaging.

The Coinage Act of 1792 established the independent monetary system of the United States, with the dollar as its basic monetary unit. Silver dollar coins were made starting in 1794. Coinage of a gold dollar coin, however, was not authorized until the Act of March 3, 1849. Its weight was set at 25.8 grains, fineness .900.

The first type, struck until 1854, is known as the Liberty Head. In 1854 the gold dollar was made larger in diameter and thinner, while keeping the same weight. Along with that modification, the design was changed to a female wearing a feather headdress, generally referred to as the Indian Princess Head type. In 1856 this was changed slightly by enlarging the size of the head.

LIBERTY HEAD (1849–1854)
Variety 1

VF-20 Very Fine: LIBERTY on headband complete and legible. Knobs on coronet defined.
EF-40 Extremely Fine: Slight wear on Liberty's hair. Knobs on coronet sharp.
AU-50 About Uncirculated: Trace of wear on headband. Nearly full luster.
AU-55 Choice About Uncirculated: Evidence of friction on design high points.
MS-60 Uncirculated: No trace of wear. Light marks and blemishes.
MS-63 Choice Uncirculated: Some distracting contact marks or blemishes in prime focal areas. Impaired luster possible.

	Mintage	VF-20	EF-40	AU-50	AU-58	MS-60	MS-63	MS-65
1849, Open Wreath, No L on Truncation	688,567	$250	$315	$390	$600	$800	$1,300	$3,700
1849, Closed Wreath	*	240	295	305	330	435	725	4,000
1849C, Open Wreath	11,634	162,000	225,000	337,500	450,000	495,000	—	—
1849C, Closed Wreath	*	1,250	2,150	3,050	6,250	7,500	15,000	—
1849D	21,588	1,300	1,850	2,500	3,700	4,000	13,500	63,500
1849O	215,000	240	320	415	700	975	2,400	10,500
1850	481,953	240	295	305	325	335	435	3,250
1850C	6,966	1,200	2,050	3,150	4,300	5,250	20,500	—
1850D	8,382	1,300	2,250	2,800	5,000	8,000	30,000	—
1850O	14,000	600	975	1,200	1,700	2,550	5,750	—
1851	3,317,671	210	265	275	295	305	430	1,400
1851C	41,267	900	1,250	1,450	2,250	2,550	4,300	19,000
1851D	9,882	1,200	1,850	2,600	3,350	4,300	14,000	69,000
1851O	290,000	240	320	330	460	650	1,300	4,950
1852	2,045,351	210	265	275	295	305	430	1,400
1852C	9,434	825	1,200	1,850	3,150	3,700	10,500	33,500
1852D	6,360	1,200	1,750	2,600	4,100	6,500	26,000	—
1852O	140,000	275	330	385	550	975	3,150	26,000
1853	4,076,051	210	265	275	295	305	430	1,500
1853C	11,515	1,000	1,650	2,150	3,350	4,300	14,000	37,000
1853D	6,583	1,300	1,850	2,800	4,450	6,500	16,500	39,000
1853O	290,000	240	295	330	415	500	1,250	5,250
1854	855,502	210	265	275	295	305	430	1,400
1854D	2,935	2,250	4,100	5,500	7,500	8,500	31,500	—
1854S	14,632	460	700	1,200	1,850	2,800	6,000	32,500

* Included in number above.

INDIAN PRINCESS HEAD, SMALL HEAD (1854–1856)
Variety 2

VF-20 Very Fine: Feather-curl tips on headdress outlined but details worn.
EF-40 Extremely Fine: Slight wear on tips of feather curls on headdress.
AU-50 About Uncirculated: Trace of wear on feathers, nearly full luster.
AU-55 Choice About Uncirculated: Evidence of friction on design high points. Most of original mint luster present.
MS-60 Uncirculated: No trace of wear. Light marks and blemishes.
MS-63 Choice Uncirculated: Some distracting contact marks or blemishes in prime focal areas. Impaired luster possible.
PF-63 Choice Proof: Reflective surfaces with only a few blemishes in secondary focal areas. No major flaws.

	Mintage	VF-20	EF-40	AU-50	AU-58	MS-60	MS-63	MS-65	PF-63
1854	783,943	$365	$435	$455	$550	$1,050	$3,250	$16,000	—
1855	758,269	365	435	455	550	1,050	3,250	16,000	$126,000
1855C	9,803	2,250	3,700	4,450	14,500	18,000	—	—	—
1855D	1,811	8,000	20,500	27,000	39,000	50,500	78,000	—	—
1855O	55,000	775	1,100	1,550	2,400	6,500	22,000	—	—
1856S	24,600	600	1,300	1,850	5,250	6,250	14,000	53,500	—

INDIAN PRINCESS HEAD, LARGE HEAD (1856–1889)
Variety 3

VF-20 Very Fine: Slight detail in curled feathers in headdress. Details worn smooth at eyebrow, hair below headdress, and behind ear and bottom curl.
EF-40 Extremely Fine: Slight wear above and to right of eye and on top of curled feathers.
AU-50 About Uncirculated: Trace of wear on feathers, nearly full luster.
AU-55 Choice About Uncirculated: Evidence of friction on design high points. Most of original mint luster present.
MS-60 Uncirculated: No trace of wear. Light marks and blemishes.
MS-63 Choice Uncirculated: Some distracting contact marks or blemishes in prime focal areas. Impaired luster possible.
PF-63 Choice Proof: Reflective surfaces with only a few blemishes in secondary focal places. No major flaws.

	Mintage	VF-20	EF-40	AU-50	AU-58	MS-60	MS-63	MS-65	PF-63
1856	1,762,936	$260	$270	$310	$320	$405	$600	$1,600	$15,500
1856D	1,460	3,900	6,750	8,250	20,500	24,000	55,000	—	—
1857	774,789	260	270	310	320	405	625	2,700	11,000
1857C	13,280	875	1,650	3,000	4,950	6,750	—	—	—
1857D	3,533	1,600	2,600	3,700	8,000	17,000	60,500	—	—
1857S	10,000	550	875	1,200	2,400	4,100	16,500	—	—
1858	117,995	260	270	310	320	405	825	3,700	11,000
1858D	3,477	1,300	2,400	3,700	5,500	7,250	19,000	51,500	—

1873, Close 3   **1873, Open 3**

	Mintage	VF-20	EF-40	AU-50	AU-58	MS-60	MS-63	MS-65	PF-63
1858S	10,000	$460	$675	$875	$1,850	$4,200	$12,500	$37,000	
1859 . . . . (80)	168,244	260	270	310	320	405	650	1,700	$3,850
1859C	5,235	1,850	2,550	3,500	5,250	6,000	26,000	—	
1859D	4,952	1,350	1,850	2,800	4,650	6,000	17,000	39,000	
1859S	15,000	345	600	925	2,400	3,900	15,000	—	
1860 . . . . (154)	36,514	275	310	335	385	460	975	6,750	5,500
1860D	1,566	2,800	5,250	7,750	13,000	20,500	46,500	—	
1860S	13,000	345	500	700	1,500	2,100	4,100	23,500	
1861 . . . . (349)	527,150	260	285	340	350	440	650	1,850	6,000
1861D	*1,250*	30,000	46,500	58,000	75,500	92,000	135,000	225,000	
1862 . . . . (35) . . .	1,361,355	260	270	310	320	415	625	1,500	4,200
1863 . . . . (50)	6,200	1,000	1,650	2,800	5,250	6,250	9,500	16,500	4,300
1864 . . . . (50)	5,900	825	1,000	1,150	2,050	2,600	6,250	7,750	5,750
1865 . . . . (25)	3,700	650	925	1,400	2,250	2,800	4,650	9,250	8,000
1866 . . . . (30)	7,100	350	500	600	750	1,050	1,950	3,450	4,300
1867 . . . . (50)	5,200	390	550	725	900	1,000	1,850	6,250	7,500
1868 . . . . (25)	10,500	355	500	600	725	800	1,950	5,250	5,250
1869 . . . . (25)	5,900	370	525	625	850	950	1,650	3,700	5,250
1870 . . . . (35)	6,300	370	500	600	725	775	1,350	3,550	3,950
1870S	3,000	650	925	1,500	2,800	3,150	7,000	20,500	
1871 . . . . (30)	3,900	335	405	500	650	825	1,550	3,050	3,950
1872 . . . . (30)	3,500	275	370	485	775	900	2,050	6,000	5,250
1873, Closed 3 . . (25)	1,800	370	575	675	800	1,200	2,800	11,000	12,000
1873, Open 3	123,300	260	270	310	320	405	600	900	
1874 . . . . (20)	198,800	260	270	310	320	405	600	800	9,500
1875 . . . . (20)	400	3,000	4,400	5,750	9,500	10,500	15,500	35,000	11,000
1876 . . . . (45)	3,200	335	495	600	750	825	1,300	3,900	3,950
1877 . . . . (20)	3,900	355	425	500	675	725	1,400	3,700	7,750
1878 . . . . (20)	3,000	330	405	500	625	700	1,150	3,700	3,950
1879 . . . . (30)	3,000	275	345	390	525	725	1,050	2,050	4,650
1880 . . . . (36)	1,600	280	305	345	415	460	1,100	1,550	7,500
1881 . . . . (87)	7,620	285	310	370	430	460	700	1,400	3,800
1882 . . . . (125)	5,000	285	310	370	430	550	850	1,400	3,050
1883 . . . . (207)	10,800	285	310	370	430	460	700	1,100	3,050
1884 . . . . (1,006)	5,230	285	310	370	450	485	750	1,250	3,050
1885 . . . . (1,105)	11,156	285	310	370	430	460	700	1,350	3,050
1886 . . . . (1,016)	5,000	285	310	370	430	460	700	1,250	3,050
1887 . . . . (1,043)	7,500	285	310	370	430	460	650	975	3,050
1888 . . . . (1,079)	15,501	285	310	370	430	460	700	975	3,050
1889 . . . . (1,779)	28,950	285	310	370	430	460	625	800	3,050

Although authorized by the Act of April 2, 1792, coinage of quarter eagles ($2.50 gold coins) was not begun until 1796.

DRAPED BUST TO RIGHT (1796–1807)

F-12 Fine: Hair worn smooth on high spots. E PLURIBUS UNUM on ribbon weak but legible.
VF-20 Very Fine: Some wear on high spots.
EF-40 Extremely Fine: Only slight wear on Liberty's hair and cheek.
AU-50 About Uncirculated: Trace of wear on cap, hair, cheek, and drapery.
AU-55 Choice About Uncirculated: Evidence of friction on design high points. Some original mint luster.
MS-60 Uncirculated: No trace of wear. Light blemishes.

No Stars on Obverse (1796)   **Stars on Obverse (1796–1807)**

	Mintage	F-12	VF-20	EF-40	AU-50	AU-58	MS-60	MS-63
1796, No Stars on Obverse	963	$53,500	$73,500	$108,000	$135,000	$202,500	$288,000	$900,000
1796, Stars on Obverse	432	46,500	55,000	73,500	94,500	139,500	144,000	450,000
1797	427	23,500	28,000	39,000	60,500	144,000	189,000	324,000
1798	1,094	6,750	8,000	14,000	22,500	44,500	77,500	180,000
1802, 2 Over "1"	3,035	6,750	8,000	11,500	14,000	24,000	26,000	58,000
1804, 13-Star Reverse	*	60,000	88,500	135,000	202,500	405,000	—	—
1804, 14-Star Reverse	3,327	7,000	9,000	12,000	15,000	24,000	32,500	102,500
1805	1,781	6,750	8,000	10,500	13,500	19,500	24,000	115,000
1806, 6/4, 8 Stars Left, 5 Right	1,136	7,000	8,500	11,500	16,000	28,000	44,500	103,500
1806, 6/5, 7 Stars Left, 6 Right	480	7,000	8,500	12,500	25,000	50,500	73,500	270,000
1807	6,812	6,750	8,000	10,500	12,000	19,500	24,000	58,000

* Included in number below.

CAPPED BUST TO LEFT, LARGE SIZE (1808)

F-12 Fine: E PLURIBUS UNUM on reverse, and LIBERTY on headband, legible but weak.
VF-20 Very Fine: Motto and LIBERTY clear.
EF-40 Extremely Fine: All details of hair plain.
AU-50 About Uncirculated: Trace of wear above eye, on top of cap, and on cheek and hair.
AU-55 Choice About Uncirculated: Evidence of friction on design high points. Some original mint luster present.
MS-60 Uncirculated: No trace of wear. Light blemishes.

	Mintage	F-12	VF-20	EF-40	AU-50	AU-58	MS-60	MS-63
1808	2,710	$41,000	$49,500	$92,000	$117,000	$198,000	$238,500	$450,000

CAPPED HEAD TO LEFT (1821–1834)

Those dated 1829 to 1834 are smaller in diameter than the 1821 to 1827 pieces.

Large Diameter   **Reduced Diameter**

See next page for chart.

	Mintage	F-12	VF-20	EF-40	AU-50	AU-58	MS-60	MS-63
1821	6,448	$6,000	$7,000	$9,750	$11,500	$19,000	$23,500	$92,000
1824, 4 Over 1	2,600	6,000	7,000	9,750	11,500	19,000	26,500	60,500
1825	4,434	6,000	7,500	11,000	13,500	24,000	26,000	55,000
1826, 6 Over 6	760	12,000	16,500	23,500	32,500	50,500	78,000	216,000
1827	2,800	6,250	7,500	12,500	15,000	26,000	28,000	55,000
1829	3,403	4,950	6,000	8,500	11,500	16,500	19,000	33,500
1830	4,540	4,950	6,000	8,500	12,000	17,500	19,500	30,500
1831	4,520	4,950	6,000	8,500	11,500	16,500	19,000	37,000
1832	4,400	4,950	6,000	8,500	11,500	18,000	20,500	37,000
1833	4,160	4,950	6,000	8,500	11,500	16,500	19,000	30,500
1834, With Motto	4,000	24,000	32,500	53,500	103,500	148,500	180,000	247,500

CLASSIC HEAD (1834–1839)

In 1834, the quarter eagle was redesigned. A ribbon binding the hair, bearing the word LIBERTY, replaced the Liberty cap. The motto was omitted from the reverse.

F-12 Fine: LIBERTY on headband legible and complete. Curl under ear outlined but no detail.

VF-20 Very Fine: LIBERTY plain; detail in hair curl.

EF-40 Extremely Fine: Small amount of wear on top of hair and below L in LIBERTY. Wear evident on wing.

AU-50 About Uncirculated: Trace of wear on coronet and hair above ear.

AU-55 Choice About Uncirculated: Evidence of friction on design high points. Some of original mint luster present.

MS-60 Uncirculated: No trace of wear. Light blemishes.

MS-63 Choice Uncirculated: Some distracting contact marks or blemishes in prime focal areas. Impaired luster possible.

Mintmark location.

	Mintage	VF-20	EF-40	AU-50	AU-58	MS-60	MS-63
1834, No Motto	112,234	$550	$725	$925	$1,650	$2,400	$6,500
1835	131,402	550	775	1,000	2,050	2,600	9,000
1836	547,986	550	725	925	1,750	2,400	6,500
1837	45,080	650	875	1,500	3,000	3,700	8,000
1838	47,030	600	775	1,300	2,100	2,550	8,000
1838C	7,880	4,450	6,750	9,500	17,500	25,000	55,000
1839	27,021	925	1,650	2,700	5,250	11,500	41,000
1839C	18,140	4,100	6,250	7,500	12,500	20,500	57,000
1839D	13,674	4,300	6,250	8,500	22,500	28,000	64,500
1839O	17,781	1,600	3,050	4,200	9,500	11,500	35,500

LIBERTY HEAD (1840–1907)

Mintmark location.

4 Plain 4

4 Crosslet 4

	Mintage	VF-20	EF-40	AU-50	AU-58	MS-60	MS-63
1840	18,859	$700	$800	$1,450	$3,250	$5,250	$10,500
1840C	12,822	1,350	2,450	2,750	6,000	8,250	19,500
1840D	3,532	4,650	8,500	13,000	37,000	60,000	—
1840O	33,580	600	1,550	1,950	4,650	6,750	19,500

QUARTER EAGLES ($2.50)

	Mintage	VF-20	EF-40	AU-50	AU-58	MS-60	MS-63
1841	*10–12 known*	—	$144,000	$171,000	$225,000	$252,000	—
1841C	10,281	$1,850	2,550	3,650	6,750	17,000	$48,000
1841D	4,164	3,350	6,000	7,750	15,000	30,500	66,000
1842	2,823	1,850	3,700	5,500	12,500	15,000	36,500
1842C	6,729	1,550	2,800	5,750	12,000	17,500	46,500
1842D	4,643	2,250	3,700	6,250	14,000	28,000	—
1842O	19,800	600	925	1,400	3,700	6,500	17,000
1843	100,546	415	485	625	1,300	1,650	9,000
1843C, Large Date	23,076	1,400	1,850	2,500	3,600	5,750	16,500
1843C, Small Date	2,988	2,800	4,400	6,250	13,000	19,000	—
1843D	36,209	1,500	2,150	2,700	4,300	5,750	28,000
1843O	364,002	460	525	650	1,000	1,500	6,250
1844	6,784	650	925	1,850	5,750	7,000	20,500
1844C	11,622	1,400	2,250	3,400	6,250	10,500	33,500
1844D	17,332	1,350	1,700	2,800	4,650	7,000	19,500
1845	91,051	415	460	525	725	1,200	3,700
1845D	19,460	1,450	1,950	2,400	5,750	7,500	34,000
1845O	4,000	2,800	6,000	7,500	20,500	26,000	78,000
1846	21,598	550	650	775	1,650	3,150	16,000
1846C	4,808	1,400	2,500	4,300	11,500	16,000	32,500
1846D	19,303	2,000	2,700	3,700	7,500	9,750	28,000
1846O	62,000	500	650	925	2,250	5,000	15,000
1847	29,814	415	550	725	1,150	2,450	9,500
1847C	23,226	1,400	1,750	2,300	3,250	3,900	12,000
1847D	15,784	1,400	1,750	2,200	4,200	6,750	18,000
1847O	124,000	500	625	1,000	2,300	4,650	14,000
1848	6,500	725	1,150	2,050	4,200	4,650	12,500

CAL. Gold Quarter Eagle (1848)

In 1848, about 230 ounces of gold were sent to Secretary of War William L. Marcy by Colonel R.B. Mason, military governor of California. The gold was turned over to the Mint and made into quarter eagles. The distinguishing mark CAL. was punched above the eagle on the reverse side while the coins were in the die.

CAL. Above Eagle on Reverse (1848)

	Mintage	VF-20	EF-40	AU-50	AU-58	MS-60	MS-63
1848, CAL. Above Eagle	1,389	$33,500	$46,500	$55,000	$64,500	$69,000	$153,000
1848C	16,788	1,850	2,400	3,000	6,250	9,500	31,500
1848D	13,771	1,400	1,950	2,500	4,000	6,750	20,500
1849	23,294	550	725	825	1,500	2,150	6,000
1849C	10,220	1,850	3,050	5,750	8,500	10,500	28,000
1849D	10,945	1,600	2,150	2,400	6,000	10,500	—
1850	252,923	415	460	525	625	700	3,250
1850C	9,148	1,300	2,400	3,250	5,750	9,750	32,500
1850D	12,148	1,500	2,250	3,250	5,750	9,500	30,500

Chart continued on next page.

	Mintage	VF-20	EF-40	AU-50	AU-58	MS-60	MS-63	PF-63
1850O 84,000		$485	$575	$750	$1,450	$3,150	$15,000	
1851 1,372,748		415	460	525	600	625	775	
1851C 14,923		1,300	1,950	2,800	4,650	7,000	28,000	
1851D 11,264		1,400	2,250	3,350	7,250	15,000	26,000	
1851O 148,000		550	650	725	1,500	3,000	9,750	
1852 1,159,681		415	460	525	600	625	875	
1852C 9,772		1,100	1,850	2,800	5,500	7,000	28,000	
1852D 4,078		1,350	2,550	5,250	7,000	14,000	37,000	
1852O 140,000		460	550	725	1,500	3,350	8,750	
1853 1,404,668		415	460	525	600	625	775	
1853D 3,178		1,650	2,700	4,650	7,000	12,000	44,000	
1854 596,258		415	460	525	600	650	925	
1854C 7,295		1,600	2,250	2,900	4,650	8,000	55,000	
1854D 1,760		2,800	5,750	8,250	17,000	23,500	62,000	
1854O 153,000		550	650	725	975	1,300	8,000	
1854S 246		270,000	378,000	432,000	—	—	—	
1855 235,480		395	420	430	525	575	1,300	
1855C 3,677		1,850	2,800	4,000	8,000	14,000	37,000	
1855D 1,123		3,550	7,500	14,000	36,000	43,000	70,000	
1856 384,240		415	460	525	600	625	1,000	
1856C 7,913		1,500	2,400	3,350	6,750	9,500	24,000	
1856D 874		20,500	30,000	42,000	92,000	108,000	—	
1856O 21,100		550	825	1,350	3,000	7,000	—	
1856S 72,120		460	550	725	2,050	3,350	9,750	
1857 214,130		415	460	525	600	625	1,100	
1857D 2,364		1,350	2,150	3,700	8,500	9,500	23,500	
1857O 34,000		500	600	825	1,850	3,700	11,500	
1857S 69,200		395	450	825	2,000	3,100	11,000	
1858 . . . . (8–10). . . .47,377		415	460	550	700	800	2,800	$28,000
1858C 9,056		1,400	2,050	2,800	3,600	6,000	18,000	
1859 . . . . (80). . . .39,364		415	460	525	750	925	3,150	19,000
1859D 2,244		2,050	3,150	4,650	11,000	17,000	—	
1859S 15,200		430	825	1,400	2,800	4,100	14,000	
1860 . . . . (112). 22,563		415	460	550	1,000	1,100	3,000	14,000
1860C 7,469		1,400	2,150	2,900	7,000	11,500	25,500	
1860S 35,600		385	550	975	1,850	3,050	13,000	
1861 . . . . (90). . . 1,283,788		415	460	525	600	625	1,150	23,500
1861S 24,000		800	1,650	3,050	8,000	15,000	—	
1862 . . . . (35). 98,508		405	450	1,200	2,250	3,050	7,750	14,000
1862, 2 Over 1 . . . . *		700	1,400	2,800	5,000	8,500	23,500	
1862S 8,000		2,100	3,700	4,550	7,500	13,000	35,500	
1863, Proof only (30).								50,500
1863S 10,800		1,400	2,600	4,100	7,000	12,000	23,500	
1864 . . . . (50). 2,774		17,000	32,500	55,000	78,000	103,500	—	14,000
1865 . . . . (25). 1,520		3,700	8,000	15,000	42,000	64,500	—	14,000
1865S 23,376		650	1,100	1,750	2,600	4,400	16,000	
1866 . . . . (30). 3,080		900	2,700	4,200	8,000	11,500	22,500	12,000
1866S 38,960		405	550	875	2,900	6,750	20,500	
1867 . . . . (50). 3,200		525	825	1,300	3,700	5,500	14,000	11,500
1867S 28,000		425	650	975	1,650	3,150	12,000	
1868 . . . . (25). 3,600		405	475	650	1,350	2,050	9,500	15,000

* Included in number above.

QUARTER EAGLES ($2.50)

	Mintage	VF-20	EF-40	AU-50	AU-58	MS-60	MS-63	PF-63
1868S	34,000	$395	$430	$725	$1,350	$2,450	$6,250	
1869	(25) 4,320	405	450	650	1,250	2,400	8,500	$12,000
1869S	29,500	405	550	600	1,150	2,250	9,000	
1870	(35) 4,520	395	500	700	1,450	3,250	9,500	12,000
1870S	16,000	395	430	700	2,400	3,250	12,000	
1871	(30) 5,320	405	550	675	975	1,500	3,900	12,000
1871S	22,000	370	435	455	925	1,650	3,450	
1872	(30) 3,000	525	850	1,600	3,000	3,900	15,000	11,500
1872S	18,000	405	500	700	1,500	3,700	8,500	
1873	(25) 178,000	370	380	385	415	430	525	14,000
1873S	27,000	370	410	550	975	1,350	4,650	
1874	(20) 3,920	395	525	575	825	1,700	5,000	17,000
1875	(20) 400	6,750	11,500	14,000	22,500	31,500	112,500	37,000
1875S	11,600	370	405	550	1,500	2,600	5,250	
1876	(45) 4,176	460	700	850	1,500	2,800	8,250	12,000
1876S	5,000	405	600	750	1,600	1,850	7,500	
1877	(20) 1,632	440	875	1,200	1,850	2,600	10,500	12,000
1877S	35,400	370	380	405	445	600	1,850	
1878	(20) 286,240	370	380	385	390	400	475	12,000
1878S	178,000	370	380	385	390	400	725	
1879	(30) 88,960	370	380	385	390	400	600	9,500
1879S	43,500	370	380	395	650	1,400	3,800	
1880	(36) 2,960	440	600	800	1,400	1,550	3,050	6,250
1881	(51) 640	1,950	2,800	4,300	7,000	10,500	24,000	6,250
1882	(67) 4,000	370	380	430	825	975	2,150	6,250
1883	(82) 1,920	650	1,200	2,500	6,250	6,750	9,500	6,250
1884	(73) 1,950	460	625	725	1,200	1,600	3,250	6,250
1885	(87) 800	725	1,850	3,000	4,200	5,250	10,500	6,250
1886	(88) 4,000	400	500	600	925	1,100	3,050	6,250
1887	(122) 6,160	395	500	625	875	925	1,600	6,250
1888	(97) 16,001	370	380	385	435	470	725	6,250
1889	(48) 17,600	370	380	385	440	470	650	6,250
1890	(93) 8,720	370	380	385	525	550	1,400	5,500
1891	(80) 10,960	370	380	385	390	525	1,050	5,500
1892	(105) 2,440	370	380	385	575	850	1,700	5,500
1893	(106) 30,000	370	380	385	390	400	475	5,500
1894	(122) 4,000	370	380	395	550	600	1,750	5,500
1895	(119) 6,000	370	380	385	410	500	1,100	5,500
1896	(132) 19,070	370	380	385	420	430	495	3,900
1897	(136) 29,768	370	380	385	415	425	495	3,900
1898	(165) 24,000	370	380	385	420	430	495	3,900
1899	(150) 27,200	370	380	385	410	430	495	3,900
1900	(205) 67,000	370	380	385	390	400	450	3,900
1901	(223) 91,100	370	380	385	390	400	450	3,900
1902	(193) 133,540	370	380	385	390	400	450	3,900
1903	(197) 201,060	370	380	385	390	400	450	3,900
1904	(170) 160,790	370	380	385	390	400	450	3,900
1905	(144) 217,800	370	380	385	390	400	450	3,900
1906	(160) 176,330	370	380	385	390	400	450	3,900
1907	(154) 336,294	370	380	385	390	400	470	3,900

INDIAN HEAD (1908–1929)

American sculptor Bela Lyon Pratt, a former student of Augustus Saint-Gaudens, designed this coin and the similar five-dollar gold piece. It features no raised rim, and the main devices and legends are in sunken relief below the surface of the coin. President Theodore Roosevelt, who sought to improve the overall aesthetic quality of American coinage, was enthusiastic about the innovative new design. Collectors and the public were not as pleased. Some feared that the recessed design would collect dirt and germs—an unfounded concern. Over time the design has been recognized as a classic, and part of the early 20th-century renaissance of American coinage.

VF-20 Very Fine: Hair-cord knot distinct. Feathers at top of head clear. Cheekbone worn.

EF-40 Extremely Fine: Cheekbone, war bonnet, and headband feathers slightly worn.

AU-50 About Uncirculated: Trace of wear on cheekbone and headdress.

MS-60 Uncirculated: No trace of wear. Light blemishes.

MS-63 Choice Uncirculated: Some distracting contact marks or blemishes in prime focal areas. Impaired luster possible.

MS-64 Uncirculated: A few scattered contact marks visible. Good eye appeal and attractive luster.

Matte PF-63 Choice Proof: Few blemishes in secondary focal areas. No major flaws. Matte surfaces.

Mintmark location is on reverse, to left of arrows.

	Mintage	EF-40	AU-50	AU-58	MS-60	MS-63	MS-64	MATTE PF-63
1908 . . . . (236) 564,821		$385	$395	$400	$420	$1,100	$1,750	$9,500
1909 . . . . (139) 441,760		385	395	400	430	1,650	2,600	9,500
1910 . . . . (682) 492,000		385	395	400	420	1,200	1,700	9,500
1911 . . . . (191) 704,000		385	395	400	440	925	1,600	9,500
1911D 55,680		1,300	1,450	1,950	2,200	—	—	
1912 . . . . (197) 616,000		385	395	410	440	1,500	3,000	9,500
1913 . . . . (165) 722,000		385	395	400	420	900	1,600	9,500
1914 . . . . (117) 240,000		385	405	420	485	2,150	3,650	9,500
1914D 448,000		385	395	460	500	1,500	2,850	
1915 . . . . (100) 606,000		385	395	400	435	900	1,600	9,500
1925D 578,000		385	395	400	420	500	625	
1926 446,000		385	395	400	420	500	625	
1927 388,000		385	395	400	420	500	625	
1928 416,000		385	395	400	420	500	625	
1929 532,000		385	395	400	420	500	625	

The three-dollar gold piece was authorized by the Act of February 21, 1853. Coinage was struck beginning in 1854. It was never popular and saw very little circulation.

VF-20 Very Fine: Eyebrow, hair about forehead and ear, and bottom curl all worn smooth. Faint details visible on curled feather-ends of headdress.

EF-40 Extremely Fine: Light wear above and to right of eye, and on top of curled feathers.

AU-50 About Uncirculated: Trace of wear on top of curled feathers and in hair above and to right of eye.

AU-55 Choice About Uncirculated: Evidence of friction on design high points. Much of original mint luster present.

MS-60 Uncirculated: No trace of wear. Light blemishes.

MS-63 Choice Uncirculated: Some distracting contact marks or blemishes in prime focal areas. Impaired luster possible.

Mintmark location is on reverse, below wreath.

PF-63 Choice Proof: Reflective surfaces with only a few blemishes in secondary focal places. No major flaws.

	Mintage	VF-20	EF-40	AU-50	AU-58	MS-60	MS-63	PF-63
1854	138,618	$800	$1,000	$1,150	$1,550	$1,950	$3,000	$75,500
1854D	1,120	20,500	28,000	37,000	104,500	108,000	—	
1854O	24,000	1,850	2,600	3,550	21,000	42,000	126,000	
1855	50,555	800	1,000	1,150	1,550	1,950	4,650	108,000
1855S	6,600	1,650	2,600	4,650	19,000	33,500	92,000	
1856	26,010	800	1,000	1,250	2,150	2,400	5,750	92,000
1856S	34,500	1,100	1,600	2,400	8,250	9,750	50,500	
1857	20,891	800	1,000	1,200	1,950	2,300	4,650	28,000
1857S	14,000	900	1,750	4,050	11,000	19,000	50,500	
1858	*(8–12)* 2,133	1,300	2,050	3,100	9,500	12,000	17,000	19,000
1859	(80) 15,558	875	1,100	1,400	2,150	2,550	7,000	12,500
1860	(119) 7,036	925	1,400	2,250	4,300	4,650	8,500	15,000
1860S	7,000	1,850	4,300	7,500	16,000	30,000	108,000	
1861	(113) 5,959	1,650	3,250	4,650	8,750	9,000	13,000	17,000
1862	(35) 5,750	1,600	3,350	4,650	8,000	8,500	15,000	14,000
1863	(39) 5,000	1,100	1,950	3,000	8,250	8,750	12,500	11,500
1864	(50) 2,630	1,350	2,800	4,100	8,500	8,750	12,000	11,500
1865	(25) 1,140	2,400	4,300	7,500	11,000	13,000	21,500	14,000
1866	(30) 4,000	875	1,100	1,650	4,300	4,300	8,000	17,000
1867	(50) 2,600	1,200	1,850	2,800	7,250	7,500	13,000	13,500
1868	(25) 4,850	925	1,200	1,450	5,250	5,250	6,500	13,500
1869	(25) 2,500	1,200	1,700	2,300	4,550	4,650	10,000	19,000
1870	(35) 3,500	925	1,250	1,750	5,250	5,250	8,250	23,500
1870S *(unique)*				4,950,000				
1871	(30) 1,300	1,300	1,700	2,300	6,500	7,000	10,500	20,500
1872	(30) 2,000	1,500	2,050	2,600	5,000	5,750	11,500	15,500
1873, Open 3 (Original)	(25)							46,500
1873, Closed 3		5,750	9,500	13,000	22,500	25,500	44,500	69,000
1874	(20) 41,800	800	1,000	1,150	1,550	1,950	3,000	15,000
1875, Proof only	(20)							112,500
1876, Proof only	(45)							49,500
1877	(20) 1,468	4,650	6,750	9,750	20,500	24,000	55,000	19,000
1878	(20) 82,304	800	1,000	1,150	1,550	1,950	3,000	20,500
1879	(30) 3,000	875	1,200	1,400	3,350	3,550	6,000	11,500
1880	(36) 1,000	1,250	1,700	2,950	5,750	6,000	9,000	15,000
1881	(54) 500	2,550	4,650	7,500	12,000	12,000	19,500	13,000
1882	(76) 1,500	1,500	2,050	2,600	4,900	5,000	8,250	10,500
1883	(89) 900	1,650	2,300	3,000	6,000	6,000	8,500	10,500
1884	(106) 1,000	1,650	2,400	3,150	6,250	7,000	13,000	10,500
1885	(110) 800	1,400	2,050	2,800	6,500	6,750	8,750	10,500
1886	(142) 1,000	1,350	2,100	2,800	4,950	5,250	9,750	10,500
1887	(160) 6,000	1,000	1,500	1,850	3,550	3,600	6,000	10,500
1888	(291) 5,000	1,100	1,350	1,650	3,150	3,350	4,950	10,500
1889	(129) 2,300	1,150	1,500	2,050	3,150	3,550	5,000	10,500

STELLA (1879–1880)

These pattern pieces were first suggested by the Hon. John A. Kasson, then U.S. envoy extraordinary and minister plenipotentiary to Austria-Hungary. It was through the efforts of Dr. W.W. Hubbell, who patented the alloy goloid (used in making another pattern piece, the goloid metric dollar) that we have these beautiful and interesting coins.

The four-dollar Stella—so called because of the five-pointed star on the reverse—was envisioned by Kasson as America's answer to various foreign gold coins popular in the international market. The British sovereign, Italy's 20 lire, and the 20 pesetas of Spain were three such coins: each smaller than a U.S. five-dollar gold piece, they were used widely in international trade.

The Stella was one of many proposals made to Congress for an international trade coin, and one of only several that made it to pattern coin form (others include the 1868 five dollar and 1874 Bickford ten dollar).

Odds were stacked against the Stella from the start. The denomination of four U.S. dollars didn't match any of the coin's European counterparts, and at any rate the U.S. double eagle (twenty-dollar coin)—already used in international commerce—was a more convenient medium of exchange. The Stella was never minted in quantities for circulation.

There are two distinct types in both years of issue. Charles E. Barber is thought to have designed the Flowing Hair type, and George T. Morgan the Coiled Hair. They were struck as patterns in gold, aluminum, copper, and white metal. Only those struck in gold are listed.

Flowing Hair   **Coiled Hair**

	Mintage	PF-60	PF-63	PF-65	PF-66	PF-67
1879, Flowing Hair	425 est. known	$95,500	$126,000	$166,500	$193,500	$288,000
1879, Coiled Hair	12 known	180,000	270,000	657,000	810,000	900,000
1880, Flowing Hair	17 known	117,000	157,500	382,500	450,000	810,000
1880, Coiled Hair	8 known	360,000	585,000	990,000	1,215,000	1,575,000

While the 1856 Flying Eagle cent, the 1879 and 1880 four-dollar Stellas, and a few other patterns are listed in this book, there are more than 1,800 other trial pieces that were minted from 1792 to the present. These are listed in Whitman's *United States Pattern Coins* book and are a fascinating numismatic specialty. Most patterns are rare, and most were made in Proof formats.

The half eagle (five-dollar gold coin) was the first gold coin struck for the United States. It was authorized to be coined by the Act of April 2, 1792. The first type weighed 135 grains, of .91667 fineness. The weight was changed by the Act of June 28, 1834, to 129 grains, of .899225 fineness. Fineness became .900 by the Act of January 18, 1837.

DRAPED BUST TO RIGHT (1795–1807)

F-12 Fine: Liberty's hair worn smooth but with distinct outline. For heraldic type, E PLURIBUS UNUM faint but legible.
VF-20 Very Fine: Slight to noticeable wear on high spots such as hair, turban, and eagle's head and wings.
EF-40 Extremely Fine: Slight wear on hair and highest part of cheek.
AU-50 About Uncirculated: Trace of wear on cap, hair, cheek, and drapery.
MS-60 Uncirculated: No trace of wear. Light blemishes.
MS-63 Choice Uncirculated: Some distracting marks or blemishes in focal areas. Impaired luster possible.

Small Eagle Reverse (1795–1798)

1795
Obverse

1795
Reverse

1796, 6 Over 5

1797, 15 Stars

1797, 16 Stars

	Mintage	F-12	VF-20	EF-40	AU-50	AU-58	MS-60	MS-63
1795, Small Eagle	8,707	$21,500	$24,000	$30,000	$37,000	$55,000	$64,500	$157,500
1796, 6 Over 5	6,196	23,500	26,500	32,500	41,000	60,500	78,000	225,000
1797, 15 Stars	3,609	23,500	32,500	55,000	99,000	157,500	202,500	—
1797, 16 Stars	*	23,500	32,500	60,000	99,000	216,000	270,000	—
1798, Small Eagle *(6 known)*	225,000	360,000	585,000	1,530,000	—	—	—

* Included in number above.

Heraldic Eagle Reverse (1795–1807)

	Mintage	F-12	VF-20	EF-40	AU-50	AU-58	MS-60	MS-63
1795, Heraldic Eagle	*unknown*	$9,500	$17,000	$31,500	$66,000	$103,500	$112,500	$198,000
1797, 7 Over 5	*20 est. known*	24,000	30,000	43,000	69,000	135,000	162,000	—
1798, Large 8, 13-Star Reverse	24,867	4,100	5,250	9,750	13,500	19,000	24,000	59,000
1798, Large 8, 14-Star Reverse	*	5,250	6,750	11,000	21,500	35,500	92,000	—
1799	7,451	4,950	6,000	8,500	11,500	19,000	25,500	66,000
1800	37,628	3,700	4,650	6,750	8,750	11,500	12,000	32,500

* Included in number above.

Chart continued on next page.

	Mintage	F-12	VF-20	EF-40	AU-50	AU-58	MS-60	MS-63
1802, 2 Over 1	53,176	$3,700	$4,500	$6,500	$8,500	$11,000	$12,000	$30,500
1803, 3 Over 2	33,506	3,350	4,100	6,000	7,750	9,750	11,000	21,000
1804	30,475	3,350	4,100	6,000	8,000	13,000	14,000	30,000
1805	33,183	3,350	4,100	6,000	8,750	11,000	12,000	21,000
1806	64,093	3,350	4,100	6,000	7,750	9,750	11,000	21,000
1807	32,488	3,350	4,100	6,000	7,750	9,750	11,000	21,000

CAPPED BUST TO LEFT (1807–1812)

F-12 Fine: LIBERTY on cap legible but partly weak.

VF-20 Very Fine: Headband edges slightly worn. LIBERTY bold.

EF-40 Extremely Fine: Slight wear on highest portions of hair; 80% of major curls plain.

AU-50 About Uncirculated: Trace of wear above eye and on top of cap, cheek, and hair.

AU-55 Choice About Uncirculated: Evidence of friction on design high points. Some mint luster present.

MS-60 Uncirculated: No trace of wear. Light blemishes.

MS-63 Choice Uncirculated: Some distracting contact marks or blemishes in prime focal areas. Impaired luster possible.

	Mintage	F-12	VF-20	EF-40	AU-50	AU-58	MS-60	MS-63
1807	51,605	$3,150	$3,900	$6,000	$7,500	$9,250	$10,000	$15,500
1808, All kinds.	55,578							
1808, 8 Over 7		3,150	3,900	6,000	7,500	12,500	14,500	32,500
1808		3,150	3,900	6,000	7,500	9,000	9,750	23,500
1809, 9 Over 8	33,875	3,300	4,100	6,250	8,000	9,750	11,000	22,500
1810	100,287	3,150	3,900	6,000	7,500	9,000	9,750	19,000
1811	99,581	3,150	3,900	6,000	7,500	9,000	9,750	20,500
1812	58,087	3,150	3,900	6,000	7,500	9,000	9,750	19,000

CAPPED HEAD TO LEFT (1813–1834)

Large Diameter — Reduced Diameter

Large Diameter (1813–1829)

	Mintage	F-12	VF-20	EF-40	AU-50	AU-58	MS-60	MS-63
1813	95,428	$3,500	$4,400	$7,000	$8,000	$11,500	$12,000	$20,500
1814, 4 Over 3	15,454	3,900	5,250	7,250	9,500	14,500	17,500	37,000
1815	10 est. known	78,000	112,500	207,000	238,500	297,000	324,000	540,000
1818	48,588	4,300	6,000	11,500	13,500	17,500	20,500	46,500
1819	51,723	23,500	32,500	46,500	55,000	78,000	99,000	189,000
1820	263,806	5,250	6,500	9,750	12,000	20,500	20,500	43,000
1821	34,641	23,500	37,000	50,500	87,500	135,000	157,500	247,500
1822	3 known	—	—	—	7,200,000	—	—	—
1823	14,485	3,900	5,250	10,500	12,000	19,500	21,500	39,000

	Mintage	F-12	VF-20	EF-40	AU-50	AU-58	MS-60	MS-63
1824 17,340		$6,250	$9,750	$26,000	$30,000	$35,500	$42,000	$87,500
1825, 5 Over Partial 4 29,060		8,500	12,000	28,000	35,500	62,500	78,000	126,000
1825, 5 Over 4 *(2 known)* . . . . *		—	—	—	630,000	—	—	—
1826 18,069		4,650	9,500	20,000	25,500	46,500	58,000	117,000
1827 24,913		4,650	8,500	19,000	24,000	35,000	42,000	108,000
1828, 8 Over 7 *(5 known)* . . . .**		11,000	24,000	53,500	60,000	78,000	112,500	292,500
1828 28,029		9,500	19,000	32,500	46,500	69,000	92,000	180,000
1829, Large Date 57,442		—	—	—	—	—	270,000	—

* Included in number above.   ** Included in number below.

Reduced Diameter (1829–1834)

	Mintage	F-12	VF-20	EF-40	AU-50	AU-58	MS-60	MS-63
1829, Small Date . . . . . . *10–12 known*		—	—	—	$112,500	$180,000	$234,000	$432,000
1830 126,351		$17,000	$26,000	$42,000	55,000	64,500	68,000	103,500
1831 140,594		17,000	26,000	42,000	55,000	64,500	69,000	135,000
1832, Curved-Base 2, 12 Stars *(5 known)* 157,487		92,000	135,000	216,000	306,000	472,500	—	720,000
1832, Square-Base 2, 13 Stars . . . . . *		17,000	26,000	42,000	55,000	64,500	68,000	103,500
1833 193,630		17,000	26,000	42,000	55,000	64,500	68,000	103,500
1834 50,141		17,000	26,000	42,000	55,000	64,500	68,000	103,500

* Included in number above.

CLASSIC HEAD (1834–1838)

	Mintage	VF-20	EF-40	AU-50	AU-58	MS-60	MS-63	MS-65
1834 657,460		$650	$875	$1,300	$2,250	$3,050	$9,500	$46,500
1835 371,534		650	875	1,350	2,600	4,100	13,500	64,500
1836 553,147		650	1,000	1,250	2,400	3,700	12,000	60,500
1837 207,121		675	1,100	1,550	3,350	4,650	19,000	73,500
1838 286,588		700	1,200	1,850	3,150	3,900	9,500	87,500
1838C 17,179		6,250	12,000	15,500	28,000	55,000	198,000	—
1838D 20,583		4,650	9,500	15,500	24,500	28,000	99,000	—

LIBERTY HEAD (1839–1908)
Variety 1 – No Motto Above Eagle (1839–1866)

VF-20 Very Fine: LIBERTY on coronet bold. Major lines show in curls on neck.

EF-40 Extremely Fine: Details clear in curls on neck. Slight wear on top and lower part of coronet and on hair.

AU-50 About Uncirculated: Trace of wear on coronet and hair above eye.

AU-55 Choice About Uncirculated: Evidence of friction on design high points. Some original mint luster.

MS-60 Uncirculated: No trace of wear. Light blemishes.

MS-63 Choice Uncirculated: Some distracting contact marks or blemishes in prime focal areas. Impaired luster possible.

PF-63 Choice Proof: Attractive reflective surfaces with only a few blemishes in secondary focal places. No major flaws.

Mintmark: 1839, above date; 1840–1908, below eagle.

1842, Large Date

Small Letters

Large Letters

	Mintage	VF-20	EF-40	AU-50	AU-58	MS-60	MS-63
1839	118,143	$825	$1,200	$1,600	$5,500	$6,750	$26,000
1839C	17,205	3,550	6,750	13,000	20,500	26,000	44,500
1839D	18,939	4,950	7,500	11,500	29,000	37,000	—
1840	137,382	625	800	1,000	2,050	3,000	8,250
1840C	18,992	2,250	3,700	6,250	11,500	17,000	42,000
1840D	22,896	2,050	3,150	4,950	8,000	12,000	43,000
1840O	40,120	725	1,100	1,950	4,100	8,500	32,000
1841	15,833	650	1,000	1,300	2,150	3,400	9,500
1841C	21,467	1,300	1,750	3,700	7,000	12,000	—
1841D	29,392	1,850	3,250	4,450	7,500	13,000	31,500
1842, Small Letters	27,578	1,250	2,050	2,800	8,000	11,500	28,000
1842, Large Letters	*	650	1,400	2,550	5,250	8,000	19,000
1842C, Small Date	27,432	7,000	14,500	22,000	42,000	64,500	99,000
1842C, Large Date	*	1,500	2,050	3,150	5,250	8,500	22,500
1842D, Small Date	59,608	2,400	3,150	4,100	7,000	12,000	30,000
1842D, Large Date	*	3,700	7,000	10,000	28,000	37,000	—
1842O	16,400	1,850	2,850	7,750	10,500	18,500	33,500
1843	611,205	625	700	750	975	1,300	9,000
1843C	44,277	1,300	1,950	2,800	4,400	8,000	23,500
1843D	98,452	1,950	2,600	3,350	6,250	8,500	26,000
1843O, Small Letters	19,075	825	1,650	3,250	7,000	15,500	30,000
1843O, Large Letters	82,000	750	975	2,600	5,250	8,500	21,500
1844	340,330	625	700	750	1,100	1,400	8,250
1844C	23,631	1,650	2,500	3,950	6,750	12,000	25,000
1844D	88,982	1,850	2,600	3,550	6,000	6,750	21,500
1844O	364,600	650	800	1,100	2,400	4,100	13,000
1845	417,099	625	700	775	1,000	1,300	6,750
1845D	90,629	2,800	3,250	4,100	6,500	7,250	23,500
1845O	41,000	975	1,500	3,350	8,500	13,000	60,000
1846, Large Date	395,942	625	700	750	975	1,700	10,500
1846, Small Date	*	625	700	775	1,400	2,400	11,500
1846C	12,995	1,600	3,000	4,200	6,750	12,000	46,500
1846D	80,294	1,400	1,750	2,600	5,500	9,000	—
1846O	58,000	825	1,650	3,000	8,500	11,500	50,500
1847	915,981	625	700	750	975	1,100	3,900
1847C	84,151	1,300	1,850	2,500	3,950	7,500	23,500
1847D	64,405	1,850	2,800	3,600	5,750	8,500	23,500
1847O	12,000	6,250	10,500	12,500	20,500	28,000	—
1848	260,775	625	700	750	975	1,300	8,000
1848C	64,472	2,100	3,150	4,200	8,500	12,000	30,000
1848D	47,465	2,050	2,700	3,700	9,500	12,500	28,000
1849	133,070	650	750	975	1,650	2,300	12,000
1849C	64,823	1,300	1,650	2,400	4,950	7,250	19,000
1849D	39,036	2,300	3,150	3,900	9,000	14,000	46,500
1850	64,491	625	775	925	1,850	2,600	15,000

* Included in number above.

HALF EAGLES ($5)

	Mintage	VF-20	EF-40	AU-50	AU-58	MS-60	MS-63	PF-63
1850C	63,591	$1,400	$1,600	$2,250	$4,000	$8,250	$16,000	
1850D	43,984	1,350	1,700	3,000	5,750	19,000	—	
1851	377,505	625	700	750	975	1,500	7,000	
1851C	49,176	1,750	2,100	2,800	6,250	9,500	29,000	
1851D	62,710	2,350	2,900	3,950	6,750	9,500	22,500	
1851O	41,000	775	1,650	3,050	6,500	8,000	20,500	
1852	573,901	625	700	750	975	1,100	3,900	
1852C	72,574	1,850	2,800	3,550	4,550	5,750	19,000	
1852D	91,584	1,650	2,350	2,750	6,000	6,750	24,000	
1853	305,770	625	700	750	1,000	1,100	5,250	
1853C	65,571	1,850	2,550	3,350	5,250	7,000	19,000	
1853D	89,678	1,750	2,550	3,150	5,250	6,750	17,000	
1854	160,675	625	700	750	1,000	1,350	6,750	
1854C	39,283	1,400	2,050	2,950	3,700	9,750	33,000	
1854D	56,413	1,400	1,800	2,450	3,850	4,550	—	
1854O	46,000	825	1,100	2,700	6,750	8,500	33,500	
1854S	2 known	—	—	—	2,700,000	—	—	
1855	117,098	625	700	750	975	1,400	5,500	
1855C	39,788	1,400	1,850	2,450	5,500	7,500	28,000	
1855D	22,432	2,050	3,000	4,650	11,500	15,000	35,500	
1855O	11,100	1,250	2,800	4,200	8,500	17,500	—	
1855S	61,000	925	1,550	2,550	5,500	9,500	—	
1856	197,990	625	700	750	1,050	1,100	5,750	
1856C	28,457	1,500	1,850	2,600	4,650	9,500	39,000	
1856D	19,786	1,650	2,250	3,050	5,500	7,500	20,500	
1856O	10,000	1,200	1,850	3,350	9,500	12,000	112,500	
1856S	105,100	725	875	1,550	4,650	6,750	31,500	
1857	98,188	625	700	750	1,000	1,500	4,650	
1857C	31,360	1,500	2,250	3,050	5,500	9,500	30,500	
1857D	17,046	1,850	2,600	3,550	6,750	12,000	37,000	
1857O	13,000	1,300	2,250	3,700	6,750	11,500	38,000	
1857S	87,000	800	1,050	1,750	5,750	7,000	17,500	
1858	15,136	700	925	1,400	2,300	3,000	7,500	—
1858C	38,856	1,650	2,600	3,200	6,250	8,000	28,000	
1858D	15,362	1,850	2,400	3,050	6,750	11,500	51,500	
1858S	18,600	1,500	3,700	5,250	15,000	26,000	—	
1859	(80) 16,734	875	1,150	1,550	3,250	5,250	19,000	$46,500
1859C	31,847	2,100	3,050	4,200	8,250	9,500	31,500	
1859D	10,366	2,250	3,000	4,100	7,500	13,000	37,000	
1859S	13,220	1,850	4,200	6,250	11,500	24,000	108,000	
1860	(62) 19,763	650	1,100	1,500	3,050	5,750	14,000	46,500
1860C	14,813	2,150	3,050	4,650	7,750	11,000	22,500	
1860D	14,635	1,850	3,350	4,300	7,500	8,000	43,000	
1860S	21,200	2,250	4,300	8,000	19,000	26,000	—	
1861	(66) 688,084	625	700	750	975	1,200	3,900	64,500
1861C	6,879	6,750	12,500	18,000	25,500	30,000	92,000	
1861D	1,597	24,000	37,000	44,500	69,000	83,000	247,500	
1861S	18,000	4,100	7,000	10,500	19,000	—	—	
1862	(35) 4,430	2,250	5,250	8,500	17,000	25,500	—	46,500
1862S	9,500	5,750	10,500	15,500	28,000	37,000	—	
1863	(30) 2,442	5,500	11,500	20,500	39,000	49,500	78,000	46,500
1863S	17,000	3,700	7,000	17,000	28,000	39,000	—	
1864	(50) 4,170	5,250	9,750	16,500	25,500	29,000	—	46,500
1864S	3,888	30,000	44,000	64,500	180,000	198,000	—	
1865	(25) 1,270	15,000	26,000	33,500	46,500	50,500	—	46,500
1865S	27,612	3,000	5,250	8,000	12,500	17,000	48,000	
1866S	9,000	2,400	5,250	9,000	17,000	37,000	—	

187

Variety 2 – Motto Above Eagle (1866–1908)

VF-20 Very Fine: Half of hair lines above coronet missing. Hair curls under ear evident, but worn. Motto and its ribbon sharp.

EF-40 Extremely Fine: Small amount of wear on top of hair and below L in LIBERTY. Wear evident on wing tips and neck of eagle.

AU-50 About Uncirculated: Trace of wear on tip of coronet and hair above eye.

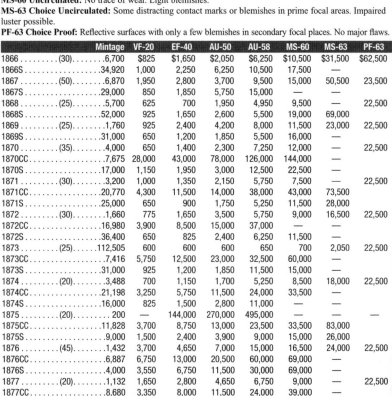

AU-55 Choice About Uncirculated: Evidence of friction on design high points. Some original mint luster present.

MS-60 Uncirculated: No trace of wear. Light blemishes.

MS-63 Choice Uncirculated: Some distracting contact marks or blemishes in prime focal areas. Impaired luster possible.

PF-63 Choice Proof: Reflective surfaces with only a few blemishes in secondary focal places. No major flaws.

	Mintage	VF-20	EF-40	AU-50	AU-58	MS-60	MS-63	PF-63
1866 . . . . (30) 6,700		$825	$1,650	$2,050	$6,250	$10,500	$31,500	$62,500
1866S 34,920		1,000	2,250	6,250	10,500	17,500	—	
1867 . . . . (50) 6,870		1,950	2,800	3,700	9,500	15,000	50,500	23,500
1867S 29,000		850	1,850	5,750	15,000	—	—	
1868 . . . . (25) 5,700		625	700	1,950	4,950	9,500	—	22,500
1868S 52,000		925	1,650	2,600	5,500	19,000	69,000	
1869 . . . . (25) 1,760		925	2,400	4,200	8,000	11,500	23,000	22,500
1869S 31,000		650	1,200	1,850	5,500	16,000	—	
1870 . . . . (35) 4,000		650	1,400	2,300	7,250	12,000	—	22,500
1870CC 7,675		28,000	43,000	78,000	126,000	144,000	—	
1870S 17,000		1,150	1,950	3,000	12,500	22,500	—	
1871 . . . . (30) 3,200		1,000	1,350	2,150	5,750	7,500	—	22,500
1871CC 20,770		4,300	11,500	14,000	38,000	43,000	73,500	
1871S 25,000		650	900	1,750	5,250	11,500	28,000	
1872 . . . . (30) 1,660		775	1,650	3,500	5,750	9,000	16,500	22,500
1872CC 16,980		3,900	8,500	15,000	37,000	—	—	
1872S 36,400		650	825	2,400	6,250	11,500	—	
1873 . . . . (25) 112,505		600	600	600	650	700	2,050	22,500
1873CC 7,416		5,750	12,500	23,000	32,500	60,000	—	
1873S 31,000		925	1,200	1,850	11,500	15,000	—	
1874 . . . . (20) 3,488		700	1,150	1,700	5,250	8,500	18,000	22,500
1874CC 21,198		3,250	5,750	11,500	24,000	33,500	—	
1874S 16,000		825	1,400	2,800	11,000	—	—	
1875 . . . . (20) 200		—	144,000	270,000	495,000	—	—	
1875CC 11,828		3,700	8,750	13,000	23,500	33,500	83,000	
1875S 9,000		1,500	2,400	3,900	9,000	15,000	26,000	
1876 . . . . (45) 1,432		3,700	4,650	7,000	15,000	16,500	24,000	22,500
1876CC 6,887		6,750	13,000	20,500	60,000	69,000	—	
1876S 4,000		3,550	6,750	11,500	30,000	69,000	—	
1877 . . . . (20) 1,132		1,650	2,800	4,650	6,750	9,000	—	22,500
1877CC 8,680		3,350	8,000	11,500	24,000	39,000	—	
1877S 26,700		650	750	1,200	5,250	6,250	15,500	
1878 . . . . (20) 131,720		600	600	625	700	725	1,750	22,500
1878CC 9,054		4,650	11,500	19,000	60,000	—	—	
1878S 144,700		600	600	600	675	675	2,050	
1879 . . . . (30) 301,920		600	600	600	600	625	875	22,500
1879CC 17,281		2,800	4,100	6,000	15,000	21,000	—	
1879S 426,200		600	600	600	625	650	1,200	
1880 . . . . (36) 3,166,400		600	600	600	600	600	675	12,000
1880CC 51,017		1,600	2,150	3,650	7,500	11,500	43,000	
1880S 1,348,900		600	600	600	600	600	675	

	Mintage	VF-20	EF-40	AU-50	AU-58	MS-60	MS-63	PF-63
1881 . . . . (42). . . .	5,708,760	$600	$600	$600	$600	$600	$650	$11,000
1881CC	13,886	3,000	5,750	7,500	13,000	19,000	40,000	
1881S	969,000	600	600	600	600	600	675	
1882 . . . . (48). . . .	2,514,520	600	600	600	600	600	650	11,000
1882CC	82,817	925	1,650	2,200	6,500	10,500	30,000	
1882S	969,000	600	600	600	600	600	675	
1883 . . . . (61).	233,400	600	600	600	600	625	975	11,000
1883CC	12,598	2,050	3,700	5,750	9,500	17,000	44,500	
1883S	83,200	600	600	600	650	650	1,000	
1884 . . . . (48). . . .	191,030	600	600	600	600	600	1,100	11,000
1884CC	16,402	1,850	3,000	4,300	10,500	16,000	—	
1884S	177,000	600	600	600	600	600	800	
1885 . . . . (66). . . .	601,440	600	600	600	600	600	725	11,000
1885S	1,211,500	600	600	600	600	600	650	
1886 . . . . (72). . . .	388,360	600	600	600	600	600	650	11,000
1886S	3,268,000	600	600	600	600	600	650	
1887, Proof only (87).								35,500
1887S	1,912,000	600	600	600	600	600	700	
1888 . . . . (95). . . .	18,201	600	600	625	675	725	2,050	12,000
1888S	293,900	600	600	600	625	700	2,800	
1889 . . . . (45).	7,520	600	650	700	975	1,300	3,250	11,000
1890 . . . . (88).	4,240	650	825	1,100	2,050	2,300	6,250	12,000
1890CC	53,800	650	775	1,050	1,650	1,850	6,750	
1891 . . . . (53).	61,360	600	600	600	600	600	875	9,750
1891CC	208,000	700	925	1,300	1,850	2,050	3,850	
1892 . . . . (92).	753,480	600	600	600	600	600	700	9,750
1892CC	82,968	975	1,350	1,650	2,400	2,800	10,500	
1892O	10,000	1,750	2,400	3,250	6,250	6,750	24,000	
1892S	298,400	600	600	600	600	600	1,100	
1893 . . . . (77). . . .	1,528,120	600	600	600	600	600	675	9,750
1893CC	60,000	875	1,250	1,650	2,900	3,150	11,500	
1893O	110,000	600	625	675	875	1,000	5,500	
1893S	224,000	600	600	600	600	625	700	
1894 . . . . (75). . . .	957,880	600	600	600	600	600	675	9,750
1894O	16,600	600	675	800	925	1,300	8,500	
1894S	55,900	600	600	600	600	1,850	8,000	
1895 . . . . (81). . . .	1,345,855	600	600	600	600	600	650	9,000
1895S	112,000	600	600	600	650	800	3,900	
1896 . . . . (103). . . .	58,960	600	600	600	600	600	750	9,000
1896S	155,400	600	600	600	650	675	2,800	
1897 . . . . (83). . . .	867,800	600	600	600	600	600	650	9,000
1897S	354,000	600	600	600	600	650	2,650	
1898 . . . . (75). . . .	633,420	600	600	600	600	600	700	9,000
1898S	1,397,400	600	600	600	600	600	675	
1899 . . . . (99). . . .	1,710,630	600	600	600	600	600	650	9,000
1899S	1,545,000	600	600	600	600	600	675	
1900 . . . . (230). . . .	1,405,500	600	600	600	600	600	650	9,000
1900S	329,000	600	600	600	600	600	700	
1901 . . . . (140).	615,900	600	600	600	600	600	650	9,000
1901S, 1 Over 0	3,648,000	600	600	600	650	650	825	
1901S . . . . *		600	600	600	600	600	650	
1902 . . . . (162). . . .	172,400	600	600	600	600	600	700	9,000
1902S	939,000	600	600	600	600	600	650	
1903 . . . . (154). . . .	226,870	600	600	600	600	600	700	9,000
1903S	1,855,000	600	600	600	600	600	700	

Included in number above.

Chart continued on next page.

	Mintage	VF-20	EF-40	AU-50	AU-58	MS-60	MS-63	PF-63
1904 . . . .(136). 392,000		$600	$600	$600	$600	$600	$650	$9,000
1904S 97,000		600	600	600	650	725	2,250	
1905 . . . .(108). 302,200		600	600	600	600	600	650	9,000
1905S 880,700		600	600	600	600	625	925	
1906 . . . .(85). 348,735		600	600	600	600	600	650	9,000
1906D 320,000		600	600	600	600	600	650	
1906S 598,000		600	600	600	600	625	775	
1907 . . . .(92). 626,100		600	600	600	600	600	650	9,000
1907D 888,000		600	600	600	600	600	650	
1908 421,874		600	600	600	600	600	650	

INDIAN HEAD (1908–1929)

This type conforms in design to the quarter eagle of the same date. The sunken-relief designs and lettering make the Indian Head a unique series, along with the quarter eagle, in United States coinage.

VF-20 Very Fine: Noticeable wear on large middle feathers and tip of eagle's wing.

EF-40 Extremely Fine: Cheekbone, war bonnet, and head-band feathers slightly worn. Feathers on eagle's upper wing show considerable wear.

AU-50 About Uncirculated: Trace of wear on cheekbone and headdress.

AU-55 Choice About Uncirculated: Evidence of friction on design high points. Much of original mint luster present.

MS-60 Uncirculated: No trace of wear. Light blemishes.

MS-63 Choice Uncirculated: Some distracting contact marks or blemishes in prime focal areas. Impaired luster possible.

Mintmark Location

Matte PF-63 Choice Proof: Matte surfaces with few blemishes in secondary focal places. No major flaws.

Coin dealers usually pay higher prices than those listed for scarcer coins with well-struck mintmarks.

	Mintage	EF-40	AU-50	AU-58	MS-60	MS-63	MS-64	MATTE PF-63
1908 . . . .(167). 577,845		$525	$550	$575	$575	$1,450	$2,300	$17,000
1908D 148,000		525	550	575	575	1,500	2,650	
1908S 82,000		575	1,100	2,900	4,300	9,750	11,500	
1909 . . . .(78). 627,060		525	550	575	575	1,400	2,400	17,000
1909D 3,423,560		525	550	575	575	825	1,250	
1909O 34,200		6,000	8,000	14,000	18,000	64,500	112,500	
1909S 297,200		550	600	1,000	3,050	10,500	15,000	
1910 . . . .(250). 604,000		525	550	575	575	1,550	2,900	17,000
1910D 193,600		525	550	575	600	2,300	7,750	
1910S 770,200		525	575	700	925	8,000	22,500	
1911 . . . .(139). 915,000		525	550	575	575	1,400	2,450	17,000
1911D 72,500		775	1,450	3,450	4,450	22,500	46,500	
1911S 1,416,000		525	600	700	775	4,100	8,750	
1912 . . . .(144). 790,000		525	550	575	575	1,550	2,600	17,000
1912S 392,000		550	600	1,050	1,300	11,500	28,000	
1913 . . . .(99). 915,901		525	550	575	600	1,400	2,650	17,000
1913S 408,000		525	575	925	1,600	9,750	16,500	
1914 . . . .(125). 247,000		525	550	575	575	1,600	2,500	17,000
1914D 247,000		525	550	575	575	2,650	3,200	
1914S 263,000		550	575	1,150	1,500	9,500	39,000	
1915 . . . .(75). 588,000		525	550	575	575	1,450	2,400	17,000
1915S 164,000		550	575	1,400	2,150	9,500	31,000	
1916S 240,000		575	625	850	1,050	4,650	5,750	
1929 662,000		14,000	17,500	22,500	24,000	33,500	39,000	

Coinage authorization, specified weights, and fineness of the eagle coins conform to those of the half eagle. The Small Eagle reverse was used until 1797, when the large, Heraldic Eagle replaced it.

DRAPED BUST TO RIGHT (1795–1804)

F-12 Fine: Details on turban and head obliterated.
VF-20 Very Fine: Hair lines in curls on neck and details under turban and over forehead worn but distinguishable.
EF-40 Extremely Fine: Definite wear on hair to left of eye and strand of hair across and around turban, as well as on eagle's wing tips.
AU-50 About Uncirculated: Trace of wear on cap, hair, cheek, and drapery.
AU-55 Choice About Uncirculated: Evidence of friction on design high points. Most of original mint luster present.
MS-60 Uncirculated: No trace of wear. Light blemishes.
MS-63 Choice Uncirculated: Some distracting contact marks or blemishes in prime focal areas. Impaired luster possible.

Small Eagle Reverse (1795–1797)

	Mintage	F-12	VF-20	EF-40	AU-50	AU-58	MS-60	MS-63
1795	5,583	$25,000	$30,500	$49,500	$60,500	$99,000	$108,000	$291,500
1796	4,146	25,000	30,500	49,500	60,500	99,000	108,000	321,000
1797, Small Eagle	3,615	33,500	44,500	60,000	76,000	151,000	198,000	391,500

Heraldic Eagle Reverse (1797–1804)

	Mintage	F-12	VF-20	EF-40	AU-50	AU-58	MS-60	MS-63
1797, Large Eagle	10,940	$9,500	$12,500	$19,500	$24,000	$40,000	$46,500	$171,000
1798, 8 Over 7, 9 Stars Left, 4 Right	900	10,500	14,500	30,000	49,000	94,500	117,000	256,500
1798, 8 Over 7, 7 Stars Left, 6 Right	842	37,000	55,000	108,000	180,000	378,000	562,500	—
1799	37,449	8,500	9,500	12,500	15,000	20,500	23,500	52,500
1800	5,999	8,500	9,500	12,500	15,000	21,000	28,000	64,500
1801	44,344	9,000	10,000	13,500	17,000	20,500	23,500	46,500
1803	15,017	10,500	12,000	14,500	18,000	25,500	27,000	54,500
1804	3,757	19,000	22,000	26,000	40,000	66,000	87,500	247,500

LIBERTY HEAD, NO MOTTO ABOVE EAGLE (1838–1866)

In 1838 the weight and diameter of the eagle were reduced and the obverse and reverse were redesigned. Liberty now faced left and the word LIBERTY was placed on the coronet.

VF-20 Very Fine: Hair lines above coronet partly worn. Curls under ear worn but defined.

EF-40 Extremely Fine: Small amount of wear on top of hair and below L in LIBERTY. Wear evident on wing tips and neck of eagle.

AU-50 About Uncirculated: Trace of wear on tip of coronet and hair above eye.

AU-55 Choice About Uncirculated: Evidence of friction on design high points. Some of original mint luster present.

MS-60 Uncirculated: No trace of wear. Light blemishes.

Mintmark is on reverse, below eagle.

MS-63 Choice Uncirculated: Some distracting contact marks or blemishes in prime focal areas. Impaired luster possible.

PF-63 Choice Proof: Attractive reflective surfaces with only a few blemishes in secondary focal places. No major flaws.

	Mintage	VF-20	EF-40	AU-50	AU-58	MS-60	MS-63	MS-64
1838	7,200	$2,800	$7,000	$12,000	$42,000	$55,000	$87,500	—
1839, Large Letters	25,801	1,500	4,200	5,250	15,000	28,000	83,000	$130,500
1839, Small Letters	12,447	4,650	7,500	8,500	35,500	55,000	108,000	171,000
1840	47,338	1,350	1,650	1,950	5,000	14,000	—	—
1841	63,131	1,250	1,300	1,650	5,250	9,500	46,500	—
1841O	2,500	9,500	17,000	35,500	78,000	—	—	—
1842	81,507	1,250	1,300	1,500	5,750	9,500	24,000	41,000
1842O	27,400	1,550	2,300	4,650	14,000	46,500	225,000	—
1843	75,462	1,250	1,350	1,750	13,000	23,500	—	—
1843O	175,162	1,300	1,400	2,150	6,750	14,500	83,000	135,000
1844	6,361	2,400	4,100	7,500	19,000	22,500	72,000	—
1844O	118,700	1,350	1,500	2,050	5,250	13,000	69,000	—
1845	26,153	1,450	1,650	2,250	7,000	12,500	—	—
1845O	47,500	1,650	2,150	3,350	9,000	19,000	53,500	—
1846	20,095	1,300	1,650	4,000	10,500	28,000	—	—
1846O	81,780	1,400	2,250	3,350	15,000	25,500	69,000	108,000
1847	862,258	1,250	1,300	1,350	1,650	3,350	20,500	37,000
1847O	571,500	1,300	1,350	1,550	3,700	6,250	32,500	69,000
1848	145,484	1,250	1,300	1,350	1,750	5,250	23,500	37,000
1848O	35,850	1,600	3,000	3,700	9,750	14,000	44,500	62,500
1849	653,618	1,250	1,300	1,450	2,050	3,550	18,000	31,500
1849O	23,900	2,400	3,700	4,650	19,500	35,500	—	—
1850	291,451	1,250	1,300	1,350	1,650	5,750	26,000	50,500
1850O	57,500	1,550	2,050	3,550	17,000	19,000	46,500	92,000
1851	176,328	1,250	1,300	1,450	2,250	4,450	31,500	—
1851O	263,000	1,350	1,450	1,600	3,550	11,500	32,500	60,000
1852	263,106	1,250	1,300	1,350	1,650	2,650	23,500	35,500
1852O	18,000	2,400	4,650	6,500	19,000	78,000	—	—
1853, 3 Over 2	201,253	1,350	1,450	1,650	3,500	9,500	—	—
1853	*	1,250	1,300	1,350	1,650	2,400	21,500	44,500
1853O	51,000	1,350	1,550	1,850	8,500	19,000	—	—
1854	54,250	1,350	1,400	1,500	2,250	6,250	26,000	44,500
1854O	52,500	1,500	1,950	2,400	6,000	15,000	—	—
1854S	123,826	1,350	1,450	1,850	5,500	18,000	—	—
1855	121,701	1,250	1,300	1,350	1,650	2,900	18,000	33,500
1855O	18,000	2,600	3,700	7,000	24,000	28,000	—	—

* Included in number above.

	Mintage	VF-20	EF-40	AU-50	AU-58	MS-60	MS-63	PF-63
1855S	9,000	$3,000	$3,900	$6,000	$24,000	—	—	
1856	60,490	1,250	1,300	1,350	1,650	$2,400	$16,500	
18560	14,500	1,500	2,800	4,450	15,000	32,500	—	
1856S	68,000	1,400	1,500	1,600	4,650	10,500	44,500	
1857	16,606	1,350	1,550	2,400	5,750	9,500	—	
18570	5,500	2,800	5,750	8,000	24,000	—	—	
1857S	26,000	1,500	2,600	3,550	8,500	10,500	30,000	
1858	2,521	4,100	5,750	8,000	20,500	28,000	126,000	
18580	20,000	1,350	1,600	2,400	6,750	13,000	41,000	
1858S	11,800	1,650	3,150	7,750	16,500	23,500	—	
1859 (80)	16,013	1,250	1,350	1,750	3,700	14,000	55,000	$109,000
18590	2,300	7,500	15,000	22,500	50,500	—	—	
1859S	7,000	4,650	7,500	12,000	26,000	41,000	—	
1860 (50)	15,055	1,250	1,300	1,650	4,200	7,500	26,000	109,000
18600	11,100	1,850	3,000	3,900	11,500	19,000	—	
1860S	5,000	6,750	12,000	16,000	30,000	37,000	—	
1861 (69)	113,164	1,250	1,300	1,450	3,000	4,650	19,500	109,000
1861S	15,500	4,300	6,750	9,000	20,500	41,000	—	
1862 (35)	10,960	2,800	3,700	5,250	8,500	15,000	46,500	99,000
1862S	12,500	4,650	7,000	10,500	39,000	64,500	—	
1863 (30)	1,218	13,000	33,500	45,500	77,500	99,000	157,500	109,000
1863S	10,000	7,500	12,000	16,500	37,000	92,000	—	
1864 (50)	3,530	6,750	10,500	21,500	44,500	55,000	—	109,000
1864S	2,500	55,000	72,000	126,000	—	—	—	
1865 (25)	3,980	3,700	6,750	16,000	26,000	37,000	—	99,000
1865S	16,700	6,750	13,000	16,500	35,500	87,500	—	
1866S	8,500	6,250	10,000	13,500	33,500	55,000	—	

LIBERTY HEAD, MOTTO ABOVE EAGLE (1866–1907)

VF-20 Very Fine: Half of hair lines over coronet visible. Curls under ear worn but defined. IN GOD WE TRUST and its ribbon sharp.

EF-40 Extremely Fine: Small amount of wear on top of hair and below L in LIBERTY. Wear evident on wing tips and neck of eagle.

AU-50 About Uncirculated: Trace of wear on hair above eye and on coronet.

AU-55 Choice About Uncirculated: Evidence of friction on design high points. Some of original mint luster present.

MS-60 Uncirculated: No trace of wear. Light blemishes.

Mintmark is on reverse, below eagle.

MS-63 Choice Uncirculated: Some distracting marks or blemishes in focal areas. Impaired luster possible.

PF-63 Choice Proof: Reflective surfaces with only a few blemishes in secondary focal areas. No major flaws.

	Mintage	VF-20	EF-40	AU-50	AU-58	MS-60	MS-63	PF-63
1866 (30)	3,750	$1,850	$3,700	$5,250	$15,000	$31,500	—	$42,000
1866S	11,500	3,050	5,250	7,500	17,000	22,500	—	
1867 (50)	3,090	3,000	3,900	5,750	20,500	26,000	—	42,000
1867S	9,000	4,450	6,750	11,500	42,000	—	—	
1868 (10–12 known)	10,630	1,300	1,400	1,850	5,500	9,750	—	42,000
1868S	13,500	1,650	2,400	3,900	16,000	—	—	
1869 (25)	1,830	2,250	5,250	7,500	22,500	37,000	$64,500	42,000
1869S	6,430	2,400	4,100	6,000	12,000	33,500	135,000	
1870 (35)	3,990	1,850	2,400	4,300	13,000	30,000	—	39,000
1870CC	5,908	77,500	94,500	157,500	765,000	—	—	
1870S	8,000	2,250	3,550	4,550	20,500	33,500	—	
1871 (30)	1,790	1,500	2,800	5,750	12,500	31,500	—	39,000
1871CC	8,085	5,750	15,000	21,500	39,000	51,500	—	

Chart continued on next page.

	Mintage	VF-20	EF-40	AU-50	AU-58	MS-60	MS-63	PF-63
1871S 16,500	$1,450	$2,050	$4,650	$19,000	—	—	
1872 . . . . (30). 1,620	2,800	6,000	8,000	22,500	$28,000	$43,000	$39,000
1872CC 4,600	11,500	16,000	20,500	50,500	—	—	
1872S 17,300	1,400	1,650	3,000	8,250	25,500	—	
1873 . . . . (25). 800	9,000	12,500	20,500	60,000	77,500	—	39,000
1873CC 4,543	19,000	30,000	42,000	92,000	—	—	
1873S 12,000	1,500	3,550	5,250	13,000	26,000	—	
1874 . . . . (20). 53,140	1,200	1,200	1,200	1,350	1,350	12,000	42,000
1874CC 16,767	3,050	6,250	9,750	37,000	57,000	162,000	
1874S 10,000	1,500	2,250	4,650	17,000	—	—	
1875 . . . . (20). 100	135,000	216,000	450,000	945,000	—	—	50,500
1875CC 7,715	6,750	14,000	22,500	69,000	86,500	153,000	
1876 . . . . (45). 687	4,650	9,000	19,000	37,000	69,000	—	33,500
1876CC 4,696	6,750	13,000	19,000	69,000	—	—	
1876S 5,000	2,600	4,300	7,750	30,000	—	—	
1877 . . . . (20). 797	3,700	6,500	11,000	20,500	41,000	—	33,500
1877CC 3,332	8,750	13,000	33,500	108,000	—	—	
1877S 17,000	1,300	1,450	2,600	9,750	23,500	—	
1878 . . . . (20). 73,780	1,200	1,200	1,200	1,250	1,350	3,900	33,500
1878CC 3,244	7,000	16,500	22,500	62,500	108,000	—	
1878S 26,100	1,200	1,250	1,300	3,000	17,000	42,000	
1879 . . . . (30). 384,740	1,200	1,200	1,200	1,200	1,200	2,400	33,500
1879CC 1,762	19,000	30,000	40,000	60,500	—	—	
18790 1,500	9,750	15,500	23,000	50,500	66,000	—	
1879S 224,000	1,200	1,200	1,200	1,250	1,300	5,750	
1880 . . . . (36). . . .1,644,840	1,200	1,200	1,200	1,200	1,200	1,600	33,500
1880CC 11,190	1,650	2,800	4,650	12,500	33,500	—	
18800 9,200	1,350	2,150	3,050	6,250	14,000	60,000	
1880S 506,250	1,200	1,200	1,200	1,200	1,200	1,650	
1881 . . . . (40). . . .3,877,220	1,200	1,200	1,200	1,200	1,200	1,350	33,500
1881CC 24,015	1,650	2,800	4,000	6,250	8,000	42,000	
18810 8,350	1,600	2,250	3,250	4,950	10,500	—	
1881S 970,000	1,200	1,200	1,200	1,200	1,200	1,650	
1882 . . . . (40). . . .2,324,440	1,200	1,200	1,200	1,200	1,200	1,300	33,500
1882CC 6,764	2,800	5,250	7,500	17,000	28,000	64,500	
18820 10,820	1,400	1,650	2,250	6,750	8,250	39,000	
1882S 132,000	1,200	1,200	1,200	1,200	1,200	1,650	
1883 . . . . (40). 208,700	1,200	1,200	1,200	1,200	1,200	1,350	33,500
1883CC 12,000	2,050	3,500	6,250	17,000	30,000	—	
18830 800	23,500	42,000	78,000	148,500	180,000	—	
1883S 38,000	1,200	1,200	1,200	1,250	1,300	6,750	
1884 . . . . (45). 76,860	1,200	1,200	1,200	1,200	1,250	3,050	33,500
1884CC 9,925	1,650	2,950	5,500	12,000	17,000	64,500	
1884S 124,250	1,200	1,200	1,200	1,200	1,250	2,800	
1885 . . . . (65). . . .253,462	1,200	1,200	1,200	1,200	1,200	1,350	28,000
1885S 228,000	1,200	1,200	1,200	1,200	1,200	1,350	
1886 . . . . (60). . . .236,100	1,200	1,200	1,200	1,200	1,200	1,750	33,500
1886S 826,000	1,200	1,200	1,200	1,200	1,200	1,350	
1887 . . . . (80). 53,600	1,200	1,200	1,300	1,350	1,500	5,750	33,500
1887S 817,000	1,200	1,200	1,200	1,200	1,200	1,300	
1888 . . . . (75). . . .132,921	1,200	1,200	1,200	1,200	1,200	5,000	31,500
18880 21,335	1,250	1,250	1,250	1,350	1,400	6,250	
1888S 648,700	1,200	1,200	1,200	1,200	1,200	1,350	
1889 . . . . (45). 4,440	1,300	1,350	1,550	2,250	3,150	9,500	33,500
1889S 425,400	1,200	1,200	1,200	1,200	1,200	1,300	
1890 . . . . (63). 57,980	1,200	1,200	1,200	1,200	1,200	2,600	23,500
1890CC 17,500	1,400	1,850	2,550	4,650	5,500	20,500	
1891 . . . . (48). 91,820	1,200	1,200	1,200	1,200	1,200	1,850	23,500

EAGLES ($10)

	Mintage	VF-20	EF-40	AU-50	AU-58	MS-60	MS-63	PF-63
1891CC	103,732	$1,300	$1,650	$2,050	$2,600	$2,800	$6,750	
1892 ......(72)	797,480	1,200	1,200	1,200	1,200	1,200	1,300	$23,500
1892CC	40,000	1,550	1,750	2,250	4,650	7,000	28,000	
1892O	28,688	1,250	1,250	1,250	1,350	1,350	8,500	
1892S	115,500	1,200	1,200	1,200	1,200	1,200	2,250	
1893 ......(55)	1,840,840	1,200	1,200	1,200	1,200	1,200	1,300	23,500
1893CC	14,000	1,850	3,150	4,650	10,500	18,000	—	
1893O	17,000	1,250	1,250	1,300	1,350	1,400	5,250	
1893S	141,350	1,200	1,200	1,200	1,200	1,200	1,750	
1894 ......(43)	2,470,735	1,200	1,200	1,200	1,200	1,200	1,300	23,500
1894O	107,500	1,250	1,250	1,250	1,300	1,350	5,250	
1894S	25,000	1,200	1,200	1,250	2,050	3,900	—	
1895 ......(56)	567,770	1,200	1,200	1,200	1,200	1,200	1,300	14,000
1895O	98,000	1,250	1,250	1,300	1,350	1,500	6,250	
1895S	49,000	1,200	1,200	1,250	1,350	2,800	8,000	
1896 ......(78)	76,270	1,200	1,200	1,200	1,200	1,200	1,350	14,000
1896S	123,750	1,200	1,200	1,200	1,200	1,550	7,000	
1897 ......(69)	1,000,090	1,200	1,200	1,200	1,200	1,200	1,300	15,000
1897O	42,500	1,250	1,250	1,300	1,450	1,650	5,750	
1897S	234,750	1,200	1,200	1,200	1,200	1,200	4,450	
1898 ......(67)	812,130	1,200	1,200	1,200	1,200	1,200	1,300	14,000
1898S	473,600	1,200	1,200	1,200	1,200	1,200	1,650	
1899 ......(86)	1,262,219	1,200	1,200	1,200	1,200	1,200	1,300	12,500
1899O	37,047	1,250	1,250	1,300	1,350	1,550	7,750	
1899S	841,000	1,200	1,200	1,200	1,200	1,200	1,650	
1900 ......(120)	293,840	1,200	1,200	1,200	1,200	1,200	1,300	12,500
1900S	81,000	1,200	1,200	1,200	1,250	1,400	3,000	
1901 ......(85)	1,718,740	1,200	1,200	1,200	1,200	1,200	1,300	12,500
1901O	72,041	1,250	1,250	1,300	1,350	1,400	2,550	
1901S	2,812,750	1,200	1,200	1,200	1,200	1,200	1,300	
1902 ......(113)	82,400	1,200	1,200	1,200	1,200	1,200	1,300	12,500
1902S	469,500	1,200	1,200	1,200	1,200	1,200	1,300	
1903 ......(96)	125,830	1,200	1,200	1,200	1,200	1,200	1,300	12,500
1903O	112,771	1,250	1,250	1,300	1,350	1,350	1,950	
1903S	538,000	1,200	1,200	1,200	1,200	1,200	1,300	
1904 ......(108)	161,930	1,200	1,200	1,200	1,200	1,200	1,300	12,500
1904O	108,950	1,250	1,250	1,300	1,350	1,350	1,950	
1905 ......(86)	200,992	1,200	1,200	1,200	1,200	1,200	1,300	13,500
1905S	369,250	1,200	1,200	1,200	1,200	1,200	3,900	
1906 ......(77)	165,420	1,200	1,200	1,200	1,200	1,200	1,300	12,500
1906D	981,000	1,200	1,200	1,200	1,200	1,200	1,300	
1906O	86,895	1,250	1,250	1,300	1,350	1,650	4,650	
1906S	457,000	1,200	1,200	1,200	1,200	1,250	1,650	
1907 ......(74)	1,203,899	1,200	1,200	1,200	1,200	1,200	1,300	12,500
1907D	1,030,000	1,200	1,200	1,200	1,200	1,200	1,300	
1907S	210,500	1,200	1,200	1,200	1,200	1,200	2,700	

INDIAN HEAD (1907–1933)

VF-20 Very Fine: Bonnet feathers worn near band. Wear visible on high points of hair.

EF-40 Extremely Fine: Slight wear on cheekbone and headdress feathers. Slight wear visible on eagle's eye and left wing.

AU-50 About Uncirculated: Trace of wear on hair above eye and on forehead.

AU-55 Choice About Uncirculated: Evidence of friction on design high points. Much of original mint luster present.

MS-60 Uncirculated: No trace of wear. Light blemishes.

MS-63 Choice Uncirculated: Some distracting contact marks or blemishes in prime focal areas. Impaired luster possible.

Matte PF-63 Choice Proof: Matte surfaces with few blemishes in secondary focal places. No major flaws.

No Motto
Mintmark is above left tip of branch on 1908-D No Motto.

With Motto
IN GOD WE TRUST
Mintmark is at left of arrow points.

Gem Uncirculated (MS-65) coins are rare, and dealers usually pay substantial premiums for them.

	Mintage	EF-40	AU-50	AU-58	MS-60	MS-63	MS-64
1907, Wire Rim, Periods	500	$17,000	$26,000	$33,500	$35,500	$46,500	$55,000
1907, Rounded Rim, Periods Before and After •E•PLURIBUS•UNUM•	50	37,000	44,500	73,500	78,000	126,000	234,000
1907, No Periods	239,406	1,250	1,250	1,250	1,300	1,900	3,350
1908, No Motto	33,500	1,250	1,250	1,300	1,350	4,450	7,000
1908D, No Motto	210,000	1,250	1,250	1,300	1,400	5,750	10,500

Variety 2 – Motto on Reverse (1908–1933)

	Mintage	EF-40	AU-50	AU-58	MS-60	MS-63	MS-64	MS-65	MATTE PF-63
1908 . . . . (116)	341,370	$1,250	$1,250	$1,300	$1,300	$1,700	$2,800	$6,250	$25,000
1908D	836,500	1,250	1,250	1,300	1,350	4,650	9,000	21,500	
1908S	59,850	1,350	1,400	2,400	3,900	9,500	12,000	19,500	
1909 . . . . (74)	184,789	1,250	1,250	1,250	1,300	2,250	5,500	9,750	25,000
1909D	121,540	1,250	1,250	1,300	1,350	3,700	8,250	21,500	
1909S	292,350	1,250	1,300	1,500	1,550	4,450	6,250	18,000	
1910 . . . . (204)	318,500	1,250	1,250	1,250	1,300	1,350	1,600	6,000	25,000
1910D	2,356,640	1,250	1,250	1,250	1,300	1,500	1,650	5,750	
1910S	811,000	1,250	1,250	1,300	1,400	5,500	10,500	46,500	
1911 . . . . (95)	505,500	1,250	1,250	1,250	1,300	1,300	1,550	5,000	23,500
1911D	30,100	1,750	2,450	4,950	5,250	13,500	60,500	180,000	
1911S	51,000	1,400	1,500	2,600	3,050	12,000	13,000	20,500	
1912 . . . . (83)	405,000	1,250	1,250	1,250	1,300	1,600	2,750	8,250	25,000
1912S	300,000	1,250	1,250	1,500	1,550	5,750	6,750	28,000	
1913 . . . . (71)	442,000	1,250	1,250	1,250	1,300	1,350	2,150	6,750	23,500
1913S	66,000	1,400	1,500	2,900	3,700	15,500	25,500	121,500	
1914 . . . . (50)	151,000	1,250	1,250	1,250	1,300	1,400	3,800	7,750	25,000
1914D	343,500	1,250	1,250	1,250	1,300	1,850	3,350	8,250	
1914S	208,000	1,250	1,300	1,400	1,450	4,850	8,500	27,000	
1915 . . . . (75)	351,000	1,250	1,250	1,250	1,300	1,650	3,550	6,750	27,000
1915S	59,000	1,500	1,850	4,300	5,250	13,500	18,000	57,000	
1916S	138,500	1,250	1,300	1,400	2,050	5,000	7,750	20,500	
1920S	126,500	33,500	38,000	55,000	73,500	121,500	180,000	324,000	
1926	1,014,000	1,250	1,250	1,250	1,300	1,300	1,500	2,450	
1930S	96,000	21,500	24,000	30,500	35,500	49,500	71,000	83,000	
1932	4,463,000	1,250	1,250	1,250	1,300	1,300	1,500	2,450	
1933	312,500	—	121,500	130,500	157,500	216,000	324,000	450,000	

This largest denomination of all regular United States issues was authorized to be coined by the Act of March 3, 1849. The coin's weight was set at 516 grains, and its fineness at .900. A single twenty-dollar gold specimen of 1849 resides in the Smithsonian.

LIBERTY HEAD (1850–1907)

VF-20 Very Fine: LIBERTY on crown bold; prongs on crown defined; lower half worn flat. Hair worn about ear.

EF-40 Extremely Fine: Trace of wear on rounded prongs of crown and down hair curls. Minor bagmarks.

AU-50 About Uncirculated: Trace of wear on hair over eye and on coronet.

AU-55 Choice About Uncirculated: Evidence of friction on design high points. Some of original mint luster present.

MS-60 Uncirculated: No trace of wear. Light blemishes.

MS-63 Choice Uncirculated: Some distracting marks or blemishes in focal areas. Impaired luster possible.

PF-63 Choice Proof: Reflective surfaces with only a few blemishes in secondary focal areas. No major flaws.

Without Motto on Reverse (1850–1866)

Mintmark is below eagle.

	Mintage	VF-20	EF-40	AU-50	AU-58	MS-60	MS-63	PF-63
1850	1,170,261	$2,500	$2,900	$3,250	$7,500	$13,500	$50,500	
1850O	141,000	4,100	6,000	9,500	33,500	46,500	—	
1851	2,087,155	2,400	2,450	2,500	3,650	5,750	26,000	
1851O	315,000	2,500	3,150	3,900	12,000	19,500	87,500	
1852	2,053,026	2,400	2,450	2,650	2,800	4,100	22,500	
1852O	190,000	2,600	3,700	5,250	9,000	24,000	112,500	
1853	1,261,326	2,400	2,450	2,500	3,700	4,250	31,000	
1853O	71,000	3,150	4,650	8,250	20,500	33,500	117,000	
1854	757,899	2,400	2,450	2,500	2,700	4,100	30,000	
1854O	3,250	112,500	180,000	270,000	405,000	—	—	
1854S	141,468	4,300	7,750	9,750	18,000	22,500	46,500	
1855	364,666	2,400	2,450	2,750	5,250	8,500	44,500	
1855O	8,000	12,000	28,000	41,000	78,000	99,000	—	
1855S	879,675	2,400	2,450	2,650	3,100	4,650	20,500	
1856	329,878	2,400	2,550	2,850	4,450	7,000	35,500	
1856O	2,250	144,000	202,500	292,500	382,500	—	—	
1856S	1,189,750	2,400	2,450	2,500	3,050	5,250	14,500	
1857	439,375	2,400	2,450	2,500	2,800	3,650	33,500	
1857O	30,000	5,000	7,000	12,000	26,000	64,500	180,000	
1857S (a)	970,500	2,400	2,450	2,500	2,600	2,900	5,500	
1858	211,714	2,500	2,750	2,850	5,250	8,000	41,000	
1858O	35,250	6,250	9,000	12,000	31,500	46,500	162,000	
1858S	846,710	2,400	2,550	2,600	3,050	4,850	43,000	
1859	(80)	43,597	3,350	6,250	9,000	15,500	19,000	—	$202,500
1859O	9,100	15,000	23,500	28,000	72,000	112,500	—	
1859S	636,445	2,400	2,450	2,700	6,250	6,500	88,500	
1860	(59)	577,611	2,400	2,450	2,600	2,800	4,300	19,000	148,500
1860O	6,600	15,000	26,000	35,500	77,500	108,000	—	
1860S	544,950	2,400	2,650	2,800	4,200	5,450	41,000	

a. Different size mintmarks exists; the Large S variety is rarest.

Chart continued on next page.

	Mintage	VF-20	EF-40	AU-50	AU-58	MS-60	MS-63	PF-63
1861 . . . . (66) 2,976,387		$2,400	$2,450	$2,500	$2,600	$3,050	$20,500	$148,500
1861O 17,741		19,000	28,000	42,000	70,000	193,500	—	
1861S 768,000		2,400	2,700	2,750	4,650	8,250	46,500	
1862 . . . .(35) 92,098		5,750	11,500	19,000	30,000	33,500	87,500	148,500
1862S 854,173		2,400	2,700	2,900	5,250	9,500	51,500	
1863 . . . .(30) 142,760		4,300	6,250	9,500	18,000	23,500	83,000	148,500
1863S 966,570		2,400	2,700	2,750	4,650	5,250	39,000	
1864 . . . .(50) 204,235		3,550	5,250	8,000	16,000	20,500	60,500	148,500
1864S 793,660		2,400	2,450	2,600	5,500	6,000	42,000	
1865 . . . .(25) 351,175		2,400	2,700	2,750	5,750	7,000	15,000	148,500
1865S 1,042,500		2,400	2,600	2,750	3,700	4,650	13,500	
1866S 120,000		9,500	17,000	24,000	66,000	126,000	—	

Motto Above Eagle (1866–1907)
Value TWENTY D. (1866–1876)

	Mintage	VF-20	EF-40	AU-50	AU-58	MS-60	MS-63	PF-63
1866 . . . .(30) 698,745		$2,400	$2,500	$2,650	$5,250	$6,750	$44,500	$108,000
1866S 842,250		2,400	2,450	2,800	7,500	9,500	—	
1867 . . . .(50) 251,015		2,400	2,400	2,600	4,300	4,950	23,500	78,000
1867S 920,750		2,400	2,400	2,500	3,800	8,000	66,000	
1868 . . . .(25) 98,575		2,400	2,400	2,800	8,000	12,500	15,000	50,500	78,000
1868S 837,500		2,400	2,400	2,400	3,050	5,250	41,000	
1869 . . . .(25) 175,130		2,400	2,450	2,600	7,250	9,500	33,500	78,000
1869S 686,750		2,400	2,400	2,450	3,550	5,250	28,000	
1870 . . . .(35) 155,150		2,400	2,650	4,200	7,250	8,000	40,000	78,000
1870CC 3,789		252,000	351,000	720,000	1,620,000	—	—	
1870S 982,000		2,400	2,400	2,400	3,050	4,100	46,500	
1871 . . . .(30) 80,120		2,450	2,850	4,100	7,500	9,500	37,000	78,000
1871CC 17,387		30,000	34,500	53,500	99,000	117,000	270,000	
1871S 928,000		2,400	2,400	2,400	2,450	4,350	16,500	
1872 . . . .(30) 251,850		2,400	2,400	2,400	2,550	3,800	21,500	78,000
1872CC 26,900		6,250	8,750	12,500	35,500	83,000	—	
1872S 780,000		2,400	2,400	2,400	2,550	2,900	28,000	
1873 . . . .(25) 1,709,800		2,400	2,400	2,400	2,450	2,450	4,950	78,000
1873CC 22,410		2,800	9,750	15,500	22,500	44,500	112,500	
1873S 1,040,600		2,400	2,400	2,400	2,450	2,650	16,000	
1874 . . . .(20) 366,780		2,400	2,400	2,400	2,950	3,050	17,000	78,000
1874CC 115,085		2,550	3,450	4,350	9,000	16,000	—	
1874S 1,214,000		2,400	2,400	2,400	2,450	2,650	21,000	
1875 . . . .(20) 295,720		2,400	2,400	2,400	2,450	2,600	8,500	108,000
1875CC 111,151		2,550	3,150	3,900	6,250	9,000	30,000	
1875S 1,230,000		2,400	2,400	2,400	2,450	2,650	7,500	
1876 . . . .(45) 583,860		2,400	2,400	2,400	2,450	2,850	7,000	78,000
1876CC 138,441		2,650	3,350	4,200	6,500	9,000	41,000	
1876S 1,597,000		2,400	2,400	2,400	2,450	2,450	4,950	

Value TWENTY DOLLARS (1877–1907)

	Mintage	VF-20	EF-40	AU-50	AU-58	MS-60	MS-63	PF-63
1877 . . . . (20)	. .397,650	$2,350	$2,350	$2,400	$2,400	$2,400	$11,500	$37,000
1877CC	. .42,565	2,650	4,650	7,000	18,000	26,000	—	
1877S	1,735,000	2,350	2,350	2,400	2,400	2,400	9,750	
1878 . . . . (20)	. .543,625	2,350	2,350	2,400	2,400	2,400	8,500	50,500
1878CC	. .13,180	6,750	12,500	15,500	28,000	62,500	—	
1878S	1,739,000	2,350	2,350	2,400	2,400	2,400	10,000	
1879 . . . . (30)	. .207,600	2,350	2,350	2,400	2,450	2,600	19,000	37,000
1879CC	. .10,708	8,500	12,500	15,500	26,000	55,000		
18790	. .2,325	37,000	47,500	66,000	103,500	115,000	225,000	
1879S	1,223,800	2,350	2,350	2,400	2,400	2,450	24,000	
1880 . . . . (36)	. . .51,420	2,350	2,350	2,550	4,100	8,500	28,000	37,000
1880S	. .836,000	2,350	2,350	2,400	2,400	2,450	15,000	
1881 . . . . (61)	. . .2,199	22,500	30,500	48,000	92,000	108,000	—	59,000
1881S	. .727,000	2,350	2,350	2,400	2,400	2,450	14,500	
1882 . . . . (59)	 571	37,000	68,000	87,500	106,000	112,500	—	37,000
1882CC	. .39,140	2,700	3,700	5,500	8,500	9,500	87,500	
1882S	1,125,000	2,350	2,350	2,400	2,400	2,400	8,250	
1883, Proof only . . . (92)	. . . .							69,000
1883CC	. .59,962	2,800	3,600	4,650	7,000	8,500	44,500	
1883S	1,189,000	2,350	2,350	2,400	2,400	2,450	5,500	
1884, Proof only . . . (71)	. . . .							108,000
1884CC	. .81,139	2,500	3,000	4,000	6,250	7,500	35,500	
1884S	. .916,000	2,350	2,350	2,400	2,400	2,500	4,100	
1885 . . . . (77)	 751	17,000	26,000	41,000	57,000	70,000	117,000	33,500
1885CC	. .9,450	6,750	13,000	21,000	24,000	30,000	126,000	
1885S	. .683,500	2,350	2,350	2,400	2,400	2,400	4,000	
1886 . . . . (106)	1,000	32,500	60,000	73,500	103,500	117,000	135,000	37,000
1887, Proof only . . (121)	. . . .							101,000
1887S	. .283,000	2,350	2,350	2,400	2,400	2,400	7,000	
1888 . . . . (105)	. .226,161	2,350	2,350	2,400	2,400	2,400	9,500	37,000
1888S	. .859,600	2,350	2,350	2,400	2,400	2,400	4,050	
1889 . . . . (41)	. . .44,070	2,350	2,350	2,400	2,400	2,500	14,500	43,000
1889CC	. .30,945	2,800	4,100	6,000	8,500	9,000	46,500	
1889S	. .774,700	2,350	2,350	2,400	2,400	2,400	3,250	
1890 . . . . (55)	. . .75,940	2,350	2,350	2,400	2,400	2,400	7,750	35,500
1890CC	. .91,209	2,600	2,900	3,650	4,950	6,250	35,500	
1890S	. .802,750	2,350	2,350	2,400	2,400	2,400	4,400	
1891 . . . . (52)	. . .1,390	22,500	30,500	39,500	60,500	66,000	121,500	37,000
1891CC	. . .5,000	13,000	19,500	23,500	30,000	31,500	166,500	
1891S	1,288,125	2,350	2,350	2,400	2,400	2,400	3,150	
1892 . . . . (93)	. . .4,430	3,700	6,250	8,500	14,000	19,000	35,500	35,500

Chart continued on next page.

	Mintage	VF-20	EF-40	AU-50	AU-58	MS-60	MS-63	PF-63
1892CC	27,265	$2,650	$3,450	$4,450	$8,500	$11,000	$37,000	
1892S	930,150	2,350	2,350	2,400	2,400	2,400	2,800	
1893 ....(59)	344,280	2,350	2,350	2,400	2,400	2,400	3,350	$92,000
1893CC	18,402	3,250	4,650	5,750	9,750	10,500	44,500	
1893S	996,175	2,350	2,350	2,400	2,400	2,400	2,650	
1894 ....(50)	1,368,940	2,350	2,350	2,400	2,400	2,400	2,750	33,500
1894S	1,048,550	2,350	2,350	2,400	2,400	2,400	2,900	
1895 ....(51)	1,114,605	2,350	2,350	2,400	2,400	2,400	2,750	37,000
1895S	1,143,500	2,350	2,350	2,400	2,400	2,400	2,800	
1896 ....(128)	792,535	2,350	2,350	2,400	2,400	2,400	2,800	33,500
1896S	1,403,925	2,350	2,350	2,400	2,400	2,400	2,800	
1897 ....(86)	1,383,175	2,350	2,350	2,400	2,400	2,400	2,800	33,500
1897S	1,470,250	2,350	2,350	2,400	2,400	2,400	2,600	
1898 ....(75)	170,395	2,350	2,350	2,400	2,400	2,600	3,950	33,500
1898S	2,575,175	2,350	2,350	2,400	2,400	2,400	2,650	
1899 ....(84)	1,669,300	2,350	2,350	2,400	2,400	2,400	2,650	33,500
1899S	2,010,300	2,350	2,350	2,400	2,400	2,400	2,800	
1900 ....(124)	1,874,460	2,350	2,350	2,400	2,400	2,400	2,550	33,500
1900S	2,459,500	2,350	2,350	2,400	2,400	2,400	2,650	
1901 ....(96)	111,430	2,350	2,350	2,400	2,400	2,400	2,550	33,500
1901S	1,596,000	2,350	2,350	2,400	2,400	2,400	2,950	
1902 ....(114)	31,140	2,350	2,350	2,400	2,500	2,500	11,500	33,500
1902S	1,753,625	2,350	2,350	2,400	2,400	2,400	3,650	
1903 ....(158)	287,270	2,350	2,350	2,400	2,400	2,400	2,650	33,500
1903S	954,000	2,350	2,350	2,400	2,400	2,400	2,950	
1904 ....(98)	6,256,699	2,350	2,350	2,400	2,400	2,400	2,550	33,500
1904S	5,134,175	2,350	2,350	2,400	2,400	2,400	2,550	
1905 ....(92)	58,919	2,350	2,350	2,400	2,450	2,600	9,000	33,500
1905S	1,813,000	2,350	2,350	2,400	2,400	2,400	3,000	
1906 ....(94)	69,596	2,350	2,350	2,400	2,400	2,450	7,000	37,000
1906D	620,250	2,350	2,350	2,400	2,400	2,400	3,850	
1906S	2,065,750	2,350	2,350	2,400	2,400	2,400	2,800	
1907 ....(78)	1,451,786	2,350	2,350	2,400	2,400	2,400	2,600	33,500
1907D	842,250	2,350	2,350	2,400	2,400	2,400	3,050	
1907S	2,165,800	2,350	2,350	2,400	2,400	2,400	3,150	

SAINT-GAUDENS (1907–1933)

The twenty-dollar gold piece designed by Augustus Saint-Gaudens is considered by many to be the most beautiful United States coin. The first coins issued were slightly more than 12,000 high-relief pieces struck for general circulation. The relief is much higher than that of later issues and the date 1907 is in Roman numerals. A few of the Proof coins were made using the lettered-edge collar from the Ultra High Relief version. These can be distinguished by a pronounced bottom left serif on the N in UNUM, and other minor differences. Flat-relief double eagles were issued later in 1907 with Arabic numerals, and continued through 1933.

The field of the rare, Ultra High Relief experimental pieces is extremely concave and connects directly with the edge without any border, giving it a sharp knifelike appearance. Liberty's skirt shows two folds on the side of her right leg; the Capitol building in the background at left is very small; the sun, on the reverse side, has 14 rays, as opposed to the regular high-relief coins, which have only 13 rays extending from the sun. High-relief Proofs are trial or experimental pieces.

VF-20 Very Fine: Minor wear on Liberty's legs and toes. Eagle's left wing and breast feathers worn.
EF-40 Extremely Fine: Drapery lines on chest visible. Wear on left breast, knee, and below. Eagle's feathers on breast and right wing bold.
AU-50 About Uncirculated: Trace of wear on nose, breast, and knee. Wear visible on eagle's wings.
AU-55 Choice About Uncirculated: Evidence of friction on design high points. Most of mint luster remains.
MS-60 Uncirculated: No trace of wear. Light marks or blemishes.
MS-63 Select Uncirculated: Some distracting contact marks or blemishes in prime focal areas. Impaired luster possible.
Matte PF-63 Choice Proof: Matte surfaces with only a few blemishes in secondary focal places. No major flaws.

Ultra High Relief Pattern, MCMVII (1907)

	PF-66
1907, Ultra High Relief, Plain Edge *(unique)*.	—
1907, Ultra High Relief, Lettered Edge.	$2,025,000

No Motto IN GOD WE TRUST (1907–1908) and With Motto IN GOD WE TRUST (1908–1933)

High Relief, MCMVII (1907)

	Mintage	AU-50	AU-58	MS-60	MS-63	MS-64	MS-65	PF-63
1907, High Relief, Roman Numerals (MCMVII), Wire Rim	12,367	$9,250	$11,500	$13,000	$21,000	$28,000	$41,000	$37,000

Arabic Numerals (1907–1933) No Motto (1907–1908) With Motto IN GOD WE TRUST (1908–1933)

Mintmark is on obverse, above date. 1909, 9 Over 8

See next page for chart.

	Mintage	AU-50	AU-58	MS-60	MS-63	MS-64	MS-65	MATTE PF-63
1907	361,667	$2,400	$2,400	$2,500	$2,800	$2,900	$3,700	
1908	4,271,551	2,400	2,400	2,400	2,550	2,550	2,600	
1908D	663,750	2,400	2,400	2,400	2,750	3,000	6,750	
1908, With Motto (101)	156,258	2,350	2,350	2,400	2,950	4,950	11,500	$270,000
1908D, With Motto	349,500	2,350	2,350	2,400	2,750	3,000	6,000	
1908S, With Motto	22,000	4,150	6,500	8,000	24,000	32,500	64,500	
1909, 9 Over 8	*	2,500	2,500	2,500	4,650	9,750	34,500	
1909 (67)	161,282	2,350	2,350	2,400	3,900	9,500	34,500	43,500
1909D	52,500	2,500	2,900	3,700	8,250	9,500	34,500	
1909S	2,774,925	2,350	2,350	2,400	2,500	2,600	4,850	
1910 (167)	482,000	2,350	2,350	2,400	2,550	2,700	7,500	39,000
1910D	429,000	2,350	2,350	2,400	2,500	2,700	3,350	
1910S	2,128,250	2,350	2,350	2,400	2,550	2,900	7,500	
1911 (100)	197,250	2,350	2,350	2,400	2,700	3,500	12,500	39,000
1911D	846,500	2,350	2,350	2,400	2,550	2,650	2,800	
1911S	775,750	2,350	2,350	2,400	2,500	2,800	3,700	
1912 (74)	149,750	2,350	2,350	2,400	2,650	6,000	20,000	39,000
1913 (58)	168,780	2,350	2,350	2,400	2,950	5,500	40,000	39,000
1913D	393,500	2,350	2,350	2,400	2,700	2,700	4,900	
1913S	34,000	2,400	2,650	2,700	5,250	8,000	33,500	
1914 (70)	95,250	2,350	2,350	2,550	3,000	4,850	21,500	43,500
1914D	453,000	2,350	2,350	2,400	2,500	2,500	3,050	
1914S	1,498,000	2,350	2,350	2,400	2,500	2,550	3,000	
1915 (50)	152,000	2,350	2,350	2,450	2,900	4,850	20,000	43,000
1915S	567,500	2,350	2,350	2,400	2,550	2,700	2,800	
1916S	796,000	2,350	2,350	2,450	2,650	2,750	3,450	
1920	228,250	2,350	2,350	2,450	2,750	2,900	162,000	
1920S	558,000	31,500	46,500	55,000	99,000	162,000	486,000	
1921	528,500	44,000	72,000	77,500	234,000	297,000	540,000	
1922	1,375,500	2,350	2,350	2,400	2,500	2,500	3,050	
1922S	2,658,000	2,500	2,900	2,950	3,450	6,500	39,000	
1923	566,000	2,350	2,350	2,400	2,500	2,500	4,100	
1923D	1,702,250	2,350	2,350	2,400	2,500	2,500	2,900	
1924	4,323,500	2,350	2,350	2,400	2,500	2,500	2,600	
1924D	3,049,500	3,100	3,550	4,650	7,500	12,000	83,000	
1924S	2,927,500	3,250	4,650	6,000	10,500	17,500	92,000	
1925	2,831,750	2,350	2,350	2,400	2,500	2,500	2,700	
1925D	2,938,500	3,700	5,250	6,000	9,750	26,000	94,500	
1925S	3,776,500	4,300	6,250	6,750	13,000	46,500	162,000	
1926	816,750	2,350	2,350	2,400	2,500	2,500	3,000	
1926D	481,000	11,500	12,500	14,000	24,000	37,000	162,000	
1926S	2,041,500	2,850	3,550	3,900	7,000	8,500	20,500	
1927	2,946,750	2,350	2,350	2,400	2,500	2,500	2,600	
1927D	180,000	675,000	855,000	900,000	1,260,000	1,620,000	2,160,000	
1927S	3,107,000	17,500	23,500	26,500	49,500	97,000	180,000	
1928	8,816,000	2,350	2,350	2,400	2,500	2,500	2,600	
1929	1,779,750	20,500	29,000	31,500	41,000	60,500	83,000	
1930S	74,000	46,500	64,500	70,000	117,000	157,500	216,000	
1931	2,938,250	28,000	42,000	48,000	83,000	103,500	171,000	
1931D	106,500	37,000	51,500	60,500	88,500	105,500	162,000	
1932	1,101,750	41,000	57,000	60,500	101,000	129,500	151,000	
1933	445,500	—	—	—	—	—	16,200,000	

* Included in number below.

Collecting U.S. commemoratives is like gathering snapshots for an album of important events, places, and people in the nation's history, from historical events and landmarks to presidents and Olympic games.

All U.S. commemoratives are legal tender; in the case of silver and gold coins, their precious-metal value surpasses their face value. The weight and finenesses for commemoratives are the same as those for standard-issue clad, silver, and gold coins. Prices for modern commemoratives are for coins or sets in their original, unopened Mint packaging, as indicated by the initials OGP ("original government packaging") in the charts.

CLASSIC COMMEMORATIVE SILVER AND GOLD

(1892–1893) World's Columbian Exposition Half Dollar

	Mintage	AU-50	MS-60	MS-63	MS-65
1892, World's Columbian Exposition half dollar	950,000	$14.50	$27	$70	$195
1893, Same type	1,550,405	14.50	32	70	215

(1893) World's Columbian Exposition, Isabella Quarter Dollar

	Mintage	AU-50	MS-60	MS-63	MS-65
1893, World's Columbian Exposition, Chicago, quarter dollar . .	24,214	$200	$315	$525	$875

(1900) Lafayette Dollar

	Mintage	AU-50	MS-60	MS-63	MS-65
1900, Lafayette silver dollar	36,026	$385	$700	$1,250	$3,900

(1903) Louisiana Purchase Exposition

	Mintage	MS-60	MS-63	MS-65	MS-66
1903, Louisiana Purchase / Thomas Jefferson gold dollar.....	17,500	$450	$550	$825	$975
1903, Louisiana Purchase / William McKinley gold dollar	17,500	335	390	625	825

(1904–1905) Lewis and Clark Exposition

	Mintage	MS-60	MS-63	MS-65	MS-66
1904, Lewis and Clark Exposition gold dollar...............	10,025	$625	$775	$2,050	$3,700
1905, Lewis and Clark Exposition gold dollar...............	10,041	550	875	2,550	6,750

(1915) Panama-Pacific Exposition

	Mintage	AU-50	MS-60	MS-63	MS-65
1915S, Panama-Pacific Exposition half dollar	27,134	$330	$525	$775	$1,700

	Mintage	MS-60	MS-63	MS-65	MS-66
1915S, Panama-Pacific Exposition gold dollar..............	15,000	$390	$485	$825	$1,150
1915S, Panama-Pacific Exposition gold $2.50...............	6,749	2,050	3,000	4,000	5,250
1915S, Panama-Pacific Exposition gold $50 Round............	483	53,500	66,000	130,500	193,500

(1915) Panama-Pacific Exposition

	Mintage	MS-60	MS-63	MS-65	MS-66
1915S, Panama-Pacific Exposition gold $50 Octagonal 645		$53,500	$70,000	$126,000	$171,000

(1916–1917) McKinley Memorial

	Mintage	MS-60	MS-63	MS-65	MS-66
1916, McKinley Memorial gold dollar.	15,000	$285	$385	$500	$675
1917, McKinley Memorial gold dollar.	5,000	370	395	600	875

(1918) Illinois Centennial

	Mintage	AU-50	MS-60	MS-63	MS-65
1918, Illinois Centennial half dollar	100,058	$110	$135	$180	$350

(1920) Maine Centennial

	Mintage	AU-50	MS-60	MS-63	MS-65
1920, Maine Centennial half dollar	50,028	$90	$110	$160	$265

(1920–1921) Pilgrim Tercentenary

With 1921 in Field
on Obverse

	Mintage	AU-50	MS-60	MS-63	MS-65
1920, Pilgrim Tercentenary half dollar................. 152,112		$60	$65	$80	$200
1921, Same, With Date Added in Field 20,053		125	135	160	240

(1921) Missouri Centennial

With 2★4 in Field

	Mintage	AU-50	MS-60	MS-63	MS-65
1921, Missouri Centennial half dollar, "2★4" in Field 9,400		$490	$600	$800	$1,150
1921, Missouri Centennial half dollar, Plain............... 11,400		290	370	485	1,050

(1921) Alabama Centennial

Without 2X2 in Field

	Mintage	AU-50	MS-60	MS-63	MS-65
1921, Alabama Centennial half dollar, With "2X2" in Field of Obverse..... 6,006		$165	$245	$330	$775
1921, Alabama Centennial half dollar, Plain....................... 16,014		100	150	275	600

Star in Field

(1922) Grant Memorial

	Mintage	AU-50	MS-60	MS-63	MS-65
1922, Grant Memorial, With Star* half dollar	4,256	$775	$1,050	$2,000	$3,350
1922, Same type, No Star in Obverse Field	67,405	90	110	170	385

* Fake stars usually have a flattened spot on the reverse.

	Mintage	MS-60	MS-63	MS-65	MS-66
1922, Grant Memorial, With Star* gold dollar.	5,016	$775	$1,050	$1,550	$1,750
1922, Grant Memorial, No Star in Obverse Field	5,016	700	900	1,200	1,400

* Fake stars usually have a flattened spot on the reverse.

(1923) Monroe Doctrine Centennial

	Mintage	AU-50	MS-60	MS-63	MS-65
1923S, Monroe Doctrine Centennial half dollar	274,077	$34	$43	$65	$405

(1924) Huguenot-Walloon Tercentenary

	Mintage	AU-50	MS-60	MS-63	MS-65
1924, Huguenot-Walloon Tercentenary half dollar	142,080	$70	$80	$110	$130

(1925) Lexington-Concord Sesquicentennial

	Mintage	AU-50	MS-60	MS-63	MS-65
1925, Lexington-Concord Sesquicentennial half dollar....... 162,013		$55	$65	$80	$160

(1925) Stone Mountain Memorial

	Mintage	AU-50	MS-60	MS-63	MS-65
1925, Stone Mountain Memorial half dollar............. 1,314,709		$43	$60	$75	$170

(1925) California Diamond Jubilee

	Mintage	AU-50	MS-60	MS-63	MS-65
1925S, California Diamond Jubilee half dollar............. 86,594		$140	$155	$170	$415

(1925) Fort Vancouver Centennial

	Mintage	AU-50	MS-60	MS-63	MS-65
1925, Fort Vancouver Centennial half dollar 14,994		$200	$270	$305	$575

**(1926) Sesquicentennial
of American Independence**

	Mintage	AU-50	MS-60	MS-63	MS-65
1926, Sesquicentennial of American Independence half dollar	141,120	$60	$80	$90	$825
1926, Sesquicentennial of American Independence gold $2.50	46,019		485	975	3,650

(1926–1939) Oregon Trail Memorial

	Mintage	AU-50	MS-60	MS-63	MS-65
1926, Oregon Trail Memorial half dollar	47,955	$110	$130	$170	$215
1926S, Same type, S Mint	83,055	110	145	185	235
1928, Oregon Trail Memorial half dollar (same as 1926)	6,028	135	160	190	285
1933D, Oregon Trail Memorial half dollar	5,008	275	290	340	395
1934D, Oregon Trail Memorial half dollar	7,006	140	160	200	250
1936, Oregon Trail Memorial half dollar	10,006	130	150	190	240
1936S, Same type, S Mint	5,006	130	150	190	240
1937D, Oregon Trail Memorial half dollar	12,008	130	150	190	240
1938, Oregon Trail Memorial half dollar (same as 1926)	6,006	140	160	190	235
1938D, Same type, D Mint	6,005	130	150	190	240
1938S, Same type, S Mint	6,006	140	160	200	260
1939, Oregon Trail Memorial half dollar (same as 1926)	3,004	335	340	370	495
1939D, Same type, D Mint	3,004	335	340	370	405
1939S, Same type, S Mint	3,005	335	340	370	415
Oregon Trail Memorial half dollar, single type coin		100	115	140	180

(1927) Vermont Sesquicentennial

	Mintage	AU-50	MS-60	MS-63	MS-65
1927, Vermont Sesquicentennial (Battle of Bennington) half dollar . .	28,142	$175	$185	$200	$285

(1928) Hawaiian Sesquicentennial

	Mintage	AU-50	MS-60	MS-63	MS-65
1928, Hawaiian Sesquicentennial half dollar	10,008	$1,300	$1,750	$2,150	$3,000
1928, Hawaiian Sesquicentennial, Sandblast Proof Presentation Piece	(50)	—	—	10,000	20,000

(1934) Maryland Tercentenary

	Mintage	AU-50	MS-60	MS-63	MS-65
1934, Maryland Tercentenary half dollar	25,015	$100	$110	$130	$145

(1934–1938) Texas Independence Centennial

	Mintage	AU-50	MS-60	MS-63	MS-65
1934, Texas Independence Centennial half dollar	61,463	$105	$115	$135	$180
1935, Texas Independence Centennial half dollar (same as 1934)	9,996	105	115	125	200
1935D, Same type, D Mint	10,007	105	115	125	190
1935S, Same type, S Mint	10,008	105	115	125	170
1936, Texas Independence Centennial half dollar (same as 1934)	8,911	105	115	135	210
1936D, Same type, D Mint	9,039	105	115	125	170
1936S, Same type, S Mint	9,055	105	115	125	190
1937, Texas Independence Centennial half dollar (same as 1934)	6,571	105	120	130	180
1937D, Same type, D Mint	6,605	105	120	130	180
1937S, Same type, S Mint	6,637	105	120	140	200

	Mintage	AU-50	MS-60	MS-63	MS-65
1938, Texas Independence Centennial half dollar (same as 1934)..... 3,780		$160	$170	$200	$275
1938D, Same type, D Mint 3,775		160	170	200	330
1938S, Same type, S Mint................................. 3,814		160	170	205	285
Texas Independence Centennial half dollar, single type coin		88	90	100	140

(1934–1938) Daniel Boone Bicentennial   1934 Added on Reverse

	Mintage	AU-50	MS-60	MS-63	MS-65
1934, Daniel Boone Bicentennial half dollar..................... 10,007		$95	$105	$110	$135
1935, Daniel Boone Bicentennial half dollar..................... 10,010		95	105	110	140
1935D, Same type, D Mint 5,005		95	105	110	165
1935S, Same type, S Mint................................. 5,005		95	105	110	150
1935, Same as 1934 but Small 1934 on reverse................. 10,008		95	105	110	145
1935D, Same type, D Mint 2,003		190	215	275	450
1935S, Same type, S Mint................................. 2,004		190	240	315	525
1936, Daniel Boone Bicentennial half dollar (same as preceding) 12,012		95	105	110	140
1936D, Same type, D Mint 5,005		95	105	125	170
1936S, Same type, S Mint................................. 5,006		95	105	145	170
1937, Daniel Boone Bicentennial half dollar (same as preceding) 9,810		110	115	120	160
1937D, Same type, D Mint 2,506		175	180	195	285
1937S, Same type, S Mint................................. 2,506		175	180	200	310
1938, Daniel Boone Bicentennial half dollar (same as preceding) 2,100		240	250	270	330
1938D, Same type, D Mint 2,100		240	250	270	345
1938S, Same type, S Mint................................. 2,100		240	250	280	355
Daniel Boone Bicentennial half dollar, single type coin		88	95	100	120

(1935) Connecticut Tercentenary

	Mintage	AU-50	MS-60	MS-63	MS-65
1935, Connecticut Tercentenary half dollar 25,018		$160	$165	$185	$275

**(1935–1939)
Arkansas Centennial**

	Mintage	AU-50	MS-60	MS-63	MS-65
1935, Arkansas Centennial half dollar 13,012		$70	$75	$85	$145
1935D, Same type, D Mint 5,505		70	75	85	145
1935S, Same type, S Mint. 5,506		70	75	85	160
1936, Arkansas Centennial half dollar (same as 1935 but 1936 on rev) 9,660		70	75	85	160
1936D, Same type, D Mint 9,660		70	75	85	160
1936S, Same type, S Mint. 9,662		70	75	95	160
1937, Arkansas Centennial half dollar (same as 1935) 5,505		80	85	95	190
1937D, Same type, D mint 5,505		80	85	95	160
1937S, Same type, S mint. 5,506		80	85	110	215
1938, Arkansas Centennial half dollar (same as 1935) 3,156		100	105	120	180
1938D, Same type, D Mint 3,155		100	105	150	225
1938S, Same type, S Mint. 3,156		100	110	140	255
1939, Arkansas Centennial half dollar (same as 1935) 2,104		170	180	200	360
1939D, Same type, D Mint 2,104		170	180	240	315
1939S, Same type, S Mint. 2,105		170	180	210	460
Arkansas Centennial half dollar, single type coin.		70	75	85	125

**(1936) Arkansas
Centennial – Robinson**

	Mintage	AU-50	MS-60	MS-63	MS-65
1936, Arkansas Centennial (Robinson) half dollar 25,265		$75	$80	$85	$105

**(1935) Hudson, New
York, Sesquicentennial**

	Mintage	AU-50	MS-60	MS-63	MS-65
1935, Hudson, New York, Sesquicentennial half dollar 10,008		$525	$525	$550	$675

(1935–1936) California-Pacific International Exposition

	Mintage	AU-50	MS-60	MS-63	MS-65
1935S, California-Pacific International Exposition half dollar . . .	70,132	$75	$75	$90	$125
1936D, California-Pacific International Exposition half dollar . . .	30,092	75	80	105	165

(1935) Old Spanish Trail

	Mintage	AU-50	MS-60	MS-63	MS-65
1935, Old Spanish Trail half dollar.	10,008	$725	$775	$825	$1,050

(1936) Providence, Rhode Island, Tercentenary

	Mintage	AU-50	MS-60	MS-63	MS-65
1936, Providence, Rhode Island, Tercentenary half dollar	20,013	$70	$80	$110	$130
1936D, Same type, D Mint	15,010	70	80	100	120
1936S, Same type, S Mint.	15,011	75	85	110	130
Providence, Rhode Island, Tercentenary half dollar, single type coin . . .		65	68	72	90

(1936) Cleveland Centennial / Great Lakes Exposition

	Mintage	AU-50	MS-60	MS-63	MS-65
1936, Cleveland Centennial / Great Lakes Exposition half dollar	50,030	$65	$70	$80	$100

(1936) Wisconsin Territorial Centennial

	Mintage	AU-50	MS-60	MS-63	MS-65
1936, Wisconsin Territorial Centennial half dollar	25,015	$100	$110	$120	$145

(1936) Cincinnati Music Center

	Mintage	AU-50	MS-60	MS-63	MS-65
1936, Cincinnati Music Center half dollar	5,005	$220	$240	$275	$330
1936D, Same type, D Mint	5,005	220	240	260	330
1936S, Same type, S Mint.	5,006	220	240	270	370
Cincinnati Music Center half dollar, single type coin		190	200	240	300

COMMEMORATIVES

(1936) Long Island Tercentenary

	Mintage	AU-50	MS-60	MS-63	MS-65
1936, Long Island Tercentenary half dollar	81,826	$60	$70	$75	$115

(1936) York County, Maine, Tercentenary

	Mintage	AU-50	MS-60	MS-63	MS-65
1936, York County, Maine, Tercentenary half dollar.	25,015	$105	$110	$115	$145

(1936) Bridgeport, Connecticut, Centennial

	Mintage	AU-50	MS-60	MS-63	MS-65
1936, Bridgeport, Connecticut, Centennial half dollar	25,015	$100	$110	$135	$190

(1936) Lynchburg, Virginia, Sesquicentennial

	Mintage	AU-50	MS-60	MS-63	MS-65
1936, Lynchburg, Virginia, Sesquicentennial half dollar.	20,013	$120	$135	$165	$190

(1936) Elgin, Illinois, Centennial

	Mintage	AU-50	MS-60	MS-63	MS-65
1936, Elgin, Illinois, Centennial half dollar	20,015	$115	$125	$150	$165

(1936) Albany, New York, Charter

	Mintage	AU-50	MS-60	MS-63	MS-65
1936, Albany, New York, Charter half dollar	17,671	$150	$155	$175	$215

(1936) San Francisco – Oakland Bay Bridge Opening

	Mintage	AU-50	MS-60	MS-63	MS-65
1936S, San Francisco–Oakland Bay Bridge Opening half dollar	71,424	$115	$125	$150	$205

(1936) Delaware Tercentenary

	Mintage	AU-50	MS-60	MS-63	MS-65
1936, Delaware Tercentenary half dollar	20,993	$155	$160	$175	$200

(1936) Columbia, South Carolina, Sesquicentennial

	Mintage	AU-50	MS-60	MS-63	MS-65
1936, Columbia, South Carolina, Sesquicentennial half dollar 9,007		$135	$160	$165	$175
1936D, Same type, D Mint 8,009		135	145	150	165
1936S, Same type, S Mint................................. 8,007		135	160	160	190
Columbia, South Carolina, Sesquicentennial half dollar, single type coin		120	140	145	175

(1936) Battle of Gettysburg Anniversary

	Mintage	AU-50	MS-60	MS-63	MS-65
1936, Battle of Gettysburg Anniversary half dollar 26,928		$365	$380	$460	$600

(1936) Norfolk, Virginia, Bicentennial

	Mintage	AU-50	MS-60	MS-63	MS-65
1936, Norfolk, Virginia, Bicentennial half dollar 16,936		$200	$210	$220	$240

(1937) Roanoke Island, North Carolina, 350th Anniversary

	Mintage	AU-50	MS-60	MS-63	MS-65
1937, Roanoke Island, NC, 350th Anniversary half dollar...........	29,030	$120	$125	$130	$160

(1937) Battle of Antietam Anniversary

	Mintage	AU-50	MS-60	MS-63	MS-65
1937, Battle of Antietam Anniversary half dollar	18,028	$385	$405	$435	$500

(1938) New Rochelle, New York, 250th Anniversary

	Mintage	AU-50	MS-60	MS-63	MS-65
1938, New Rochelle, NY, 250th Anniversary half dollar.......	15,266	$175	$185	$215	$265

(1946) Iowa Centennial

	Mintage	AU-50	MS-60	MS-63	MS-65
1946, Iowa Centennial half dollar	100,057	$65	$70	$70	$95

(1946–1951) Booker T. Washington Memorial

	Mintage	AU-50	MS-60	MS-63	MS-65
1946, Booker T. Washington Memorial half dollar **(a)**	700,546	$14.50	$18	$22	$27
1946D, Same type, D Mint	50,000	14.50	18	22	32
1946S, Same type, S Mint	500,279	14.50	18	22	27
1947, Booker T. Washington Memorial half dollar (same as 1946)	6,000	14.50	18	27	40
1947D, Same type, D Mint	6,000	14.50	18	27	40
1947S, Same type, S Mint	6,000	14.50	18	27	55
1948, Booker T. Washington Memorial half dollar (same as 1946)	8,005	14.50	18	27	45
1948D, Same type, D Mint	8,005	19.00	22	27	65
1948S, Same type, S Mint	8,005	19.00	22	27	36
1949, Booker T. Washington Memorial half dollar (same as 1946)	6,004	23.00	27	43	80
1949D, Same type, D Mint	6,004	28.00	34	38	43
1949S, Same type, S Mint	6,004	28.00	36	43	70
1950, Booker T. Washington Memorial half dollar (same as 1946)	6,004	19.00	23	28	31
1950D, Same type, D Mint	6,004	17.00	20	34	55
1950S, Same type, S Mint	62,091	17.00	20	23	45
1951, Booker T. Washington Memorial half dollar (same as 1946) . .	210,082	14.50	19	22	27
1951D, Same type, D Mint	7,004	19.00	27	40	60
1951S, Same type, S Mint	7,004	17.00	23	35	45
Booker T. Washington Memorial, single type coin		12.00	13	15	40

a. Minted; quantity melted unknown.

(1951–1954) Carver/Washington Commemorative

	Mintage	AU-50	MS-60	MS-63	MS-65
1951, Carver/Washington half dollar	20,018	$16	$22	$29	$55
1951D, Same type, D Mint	10,004	19	25	34	55
1951S, Same type, S Mint	10,004	19	25	39	50
1952, Carver/Washington half dollar (same as 1951)	1,106,292	16	22	30	45
1952D, Same type, D Mint	8,006	21	27	39	50
1952S, Same type, S Mint	8,006	21	27	34	55

Chart continued on next page.

	Mintage	AU-50	MS-60	MS-63	MS-65
1953, Carver/Washington half dollar (same as 1951)	8,003	$19	$26	$34	$55
1953D, Same type, D Mint	8,003	16	31	39	55
1953S, Same type, S Mint	88,020	19	25	32	55
1954, Carver/Washington half dollar (same as 1951)	12,006	18	24	32	48
1954D, Same type, D Mint	12,006	18	24	32	50
1954S, Same type, S Mint	42,024	18	24	32	50
Carver/Washington half dollar, single type coin		12	13	15	40

MODERN COMMEMORATIVES

(1982) George Washington 250th Anniversary of Birth

	Mintage	OGP
1982D, George Washington 250th Anniversary silver half dollar, Uncirculated	2,210,458	$11
1982S, George Washington 250th Anniversary silver half dollar, Proof	(4,894,044)	11

(1983–1984) Los Angeles Olympiad

COMMEMORATIVES

	Mintage	OGP
1983P, Discus Thrower silver dollar, Uncirculated	294,543	$26
1983D, Discus Thrower silver dollar, Uncirculated	174,014	26
1983S, Discus Thrower silver dollar, Uncirculated	174,014	26
1983S, Discus Thrower silver dollar, Proof.	(1,577,025)	26
1984P, Olympic Coliseum silver dollar, Uncirculated.	217,954	26
1984D, Olympic Coliseum silver dollar, Uncirculated	116,675	26
1984S, Olympic Coliseum silver dollar, Uncirculated	116,675	26
1984S, Olympic Coliseum silver dollar, Proof.	(1,801,210)	26
1984P, Olympic Torch Bearers gold $10, Proof.	(33,309)	1,250
1984D, Olympic Torch Bearers gold $10, Proof	(34,533)	1,250
1984S, Olympic Torch Bearers gold $10, Proof	(48,551)	1,250
1984W, Olympic Torch Bearers gold $10, Uncirculated	75,886	1,250
1984W, Olympic Torch Bearers gold $10, Proof	(381,085)	1,250
1983–1984 2-coin set. Both Proof silver dollars		50
1983–1984 6-coin set. One each of Proof and Uncirculated silver dollars, Proof and Uncirculated gold $10 **(a)**		2,550
1983 3-piece Collector set. P, D, and S Uncirculated silver dollars.		75
1984 3-piece Collector set. P, D, and S Uncirculated silver dollars.		75
1983–1984 Gold and Silver set. Uncirculated 1983 and 1984 silver dollars and Uncirculated gold $10 . .		1,300
1983–1984 Gold and Silver set. Proof 1983 and 1984 silver dollars and Proof gold $10.		1,300

Note: Proof Los Angeles Olympiad silver dollars for 1983 and 1984 were also included in Prestige Sets; see page 248.
a. Packaged in a cherrywood box.

(1986) Statue of Liberty Centennial

	Mintage	OGP
1986D, Statue of Liberty Centennial clad half dollar, Uncirculated	928,008	1.70
1986S, Statue of Liberty Centennial clad half dollar, Proof.	(6,925,627)	1.70
1986P, Statue of Liberty Centennial silver dollar, Uncirculated	723,635	26.00
1986S, Statue of Liberty Centennial silver dollar, Proof	(6,414,638)	26.00
1986W, Statue of Liberty Centennial gold $5, Uncirculated	95,248	575.00
1986W, Statue of Liberty Centennial gold $5, Proof.	(404,013)	600.00
2-coin set. Uncirculated silver dollar and clad half dollar.		28.00
2-coin set. Uncirculated and Proof gold $5		900.00

Note: Proof Statue of Liberty Centennial clad half dollars and silver dollars were also included in Prestige Sets; see page 248.

Chart continued on next page.

	Mintage	OGP
2-coin set. Proof silver dollar and clad half dollar		$28
3-coin set. Uncirculated silver dollar, clad half dollar, and gold $5		600
3-coin set. Proof silver dollar, clad half dollar, and gold $5.		625
6-coin set. One each of Proof and Uncirculated clad half dollar, silver dollar, and gold $5 **(a)**		1,250

Note: Proof Statue of Liberty Centennial clad half dollars and silver dollars were also included in Prestige Sets; see page 248. **a.** Packaged in a cherrywood box.

(1987) U.S. Constitution Bicentennial

	Mintage	OGP
1987P, U.S. Constitution Bicentennial silver dollar, Uncirculated 451,629		$26
1987S, U.S. Constitution Bicentennial silver dollar, Proof . . . .(2,747,116)		26
1987W, U.S. Constitution Bicentennial gold $5, Uncirculated 214,225		575
1987W, U.S. Constitution Bicentennial gold $5, Proof. . . . .(651,659)		600
2-coin set. Uncirculated silver dollar and gold $5		600
2-coin set. Proof silver dollar and gold $5		625
4-coin set. One each of Proof and Uncirculated silver dollar and gold $5 **(a)**		1,250

Note: Proof U.S. Constitution Bicentennial silver dollars were also included in Prestige Sets; see page 248. **a.** Packaged in a cherrywood box.

(1988) Seoul Olympiad

	Mintage	OGP
1988D, Seoul Olympiad silver dollar, Uncirculated 191,368		$26
1988S, Seoul Olympiad silver dollar, Proof. . . . .(1,359,366)		26
1988W, Seoul Olympiad gold $5, Uncirculated. 62,913		575
1988W, Seoul Olympiad gold $5, Proof . . . .(281,465)		600
2-coin set. Uncirculated silver dollar and gold $5		600
2-coin set. Proof silver dollar and gold $5		625
4-coin set. One each of Proof and Uncirculated silver dollar and gold $5 **(a)**		1,250

Note: Proof Seoul Olympiad silver dollars were also included in Prestige Sets; see page 248. **a.** Packaged in a cherry wood box.

COMMEMORATIVES

(1989) Congress Bicentennial

	Mintage	OGP
1989D, Congress Bicentennial clad half dollar, Uncirculated 163,753		$5.50
1989S, Congress Bicentennial clad half dollar, Proof................................. (767,897)		3.40
1989D, Congress Bicentennial silver dollar, Uncirculated............................. 135,203		26.00
1989S, Congress Bicentennial silver dollar, Proof................................... (762,198)		26.00
1989W, Congress Bicentennial gold $5, Uncirculated................................. 46,899		575.00
1989W, Congress Bicentennial gold $5, Proof .... (164,690)		600.00
2-coin set. Proof clad half dollar and silver dollar		31.00
3-coin set. Proof clad half dollar, silver dollar, and gold $5.............................		625.00
2-coin set. Uncirculated clad half dollar and silver dollar		30.00
3-coin set. Uncirculated clad half dollar, silver dollar, and gold $5......................		625.00
6-coin set. One each of Proof and Uncirculated clad half dollar, silver dollar, and gold $5 **(a)**		1,250.00

Note: Proof Congress Bicentennial clad half dollars and silver dollars were also included in Prestige Sets; see page 248.
a. Packaged in a cherrywood box.

(1990) Eisenhower Centennial

	Mintage	OGP
1990W, Eisenhower Centennial silver dollar, Uncirculated 241,669		$28
1990P, Eisenhower Centennial silver dollar, Proof .... (1,144,461)		26

Note: Proof Eisenhower Centennial silver dollars were also included in Prestige Sets; see page 248.

223

(1991) Mount Rushmore Golden Anniversary

	Mintage	OGP
1991D, Mount Rushmore Golden Anniversary clad half dollar, Uncirculated	172,754	$10
1991S, Mount Rushmore Golden Anniversary clad half dollar, Proof	(753,257)	7
1991P, Mount Rushmore Golden Anniversary silver dollar, Uncirculated	133,139	29
1991S, Mount Rushmore Golden Anniversary silver dollar, Proof	(738,419)	26
1991W, Mount Rushmore Golden Anniversary gold $5, Uncirculated	31,959	575
1991W, Mount Rushmore Golden Anniversary gold $5, Proof	(111,991)	600
2-coin set. Uncirculated clad half dollar and silver dollar		39
2-coin set. Proof clad half dollar and silver dollar		33
3-coin set. Uncirculated clad half dollar, silver dollar, and gold $5		625
3-coin set. Proof clad half dollar, silver dollar, and gold $5		650
6-coin set. One each of Proof and Uncirculated clad half dollar, silver dollar, and gold $5 **(a)**		1,250

Note: Proof Mount Rushmore Golden Anniversary clad half dollars and silver dollars were also included in Prestige Sets; see page 248. **a.** Packaged in a cherrywood box.

(1991) Korean War Memorial

	Mintage	OGP
1991D, Korean War Memorial silver dollar, Uncirculated	213,049	$26
1991P, Korean War Memorial silver dollar, Proof	(618,488)	26

(1991) United Service Organizations

	Mintage	OGP
1991D, United Service Organizations silver dollar, Uncirculated	124,958	$26
1991S, United Service Organizations silver dollar, Proof	(321,275)	26

(1992) XXV Olympiad

	Mintage	OGP
1992P, XXV Olympiad clad half dollar, Uncirculated	161,607	$4.30
1992S, XXV Olympiad clad half dollar, Proof	(519,645)	5.00
1992D, XXV Olympiad silver dollar, Uncirculated	187,552	26.00
1992S, XXV Olympiad silver dollar, Proof	(504,505)	26.00
1992W, XXV Olympiad gold $5, Uncirculated	27,732	575.00
1992W, XXV Olympiad gold $5, Proof	(77,313)	600.00
2-coin set. Uncirculated clad half dollar and silver dollar		30.00
2-coin set. Proof clad half dollar and silver dollar		31.00
3-coin set. Uncirculated clad half dollar, silver dollar, and gold $5		600.00
3-coin set. Proof clad half dollar, silver dollar, and gold $5		625.00
6-coin set. One each of Proof and Uncirculated clad half dollar, silver dollar, and gold $5 **(a)**		1,250.00

Note: Proof XXV Olympiad half dollars and silver dollars were also included in Prestige Sets; see page 248. **a.** Packaged in a cherrywood box.

(1992) White House 200th Anniversary

	Mintage	OGP
1992D, White House 200th Anniversary silver dollar, Uncirculated	123,803	$26
1992W, White House 200th Anniversary silver dollar, Proof	(375,851)	26

(1992) Christopher Columbus Quincentenary

	Mintage	OGP
1992D, Christopher Columbus Quincentenary clad half dollar, Uncirculated	135,702	$8
1992S, Christopher Columbus Quincentenary clad half dollar, Proof	(390,154)	8
1992D, Christopher Columbus Quincentenary silver dollar, Uncirculated	106,949	28
1992P, Christopher Columbus Quincentenary silver dollar, Proof	(385,241)	26
1992W, Christopher Columbus Quincentenary gold $5, Uncirculated	24,329	575
1992W, Christopher Columbus Quincentenary gold $5, Proof	(79,730)	600
2-coin set. Uncirculated clad half dollar and silver dollar		36
2-coin set. Proof clad half dollar and silver dollar		34
3-coin set. Uncirculated clad half dollar, silver dollar, and gold $5		625
3-coin set. Proof clad half dollar, silver dollar, and gold $5		650
6-coin set. One each of Proof and Uncirculated clad half dollar, silver dollar, and gold $5 **(a)**		1,250

a. Packaged in a cherrywood box.

(1993) Bill of Rights

	Mintage	OGP
1993W, Bill of Rights silver half dollar, Uncirculated	193,346	$11.00
1993S, Bill of Rights silver half dollar, Proof	(586,315)	9.75
1993D, Bill of Rights silver dollar, Uncirculated	98,383	27.00
1993S, Bill of Rights silver dollar, Proof	(534,001)	26.00
1993W, Bill of Rights gold $5, Uncirculated	23,266	575.00
1993W, Bill of Rights gold $5, Proof	(78,651)	600.00
2-coin set. Uncirculated silver half dollar and silver dollar		37.00
2-coin set. Proof silver half dollar and silver dollar		36.00
3-coin set. Uncirculated silver half dollar, silver dollar, and gold $5		625.00
3-coin set. Proof silver half dollar, silver dollar, and gold $5		650.00
6-coin set. One each of Proof and Uncirculated silver half dollar, silver dollar, and gold $5 **(a)**		1,250.00
Young Collector set. Uncirculated silver half dollar		11.00
Coin and Medal set. Silver half dollar and bronze James Madison Peace medal replica		12.50
Coin and Stamp set. Proof silver half dollar and themed 25¢ postage stamp		10.50

Note: Proof Bill of Rights half dollars and silver dollars were also included in Prestige Sets; see page 248. **a.** Packaged in a cherrywood box.

(1993) 50th Anniversary of World War II, 1991–1995

	Mintage	OGP
1993P) 1991–1995 World War II clad half dollar, Uncirculated	197,072	$9
1993P) 1991–1995 World War II clad half dollar, Proof	(317,396)	11

(1993) 50th Anniversary of World War II, 1991–1995

	Mintage	OGP
(1993D) 1991–1995 World War II silver dollar, Uncirculated	107,240	$26
(1993W) 1991–1995 World War II silver dollar, Proof	(342,041)	28
(1993W) 1991–1995 World War II gold $5, Uncirculated	23,672	575
(1993W) 1991–1995 World War II gold $5, Proof	(67,026)	600
2-coin set. Uncirculated clad half dollar and silver dollar		35
2-coin set. Proof clad half dollar and silver dollar		39
3-coin set. Uncirculated clad half dollar, silver dollar, and gold $5		625
3-coin set. Proof clad half dollar, silver dollar, and gold $5		650
6-coin set. One each of Proof and Uncirculated clad half dollar, silver dollar, and gold $5 **(a)**		1,250
Young Collector's set. Uncirculated clad half dollar		9
Victory Medal set. Uncirculated clad half dollar and bronze Victory medal replica		11

a. Packaged in a cherrywood box.

(1994) Thomas Jefferson 250th Anniversary of Birth, 1993

	Mintage	OGP
1993P (1994) Thomas Jefferson 250th Anniversary of Birth, 1993 silver dollar, Uncirculated	266,927	$27
1993S (1994) Thomas Jefferson 250th Anniversary of Birth, 1993 silver dollar, Proof	(332,891)	26
Coinage and Currency set (issued in 1994). Uncirculated silver dollar, Matte Finish 1994P Jefferson nickel, and $2 Federal Reserve Note		46

(1994) World Cup Tournament

	Mintage	OGP
1994D, World Cup Tournament clad half dollar, Uncirculated	168,208	$6.25
1994P, World Cup Tournament clad half dollar, Proof	(609,354)	6.25
1994D, World Cup Tournament silver dollar, Uncirculated	81,524	27.00
1994S, World Cup Tournament silver dollar, Proof	(577,090)	27.00
1994W, World Cup Tournament gold $5, Uncirculated	22,447	575.00
1994W, World Cup Tournament gold $5, Proof	(89,614)	600.00
2-coin set. Uncirculated clad half dollar and silver dollar		33.00
2-coin set. Proof clad half dollar and silver dollar		38.00
3-coin set. Uncirculated clad half dollar, silver dollar, and gold $5		625.00
3-coin set. Proof clad half dollar, silver dollar, and gold $5		650.00
6-coin set. One each of Proof and Uncirculated clad half dollar, silver dollar, and gold $5 **(a)**		1,250.00
Young Collector set. Uncirculated clad half dollar		6.25
Special Edition set. Proof clad half dollar and silver dollar		33.00

Note: Proof World Cup Tournament half dollars and silver dollars were also included in Prestige Sets; see page 249. The Mint also issued other minor sets under this program; they are not listed here. **a.** Packaged in a cherrywood box.

(1994) Vietnam Veterans Memorial

	Mintage	OGP
1994W, Vietnam Veterans Memorial silver dollar, Uncirculated	57,290	$34
1994P, Vietnam Veterans Memorial silver dollar, Proof	(227,671)	40

Chart continued on next page.

229

	Mintage	OGP
U.S. Veterans set. Uncirculated Vietnam, POW, and Women in Military Service silver dollars **(a)**		$100
U.S. Veterans set. Proof Vietnam, POW, and Women in Military Service silver dollars **(a)**		105

a. Same set as listed under U.S. Prisoner of War Museum and Women in Military Service Memorial.

(1994) U.S. Prisoner of War Museum

	Mintage	OGP
1994W, U.S. Prisoner of War Museum silver dollar, Uncirculated	54,893	$36
1994P, U.S. Prisoner of War Museum silver dollar, Proof	(224,449)	34
U.S. Veterans set. Uncirculated POW, Vietnam, and Women in Military Service silver dollars **(a)**		100
U.S. Veterans set. Proof POW, Vietnam, and Women in Military Service silver dollars **(a)**		105

a. Same set as listed under Vietnam Veterans Memorial and Women in Military Service Memorial.

(1994) Women in Military Service Memorial

	Mintage	OGP
1994W, Women in Military Service Memorial silver dollar, Uncirculated	69,860	$29
1994P, Women in Military Service Memorial silver dollar, Proof	(241,278)	28
U.S. Veterans set. Uncirculated Women in Military Service, POW, and Vietnam silver dollars **(a)**		100
U.S. Veterans set. Proof Women in Military Service, POW, and Vietnam silver dollars **(a)**		105

a. Same set as listed under Vietnam Veterans Memorial and U.S. Prisoner of War Museum.

(1994) U.S. Capitol Bicentennial

	Mintage	OGP
1994D, U.S. Capitol Bicentennial silver dollar, Uncirculated	68,332	$27
1994S, U.S. Capitol Bicentennial silver dollar, Proof	(279,579)	27

(1995) Civil War Battlefield Preservation

	Mintage	OGP
1995S, Civil War Battlefield Preservation clad half dollar, Uncirculated	119,520	$13.50
1995S, Civil War Battlefield Preservation clad half dollar, Proof	(330,002)	18.00
1995P, Civil War Battlefield Preservation silver dollar, Uncirculated	45,866	38.00
1995S, Civil War Battlefield Preservation silver dollar, Proof	(437,114)	29.00
1995W, Civil War Battlefield Preservation gold $5, Uncirculated	12,735	575.00
1995W, Civil War Battlefield Preservation gold $5, Proof	(55,246)	600.00
2-coin set. Uncirculated clad half dollar and silver dollar		47.00
2-coin set. Proof clad half dollar and silver dollar		50.00
3-coin set. Uncirculated clad half dollar, silver dollar, and gold $5		625.00
3-coin set. Proof clad half dollar, silver dollar, and gold $5		650.00
6-coin set. One each of Proof and Uncirculated clad half dollar, silver dollar, and gold $5 **(a)**		1,300.00
Young Collector set. Uncirculated clad half dollar		13.50
2-coin Union set. Proof clad half dollar and silver dollar in photo case		50.00
3-coin Union set. Proof clad half dollar, silver dollar, and gold $5 in photo case		625.00

Note: Proof Civil War Battlefield Preservation half dollars and silver dollars were also included in Prestige Sets; see page 249. **a.** Packaged in a cherrywood box.

(1995–1996) Atlanta Centennial Olympic Games

	Mintage	OGP
1995S, Basketball clad half dollar, Uncirculated	171,001	$9.00
1995S, Basketball clad half dollar, Proof	(169,655)	15.00
1995S, Baseball clad half dollar, Uncirculated	164,605	12.50
1995S, Baseball clad half dollar, Proof	(118,087)	12.50
1996S, Swimming clad half dollar, Uncirculated	49,533	32.00
1996S, Swimming clad half dollar, Proof	(114,315)	16.00
1996S, Soccer clad half dollar, Uncirculated	52,836	18.00
1996S, Soccer clad half dollar, Proof	(112,412)	18.00
1995D, Gymnastics silver dollar, Uncirculated	42,497	32.00
1995P, Gymnastics silver dollar, Proof	(182,676)	27.00
1995D, Paralympics silver dollar, Uncirculated	28,649	47.00
1995P, Paralympics silver dollar, Proof	(138,337)	27.00
1995D, Track and Field silver dollar, Uncirculated	24,976	40.00
1995P, Track and Field silver dollar, Proof	(136,935)	29.00
1995D, Cycling silver dollar, Uncirculated	19,662	55.00
1995P, Cycling silver dollar, Proof	(118,795)	28.00
1996D, Tennis silver dollar, Uncirculated	15,983	55.00
1996P, Tennis silver dollar, Proof	(92,016)	45.00
1996D, Paralympics silver dollar, Uncirculated	14,497	90.00
1996P, Paralympics silver dollar, Proof	(84,280)	26.00
1996D, Rowing silver dollar, Uncirculated	16,258	60.00
1996P, Rowing silver dollar, Proof	(151,890)	38.00
1996D, High Jump silver dollar, Uncirculated	15,697	65.00
1996P, High Jump silver dollar, Proof	(124,502)	26.00
1995W, Torch Runner gold $5, Uncirculated	14,675	575.00
1995W, Torch Runner gold $5, Proof	(57,442)	600.00
1995W, Stadium gold $5, Uncirculated	10,579	575.00
1995W, Stadium gold $5, Proof	(43,124)	600.00
1996W, Flag Bearer gold $5, Uncirculated	9,174	575.00
1996W, Flag Bearer gold $5, Proof	(32,886)	600.00

Note: Proof Atlanta Centennial Olympic Games half dollars and silver dollars were also included in Prestige Sets; see page 249.

	Mintage	OGP
1996W, Cauldron gold $5, Uncirculated	9,210	$575.00
1996W, Cauldron gold $5, Proof	(38,555)	600.00
2-coin set #1. Proof silver dollars (Gymnastics, Paralympics)		70.00
4-coin set #1. Uncirculated clad half dollar (Basketball), silver dollars (Gymnastics, Paralympics), and gold $5 (Torch Bearer)		675.00
4-coin set #2. Proof clad half dollar (Basketball), silver dollars (Gymnastics, Paralympics), and gold ($5 Torch Bearer)		675.00
4-coin set #3. Proof clad half dollar (Baseball), silver dollars (Cyclist, Track Runner), and gold $5 (Olympic Stadium)		675.00
Young Collector's set #1. Uncirculated Basketball clad half dollar		9.00
Young Collector's set #2. Uncirculated Baseball clad half dollar		12.50
Young Collector's set #3. Uncirculated Swimming clad half dollar		32.00
Young Collector's set #4. Uncirculated Soccer clad half dollar		18.00
1995–1996 16-coin set. One each of all Uncirculated coins **(a)**		2,750.00
1995–1996 16-coin set. One each of all Proof coins **(a)**		2,500
1995–1996 8-coin set. One each of all Proof silver dollars		250.00
1995–1996 32-coin set. One each of all Uncirculated and Proof coins **(a)**		5,750.00

Note: Proof Atlanta Centennial Olympic Games half dollars and silver dollars were also included in Prestige Sets; see page 249. **a.** Packaged in a cherrywood box.

(1995) Special Olympics World Games

	Mintage	OGP
1995W, Special Olympics World Games silver dollar, Uncirculated	89,301	$27
1995P, Special Olympics World Games silver dollar, Proof	(351,764)	27
2-coin set. Proof silver dollar and 1995S Kennedy half dollar		55

(1996) National Community Service

See next page for chart.

	Mintage	OGP
1996S, National Community Service silver dollar, Uncirculated	23,500	$55
1996S, National Community Service silver dollar, Proof	(101,543)	27
Coin and Stamp set. Proof silver dollar and 3¢ Saint-Gaudens postage stamp		28

(1996) Smithsonian Institution 150th Anniversary

	Mintage	OGP
1996D, Smithsonian Institution 150th Anniversary silver dollar, Uncirculated	31,320	$38
1996P, Smithsonian Institution 150th Anniversary silver dollar, Proof	(129,152)	28
1996W, Smithsonian Institution 150th Anniversary gold $5, Uncirculated	9,068	575
1996W, Smithsonian Institution 150th Anniversary gold $5, Proof	(21,772)	600
2-coin set. Proof silver dollar and gold $5		625
4-coin set. One each of Proof and Uncirculated silver dollars and gold $5 (a)		1,250
Young Collector's set. Proof silver dollar		28

a. Packaged in a cherrywood box.

(1997) U.S. Botanic Garden

	Mintage	OGP
1997P, U.S. Botanic Garden silver dollar, Uncirculated	58,505	$27
1997P, U.S. Botanic Garden silver dollar, Proof	(189,671)	29
Coinage and Currency set. Uncirculated silver dollar, Matte Finish 1997P Jefferson nickel, and $1 Federal Reserve Note		90

Note: Proof U.S. Botanic Garden silver dollars were also included in Prestige Sets; see page 249.

COMMEMORATIVES

(1997) Jackie Robinson

	Mintage	OGP
1997S, Jackie Robinson silver dollar, Uncirculated	30,180	$45
1997S, Jackie Robinson silver dollar, Proof	(110,002)	40
1997W, Jackie Robinson gold $5, Uncirculated	5,174	625
1997W, Jackie Robinson gold $5, Proof	(24,072)	600
2-coin set. Proof silver dollar and gold $5		650
4-coin set. One each of Proof and Uncirculated silver dollars and gold $5 **(a)**		1,350
Legacy set. Proof gold $5, baseball card, and pin **(a)**		700

a. Packaged in a cherrywood box.

(1997) Franklin D. Roosevelt

	Mintage	OGP
1997W, Franklin D. Roosevelt gold $5, Uncirculated	11,894	$575
1997W, Franklin D. Roosevelt gold $5, Proof	(29,474)	600
2-coin set. One each of Proof and Uncirculated gold $5		1,200

(1997) National Law Enforcement Officers Memorial

	Mintage	OGP
1997P, National Law Enforcement Officers Memorial silver dollar, Uncirculated	28,575	$65
1997P, National Law Enforcement Officers Memorial silver dollar, Proof	(110,428)	36
Insignia set. Proof silver dollar, lapel pin, and patch		70

(1998) Robert F. Kennedy

	Mintage	OGP
1998S, Robert F. Kennedy silver dollar, Uncirculated	106,422	$29
1998S, Robert F. Kennedy silver dollar, Proof.	(99,020)	29
2-coin Collector's set. Uncirculated RFK silver dollar and Matte Finish 1998S JFK silver half dollar.		110
2-coin set. Proof and Uncirculated RFK silver dollars.		55

(1998) Black Revolutionary War Patriots

	Mintage	OGP
1998S, Black Revolutionary War Patriots silver dollar, Uncirculated	37,210	$45
1998S, Black Revolutionary War Patriots silver dollar, Proof.	(75,070)	40
2-coin set. Proof and Uncirculated silver dollars		85
Young Collector set. Uncirculated silver dollar		45
Coin and Stamp set. Proof silver dollar and four themed postage stamps (10¢, 13¢, 15¢, and 25¢)		55

(1999) Dolley Madison

	Mintage	OGP
1999P, Dolley Madison silver dollar, Uncirculated	89,104	$29
1999P, Dolley Madison silver dollar, Proof	(224,403)	31
2-coin set. Proof and Uncirculated silver dollars		60

(1999) George Washington Death Bicentennial

	Mintage	OGP
1999W, George Washington Death Bicentennial gold $5, Uncirculated	22,511	575
1999W, George Washington Death Bicentennial gold $5, Proof	(41,693)	600
2-coin set. One each of Proof and Uncirculated gold $5		1,200

(1999) Yellowstone National Park

	Mintage	OGP
1999P, Yellowstone National Park silver dollar, Uncirculated	82,563	$28
1999P, Yellowstone National Park silver dollar, Proof	(187,595)	29
2-coin set. One each of Proof and Uncirculated gold $5		55

(2000) Library of Congress Bicentennial

See next page for chart.

	Mintage	OGP
2000P, Library of Congress Bicentennial silver dollar, Uncirculated	53,264	$27
2000P, Library of Congress Bicentennial silver dollar, Proof	(198,503)	28
2000W, Library of Congress Bicentennial bimetallic (gold/platinum) $10, Uncirculated	7,261	925
2000W, Library of Congress Bicentennial bimetallic (gold/platinum) $10, Proof	(27,445)	725

(2000) Leif Ericson Millennium

	Mintage	OGP
2000P, Leif Ericson Millennium silver dollar, Uncirculated	28,150	$50
2000P, Leif Ericson Millennium silver dollar, Proof	(144,748)	36
2-coin set. Proof silver dollar and Icelandic 1,000 krónur		55

(2001) American Buffalo Commemorative

	Mintage	OGP
2001D, American Buffalo silver dollar, Uncirculated	227,131	$75
2001P, American Buffalo silver dollar, Proof	(272,869)	75
2-coin set. One each of Proof and Uncirculated silver dollars		155
Coinage and Currency set. Uncirculated silver dollar, face reprint of 1899 $5 Indian Chief Silver Certificate, 1987 Chief Red Cloud 10¢ stamp, and 2001 Bison 21¢ stamp		100

COMMEMORATIVES

(2001) Capitol Visitor Center

	Mintage	OGP
2001P, U.S. Capitol Visitor Center clad half dollar, Uncirculated	99,157	$11.50
2001P, U.S. Capitol Visitor Center clad half dollar, Proof	(77,962)	11.00
2001P, U.S. Capitol Visitor Center silver dollar, Uncirculated	35,380	27.00
2001P, U.S. Capitol Visitor Center silver dollar, Proof	(143,793)	28.00
2001W, U.S. Capitol Visitor Center gold $5, Uncirculated	6,761	575.00
2001W, U.S. Capitol Visitor Center gold $5, Proof	(27,652)	600.00
3-coin set. Proof clad half dollar, silver dollar, and gold $5.		650.00

(2002) Salt Lake Olympic Games

	Mintage	OGP
2002P, Salt Lake Olympic Games silver dollar, Uncirculated	40,257	$27
2002P, Salt Lake Olympic Games silver dollar, Proof	(166,864)	27
2002W, Salt Lake Olympic Games gold $5, Uncirculated	10,585	575
2002W, Salt Lake Olympic Games gold $5, Proof	(32,877)	600
2-coin set. Proof silver dollar and gold $5		625
4-coin set. One each of Proof and Uncirculated silver dollar and gold $5		1,250

(2002) West Point Bicentennial

	Mintage	OGP
2002W, West Point Bicentennial silver dollar, Uncirculated...............................	103,201	$27
2002W, West Point Bicentennial silver dollar, Proof...................................	(288,293)	29

(2003) First Flight Centennial

	Mintage	OGP
2003P, First Flight Centennial clad half dollar, Uncirculated............................	57,122	$12.50
2003P, First Flight Centennial clad half dollar, Proof................................	(109,710)	10.00
2003P, First Flight Centennial silver dollar, Uncirculated.............................	53,533	28.00
2003P, First Flight Centennial silver dollar, Proof..................................	(190,240)	29.00
2003W, First Flight Centennial gold $10, Uncirculated...............................	10,009	1,250.00
2003W, First Flight Centennial gold $10, Proof....................................	(21,676)	1,250.00
3-coin set. Proof clad half dollar, silver dollar, and gold $10...................................		1,250.00

(2004) Thomas Alva Edison

	Mintage	OGP
2004P, Thomas Alva Edison silver dollar, Uncirculated	92,510	$27
2004P, Thomas Alva Edison silver dollar, Proof.	(211,055)	27
Collector's set. Uncirculated silver dollar in case with functioning light bulb		35

(2004) Lewis and Clark Bicentennial

	Mintage	OGP
2004P, Lewis and Clark Bicentennial silver dollar, Uncirculated	142,015	$27
2004P, Lewis and Clark Bicentennial silver dollar, Proof.	(351,989)	27
Coin and Pouch set. Proof silver dollar and beaded pouch		55
Coinage and Currency set. Uncirculated silver dollar, 2004D Sacagawea dollar, 2005P and 2005D nickels, Series of 1901 $10 Bison note replica, silver-plated Thomas Jefferson Peace Medal replica, three themed 37¢ postage stamps, and two booklets		29

(2005) Chief Justice John Marshall

See next page for chart.

	Mintage	OGP
2005P, Chief Justice John Marshall silver dollar, Uncirculated 67,096		$27
2005P, Chief Justice John Marshall silver dollar, Proof. . . . . (196,753)		27
Coin and Chronicles set. Uncirculated silver dollar, booklet, and BEP intaglio portrait.		17
American Legacy set. Proof Marine Corps and John Marshall dollars, 11-piece Proof set **(a)**		49

a. Same set as listed under Marine Corps 230th Anniversary.

(2005) Marine Corps 230th Anniversary

	Mintage	OGP
2005P, Marine Corps 230th Anniversary silver dollar, Uncirculated 49,671		$41
2005P, Marine Corps 230th Anniversary silver dollar, Proof . . . . (548,810)		41
Coin and Stamp set. Uncirculated silver dollar and themed 3¢ postage stamp		43
American Legacy set. Proof Marine Corps and John Marshall silver dollars, 11-piece Proof set **(a)**.		49

a. Same set as listed under Chief Justice James Marshall.

(2006) Benjamin Franklin Tercentenary

	Mintage	OGP
2006P, Benjamin Franklin "Scientist" silver dollar, Uncirculated. 58,000		$27
2006P, Benjamin Franklin "Scientist" silver dollar, Proof . . . . (142,000)		27

COMMEMORATIVES

	Mintage	OGP
2006P, Benjamin Franklin "Founding Father" silver dollar, Uncirculated 58,000		$26
2006P, Benjamin Franklin "Founding Father" silver dollar, Proof. . . . . (142,000)		31
Coin and Chronicles set. Uncirculated "Scientist" silver dollar, four themed 39¢ postage		
stamps, *Poor Richard's Almanack* replica, and intaglio print		35
American Legacy set. Proof "Founding Father" silver dollar; Proof San Francisco Old Mint		
silver dollar; and Proof cent, nickel, dime, quarter, half dollar, and Sacagawea dollar **(a)**.		49

a. Same set as listed under San Francisco Old Mint Centennial.

(2006) San Francisco Old Mint Centennial

	Mintage	OGP
2006S, San Francisco Old Mint Centennial silver dollar, Uncirculated 67,100		$29.00
2006S, San Francisco Old Mint Centennial silver dollar, Proof. . . . . (160,870)		29.00
2006S, San Francisco Old Mint Centennial gold $5, Uncirculated 17,500		575.00
2006S, San Francisco Old Mint Centennial gold $5, Proof . . . . (44,174)		600.00
American Legacy set. Proof San Francisco Old Mint silver dollar; Proof "Founding Father"		
silver dollar; and Proof cent, nickel, dime, quarter, half dollar, and Sacagawea dollar **(a)**.		49.00
2007P, Jamestown 400th Anniversary silver dollar, Uncirculated 81,034		27.00
2007P, Jamestown 400th Anniversary silver dollar, Proof. . . . . (260,363)		31.00
2007W, Jamestown 400th Anniversary gold $5, Uncirculated 18,623		575.00
2007W, Jamestown 400th Anniversary gold $5, Proof. . . . . (47,123)		600.00
American Legacy set. Proof Jamestown silver dollar; Proof Little Rock Central High School		
Desegregation silver dollar; and 14-piece Proof Set **(b)**.		45.00
2007P, Little Rock Central High School Desegregation silver dollar, Uncirculated 66,093		27.00
2007P, Little Rock Central High School Desegregation silver dollar, Proof . . . . (124,678)		27.00
Coin and Medal set. Uncirculated silver dollar, bronze medal.		28.00
American Legacy set. Proof Little Rock Central High School Desegregation silver dollar;		
Proof Jamestown silver dollar; and 14-piece Proof Set **(c)**		45.00
2008S, Bald Eagle Recovery and National Emblem clad half dollar, Uncirculated 120,180		9.00
2008S, Bald Eagle Recovery and National Emblem clad half dollar, Proof . . . . (220,577)		13.50
2008P, Bald Eagle Recovery and National Emblem silver dollar, Uncirculated 119,204		27.00
2008P, Bald Eagle Recovery and National Emblem silver dollar, Proof . . . . (294,601)		27.00
2008W, Bald Eagle Recovery and National Emblem gold $5, Uncirculated 15,009		575.00
2008W, Bald Eagle Recovery and National Emblem gold $5, Proof. . . . . (59,269)		600.00
3-coin set. Proof clad half dollar, silver dollar, and gold $5.		650.00
Coin and Medal set. Uncirculated silver dollar and bronze Bald Eagle medal		31.00
Young Collector set. Uncirculated clad half dollar.		27.00
American Legacy set. Proof Bald Eagle silver dollar and 14-piece Proof Set		27.00

a. Same set as listed under Benjamin Franklin Tercentenary. **b.** Same set as listed under Little Rock Central High School Desegregation. **c.** Same set as listed under Jamestown 400th Anniversary.

Chart continued on next page.

	Mintage	OGP
2009P, Louis Braille Bicentennial silver dollar, Uncirculated	82,639	$27.00
2009P, Louis Braille Bicentennial silver dollar, Proof	(135,235)	27.00
Education set. Uncirculated silver dollar in tri-fold package		31.00
2009P, Abraham Lincoln Bicentennial silver dollar, Uncirculated	125,000	29.00
2009P, Abraham Lincoln Bicentennial silver dollar, Proof	(325,000)	29.00
Coin and Chronicles set. Proof silver dollar and the four Proof 2009S Lincoln Bicentennial cents		43.00
2010W, American Veterans Disabled for Life silver dollar, Uncirculated	78,301	27.00
2010W, American Veterans Disabled for Life silver dollar, Proof	(202,770)	26.00
2010P, Boy Scouts of America Centennial silver dollar, Uncirculated	105,020	29.00
2010P, Boy Scouts of America Centennial silver dollar, Proof	(244,963)	30.00
2011S, Medal of Honor silver dollar, Uncirculated	44,752	32.00
2011P, Medal of Honor silver dollar, Proof	(112,833)	32.00
2011P, Medal of Honor gold $5, Uncirculated	8,233	575.00
2011W, Medal of Honor gold $5, Proof	(17,999)	600.00
2011D, U.S. Army clad half dollar, Uncirculated	39,442	21.00
2011S, U.S. Army clad half dollar, Proof	(68,332)	14.50
2011S, U.S. Army silver dollar, Uncirculated	43,512	32.00
2011P, U.S. Army silver dollar, Proof	(119,829)	31.00
2011P, U.S. Army gold $5, Uncirculated	8,052	575.00
2011W, U.S. Army gold $5, Proof	(17,148)	600.00
2012W, Infantry Soldier silver dollar, Uncirculated	44,348	29.00
2012W, Infantry Soldier silver dollar, Proof	(161,151)	34.00
2012P, Star-Spangled Banner silver dollar, Uncirculated	41,686	32.00
2012P, Star-Spangled Banner silver dollar, Proof	(169,065)	31.00
2012W, Star-Spangled Banner gold $5, Uncirculated	7,027	575.00
2012W, Star-Spangled Banner gold $5, Proof	(18,313)	600.00
2-coin set. Proof silver dollar and gold $5		625.00
2013W, Girl Scouts of the U.S.A. Centennial silver dollar, Uncirculated	37,462	28.00
2013W, Girl Scouts of the U.S.A. Centennial silver dollar, Proof	(86,355)	33.00
Young Collectors set. Uncirculated silver dollar		36.00
2013D, 5-Star Generals clad half dollar, Uncirculated	38,095	13.50
2013S, 5-Star Generals clad half dollar, Proof	(47,326)	26.00
2013W, 5-Star Generals silver dollar, Uncirculated	34,638	39.00
2013P, 5-Star Generals silver dollar, Proof	(69,283)	44.00
2013P, 5-Star Generals gold $5, Uncirculated	5,667	575.00
2013W, 5-Star Generals gold $5, Proof	(15,844)	600.00
3-coin set. Proof clad half dollar, silver dollar, and gold $5		675.00
Profile Collection. Unc. half dollar and silver dollar, bronze MacArthur Congressional Gold Medal replica		45.00
2014D, National Baseball Hall of Fame clad half dollar, Uncirculated (d)	142,405	18.00
2014S, National Baseball Hall of Fame clad half dollar, Proof (d)	(249,049)	16.00
2014P, National Baseball Hall of Fame silver dollar, Uncirculated (d)	131,910	30.00
2014P, National Baseball Hall of Fame silver dollar, Proof (d)	(267,847)	30.00
2014W, National Baseball Hall of Fame gold $5, Uncirculated (d)	17,674	575.00
2014W, National Baseball Hall of Fame gold $5, Proof (d)	(32,428)	600.00
Young Collectors set. Uncirculated clad half dollar (d)		16.00

d. The obverse of each denomination is concave; the reverse is convex.

COMMEMORATIVES

	Mintage	OGP
2014P, Civil Rights Act of 1964 silver dollar, Uncirculated	24,720	$40.00
2014P, Civil Rights Act of 1964 silver dollar, Proof	(61,992)	48.00
2015D, U.S. Marshals Service 225th Anniversary clad half dollar, Uncirculated	30,231	14.50
2015S, U.S. Marshals Service 225th Anniversary clad half dollar, Proof	(76,549)	11.50
2015P, U.S. Marshals Service 225th Anniversary silver dollar, Uncirculated	38,149	36.00
2015P, U.S. Marshals Service 225th Anniversary silver dollar, Proof	(124,329)	37.00
2015W, U.S. Marshals Service 225th Anniversary gold $5, Uncirculated	6,743	575.00
2015W, U.S. Marshals Service 225th Anniversary gold $5, Proof	(24,959)	600.00
3-coin set. Proof clad half dollar, silver dollar, and gold $5.		650.00
2015P, March of Dimes 75th Anniversary silver dollar, Uncirculated.	24,742	36.00
2015W, March of Dimes 75th Anniversary silver dollar, Proof.	(32,030)	29.00
Special Silver set. Proof silver dollar, silver Proof and Reverse Proof dimes		45.00
2016P, Mark Twain silver dollar, Uncirculated.	26,291	32.00
2016P, Mark Twain silver dollar, Proof	(78,549)	29.00
2016W, Mark Twain gold $5, Uncirculated	5,701	575.00
2016W, Mark Twain gold $5, Proof	(13,271)	600.00
2016D, National Park Service 100th Anniversary clad half dollar, Uncirculated	21,328	15.50
2016S, National Park Service 100th Anniversary clad half dollar, Proof	(54,946)	22.00
2016P, National Park Service 100th Anniversary silver dollar, Uncirculated	20,979	30.00
2016P, National Park Service 100th Anniversary silver dollar, Proof	(77,319)	32.00
2016W, National Park Service 100th Anniversary gold $5, Uncirculated.	5,195	575.00
2016W, National Park Service 100th Anniversary gold $5, Proof	(19,503)	600.00
3-coin set. Proof clad half dollar, silver dollar, and gold $5.		650.00
2017P, Lions Club International Century of Service silver dollar, Uncirculated	68,330	36.00
2017P, Lions Club International Century of Service silver dollar, Proof	(17,224)	43.00
2017S, Boys Town Centennial clad half dollar, Uncirculated.	15,561	18.00
2017D, Boys Town Centennial clad half dollar, Proof	(23,212)	13.50
2017P, Boys Town Centennial silver dollar, Uncirculated	12,307	32.00
2017P, Boys Town Centennial silver dollar, Proof	(31,648)	39.00
2017W, Boys Town Centennial gold $5, Uncirculated	2,939	600.00
2017W, Boys Town Centennial gold $5, Proof	(7,377)	600.00
3-coin set. Proof clad half dollar, silver dollar, and gold $5.		650.00
2018P, World War I Centennial silver dollar, Uncirculated	22,338	42.00
2018P, World War I Centennial silver dollar, Proof.	(127,867)	42.00
Air Service Medal set. Proof silver dollar and silver Air Service medal		50.00
Army Medal set. Proof silver dollar and silver Army medal.		50.00
Coast Guard Medal set. Proof silver dollar and silver Coast Guard medal.		50.00
Marine Corps Medal set. Proof silver dollar and silver Marine Corps medal		50.00
Navy Medal set. Proof silver dollar and silver Navy medal		50.00
2018D, Breast Cancer Awareness clad half dollar, Uncirculated.	11,301	18.00
2018S, Breast Cancer Awareness clad half dollar, Proof	(22,391)	22.00
2018P, Breast Cancer Awareness silver dollar, Uncirculated.	12,521	32.00
2018P, Breast Cancer Awareness silver dollar, Proof	(34,548)	50.00
2018W, Breast Cancer Awareness gold $5, Uncirculated (e)	4,477	575.00
2018W, Breast Cancer Awareness gold $5, Proof (e)	(10,381)	600.00
Coin and Stamp set. Proof clad half dollar and themed First Class postage stamp.		60.00

e. Produced in "rose pink" gold, composed of .850 gold, .148 copper, and .002 zinc.

Chart continued on next page.

	Mintage	OGP
2019D, Apollo 11 50th Anniversary clad half dollar, Uncirculated **(d)**	41,748	$18.00
2019S, Apollo 11 50th Anniversary clad half dollar, Proof **(d)**	(181,735)	20.00
2019P, Apollo 11 50th Anniversary silver dollar, Uncirculated **(d)**	59,711	38.00
2019P, Apollo 11 50th Anniversary silver dollar, Proof **(d)**	(224,010)	55.00
2019P, Apollo 11 50th Anniversary 5-oz. silver dollar, Proof **(d,f)**	(68,308)	180.00
2019W, Apollo 11 50th Anniversary gold $5, Uncirculated **(d)**	12,035	575.00
2019W, Apollo 11 50th Anniversary gold $5, Proof **(d)**	(34,036)	600.00
Half dollar set. Uncirculated and Proof clad half dollars **(d)**		38.00
2019D, American Legion 100th Anniversary clad half dollar, Uncirculated	11,429	27.00
2019S, American Legion 100th Anniversary clad half dollar, Proof	(27,286)	29.00
2019P, American Legion 100th Anniversary silver dollar, Uncirculated	13,790	38.00
2019P, American Legion 100th Anniversary silver dollar, Proof	(63,100)	45.00
2019W, American Legion 100th Anniversary gold $5, Uncirculated	2,929	575.00
2019W, American Legion 100th Anniversary gold $5, Proof	(10,916)	600.00
3-coin set. Proof clad half dollar, silver dollar **(d)**, and gold $5.		675.00
Silver Dollar and Medal set. Proof silver dollar **(d)** and silver American Veterans medal		55.00
2020D, Naismith Mem. Basketball Hall of Fame 60th Anniv. clad half dollar, Uncirculated **(d)**	13,639	16.00
2020S, Naismith Mem. Basketball Hall of Fame 60th Anniv. clad half dollar, Enh. Unc.	22,565	27.00
2020S, Naismith Mem. Basketball Hall of Fame 60th Anniv. clad half dollar, Proof **(d)**	(26,584)	12.50
2020S, Naismith Mem. Basketball Hall of Fame 60th Anniv. clad half dollar, Proof, Colorized **(d)**	(32,614)	25.00
2020P, Naismith Mem. Basketball Hall of Fame 60th Anniv. silver dollar, Uncirculated **(d)**	21,328	47.00
2020P, Naismith Mem. Basketball Hall of Fame 60th Anniv. silver dollar, Proof **(d)**	(68,778)	40.00
2020P, Naismith Mem. Basketball Hall of Fame 60th Anniv. silver dollar, Proof, Colorized **(d)**	(25,735)	55.00
2020W, Naismith Mem. Basketball Hall of Fame 60th Anniv. gold $5, Uncirculated **(d)**	3,263	600.00
2020W, Naismith Mem. Basketball Hall of Fame 60th Anniv. gold $5, Proof **(d)**	(8,075)	625.00
Kids set. Enhanced Uncirculated clad half dollar **(d)**		27.00
2020P, Women's Suffrage Centennial silver dollar, Uncirculated	12,625	45.00
2020P, Women's Suffrage Centennial silver dollar, Proof	(43,479)	55.00
Coin and Medal set. Proof silver dollar and silver medal		65.00
2021P, Christa McAuliffe silver dollar, Uncirculated	16,038	60.00
2021P, Christa McAuliffe silver dollar, Proof	(54,191)	65.00
2021D, National Law Enforcement Memorial and Museum clad half dollar, Uncirculated	10,217	13.50
2021S, National Law Enforcement Memorial and Museum clad half dollar, Proof	(27,705)	25.00
2021P, National Law Enforcement Memorial and Museum silver dollar, Uncirculated	9,426	60.00
2021P, National Law Enforcement Memorial and Museum silver dollar, Proof	(34,109)	65.00
2021W, National Law Enforcement Memorial and Museum gold $5, Uncirculated	1,754	600.00
2021W, National Law Enforcement Memorial and Museum gold $5, Proof.	(5,871)	625.00
3-coin set. Proof clad half dollar, silver dollar **(c)**, and gold $5.		725.00
2022D, National Purple Heart Hall of Honor clad half dollar, Uncirculated.	*12,264*	22.00
2022S, National Purple Heart Hall of Honor clad half dollar, Proof	*(27,799)*	32.00
2022W, National Purple Heart Hall of Honor silver dollar, Uncirculated	*14,168*	60.00
2022W, National Purple Heart Hall of Honor silver dollar, Proof	*(53,325)*	65.00
2022W, National Purple Heart Hall of Honor silver dollar, Proof, colorized.	*(24,871)*	90.00
2022W, National Purple Heart Hall of Honor gold $5, Uncirculated.	*1,677*	600.00
2022W, National Purple Heart Hall of Honor gold $5, Proof	*(7,675)*	625.00
3-coin set. Proof clad half dollar, silver dollar, and gold $5.		725.00

d. The obverse of each denomination is concave; the reverse is convex. **f.** Identical in design to the regular-issue dollar coin, but enlarged to 3 inches in diameter.

	Mintage	OGP
2022D, Negro Leagues Baseball clad half dollar, Uncirculated	*9,792*	$22.00
2022S, Negro Leagues Baseball clad half dollar, Proof	*(22,841)*	29.00
2022W, Negro Leagues Baseball silver dollar, Uncirculated	*8,445*	60.00
2022P, Negro Leagues Baseball silver dollar, Proof	*(37,186)*	60.00
2022P, Negro Leagues Baseball silver dollar, Proof, with privy mark	*(19,687)*	65.00
2022W, Negro Leagues Baseball gold $5, Uncirculated	*1,507*	600.00
2022W, Negro Leagues Baseball gold $5, Proof	*(5,357)*	625.00
3-coin set. Proof clad half dollar, silver dollar, and gold $5		725.00
Coin and medal set. Proof silver dollar and Jackie Robinson Proof silver medal		130.00
2024D, Greatest Generation clad half dollar, Uncirculated		22.00
2024S, Greatest Generation clad half dollar, Proof		40.00
2024P, Greatest Generation silver dollar, Uncirculated		65.00
2024P, Greatest Generation silver dollar, Proof		70.00
2024W, Greatest Generation gold $5, Uncirculated		600.00
2024W, Greatest Generation gold $5, Proof		625.00
3-coin set. Proof clad half dollar, silver dollar and gold $5		750.00
2024D, Harriet Tubman Bicentennial clad half dollar, Uncirculated		22.00
2024S, Harriet Tubman Bicentennial clad half dollar, Proof		40.00
2024P, Harriet Tubman Bicentennial silver dollar, Uncirculated		65.00
2024P, Harriet Tubman Bicentennial silver dollar, Proof		70.00
2024W, Harriet Tubman Bicentennial gold $5, Uncirculated		600.00
2024W, Harriet Tubman Bicentennial gold $5, Proof		625.00
3-coin set. Proof clad half dollar, silver dollar and gold $5		750.00

PROOF COINS AND SETS

Proof coins can usually be distinguished by their sharpness of detail, high wire edge, and extremely brilliant, mirrorlike surface. Proofs are sold by the Mint at a premium.

Proof coins were not struck during 1943–1949 or 1965–1967. Sets from 1936 through 1972 include the cent, nickel, dime, quarter, and half dollar; from 1973 through 1981 the dollar was also included. From 1999 on, Proof sets have included the year's multiple quarter dollars, and since 2000 they have included the Mint's golden dollar coins. *Values shown are for original unblemished sets.*

Figures in parentheses represent the total number of full sets minted.

	Mintage	Issue Price	OGP		Mintage	Issue Price	OGP
1936	(3,837)	$1.89	$4,950.00	1981S, Type 1	(4,063,083)	$11.00	$8.00
1937	(5,542)	1.89	2,200.00	1981S, Type 2	*	11.00	85.00
1938	(8,045)	1.89	900.00	1982S	(3,857,479)	11.00	6.25
1939	(8,795)	1.89	850.00	1983S	(3,138,765)	11.00	6.25
1940	(11,246)	1.89	700.00	1983S, Prestige set			
1941	(15,287)	1.89	675.00	(Olympic dollar)	(140,361)	59.00	32.00
1942, Both nickels	(21,120)	1.89	650.00	1984S	(2,748,430)	11.00	5.50
1942, One nickel	*	1.89	725.00	1984S, Prestige set			
1950	(51,386)	2.10	725.00	(Olympic dollar)	(316,680)	59.00	32.00
1951	(57,500)	2.10	700.00	1985S	(3,362,821)	11.00	5.50
1952	(81,980)	2.10	320.00	1986S	(2,411,180)	11.00	5.50
1953	(128,800)	2.10	225.00	1986S, Prestige set (Statue			
1954	(233,300)	2.10	135.00	of Liberty half, dollar)	(599,317)	48.50	32.00
1955, Box pack	(378,200)	2.10	110.00	1987S	(3,792,233)	11.00	5.00
1955, Flat pack	*	2.10	125.00	1987S, Prestige set			
1956	(669,384)	2.10	50.00	(Constitution dollar)	(435,495)	45.00	31.00
1957	(1,247,952)	2.10	24.00	1988S	(3,031,287)	11.00	4.30
1958	(875,652)	2.10	28.00	1988S, Prestige set			
1959	(1,149,291)	2.10	22.00	(Olympic dollar)	(231,661)	45.00	31.00
1960, With LgDt cent	(1,691,602)	2.10	22.00	1989S	(3,009,107)	11.00	4.30
1960, With SmDt cent	*	2.10	24.00	1989S, Prestige set			
1961	(3,028,244)	2.10	22.00	(Congressional half,			
1962	(3,218,019)	2.10	22.00	dollar)	(211,807)	45.00	31.00
1963	(3,075,645)	2.10	22.00	1990S	(2,793,433)	11.00	6.25
1964	(3,950,762)	2.10	22.00	1990S, With No S cent	(3,555)	11.00	4,200.00
1968S	(3,041,506)	5.00	6.25	1990S, Prestige set			
1969S	(2,934,631)	5.00	6.75	(Eisenhower dollar)	(506,126)	45.00	32.00
1970S	(2,632,810)	5.00	10.00	1990S, Prestige Set,			
1970S, With SmDt cent	*	5.00	60.00	With No S cent	*	45.00	4,650.00
1971S	(3,220,733)	5.00	4.30	1991S	(2,610,833)	11.00	5.50
1972S	(3,260,996)	5.00	3.40	1991S, Prestige set (Mt.			
1973S	(2,760,339)	7.00	8.00	Rushmore half, dollar)	(256,954)	59.00	38.00
1974S	(2,612,568)	7.00	8.00	1992S	(2,675,618)	11.00	5.50
1975S, With 1976 quarter,				1992S, Prestige set			
half, and dollar	(2,845,450)	7.00	11.00	(Olympic half, dollar)	(183,293)	56.00	37.00
1976S	(4,149,730)	7.00	8.00	1992S, Silver	(1,009,586)	21.00	17.00
1976S, 3-piece set	(3,998,621)	15.00	16.00	1992S, Silver Premier set	(308,055)	37.00	17.00
1977S	(3,251,152)	9.00	7.75	1993S	(2,409,394)	12.50	5.50
1978S	(3,127,781)	9.00	7.25	1993S, Prestige set (Bill			
1979S, Type 1	(3,677,175)	9.00	8.00	of Rights half, dollar)	(224,045)	57.00	41.00
1979S, Type 2	*	9.00	34.00	1993S, Silver	(570,213)	21.00	19.00
1980S	(3,554,806)	10.00	6.25	1993S, Silver Premier set	(191,140)	37.50	19.00

Note: OGP = Set in original government packaging. * Included in number above.

PROOF AND MINT SETS

	Mintage	Issue Price	OGP
1994S . . . . (2,308,701)		$12.50	$5.50
1994S, Prestige set (World			
Cup half, dollar) . . . . . . (175,893)		57.00	39.00
1994S, Silver . . . . (636,009)		21.00	18.00
1994S, Silver Premier set . (149,320)		37.50	18.00
1995S . . . . (2,010,384)		12.50	8.00
1995S, Prestige set (Civil			
War half, dollar) . . . . . . (107,112)		57.00	55.00
1995S, Silver . . . . (549,878)		21.00	23.00
1995S, Silver Premier set . (130,107)		37.50	23.00
1996S . . . . (1,695,244)		12.50	8.00
1996S, Prestige set			
(Olympic half, dollar). . . . (55,000)		57.00	135.00
1996S, Silver . . . . (623,655)		21.00	20.00
1996S, Silver Premier set . (151,366)		37.50	20.00
1997S . . . . (1,975,000)		12.50	9.00
1997S, Prestige set			
(Botanic dollar) . . . . (80,000)		48.00	38.00
1997S, Silver . . . . (605,473)		21.00	22.00
1997S, Silver Premier set . (136,205)		37.50	22.00
1998S . . . . (2,086,507)		12.50	8.00
1998S, Silver . . . . (638,134)		21.00	16.00
1998S, Silver Premier set . (240,658)		37.50	16.00
1999S, 9-pc set . . . . (2,543,401)		19.95	9.00
1999S, 5-pc qtr set. . . . . (1,169,958)		13.95	3.20
1999S, Silver 9-pc set . . . (804,565)		31.95	55.00
2000S, 10-pc set . . . . . . (3,082,572)		19.95	9.00
2000S, 5-pc qtr set. . . . . . (937,600)		13.95	3.40
2000S, Silver 10-pc set . . (965,421)		31.95	48.00
2001S, 10-pc set . . . . . . (2,294,909)		19.95	9.00
2001S, 5-pc qtr set. . . . . . (799,231)		13.95	3.40
2001S, Silver 10-pc set . . (889,697)		31.95	48.00
2002S, 10-pc set . . . . . . (2,319,766)		19.95	8.00
2002S, 5-pc qtr set. . . . . . (764,479)		13.95	4.10
2002S, Silver 10-pc set . . (892,229)		31.95	48.00
2003S, 10-pc set . . . . . . (2,172,684)		19.95	9.00
2003S, 5-pc qtr set. . . . . (1,235,832)		13.95	2.20
2003S, Silver 10-pc set . (1,125,755)		31.95	48.00
2004S, 11-pc set . . . . . . (1,789,488)		22.95	8.50
2004S, 5-pc qtr set. . . . . . (951,196)		15.95	3.70
2004S, Silver 11-pc set . (1,175,934)		37.95	48.00
2004S, Silver 5-pc qtr set. (593,852)		23.95	26.00
2005S, 11-pc set . . . . . . (2,275,000)		22.95	8.00
2005S, 5-pc qtr set. . . . . . (987,960)		15.95	2.20
2005S, Silver 11-pc set . (1,069,679)		37.95	48.00
2005S, Silver 5-pc qtr set. (608,970)		23.95	26.00
2006S, 10-pc set . . . . . . (2,000,428)		22.95	8.00
2006S, 5-pc qtr set. . . . . . (882,000)		15.95	2.60
2006S, Silver 10-pc set . (1,054,008)		37.95	48.00
2006S, Silver 5-pc qtr set. (531,000)		23.95	26.00
2007S, 14-pc set . . . . . . (1,702,116)		26.95	14.50

	Mintage	Issue Price	OGP
2007S, 5-pc qtr set. . . . . . (672,662)		$13.95	$5.50
2007S, 4-pc Pres set . . . (1,285,972)		14.95	4.10
2007S, Silver 14-pc set . . (875,050)		44.95	48.00
2007S, Silver 5-pc qtr set. (672,662)		25.95	26.00
2008S, 14-pc set . . . . . . (1,382,017)		26.95	25.00
2008S, 5-pc qtr set. . . . . . (672,438)		13.95	11.00
2008S, 4-pc Pres set . . . . (836,730)		14.95	8.00
2008S, Silver 14-pc set . . (763,887)		44.95	48.00
2008S, Silver 5-pc qtr set. (429,021)		25.95	26.00
2009S, 18-pc set . . . . . . (1,477,967)		29.95	26.00
2009S, 6-pc qtr set. . . . . . (635,423)		14.95	4.30
2009S, 4-pc Pres set . . . . (627,925)		14.95	5.50
2009S, Silver 18-pc set . . (694,406)		52.95	47.00
2009S, Silver 6-pc qtr set. (299,164)		29.95	31.00
2009S, 4-pc Lincoln			
Bicentennial set . . . . . . (200,000)		7.95	6.75
2010S, 14-pc set . . . . . . (1,103,950)		31.95	27.00
2010S, 5-pc qtr set. . . . . . (276,335)		14.95	9.50
2010S, 4-pc Pres set . . . . (535,463)		15.95	11.00
2010S, Silver 14-pc set . . (585,414)		56.95	42.00
2010S, Silver 5-pc qtr set. (274,003)		32.95	26.00
2011S, 14-pc set . . . . . . (1,098,835)		31.95	27.00
2011S, 5-pc qtr set. . . . . . (152,302)		14.95	10.00
2011S, 4-pc Pres set . . . . (299,853)		19.95	21.00
2011S, Silver 14-pc set . . (574,175)		67.95	42.00
2011S, Silver 5-pc qtr set. (147,901)		39.95	26.00
2012S, 14-pc set . . . . (794,002)		31.95	65.00
2012S, 5-pc qtr set. . . . . . (148,498)		14.95	11.00
2012S, 4-pc Pres set . . . . (249,298)		18.95	40.00
2012S, Silver 14-pc set . . (395,443)		67.95	90.00
2012S, Silver 8-pc			
Limited Edition set . . . . . (50,169)		149.95	110.00
2012S, Silver 5-pc qtr set. (162,448)		41.95	26.00
2013S, 14-pc set . . . . (802,460)		31.95	27.00
2013S, 5-pc qtr set. . . . . . (128,377)		14.95	10.00
2013S, 4-pc Pres set . . . . (266,618)		18.95	10.00
2013S, Silver 14-pc set . . (419,720)		67.95	50.00
2013S, Silver 8-pc			
Limited Edition set . . . . . (47,971)		139.95	110.00
2013S, Silver 5-pc qtr set. (138,451)		41.95	26.00
2014S, 14-pc set . . . . (714,661)		31.95	27.00
2014S, 5-pc qtr set. . . . . . (115,179)		14.95	11.00
2014S, 4-pc Pres set . . . . (229,415)		18.95	11.00
2014S, Silver 14-pc set . . (429,493)		67.95	41.00
2014S, Silver 8-pc			
Limited Edition set . . . . (42,614)		139.95	115.00
2014S, Silver 5-pc qtr set. (119,251)		41.95	26.00
2015S, 14-pc set . . . . (662,854)		32.95	32.00
2015S, 5-pc qtr set. . . . . . . (99,466)		14.95	9.00
2015S, 4-pc Pres set . . . . (222,068)		18.95	10.00
2015S, Silver 14-pc set . . (387,310)		53.95	41.00

Note: OGP = Set in original government packaging.

Chart continued on next page.

Year	Mintage	Issue Price	OGP
2015S, Silver 5-pc qtr set. .	(103,311)	$31.95	$26.00
2016S, 13-piece set	(595,184)	31.95	43.00
2016S, 5-piece qtr set	(91,674)	14.95	10.00
2016S, 3-piece Pres set . .	(231,549)	17.95	9.00
2016S, Silver 13-pc set . .	(369,849)	52.95	50.00
2016S, Silver 5-pc qtr set. .	(95,709)	31.95	26.00
2016S, Silver 8-pc Limited			
Edition set, with 2016W			
American Silver Eagle . . .	(49,647)	139.95	90.00
2017S, 10-piece set	(568,678)	31.95	32.00
2017S, 5-piece qtr set . . .	(88,909)	14.95	10.00
2017S, Silver 10-pc set . .	(358,085)	52.95	42.00
2017S, Silver 5-pc qtr set. .	(89,632)	31.95	26.00
2017S, Silver 8-piece			
Limited Edition set	(48,901)	139.95	110.00
2018S, 10-piece set	(517,053)	27.95	34.00
2018S, 5-piece qtr set . . .	(86,694)	15.95	11.00
2018S, Silver 10-pc set . .	(332,268)	49.95	36.00
2018S, Silver 5-pc qtr set. .	(79,300)	33.95	26.00
2018S, 50th Anniv silver			
10-piece RevPf set	(199,116)	54.95	60.00
2018S, Silver 8-piece			
Limited Edition set	(49,480)	144.95	120.00
2019S, 10-piece set, plus			
2019W Proof cent	(600,423)	27.95	40.00
2019S, 5-piece qtr set. . . .	(78,777)	15.95	12.50
2019S, 4-piece American			
Innovation dollar set . .	(137,696)	20.95	20.00
2019S, Silver 10-pc set, plus			
2019W RevPf cent. . . .	(412,508)	54.95	80.00
2019S, Silver 5-pc qtr set .	(78,585)	36.95	27.00
2019S, Silver 8-piece			
Limited Edition set	(48,417)	149.95	125.00
2020S, 10-piece set, Plus			
2020W Proof nickel . . .	(465,080)	32.00	130.00
2020S, 5-piece quarter set	(64,242)	18.50	12.50
2020S, 4-piece American			
Innovation dollar set . .	(101,593)	24.00	20.00
2020S, Silver 10-piece set,			
Plus 2020W Reverse			
Proof nickel	(313,184)	63.25	65.00

Year	Mintage	Issue Price	OGP
2020S, Silver 5-pc qtr set . .	(64,012)	$42.50	$50
2020S, Silver 8-piece			
Limited Edition set.	(49,995)	201.00	180
2021S, 7-piece set	(511,147)	32.00	28
2021S, 4-piece American			
Innovation dollar set . . .	(82,539)	24.00	20
2021S, 4-piece American			
Innovation dollar RevPf set	(50,000)	28.00	23
2021S, Silver 7-piece set	(298,710)	105.00	90
2021S, Silver 6-piece			
Limited Edition set.	(48,592)	235.00	180
2022S, 10-piece set	(398,580)	32.00	41
2022S, 5-piece quarter set	(42,606)	21.00	16
2022S, 4-piece American			
Innovation dollar set . . .	(72,948)	24.00	20
2022S, 4-piece American			
Innovation dollar RevPf set	(49,478)	28.00	23
2022S, Silver 10-piece set	(236,373)	105.00	110
2022S, Silver 5-piece qtr set	(57,532)	73.00	55
2022S, Silver 8-piece			
Limited Edition set.	(50,000)	201.00	165
2023S, 10-piece set		35.00	32
2023S, 5-piece quarter set		23.00	16
2023S, 4-piece American			
Innovation dollar set		24.00	20
2023S, 4-piece American			
Innovation dollar RevPf set		28.00	23
2023S, Silver 10-piece set		130.00	90
2023S, Silver 5-piece quarter set . .		80.00	50
2023S, Silver 8-piece			
Limited Edition set.		220.00	135
2024S, 10-piece set		35.00	27
2024S, 5-piece quarter set		23.00	27
2024S, 4-piece American			
Innovation dollar set		24.00	22
2024S, 4-piece American			
Innovation dollar RevPf set		28.00	23
2024S, Silver 10-piece set		150.00	125
2024S, Silver 5-piece quarter set . .		80.00	70
2024S, Silver 8-piece			
Limited Edition set.		220.00	200

Note: OGP = Set in original government packaging.

UNCIRCULATED MINT SETS

Official Mint Sets are specially packaged by the government for sale to collectors. They contain Uncirculated specimens of each year's coins for every denomination issued from each mint. Sets from 1947 through 1958 contain two examples of each regular-issue coin. No official sets were produced in 1950, 1982, or 1983. Privately assembled sets are valued according to individual coin prices. Only official sets are included in the following list. Unlike the Proof sets, these are normal coins intended for circulation and are not minted with any special consideration for quality. From 1942 to 1946, groups of two coins from each mint were sold in a cloth shipping bag with only minimal protection. Very few of those mailing packages were saved by collectors.

	Mintage	Issue Price	OGP
1947 P-D-S............5,000	5,000	$4.87	$1,100.00
1948 P-D-S............6,000	6,000	4.92	775.00
1949 P-D-S............5,000	5,000	5.45	925.00
1951 P-D-S............8,654	8,654	6.75	725.00
1952 P-D-S............11,499	11,499	6.14	650.00
1953 P-D-S............15,538	15,538	6.14	550.00
1954 P-D-S............25,599	25,599	6.19	300.00
1955 P-D-S............49,656	49,656	3.57	255.00
1956 P-D............45,475	45,475	3.34	255.00
1957 P-D............34,324	34,324	4.40	255.00
1958 P-D............50,314	50,314	4.43	160.00
1959 P-D............187,000	187,000	2.40	36.00
1960 P-D............260,485	260,485	2.40	35.00
1961 P-D............223,704	223,704	2.40	35.00
1962 P-D............385,285	385,285	2.40	35.00
1963 P-D............606,612	606,612	2.40	34.00
1964 P-D............1,008,108	1,008,108	2.40	31.00
1965*............2,360,000	2,360,000	4.00	9.00
1966*............2,261,583	2,261,583	4.00	8.00
1967*............1,863,344	1,863,344	4.00	8.50
1968 P-D-S............2,105,128	2,105,128	2.50	5.50
1969 P-D-S............1,817,392	1,817,392	2.50	5.50
1970 P-D-S............2,038,134	2,038,134	2.50	12.50
1971 P-D-S............2,193,396	2,193,396	3.50	3.40
1972 P-D-S............2,750,000	2,750,000	3.50	3.00
1973 P-D-S............1,767,691	1,767,691	6.00	11.00
1974 P-D-S............1,975,981	1,975,981	6.00	10.00
1975 P-D............1,921,488	1,921,488	6.00	8.50
1776–1976, 3-piece set..4,908,319	4,908,319	9.00	8.00
1976 P-D............1,892,513	1,892,513	6.00	16.00
1977 P-D............2,006,869	2,006,869	7.00	8.00
1978 P-D............2,162,609	2,162,609	7.00	8.00
1979 P-D............2,526,000	2,526,000	8.00	5.50
1980 P-D-S............2,815,066	2,815,066	9.00	5.50
1981 P-D-S............2,908,145	2,908,145	11.00	6.25
1984 P-D............1,832,857	1,832,857	7.00	2.60
1985 P-D............1,710,571	1,710,571	7.00	2.60
1986 P-D............1,153,536	1,153,536	7.00	5.50
1987 P-D............2,890,758	2,890,758	7.00	3.40
1988 P-D............1,646,204	1,646,204	7.00	3.40
1989 P-D............1,987,915	1,987,915	7.00	2.60

	Mintage	Issue Price	OGP
1990 P-D............1,809,184	1,809,184	$7.00	$2.60
1991 P-D............1,352,101	1,352,101	7.00	2.60
1992 P-D............1,500,143	1,500,143	7.00	3.40
1993 P-D............1,297,431	1,297,431	8.00	3.40
1994 P-D............1,234,813	1,234,813	8.00	2.60
1995 P-D............1,038,787	1,038,787	8.00	3.40
1996 P-D, Plus			
1996W dime.........1,457,949	1,457,949	8.00	11.00
1997 P-D............950,473	950,473	8.00	4.30
1998 P-D............1,187,325	1,187,325	8.00	3.40
1999 P-D (18 pieces)......1,243,867	1,243,867	14.95	5.50
2000 P-D (20 pieces)......1,490,160	1,490,160	14.95	8.00
2001 P-D (20 pieces)......1,116,915	1,116,915	14.95	8.00
2002 P-D (20 pieces)......1,139,388	1,139,388	14.95	8.00
2003 P-D (20 pieces)......1,001,532	1,001,532	14.95	8.00
2004 P-D (22 pieces)......842,507	842,507	16.95	8.00
2005 P-D (22 pieces)......1,160,000	1,160,000	16.95	8.00
2006 P-D (20 pieces)......847,361	847,361	16.95	8.00
2007 P-D (28 pieces)......895,628	895,628	22.95	18.00
2008 P-D (28 pieces)......745,464	745,464	22.95	22.00
2009 P-D (36 pieces)......774,844	774,844	27.95	18.00
2010 P-D (28 pieces)......583,912	583,912	31.95	18.00
2011 P-D (28 pieces)......533,529	533,529	31.95	18.00
2012 P-D (28 pieces)......392,224	392,224	27.95	40.00
2013 P-D (28 pieces)......376,844	376,844	27.95	22.00
2014 P-D (28 pieces)......345,813	345,813	27.95	22.00
2015 P-D (28 pieces)......314,029	314,029	28.95	21.00
2016 P-D (26 pieces)......296,582	296,582	28.95	25.00
2017 P-D (20 pieces)......286,813	286,813	26.95	24.00
2017S, 225th Anniversary Enhanced Uncirculated Set (10 pieces).........210,419	210,419	29.95	18.00
2018 P-D (20 pieces)......257,531	257,531	20.95	25.00
2019 P-D (20 pieces), Plus 2019W cent.......346,117	346,117	21.95	32.00
2020 P-D (20 pieces) (a)...211,787	211,787	25.25	18.00
2021 P-D (14 pieces)......232,141	232,141	25.25	18.00
2022 P-D (20 pieces)......249,923	249,923	25.25	29.00
2023 P-D (20 pieces)......184,278	184,278	29.00	22.00
2024 P-D (20 pieces)............		29.00	20.00

Notes: OGP = Set in original government packaging. Sets issued from 2005 to 2010 have a special Satin Finish that is somewhat different from the finish on Uncirculated coins made for general circulation. * Special Mint Set. **a.** An Uncirculated nickel from the West Point Mint was intended to be a premium for the 2020 Mint Set, but was canceled due to COVID-19.

OTHER COLLECTIBLE SETS

	OGP
(2000) Millennium Coin and Currency Set	
3-piece set. Uncirculated Sacagawea dollar, Uncirculated American Silver Eagle bullion coin, and $1 Federal Reserve Note	$70.00
(2003) Legacies of Freedom	
Uncirculated American Silver Eagle bullion coin and Uncirculated 2002 £2 Silver Britannia coin	60.00
(2004) Westward Journey Nickel Series	
Proof Sacagawea dollar, two 2004 Proof nickels, and silver-plated Peace Medal replica.	7.25
(2005) Westward Journey Nickel Series	
Proof Sacagawea dollar, two 2005 Proof nickels, and silver-plated Peace Medal replica.	7.25
(2013) Theodore Roosevelt Coin and Chronicles	
Uncirculated Presidential dollar, silver Presidential medal, National Wildlife Refuge System Centennial bronze medal, and Roosevelt print.	110.00
(2014) 50th Anniversary Kennedy Half Dollar Uncirculated Coin Set	
2014P and 2014D clad half dollars	22.00
(2014) 50th Anniversary Kennedy Half Dollar Silver Coin Collection	
2014P Proof, 2014D Uncirculated, 2014S Enhanced Uncirculated, and 2014W Reverse Proof silver half dollars.	70.00
(2014) Franklin D. Roosevelt Coin and Chronicles	
Proof dime and Presidential dollar, bronze Presidential medal, silver Presidential medal, four themed postage stamps (1¢, 2¢, 3¢, 5¢), and companion booklet	50.00
(2014) American $1 Coin and Currency Set	
2014D Native American – Native Hospitality Enhanced Uncirculated dollar and $1 Federal Reserve Note.	9.00
(2015) Harry S. Truman Coin and Chronicles	
Reverse Proof Presidential dollar, silver Presidential medal, 1973 Truman 8¢ postage stamp, and information booklet.	180.00
(2015) Dwight D. Eisenhower Coin and Chronicles	
Reverse Proof Presidential dollar, silver Presidential medal, 1969 Eisenhower 6¢ postage stamp, and information booklet.	115.00
(2015) John F. Kennedy Coin and Chronicles	
Reverse Proof Presidential dollar, silver Presidential medal, 1964 Kennedy 5¢ postage stamp, and information booklet.	70.00
(2015) Lyndon B. Johnson Coin and Chronicles	
Reverse Proof Presidential dollar, silver Presidential medal, 1973 Johnson 8¢ postage stamp, and information booklet.	45.00
(2015) American $1 Coin and Currency Set	
2015W Native American – Mohawk Ironworkers Enhanced Uncirculated dollar and $1 Federal Reserve Note.	9.00
(2016) Ronald Reagan Coin and Chronicles	
Reverse Proof Presidential dollar, Proof American Silver Eagle, bronze Ronald and Nancy Reagan medal, engraved Ronald Reagan Presidential portrait, and information booklet	60.00
(2016) American $1 Coin and Currency Set	
2016S Native American – Code Talkers Enhanced Uncirculated dollar and $1 Federal Reserve Note	9.00
(2019) American $1 Coin and Currency Set	
2019W Native American – American Indians in Space Enhanced Uncirculated dollar and $1 Federal Reserve Note.	9.00
(2019) Youth Coin and Currency Set	
Five Proof America the Beautiful quarters and $2 Federal Reserve Note	16.00
(2021) George Herbert Walker Bush Coin and Chronicles	
Reverse Proof Presidential dollar, silver Presidential medal, 2019 George H.W. Bush "forever" postage stamp, Barbara Bush bronze medal, and information booklet	110.00

Note: OGP = Set in original government packaging.

AMERICA THE BEAUTIFUL SILVER BULLION COINS

Values below are based on spot silver value of $30 per ounce.

**Weight and purity
incused on edge**
Actual size 3 inches.

	Mintage	OGP		Mintage	OGP
25¢ 2010(P), Hot Springs (AR)	33,000	$170	25¢ 2013P, Great Basin (NV)	(17,792)	$150
25¢ 2010P, Hot Springs (AR)	(26,788)	160	25¢ 2013(P), Fort McHenry (MD)	30,000	170
25¢ 2010(P), Yellowstone (WY)	33,000	170	25¢ 2013P, Fort McHenry (MD)	(19,802)	150
25¢ 2010P, Yellowstone (WY)	(26,711)	160	25¢ 2013(P), Mount Rushmore (SD)	35,000	170
25¢ 2010(P), Yosemite (CA)	33,000	170	25¢ 2013P, Mount Rushmore (SD)	(23,547)	150
25¢ 2010P, Yosemite (CA)	(26,716)	160	25¢ 2014(P), Great Smoky Mtns (TN)	33,000	170
25¢ 2010(P), Grand Canyon (AZ)	33,000	170	25¢ 2014P, Great Smoky Mtns (TN)	(24,710)	150
25¢ 2010P, Grand Canyon (AZ)	(25,967)	160	25¢ 2014(P), Shenandoah (VA)	25,000	170
25¢ 2010(P), Mount Hood (OR)	33,000	170	25¢ 2014P, Shenandoah (VA)	(28,276)	150
25¢ 2010P, Mount Hood (OR)	(26,637)	160	25¢ 2014(P), Arches (UT)	22,000	170
25¢ 2011(P), Gettysburg (PA)	126,700	170	25¢ 2014P, Arches (UT)	(28,183)	150
25¢ 2011P, Gettysburg (PA)	(24,625)	160	25¢ 2014(P), Great Sand Dunes (CO)	22,000	170
25¢ 2011(P), Glacier (MT)	126,700	170	25¢ 2014P, Great Sand Dunes (CO)	(24,103)	150
25¢ 2011P, Glacier (MT)	(20,856)	160	25¢ 2014(P), Everglades (FL)	34,000	170
25¢ 2011(P), Olympic (WA)	104,900	170	25¢ 2014P, Everglades (FL)	(19,772)	150
25¢ 2011P, Olympic (WA)	(18,398)	160	25¢ 2015(P), Homestead (NE)	35,000	170
25¢ 2011P, Vicksburg (MS)	58,100	170	25¢ 2015(P), Homestead (NE)	(21,286)	150
25¢ 2011P, Vicksburg (MS)	(18,594)	160	25¢ 2015(P), Kisatchie (LA)	42,000	170
25¢ 2011P, Chickasaw (OK)	48,700	170	25¢ 2015P, Kisatchie (LA)	(19,449)	150
25¢ 2011P, Chickasaw (OK)	(16,827)	160	25¢ 2015(P), Blue Ridge Pkwy (NC)	45,000	170
25¢ 2012(P), El Yunque (PR)	24,000	170	25¢ 2015P, Blue Ridge Pkwy (NC)	(17,461)	150
25¢ 2012P, El Yunque (PR)	(17,314)	175	25¢ 2015(P), Bombay Hook (DE)	45,000	170
25¢ 2012(P), Chaco Culture (NM)	24,400	170	25¢ 2015P, Bombay Hook (DE)	(17,309)	150
25¢ 2012P, Chaco Culture (NM)	(17,146)	160	25¢ 2015(P), Saratoga (NY)	45,000	170
25¢ 2012(P), Acadia (ME)	25,400	170	25¢ 2015P, Saratoga (NY)	(17,563)	150
25¢ 2012(P), Acadia (ME)	(14,978)	160	25¢ 2016(P), Shawnee (IL)	105,000	170
25¢ 2012(P), Hawai'i Volcanoes (HI)	20,000	275	25¢ 2016P, Shawnee (IL)	(18,781)	150
25¢ 2012P, Hawai'i Volcanoes (HI)	(14,863)	330	25¢ 2016(P), Cumberland Gap (KY)	75,000	170
25¢ 2012(P), Denali (AK)	20,000	170	25¢ 2016P, Cumberland Gap (KY)	(18,713)	150
25¢ 2012P, Denali (AK)	(15,225)	165	25¢ 2016(P), Harpers Ferry (WV)	75,000	170
25¢ 2013(P), White Mountain (NH)	35,000	170	25¢ 2016P, Harpers Ferry (WV)	(18,896)	150
25¢ 2013P, White Mountain (NH)	(20,530)	150	25¢ 2016(P), T. Roosevelt (ND)	40,000	170
25¢ 2013(P), Perry's Victory (OH)	30,000	170	25¢ 2016P, T. Roosevelt (ND)	(18,917)	150
25¢ 2013P, Perry's Victory (OH)	(17,707)	150	25¢ 2016(P), Fort Moultrie (SC)	35,000	170
25¢ 2013(P), Great Basin (NV)	30,000	170	25¢ 2016P, Fort Moultrie (SC)	(17,882)	150

Notes: OGP = Coin in original government packaging. Bullion strikes, which have no mintmark, have a brilliant Uncirculated finish and are sold only through dealers. Numismatic strikes carry a mintmark and are sold directly to the public. Numismatic finishes include Burnished (a special matte finish the Mint calls "Uncirculated"), Proof, Reverse Proof, and others.

	Mintage	OGP
25¢ 2017(P), Effigy Mounds (IA) 35,000		$170
25¢ 2017P, Effigy Mounds (IA) . . . . . . (17,251)		150
25¢ 2017(P), F. Douglass (DC). 20,000		170
25¢ 2017P, F. Douglass (DC) . . . .(17,678)		150
25¢ 2017(P), Ozark (MO). 20,000		170
25¢ 2017P, Ozark (MO) . . . .(17,694)		150
25¢ 2017P, Ellis Island (NJ) 40,000		170
25¢ 2017P, Ellis Island (NJ). . . . .(17,670)		150
25¢ 2017P, George Rogers Clark (IN) . .35,000		170
25¢ 2017P, George Rogers Clark (IN) . .(14,731)		150
25¢ 2018(P), Pictured Rocks (MI). 30,000		170
25¢ 2018P, Pictured Rocks (MI) . . . . . (17,773)		150
25¢ 2018(P), Apostle Islands (WI) 30,000		170
25¢ 2018P, Apostle Islands (WI) . . . . . (16,802)		150
25¢ 2018(P), Voyageurs (MN) 30,000		170
25¢ 2018P, Voyageurs (MN) . . . . (16,839)		150
25¢ 2018(P), Cumberland Island (GA) . . .52,500		170
25¢ 2018P, Cumberland Island (GA) . . (16,376)		150
25¢ 2018P, Block Island (RI) 80,000		170
25¢ 2018P, Block Island (RI). . . . . (15,912)		150
25¢ 2019(P), Lowell (MA) 80,000		170
25¢ 2019P, Lowell (MA) . . . . (16,644)		150

	Mintage	OGP
25¢ 2019(P), Am. Mem. Park (NMI) 80,000		$170
25¢ 2019P, Am. Mem. Park (NMI) . . . (16,287)		150
25¢ 2019(P), War in the Pacific (Guam) 72,500		170
25¢ 2019P, War in the Pacific (Guam) . . . . (16,277)		150
25¢ 2019(P), Frank Church River (ID) . . 25,000		170
25¢ 2019P, Frank Church River (ID) . . (16,310)		150
25¢ 2019(P), San Antonio (TX) 55,200		170
25¢ 2019P, San Antonio (TX). . . . . . . (16,211)		150
25¢ 2020P, Nat'l Pk Am. Sam. (AS) 45,000		170
25¢ 2020(P), Nat'l Pk Am. Sam. (AS). . (15,781)		150
25¢ 2020P, Weir Farm (CT) 45,000		170
25¢ 2020(P), Weir Farm (CT) . . . . (15,326)		150
25¢ 2020(P), Salt River Bay (USVI) 45,000		170
25¢ 2020(P), Salt River Bay (USVI). . . . . (13,544)		150
25¢ 2020P, Marsh-Billings-Rock. (VT) . .45,000		170
25¢ 2020(P), Marsh-Billings-Rock. (VT) (13,545)		150
25¢ 2020P, Tallgrass Prairie (KS) 45,000		170
25¢ 2020(P), Tallgrass Prairie (KS). . . (13,613)		150
25¢ 2021P, Tuskegee Airmen (AL) 52,900		170
25¢ 2021(P), Tuskegee Airmen (AL). . (19,815)		150

Notes: OGP = Coin in original government packaging. Bullion strikes, which have no mintmark, have a brilliant Uncirculated finish and are sold only through dealers. Numismatic strikes carry a mintmark and are sold directly to the public. Numismatic finishes include Burnished (a special matte finish the Mint calls "Uncirculated"), Proof, Reverse Proof, and others.

$1 AMERICAN SILVER EAGLE COINS

Values below are based on spot silver value of $30 per ounce.

Variety 1
(Heraldic Eagle Reverse),
1986–2021.

Variety 2
(Flying Eagle Reverse),
2021 to date.

	Mintage	OGP
$1 1986	5,393,005	$70
$1 1986S	(1,446,778)	70
$1 1987	11,442,335	35
$1 1987S	(904,732)	70
$1 1988	5,004,646	38
$1 1988S	(557,370)	70
$1 1989	5,203,327	30
$1 1989S	(617,694)	70
$1 1990	5,840,110	36
$1 1990S	(695,510)	70
$1 1991	7,191,066	33
$1 1991S	(511,925)	70
$1 1992	5,540,068	33
$1 1992S	(498,654)	70
$1 1993	6,763,762	30
$1 1993P	(405,913)	60
$1 1994	4,227,319	60
$1 1994P	(372,168)	90
$1 1995	4,672,051	39
$1 1995P	(438,511)	70
$1 1995W	(30,125)	2,600
$1 1996	3,603,386	55
$1 1996P	(500,000)	70
$1 1997	4,295,004	43
$1 1997P	(435,368)	75
$1 1998	4,847,549	34
$1 1998P	(450,000)	70
$1 1999	7,408,640	37
$1 1999P	(549,769)	70
$1 2000(W)	9,239,132	35
$1 2000P	(600,000)	70
$1 2001(W)	9,001,711	33
$1 2001W	(746,398)	60
$1 2002(W)	10,539,026	33
$1 2002W	(647,342)	60
$1 2003(W)	8,495,008	33
$1 2003W	(747,831)	60
$1 2004(W)	8,882,754	—
$1 2004W	(801,602)	60
$1 2005(W)	8,891,025	30
$1 2005W	(816,663)	60
$1 2006(W)	10,676,522	32
$1 2006W, Burnished	468,020	46
$1 2006W	(1,092,477)	60
$1 2006P, Reverse Proof	(248,875)	85
$1 2007(W)	9,028,036	30
$1 2007W, Burnished	621,333	37
$1 2007W	(821,759)	60
$1 2008(W)	20,583,000	$30
$1 2008W, Burnished	533,757	37
$1 2008W, Burnished, Reverse of 2007	47,000	300
$1 2008W	(700,979)	60
$1 2009(W) (a)	30,459,000	30
$1 2010(W)	34,764,500	30
$1 2010W	(849,861)	60
$1 2011(W)(S)	40,020,000	30
$1 2011W, Burnished	409,927	37
$1 2011W	(947,355)	60
$1 2011S, Burnished	99,882	110
$1 2011P, Reverse Proof	(99,882)	160
$1 2012(W)(S)	33,121,500	30
$1 2012W, Burnished	226,120	37
$1 2012W	(869,386)	60
$1 2012S	(285,184)	60
$1 2012S, Reverse Proof	(224,981)	65
$1 2013(W)(S)	42,675,000	30
$1 2013W, Burnished	281,310	37
$1 2013W, Enhanced Uncirculated	222,091	70
$1 2013W	(934,812)	60
$1 2013W, Reverse Proof	(281,310)	65
$1 2014(W)(S)	44,006,000	30
$1 2014W, Burnished	253,169	37
$1 2014W	(944,757)	60
$1 2015(W)(P)(S)	47,000,000	30
$1 2015W, Burnished	223,879	37
$1 2015W	(707,518)	60
$1 2016(W)(S)	37,701,500	30
$1 2016W, Burnished	216,501	37
$1 2016W	(595,843)	60
$1 2017(W)(S)	18,065,500	33
$1 2017W, Burnished	176,739	37
$1 2017W	(440,596)	60
$1 2017S	(123,799)	65
$1 2018(W)(S)	15,700,000	39
$1 2018W, Burnished	131,935	37
$1 2018W	(361,192)	60
$1 2018S	(158,791)	60
$1 2019(W)	14,863,500	33
$1 2019W, Burnished	141,030	37
$1 2019W	(345,380)	60
$1 2019W, Enhanced Reverse Proof	(99,675)	90
$1 2019S	(146,799)	60
$1 2019S, Enhanced Reverse Proof	(29,909)	800
$1 2020(W)(S)	30,089,500	30
$1 2020W, Burnished	154,863	37

Notes: OGP = Coin in original government packaging. Bullion strikes, which have no mintmark, have a brilliant Uncirculated finish and are sold only through dealers. Numismatic strikes carry a mintmark and are sold directly to the public. Numismatic finishes include Burnished (a special matte finish the Mint calls "Uncirculated"), Proof, Reverse Proof, and others. **a.** No Proof dollars were made in 2009. Beware of alterations made privately outside the Mint.

Chart continued on next page.   **255**

	Mintage	OGP
$1 2020W, 75th Anniversary of the End of WWII (with privy mark)	(74,742)	$300
$1 2020W	(357,111)	60
$1 2020S	(191,271)	60
$1 2021(W), Variety 1	28,275,000	30
$1 2021W, Variety 1	(299,509)	60
$1 2021W, Variety 1, Reverse Proof	124,229	90
$1 2021(W)(S), Variety 2	*	37
$1 2021W, Variety 2, Burnished	154,861	37
$1 2021W, Variety 2	(311,773)	60
$1 2021S, Variety 2	(237,244)	60
$1 2021S, Variety 2, Reverse Proof	**	90
$1 2022(W)(S)	16,000,000	30
$1 2022W, Burnished	187,430	37

	Mintage	OGP
$1 2022W	(496,686)	$60
$1 2022S	(199,398)	60
$1 2023(W)(S)	8,495,008	32
$1 2023W, Burnished	199,533	37
$1 2023W		60
$1 2023S		60
$1 2024(W)(S)		30
$1 2024W, Burnished		37
$1 2024W		70
$1 2024S		70
2024(P), Star privy mark	500,000	65
$1 2025(W)(S)		
$1 2025W, Burnished		—
$1 2024W		—
$1 2025S		—

Notes: OGP = Coin in original government packaging. Bullion strikes, which have no mintmark, have a brilliant Uncirculated finish and are sold only through dealers. Numismatic strikes carry a mintmark and are sold directly to the public. Numismatic finishes include Burnished (a special matte finish the Mint calls "Uncirculated"), Proof, Reverse Proof, and others. * Included in $1 2021(W), Variety 1. ** Included in $1 2021(W), Variety 1 Reverse Proof.

American Silver Eagle Sets

	OGP
1997 Impressions of Liberty Set	$7,000
2006 20th Anniversary Silver Coin Set. Uncirculated, Proof, Reverse Proof	1,800
2006 20th Anniversary 1-oz. Gold- and Silver-Dollar Set. Uncirculated	165
2011 25th Anniversary Five-Coin Set. 2011W Unc., Pf; 2011P RevPf; 2011S Unc.; 2011 Bullion.	435
2012 75th Anniversary of San Francisco Mint Two-Piece Set. S-Mint Pf and RevPf silver dollars	125
2013 75th Anniversary of West Point Depository Two-Coin Set. W-Mint Enhanced Uncirculated and Reverse Proof silver dollars	180
2019 Pride of Two Nations Limited Edition Two-Coin Set. W-Mint Enhanced Reverse Proof and Royal Canadian Mint Silver Maple Leaf modified Proof	145
2021 Reverse Proof Two-Coin Set. W-Mint, Heraldic Eagle, and S-Mint, Flying Eagle, Reverse Proof silver dollars	180
	180

Note: OGP = Set in original government packaging.

AMERICAN GOLD EAGLE COINS

Bullion values are based on spot gold at $2,670 per ounce.

Variety 1 Reverse, 1986–2021.

Variety 2 Reverse, 2021 to date.

$5 Tenth-Ounce Gold

	Mintage	OGP		Mintage	OGP
$5 MCMLXXXVI (1986)	912,609	$295	$5 2005W	(49,265)	$280
$5 MCMLXXXVII (1987)	580,266	285	$5 2006	285,006	265
$5 MCMLXXXVIII (1988)	159,500	345	$5 2006W, Burnished	20,643	270
$5 MCMLXXXVIII (1988)P	(143,881)	280	$5 2006W	(47,277)	280
$5 MCMLXXXIX (1989)	264,790	315	$5 2007	190,010	270
$5 MCMLXXXIX (1989)P	(84,647)	280	$5 2007W, Burnished	22,501	270
$5 MCMXC (1990)	210,210	315	$5 2007W	(58,553)	280
$5 MCMXC (1990)P	(99,349)	280	$5 2008	305,000	265
$5 MCMXCI (1991)	165,200	315	$5 2008W, Burnished	12,657	270
$5 MCMXCI (1991)P	(70,334)	280	$5 2008W	(28,116)	280
$5 1992	209,300	315	$5 2009	270,000	265
$5 1992P	(64,874)	280	$5 2010	435,000	265
$5 1993	210,709	275	$5 2010W	(54,285)	280
$5 1993P	(58,649)	280	$5 2011	350,000	265
$5 1994	206,380	275	$5 2011W	(42,697)	280
$5 1994W	(62,849)	280	$5 2012	290,000	265
$5 1995	223,025	275	$5 2012W	(20,637)	280
$5 1995W	(62,667)	280	$5 2013	555,000	265
$5 1996	401,964	275	$5 2013W	(21,738)	280
$5 1996W	(57,047)	280	$5 2014	545,000	265
$5 1997	528,266	270	$5 2014W	(22,725)	280
$5 1997W	(34,977)	280	$5 2015	980,000	265
$5 1998	1,344,520	265	$5 2015W	(26,769)	280
$5 1998W	(39,395)	280	$5 2016	925,000	265
$5 1999	2,750,338	265	$5 2016W	(38,889)	280
$5 1999W, Unc. Made from unpolished Proof dies	*14,500*	875	$5 2017	395,000	265
$5 1999W	(48,428)	280	$5 2017W	(20,974)	280
$5 2000	569,153	270	$5 2018	230,000	265
$5 2000W	(49,971)	280	$5 2018W	(22,155)	280
$5 2001	269,147	265	$5 2019	195,000	265
$5 2001W	(37,530)	280	$5 2019W	(19,612)	280
$5 2002	230,027	265	$5 2020	350,000	265
$5 2002W	(40,864)	280	$5 2020W	(24,033)	280
$5 2003	245,029	265	$5 2021, Variety 1	490,000	265
$5 2003W	(40,027)	280	$5 2021W, Variety 1	(20,062)	280
$5 2004	250,016	265	$5 2021, Variety 2		265
$5 2004W	(35,131)	280	$5 2021W, Variety 2	(26,342)	280
$5 2005	300,043	265	$5 2022	575,000	265
			$5 2022W	(23,712)	280

Note: OGP = Coin in original government packaging.

Chart continued on next page.

	Mintage	OGP
$5 2023		$265
$5 2023W	(22,821)	280

	Mintage	OGP
$5 2024		$265
$5 2024W		280

Note: OGP = Coin in original government packaging.

$10 Quarter-Ounce Gold

	Mintage	OGP
$10 MCMLXXXVI (1986)	726,031	$700
$10 MCMLXXXVII (1987)	269,255	700
$10 MCMLXXXVIII (1988)	49,000	1,750
$10 MCMLXXXVIII (1988)P	(98,028)	700
$10 MCMLXXXIX (1989)	81,789	1,750
$10 MCMLXXXIX (1989)P	(54,170)	700
$10 MCMXC (1990)	41,000	2,100
$10 MCMXC (1990)P	(62,674)	700
$10 MCMXCI (1991)	36,100	2,200
$10 MCMXCI (1991)P	(50,839)	700
$10 1992	59,546	1,600
$10 1992P	(46,269)	700
$10 1993	71,864	1,600
$10 1993P	(46,464)	700
$10 1994	72,650	1,600
$10 1994W	(48,172)	700
$10 1995	83,752	1,650
$10 1995W	(47,526)	700
$10 1996	60,318	1,600
$10 1996W	(38,219)	700
$10 1997	108,805	650
$10 1997W	(29,805)	700
$10 1998	309,829	650
$10 1998W	(29,503)	700
$10 1999	564,232	650
$10 1999W, Unc. Made from unpolished Proof dies	10,000	1,200
$10 1999W	(34,417)	700
$10 2000	128,964	650
$10 2000W	(36,036)	700
$10 2001	71,280	1,500
$10 2001W	(25,613)	700
$10 2002	62,027	675
$10 2002W	(29,242)	700
$10 2003	74,029	650
$10 2003W	(30,292)	700
$10 2004	72,014	650
$10 2004W	(28,839)	700
$10 2005	72,015	650
$10 2005W	(37,207)	700
$10 2006	60,004	650
$10 2006W, Burnished	15,188	650

	Mintage	OGP
$10 2006W	(36,127)	$700
$10 2007	34,004	675
$10 2007W, Burnished	12,766	650
$10 2007W	(46,189)	700
$10 2008	70,000	650
$10 2008W, Burnished	8,883	650
$10 2008W	(18,877)	700
$10 2009	110,000	650
$10 2010	86,000	650
$10 2010W	(44,507)	700
$10 2011	80,000	650
$10 2011W	(28,782)	700
$10 2012	90,000	650
$10 2012W	(13,926)	700
$10 2013	114,500	650
$10 2013W	(12,782)	700
$10 2014	90,000	650
$10 2014W	(14,790)	700
$10 2015	158,000	650
$10 2015W	(15,775)	700
$10 2016	152,000	650
$10 2016W	(24,405)	700
$10 2017	64,000	650
$10 2017W	(14,516)	700
$10 2018	62,000	650
$10 2018W	(12,769)	700
$10 2019	38,000	650
$10 2019W	(11,861)	700
$10 2020	106,000	650
$10 2020W	(15,806)	700
$10 2021, Variety 1	162,000	650
$10 2021W, Variety 1	(13,531)	700
$10 2021, Variety 2		650
$10 2021W, Variety 2	(10,865)	700
$10 2021W, Variety 2	(a)	2,400
$10 2022	140,000	650
$10 2022W	(14,370)	700
$10 2023		650
$10 2023W	(13,884)	700
$10 2024		650
$10 2024W		700

Note: OGP = Coin in original government packaging. **a.** The Mint reported that 7,924 bullion-strike pieces were made in error with an unfinished Proof obverse die bearing a W mintmark. To date, just over 60 have been found.

$25 Half-Ounce Gold

	Mintage	OGP		Mintage	OGP
$25 MCMLXXXVI (1986).	599,566	$1,400	$25 2006W	(34,322)	$1,400
$25 MCMLXXXVII (1987)	131,255	2,300	$25 2007	47,002	1,300
$25 MCMLXXXVII (1987)P	(143,398)	1,400	$25 2007W, Burnished	11,455	1,300
$25 MCMLXXXVIII (1988).	45,000	1,650	$25 2007W	(44,025)	1,400
$25 MCMLXXXVIII (1988)P	(76,528)	1,400	$25 2008	61,000	1,350
$25 MCMLXXXIX (1989).	44,829	3,900	$25 2008W, Burnished	15,682	1,300
$25 MCMLXXXIX (1989)P.	(44,798)	1,400	$25 2008W	(22,602)	1,400
$25 MCMXC (1990).	31,000	4,200	$25 2009	110,000	1,300
$25 MCMXC (1990)P	(51,636)	1,400	$25 2010	81,000	1,300
$25 MCMXCI (1991)	24,100	4,500	$25 2010W	(44,527)	1,400
$25 MCMXCI (1991)P	(53,125)	1,400	$25 2011	70,000	1,350
$25 1992	54,404	2,100	$25 2011W	(26,781)	1,400
$25 1992P	(40,976)	1,400	$25 2012	43,000	1,300
$25 1993	73,324	2,200	$25 2012W	(12,919)	1,400
$25 1993P	(43,819)	1,400	$25 2013	57,000	1,300
$25 1994	62,400	2,200	$25 2013W	(12,716)	1,400
$25 1994W	(44,584)	1,400	$25 2014	35,000	1,350
$25 1995	53,474	3,050	$25 2014W	(14,693)	1,400
$25 1995W	(45,388)	1,400	$25 2015	78,000	1,300
$25 1996	39,287	2,750	$25 2015W	(15,820)	1,400
$25 1996W	(35,058)	1,400	$25 2016	71,000	1,300
$25 1997	79,605	2,150	$25 2016W	(23,578)	1,400
$25 1997W	(26,344)	1,400	$25 2017	37,000	1,300
$25 1998	169,029	1,300	$25 2017W	(12,715)	1,400
$25 1998W	(25,374)	1,400	$25 2018	32,000	1,300
$25 1999	263,013	1,300	$25 2018W	(9,961)	1,400
$25 1999W	(30,427)	1,400	$25 2019	30,000	1,300
$25 2000	79,287	2,150	$25 2019W	(10,703)	1,400
$25 2000W	(32,028)	1,400	$25 2020	70,000	1,300
$25 2001	48,047	2,150	$25 2020W	(14,020)	1,400
$25 2001W	(23,240)	1,400	$25 2021, Variety 1	95,000	1,300
$25 2002	70,027	1,350	$25 2021W, Variety 1	(12,180)	1,400
$25 2002W	(29,242)	1,400	$25 2021, Variety 2		1,300
$25 2003	79,029	1,300	$25 2021W, Variety 2		1,400
$25 2003W	(28,270)	1,400	$25 2022	75,000	1,300
$25 2004	98,040	1,300	$25 2022W	(11,876)	1,400
$25 2004W	(27,330)	1,400	$25 2023		1,300
$25 2005	80,023	1,300	$25 2023W	(11,408)	1,400
$25 2005W	(34,311)	1,400	$25 2024		1,300
$25 2006	66,005	1,300	$25 2024W		1,400
$25 2006W, Burnished	15,164	1,300			

Note: OGP = Coin in original government packaging.

$50 One-Ounce Gold

	Mintage	OGP		Mintage	OGP
$50 MCMLXXXVI (1986).	1,362,650	$2,550	$50 MCMLXXXIX (1989)W	(54,570)	$2,750
$50 MCMLXXXVI (1986)W	(446,290)	2,800	$50 MCMXC (1990).	373,210	2,550
$50 MCMLXXXVII (1987)	1,045,500	2,550	$50 MCMXC (1990)W	(62,401)	2,800
$50 MCMLXXXVII (1987)W	(147,498)	2,750	$50 MCMXCI (1991)	243,100	2,550
$50 MCMLXXXVIII (1988).	465,000	2,550	$50 MCMXCI (1991)W	(50,411)	2,800
$50 MCMLXXXVIII (1988)W	(87,133)	2,750	$50 1992	275,000	2,550
$50 MCMLXXXIX (1989).	415,790	2,550	$50 1992W	(44,826)	2,750

Note: OGP = Coin in original government packaging.

Chart continued on next page.

	Mintage	OGP
$50 1993	480,192	$2,550
$50 1993W	(34,369)	2,800
$50 1994	221,633	2,550
$50 1994W	(46,674)	2,750
$50 1995	200,636	2,550
$50 1995W	(46,368)	2,800
$50 1996	189,148	2,550
$50 1996W	(36,153)	2,800
$50 1997	664,508	2,550
$50 1997W	(32,999)	2,750
$50 1998	1,468,530	2,550
$50 1998W	(25,886)	2,800
$50 1999	1,505,026	2,550
$50 1999W	(31,427)	2,800
$50 2000	433,319	2,550
$50 2000W	(33,007)	2,750
$50 2001	143,605	2,550
$50 2001W	(24,555)	2,750
$50 2002	222,029	2,550
$50 2002W	(27,499)	2,750
$50 2003	416,032	2,550
$50 2003W	(28,344)	2,750
$50 2004	417,019	2,550
$50 2004W	(28,215)	2,750
$50 2005	356,555	2,550
$50 2005W	(35,246)	2,800
$50 2006	237,510	2,550
$50 2006W, Burnished	45,053	2,550
$50 2006W	(47,092)	2,750
$50 2006W, Reverse Proof	(9,996)	2,850
$50 2007	140,016	2,600
$50 2007W, Burnished	18,066	2,550
$50 2007W	(51,810)	2,750
$50 2008	710,000	2,550
$50 2008W, Burnished	11,908	2,550
$50 2008W	(30,237)	2,750
$50 2009	1,493,000	2,550
$50 2010	1,125,000	2,550
$50 2010W	(59,480)	2,750
$50 2011	857,000	2,550
$50 2011W, Burnished	8,729	2,550
$50 2011W	(48,306)	2,750
$50 2012	675,000	2,550

	Mintage	OGP
$50 2012W, Burnished	6,118	$2,600
$50 2012W	(23,630)	2,750
$50 2013	758,500	2,550
$50 2013W, Burnished	7,293	2,550
$50 2013W	(24,710)	2,750
$50 2014	425,000	2,550
$50 2014W, Burnished	7,902	2,550
$50 2014W	(28,703)	2,750
$50 2015	626,500	2,550
$50 2015W, Burnished	6,533	2,550
$50 2015W	(32,652)	2,750
$50 2016	817,500	2,550
$50 2016W, Burnished	6,887	2,550
$50 2016W	(41,621)	2,750
$50 2017	228,500	2,550
$50 2017W, Burnished	5,800	2,550
$50 2017W	(19,056)	2,750
$50 2018	191,000	2,550
$50 2018W, Burnished	8,518	2,550
$50 2018W	(15,564)	2,750
$50 2019	108,000	2,550
$50 2019W, Burnished	6,365	2,550
$50 2019W	(14,695)	2,750
$50 2020	747,500	2,550
$50 2020W, Burnished	6,284	2,400
$50 2020W	(5,874)	2,750
$50 2020W, 75th Anniversary of the End of WWII (with privy mark)	(1,939)	10,500
$50 2021, Variety 1	1,115,500	2,550
$50 2021W, Variety 1	(4,404)	2,750
$50 2021, Variety 2		2,550
$50 2021W, Variety 2, Burnished		2,550
$50 2021W, Variety 2	(5,562)	2,750
$50 2022	850,000	2,550
$50 2022W, Burnished		2,550
$50 2022W	(15,819)	2,750
$50 2023		2,550
$50 2023W, Burnished		2,550
$50 2023W	(15,863)	2,750
$50 2024		2,550
$50 2024W, Burnished		2,550
$50 2024W		2,750

Note: OGP = Set in original government packaging.

Gold Bullion Sets

	OGP
1987 Gold Set. $50, $25	4,050
1988 Gold Set. $50, $25, $10, $5	5,000
1989 Gold Set. $50, $25, $10, $5	5,000
1990 Gold Set. $50, $25, $10, $5	5,000
1991 Gold Set. $50, $25, $10, $5	5,000
1992 Gold Set. $50, $25, $10, $5	5,000
1993 Gold Set. $50, $25, $10, $5	5,000

	OGP
1993 Bicentennial Gold Set. $25, $10, $5, $1 silver eagle, and medal	$1,850
1994 Gold Set. $50, $25, $10, $5	5,000
1995 Gold Set. $50, $25, $10, $5	5,000
1995 Anniversary Gold Set. $50, $25, $10, $5, and $1 silver eagle	8,000
1996 Gold Set. $50, $25, $10, $5	5,000

Note: OGP = Set in original government packaging.

	OGP
1997 Gold Set. $50, $25, $10, $5..........	$5,000
1997 Impressions of Liberty Set.	
$100 platinum, $50 gold, $1 silver	2,000
1998 Gold Set. $50, $25, $10, $5..........	5,000
1999 Gold Set. $50, $25, $10, $5..........	5,000
2000 Gold Set. $50, $25, $10, $5..........	5,000
2001 Gold Set. $50, $25, $10, $5..........	5,000
2002 Gold Set. $50, $25, $10, $5	5,000
2003 Gold Set. $50, $25, $10, $5..........	5,000
2004 Gold Set. $50, $25, $10, $5..........	5,000
2005 Gold Set. $50, $25, $10, $5..........	5,000
2006 Gold Set. $50, $25, $10, $5..........	5,000
2007 Gold Set. $50, $25, $10, $5..........	5,000
2008 Gold Set. $50, $25, $10, $5..........	5,000
2010 Gold Set. $50, $25, $10, $5 (a)	5,000

	OGP
2011 Gold Set. $50, $25, $10, $5..........	$5,000
2012 Gold Set. $50, $25, $10, $5..........	5,000
2013 Gold Set. $50, $25, $10, $5..........	5,000
2014 Gold Set. $50, $25, $10, $5..........	5,000
2015 Gold Set. $50, $25, $10, $5..........	5,000
2016 Gold Set. $50, $25, $10, $5..........	5,000
2017 Gold Set. $50, $25, $10, $5..........	5,000
2018 Gold Set. $50, $25, $10, $5..........	5,000
2019 Gold Set. $50, $25, $10, $5..........	5,000
2020 Gold Set. $50, $25, $10, $5..........	5,000
2021 Gold Set, Variety 1. $50, $25, $10, $5 ..	5,000
2021 Gold Set, Variety 2. $50, $25, $10, $5 ..	5,000
2022 Gold Set. $50, $25, $10, $5..........	5,000
2023 Gold Set. $50, $25, $10, $5..........	5,000
2024 Gold Set. $50, $25, $10, $5..........	5,000

Note: OGP = Set in original government packaging. **a.** The U.S. Mint did not issue a 2009 gold set.

2006 20th Anniversary Sets

	OGP
2006W $50 Gold Set. Uncirculated, Proof, Reverse Proof	$8,250
2006W 1-oz. Gold and Silver Coin Set. Burnished	2,550

Note: OGP = Set in original government packaging.

Gold Bullion Burnished Sets 2006–2008

	OGP
2006W Burnished Gold Set. $50, $25, $10, $5...	$4,900
2007W Burnished Gold Set. $50, $25, $10, $5...	4,900
2008W Burnished Gold Set. $50, $25, $10, $5...	4,900

Note: OGP = Set in original government packaging.

AMERICAN BUFFALO .9999 FINE GOLD BULLION COINS

	Mintage	OGP
$5 2008W, Burnished	17,429	$390
$5 2008W......................	(18,884)	525
$10 2008W, Burnished	9,949	975
$10 2008W.....................	(13,125)	1,100
$25 2008W, Burnished	16,908	1,300
$25 2008W.....................	(12,169)	1,850
$50 2006	337,012	2,550
$50 2006W	(246,267)	2,550
$50 2007	136,503	2,550
$50 2007W	(58,998)	2,550
$50 2008 (a)...................	214,053 (a)	2,550

	Mintage	OGP
$50 2008W, Burnished	9,074	$2,700
$50 2008W.....................	(18,863)	2,550
$50 2009	200,000	2,550
$50 2009W.....................	(49,306)	2,550
$50 2010	209,000	2,550
$50 2010W.....................	(49,263)	2,550
$50 2011	250,000	2,550
$50 2011W.....................	(28,693)	2,550
$50 2012	100,000	2,550
$50 2012W.....................	(19,765)	2,550
$50 2013	198,500	2,550

Note: OGP = Set in original government packaging. **a.** Includes 24,553 sold as Lunar New Year Celebration coins.

Chart continued on next page.

	Mintage	OGP
$50 2013W	(18,594)	$2,600
$50 2013W, Reverse Proof	(47,836)	2,650
$50 2014	180,500	2,550
$50 2014W	(20,557)	2,600
$50 2015	220,500	2,550
$50 2015W	(16,591)	2,600
$50 2016	219,500	2,550
$50 2016W	(21,878)	2,600
$50 2017	99,500	2,550
$50 2017W	(15,810)	2,600
$50 2018	121,500	2,550
$50 2018W	(15,283)	2,600

	Mintage	OGP
$50 2019	61,500	$2,550
$50 2019W	(14,836)	2,650
$50 2020	242,000	2,550
$50 2020W	(11,887)	2,750
$50 2021	350,500	2,550
$50 2021W	(16,958)	2,600
$50 2022		2,550
$50 2022W	(15,493)	2,600
$50 2023		2,550
$50 2023W	(13,731)	2,600
$50 2024		2,550
$50 2024W		2,600

Note: OGP = Set in original government packaging.

American Buffalo Gold Bullion Sets

	Mintage	OGP
2008W Four-coin set. $50, $25, $10, $5...	6,049	$5,500
2008W Four-coin set, Burnished. $50, $25, $10, $5...................................		6,250
2008W Double Prosperity Set. Uncirculated $25 Buffalo and $25 American Gold Eagle coins	7,751	3,250

Note: OGP = Set in original government packaging.

FIRST SPOUSE $10 GOLD BULLION COINS
Half-Ounce 24-Karat Gold

Martha Washington   **Abigail Adams**   **Jefferson's Liberty**   **Dolley Madison**

	Mintage	OGP-MS	OGP-PF
$10 2007W, Martha Washington.............................(19,167) 17,661		$1,250	$1,250
$10 2007W, Abigail Adams...................................(17,149) 17,142		1,250	1,250
$10 2007W, Thomas Jefferson's Liberty ....(19,815) 19,823		1,250	1,250
$10 2007W, Dolley Madison ....(17,943) 12,340		1,250	1,250
$10 2008W, Elizabeth Monroe................................(7,800) 4,462		1,250	1,250
$10 2008W, Louisa Adams ....(6,581) 3,885		1,250	1,250
$10 2008W, Andrew Jackson's Liberty ....(7,684) 4,609		1,250	1,250
$10 2008W, Martin Van Buren's Liberty ....(6,807) 3,826		1,250	1,250
$10 2009W, Anna Harrison ....(6,251) 3,645		1,250	1,250
$10 2009W, Letitia Tyler ....(5,296) 3,240		1,250	1,250
$10 2009W, Julia Tyler ....(4,844) 3,143		1,250	1,250
$10 2009W, Sarah Polk ....(5,151) 3,489		1,250	1,250
$10 2009W, Margaret Taylor ....(4,936) 3,627		1,250	1,250
$10 2010W, Abigail Fillmore ....(6,130) 3,482		1,250	1,250
$10 2010W, Jane Pierce ....(4,775) 3,338		1,250	1,250
$10 2010W, James Buchanan's Liberty.......................(7,110) 5,162		1,250	1,250
$10 2010W, Mary Lincoln ....(6,861) 3,695		1,250	1,250

Note: OGP = Set in original government packaging.

	Mintage	OGP-MS	OGP-PF
$10 2011W, Eliza Johnson . . . .(3,887)	2,905	$1,250	$1,250
$10 2011W, Julia Grant . . . .(3,943)	2,892	1,250	1,250
$10 2011W, Lucy Hayes . . . .(3,868)	2,196	1,250	1,250
$10 2011W, Lucretia Garfield . . . .(3,653)	2,168	1,250	1,250
$10 2012W, Alice Paul . . . .(3,505)	2,798	1,250	1,250
$10 2012W, Frances Cleveland, Variety 1 . . . .(3,158)	2,454	1,250	1,250
$10 2012W, Caroline Harrison . . . .(3,046)	2,436	1,250	1,250
$10 2012W, Frances Cleveland, Variety 2 . . . .(3,104)	2,425	1,250	1,250
$10 2013W, Ida McKinley . . . .(2,724)	2,008	1,250	1,250
$10 2013W, Edith Roosevelt . . . .(2,840)	2,027	1,250	1,250
$10 2013W, Helen Taft . . . .(2,598)	1,993	1,250	1,250
$10 2013W, Ellen Wilson . . . .(2,511)	1,980	1,250	1,250
$10 2013W, Edith Wilson . . . .(2,464)	1,974	1,250	1,250
$10 2014W, Florence Harding . . . .(2,372)	1,949	1,250	1,250
$10 2014W, Grace Coolidge . . . .(2,315)	1,944	1,250	1,250
$10 2014W, Lou Hoover . . . .(2,392)	1,936	1,250	1,250
$10 2014W, Eleanor Roosevelt . . . .(2,377)	1,886	1,250	1,250
$10 2015W, Elizabeth Truman . . . .(2,747)	1,946	1,250	1,250
$10 2015W, Mamie Eisenhower . . . .(2,704)	2,102	1,250	1,250
$10 2015W, Jacqueline Kennedy . . . .(11,222)	6,771	1,250	1,250
$10 2015W, Claudia Taylor "Lady Bird" Johnson . . . .(2,653)	1,927	1,250	1,250
$10 2016W, Pat Nixon . . . .(2,645)	1,839	1,250	1,250
$10 2016W, Betty Ford . . . .(2,471)	1,824	1,250	1,350
$10 2016W, Nancy Reagan . . . .(3,548)	2,009	1,250	1,350
$10 2020W, Barbara Bush . . . .(2,896)	1,932	1,250	1,350

Note: OGP = Set in original government packaging.

MMIX ULTRA HIGH RELIEF GOLD COIN (2009)

MMIX Ultra High Relief Gold Coin
*Photographed at an angle to
show the edge, lettered E PLURIBUS
UNUM, and the depth of relief.*

A modern version of the 1907 Ultra High Relief double eagle gold pattern was produced in 2009 at the Philadelphia Mint. It was made to demonstrate technical advances
in minting techniques that make possible such a coin. The original design was never
made for commercial use because it could not be made in sufficient quantities.

The design was by Augustus Saint-Gaudens. A version of it in much lower relief
was used on double eagle coins minted from 1907 to 1933. To create the coin in ultra
high relief, the 2009 version was made in a slightly smaller diameter, and composed
of 24-karat gold, making it easier to strike and maintain the fidelity of the design.
Through 21st-century technology the original Saint-Gaudens plasters were digitally
mapped by the Mint and used in the die-making process. The date was changed to
2009, and four additional stars were added to represent the current 50 states. The
inscription "In God We Trust" was not used on the 1907 version.

The MMIX Ultra High Relief gold coins are 4 mm thick and contain one ounce of
.999 fine gold. All are Uncirculated (business strikes). All are made at the West Point
Mint, and packaged by the Mint in a special mahogany box.

See next page for chart.

	Mintage	OGP
(2009) MMIX (2009), Uncirculated	114,427	$2,650

Note: OGP = Set in original government packaging.

400TH ANNIVERSARY OF THE MAYFLOWER GOLD COIN

In 2020 the United States Mint recognized the 400th anniversary of the Pilgrims' landing at Plymouth Rock aboard the *Mayflower*. Under authority granted by Congress to the secretary of the Treasury, the Mint issued two 1/4-ounce, ten-dollar gold coins from the West Point Mint, one in Proof and the other a Reverse Proof. Both have a reeded edge and a diameter of 22 mm, with a fineness of .9999. The Proof was sold individually, while the Reverse Proof was part of a two-coin set that also contained a gold £25 commemorative Proof coin from the British Royal Mint.

	Mintage	OGP
2020W, Proof . . . .*(4,743)*	$850
2020W, Reverse Proof. . . . .*(4,881)*	700
2020W, two-coin Proof set **(a)**. . . . .*(9,072)*	110

Note: OGP = Coin or set in original government packaging. **a.** Contains the 2020-W Proof coin and a £25 British commemorative Proof gold coin.

75TH ANNIVERSARY OF THE END OF WORLD WAR II GOLD COIN

Under the Treasury secretary's authority to issue gold coins "from time to time" without specific commemorative legislation, in 2020 the Mint issued a .9999 fine gold twenty-five-dollar coin to mark the 75th anniversary of the end of World War II. Struck at the West Point Mint, the Proof coin weighs one-half ounce and measures 27 mm in diameter. Its edge is reeded. The Mint also issued a related one-ounce Proof silver medal, privy-marked West Point quarter dollars, and privy-marked gold and silver American Eagles in celebration of the anniversary.

	Mintage	OGP
2020W, Proof . . . .*(7,367)*	$1,350

Note: OGP = Coin in original government packaging.

AMERICAN LIBERTY HIGH RELIEF GOLD COINS

The first American Liberty High Relief .9999-fine gold coin, with a weight of one ounce and a face value of $100, was minted at West Point in 2015. The coin was not congressionally mandated, instead being created under authority granted to the Secretary of the Treasury by federal law. Its design was created in part to show "a 'modern' Liberty that reflects the nation's diversity."

The designs for the American Liberty High Relief gold coins are created to take full advantage of the same high-relief techniques used to create the MMIX Ultra High Relief gold coin. The Mint also issues each new design as a silver medal.

2015-W

1792–2017-W

2018-W, $10

2019-W

2021-W

2023-W

	Mintage	OGP
$100 2015W, 1 oz., Uncirculated	49,325	$2,750
$100 1792–2017W, 1 oz., Proof	(30,823)	2,600
$10 2018W, 1/10 oz., Proof	(29,590)	260
$100 2019W, 1 oz., Enhanced Uncirculated	24,609	2,600
$100 2021W, 1 oz., Proof	(12,470)	5,250
$100 2023W, 1 oz., Proof	(12,500)	3,000

Note: OGP = Coin in original government packaging.

LIBERTY AND BRITANNIA GOLD COINS

In 2024, the Mint released the first issue in a new series produced in collaboration with the United Kingdom's Royal Mint. The one-ounce coins, struck at West Point with a face value of $100, are composed of .9999 fine gold and measure 32.7 mm in diameter. The obverse depicts the allegorical figures of Liberty and Britannia, representing America and Britain, respectively; this is the first time the two figures are shown on a U.S. coin. Like the American Liberty High Relief gold coins and similar series, the Liberty and Britannia coins are produced under the authority of the Treasury secretary to issue gold coins "from time to time" without specific commemorative legislation.

	Mintage	OGP
2024W, Uncirculated	10,000	$3,600

Note: OGP = Coin in original government packaging.

230TH ANNIVERSARY FLOWING HAIR HIGH RELIEF GOLD COIN

2024-W

2024-W With Privy Mark

In 2024, the Mint released a special gold coin in honor of the 230th anniversary of the first U.S. one-dollar coin: the Flowing Hair silver dollar, issued on October 15, 1794. The one-ounce bullion coins, measuring 30.61 mm in diameter, are produced in .9999 fine gold at the West Point Mint. The high-relief obverse and reverse designs are modern reproductions of those on the original dollar. The edge is lettered HUNDRED CENTS ONE DOLLAR OR UNIT, with one to three 6-pointed stars in the spaces between words. The coins are produced under the Treasury secretary's authority to issue gold coins "from time to time" without specific commemorative legislation.

	Mintage	OGP
2024W, Uncirculated	17,500	3,700
2024W, Uncirculated, with privy mark	230	—

Note: OGP = Coin in original government packaging.

AMERICAN PLATINUM EAGLE COINS

The one-ounce American Eagle platinum coin is designated $100 and contains one ounce of pure platinum. Fractional denominations containing 1/2 ounce, 1/4 ounce, or 1/10 ounce are called $50, $25, and $10, respectively.

Bullion values are based on spot platinum at $960 per ounce.

Obverse for Bullion
and Proof, All Years

Reverse for Bullion,
All Years; for Proof in 1997

$10 Tenth-Ounce Platinum

	Mintage	OGP		Mintage	OGP
$10 1997	70,250	$165	$10 2004	15,010	$120
$10 1997W	(36,993)	135	$10 2004W	(7,161)	110
$10 1998	39,525	165	$10 2005	14,013	120
$10 1998W	(19,847)	110	$10 2005W	(8,104)	140
$10 1999	55,955	125	$10 2006	11,001	120
$10 1999W	(19,133)	110	$10 2006W, Burnished	3,544	405
$10 2000	34,027	120	$10 2006W	(10,205)	110
$10 2000W	(15,651)	110	$10 2007	13,003	120
$10 2001	52,017	120	$10 2007W, Burnished	5,556	300
$10 2001W	(12,174)	110	$10 2007W	(8,176)	110
$10 2002	23,005	120	$10 2008	17,000	120
$10 2002W	(12,365)	110	$10 2008W, Burnished	3,706	370
$10 2003	22,007	120	$10 2008W	(5,138)	135
$10 2003W	(9,534)	110			

Note: OGP = Coin in original government packaging.

$25 Quarter-Ounce Platinum

	Mintage	OGP		Mintage	OGP
$25 1997	27,100	$280	$25 2004	18,010	$260
$25 1997W	(18,628)	285	$25 2004W	(5,193)	285
$25 1998	38,887	260	$25 2005	12,013	260
$25 1998W	(14,873)	285	$25 2005W	(6,592)	285
$25 1999	39,734	260	$25 2006	12,001	260
$25 1999W	(13,507)	285	$25 2006W, Burnished	2,676	725
$25 2000	20,054	260	$25 2006W	(7,813)	285
$25 2000W	(11,995)	285	$25 2007	8,402	260
$25 2001	21,815	260	$25 2007W, Burnished	3,690	625
$25 2001W	(8,847)	285	$25 2007W	(6,017)	285
$25 2002	27,405	290	$25 2007W, Frosted FREEDOM	(21)	—
$25 2002W	(9,282)	285	$25 2008	22,800	260
$25 2003	25,207	260	$25 2008W, Burnished	2,481	1,000
$25 2003W	(7,044)	285	$25 2008W	(4,153)	285

Note: OGP = Coin in original government packaging.

$50 Half-Ounce Platinum

	Mintage	OGP		Mintage	OGP
$50 1997	20,500	$490	$50 1998W	(13,836)	$575
$50 1997W	(15,431)	575	$50 1999	32,309	490
$50 1998	32,415	490	$50 1999W	(11,103)	575

Note: OGP = Coin in original government packaging.

Chart continued on next page.

267

	Mintage	OGP
$50 2000	18,892	$490
$50 2000W	(11,049)	575
$50 2001	12,815	490
$50 2001W	(8,254)	575
$50 2002	24,005	490
$50 2002W	(8,772)	575
$50 2003	17,409	490
$50 2003W	(7,131)	575
$50 2004	13,236	490
$50 2004W	(5,063)	575
$50 2005	9,013	490
$50 2005W	(5,942)	575

	Mintage	OGP
$50 2006	9,602	$490
$50 2006W, Burnished	2,577	925
$50 2006W	(7,649)	575
$50 2007	7,001	490
$50 2007W, Burnished	3,635	925
$50 2007W	(25,519)	575
$50 2007W, Reverse Proof	(19,583)	600
$50 2007W, Frosted FREEDOM	(21)	—
$50 2008	14,000	490
$50 2008W, Burnished	2,253	1,300
$50 2008W	(4,020)	575

Note: OGP = Coin in original government packaging.

$100 One-Ounce Platinum
Proof Platinum Reverse Designs

1998: Eagle Over New England. "Vistas of Liberty" series.

1999: Eagle Above Southeastern Wetlands. "Vistas of Liberty" series.

2000: Eagle Above America's Heartland. "Vistas of Liberty" series.

2001: Eagle Above America's Southwest. "Vistas of Liberty" series.

2002: Eagle Fishing in America's Northwest. "Vistas of Liberty" series.

2003.

2004.

2005.

2006: Legislative Branch. "Foundations of Democracy" series.

2007: Executive Branch. "Foundations of Democracy" series.

2008: Judicial Branch. "Foundations of Democracy" series.

2009: To Form a More Perfect Union. "Preamble to the Constitution" series.

2010: To Establish Justice. "Preamble to the Constitution" series.

2011: To Insure Domestic Tranquility. "Preamble to the Constitution" series.

2012: To Provide for the Common Defence. "Preamble to the Constitution" series.

2013: To Promote the General Welfare. "Preamble to the Constitution" series.

2014: To Secure the Blessings of Liberty to Ourselves and Our Posterity. "Preamble to the Constitution" series.

2015: Liberty Nurtures Freedom. "Torches of Liberty" series.

2016: Portrait of Liberty. "Torches of Liberty" series.

Common reverse: 2018–2020 and 2021–2025 series.

2018. Life. "Preamble to the Declaration of Independence" series.

2019. Liberty.
"Preamble to the Declaration
of Independence" series.

2020: Pursuit of Happiness.
"Preamble to the Declaration
of Independence" series.

2021: Freedom of Religion.
"First Amendment to the
U.S. Constitution" series.

2022: Freedom of Speech.
"First Amendment to the
U.S. Constitution" series.

2023: Freedom of the Press.
"First Amendment to the
U.S. Constitution" series.

2024: Right to Assemble.
"First Amendment to the
U.S. Constitution" series.

2025: Right to Petition.
"First Amendment to the
U.S. Constitution" series.

	Mintage	OGP
$100 1997	56,000	$975
$100 1997W	(20,851)	1,150
$100 1998	133,002	975
$100 1998W	(14,912)	1,150
$100 1999	56,707	975
$100 1999W	(12,363)	1,150
$100 2000	10,003	975
$100 2000W	(12,453)	1,150
$100 2001	14,070	1,550
$100 2001W	(8,969)	1,150
$100 2002	11,502	1,300
$100 2002W	(9,834)	1,150

	Mintage	OGP
$100 2003	8,007	$1,100
$100 2003W	(8,246)	1,150
$100 2004	7,009	975
$100 2004W	(6,007)	1,150
$100 2005	6,310	975
$100 2005W	(6,602)	1,200
$100 2006	6,000	975
$100 2006W, Burnished	3,068	1,850
$100 2006W	(9,152)	1,200
$100 2007	7,202	975
$100 2007W, Burnished	4,177	1,800
$100 2007W	(8,363)	1,150

Note: OGP = Coin in original government packaging.

	Mintage	OGP
$100 2007W, Frosted FREEDOM	(12)	—
$100 2008	21,800	$975
$100 2008W, Burnished	2,876	1,950
$100 2008W	(4,769)	1,150
$100 2009W	(7,945)	1,150
$100 2010W	(14,790)	1,150
$100 2011W	(14,835)	1,150
$100 2012W	(9,081)	1,150
$100 2013W	(5,763)	1,150
$100 2014	16,900	975
$100 2014W	(4,596)	1,150
$100 2015	20,000	1,750
$100 2015W	(3,881)	975
$100 2016	20,000	1,150
$100 2016W	(9,151)	1,400

	Mintage	OGP
$100 2017	20,000	$975
$100 2017W	(8,892)	1,150
$100 2018	30,000	975
$100 2018W	(14,499)	1,200
$100 2019	40,000	975
$100 2019W	(10,928)	1,150
$100 2020	56,500	975
$100 2020W	(9,825)	1,200
$100 2021	75,000	975
$100 2021W	(9,984)	1,200
$100 2022	80,000	975
$100 2022W	(9,940)	1,200
$100 2023		975
$100 2023W		1,150
$100 2024		975
$100 2024W		1,150

Note: OGP = Coin in original government packaging.

Platinum Bullion Sets

	OGP
1997 Platinum Set. $100, $50, $25, $10	$2,450
1998 Platinum Set. $100, $50, $25, $10	2,450
1999 Platinum Set. $100, $50, $25, $10	2,450
2000 Platinum Set. $100, $50, $25, $10	2,450
2001 Platinum Set. $100, $50, $25, $10	2,450
2002 Platinum Set. $100, $50, $25, $10	2,450
2003 Platinum Set. $100, $50, $25, $10	2,450
2004W Platinum Set. $100, $50, $25, $10	2,450
2005W Platinum Set. $100, $50, $25, $10	2,450
2006W Platinum Set. $100, $50, $25, $10	2,450
2006W Platinum Burnished Set. $100, $50, $25, $10	2,800
2007W Platinum Set. $100, $50, $25, $10	2,450
2007W Platinum Burnished Set. $100, $50, $25, $10	2,650
2008W Platinum Set. $100, $50, $25, $10	2,450
2008W Platinum Burnished Set. $100, $50, $25, $10	4,650

Note: OGP = Set in original government packaging.

American Eagle 10th Anniversary Platinum Set

	OGP
Two-coin set containing one Proof platinum half-ounce and one Enhanced Reverse Proof half-ounce dated 2007W. Housed in hardwood box with mahogany finish	$1,300

Note: OGP = Set in original government packaging.

AMERICAN PALLADIUM
EAGLE COINS (2017 TO DATE)

Designer Adolph A. Weinman; composition .9995 palladium; net weight 1 oz. pure palladium; diameter 32.7 mm; reeded edge; mints: Philadelphia, West Point.

The $25 American Palladium Eagle features a high-relief obverse design derived from artist Adolph Weinman's Winged Liberty dime of 1916 to 1945. The reverse is a high-relief version of Weinman's 1907 American Institute of Architects gold medal reverse, showing an eagle grasping a branch.

Bullion-strike coins are minted in Philadelphia and distributed through the Mint's authorized purchasers. Proof, Reverse Proof, and Uncirculated numismatic versions struck at the West Point Mint are sold by the Mint directly to collectors.

As of this printing, the spot price of palladium is about $980 per ounce.

	Mintage	OGP
$25 2017	*15,000*	$1,050
$25 2018W	*(14,986)*	1,350
$25 2019W, Reverse Proof	*(18,775)*	1,500
$25 2020W, Burnished	9,742	1,150
$25 2021	8,700	1,050
$25 2021W	*(5,170)*	1,050
$25 2022W, Reverse Proof	*(7,366)*	1,650
$25 2023W	6,000	1,050
$25 2024W	*(6,000)*	1,050

Note: OGP = Coin in original government packaging.

Private gold refers to the necessity pieces of various shapes, denominations, and finenesses that were coined by facilities other than official U.S. mints and circulated in isolated areas of the country by assayers, bankers, and other private individuals and organizations. Usually, private coins were circulated due to a shortage of regular federal coinage. In the Western states particularly, official money became so scarce that gold itself—the very commodity the pioneers had come so far to acquire—was converted into a local medium of exchange. Although some numismatists use the terms *territorial gold* and *state gold*, no state or territory had the authority to coin money (with the exception of the Mormon issues of Salt Lake City).

Christopher Bechtler, Carolina Gold, 5 DOLLARS

Private and territorial gold coinage is a complex series. Examples are rarely encountered and, in most cases, are very valuable. For more information on these coins, readers are urged to consult the *Guide Book of United States Coins* (popularly known as the *Red Book*), which is considered the standard reference for the series.

Moffat & Co., San Francisco, $16 Ingot

Baldwin & Co., San Francisco, TEN DOLLARS

Clark, Gruber & Co., Denver, TEN DOLLARS

Kellogg & Co., San Francisco, FIFTY DOLLARS

California Small-Denomination Gold (Various)

HARD TIMES TOKENS (1832–1844)

During the financial crises of 1832 to 1844 many government coins were hoarded, and privately made tokens were used out of necessity. The so-called Hard Times tokens of this period were slightly smaller and lighter than normal large cents. They were made of copper or brass and are of two general groups: political tokens whose theme centered on President Andrew Jackson's fight against the Bank of the United States, and tradesmen's cards, issued by merchants. Many different designs and varieties exist.

	VF	EF
Hard Times Tokens, 1832–1844, most common pieces	$20	$35

CIVIL WAR TOKENS (1860's)

Civil War tokens are generally divided into two groups: tradesmen's tokens, and anonymously issued pieces with political or patriotic themes. They came into existence only because of the scarcity of government coins and disappeared as soon as the bronze coins of 1864 met the public demand for small copper change.

These tokens vary greatly in composition and design. A number were more or less faithful imitations of the copper-nickel cent. A few of this type have the word NOT in very small letters above the words ONE CENT.

	F	VF	EF	Unc.
Copper or Brass Tokens	$5	$8	$12	$30
Nickel or German Silver Tokens..............................	20	30	60	110
White-Metal Tokens..	25	35	65	110
Copper-Nickel Tokens......................................	30	50	80	125
Silver Tokens...	80	150	225	400

Values shown are for the most common tokens in each composition.

TOP 25 U.S. COIN PRICES REALIZED AT AUCTION

Combined with dealer's buying prices, auction data can help advanced collectors understand the modern market for high-end rarities.

It is important to understand that the following prices include a buyer's premium (a surcharge which the buyer pays the auction house over the final "hammer price," or winning bid; contemporary auction houses charge around 17.5%) and the seller's commission (a small percentage of the hammer price which the individual selling the coin pays to the auction house; this fee can sometimes be negotiated to less than 5%).

Rank	Price	Coin	Grade	Firm	Date
1	$18,872,250	$20, 1933	MS-65	Sotheby's	Jun 2021
2	10,016,875	Silver $1, 1794	PCGS SP-66 CAC	Stack's Bowers	Jan 2013
3	9,360,000	Prefederal, 1787, Brasher Doubloon, EB on Wing	NGC MS-65* CAC	Heritage	Jan 2021
4	8,400,000	$5, 1822	PCGS AU-50	Stack's Bowers	Mar 2021
5	7,680,000	Silver $1, 1804, Class I	PCGS PF-68	Stack's Bowers	Aug 2021
6	7,590,020	$20, 1933	Gem BU	Sotheby's/Stack's	Jul 2002
7	7,200,000	$20, 1861, Paquet Reverse	PCGS MS-67 CAC	Heritage	Aug 2021
8	6,600,000	Silver $1, 1794	PCGS MS-66+ CAC	Heritage	Aug 2021
9	5,520,000	$3, 1870-S	PCGS SP-50 893 Engraved	Heritage	Jan 2023
10	5,280,000	$10, 1804, Plain 4, BD-2	PCGS 65+ DC CAC	Heritage	Jan 2021
11	4,993,750	Silver $1, 1794	PCGS MS-66+	Stack's/Sotheby's	Sep 2015
12	4,620,000	$5, 1821	PCGS PF-65 Cam CAC	Heritage	Sep 2022
13	4,582,500	Prefederal, 1787, Brasher Doubloon, EB on Wing	NGC MS-63 CAC	Heritage	Jan 2014
14	4,560,000	5¢, 1913, Liberty Head	PCGS PF-66 CAC	Stack's Bowers	Aug 2018
15	4,440,000	$20, 1927-D	PCGS MS-66	Heritage	Aug 2022
16	4,320,000	$20, MCMVII, Ultra High Relief, Lettered Edge, Inverted	PCGS PF-69	Heritage	Aug 2023
17	4,140,000	Silver $1, 1804, Class I	PCGS PF-68	B&M	Aug 1999
18	4,080,000	$5, 1825/4/1, BD-1	PCGS PF-67 Cam CAC	Stack's Bowers	Aug 2022
19	3,960,000	Trade $1, 1885	NGC PF-66	Heritage	Jan 2019
20	3,877,500	Silver $1, 1804, Class I	PCGS PF-62	Heritage	Aug 2013
21	3,840,000	$5, 1829, Small Date, BD-2	PCGS PF-66+ CAC	Heritage	Aug 2023
22	3,737,500	5¢, 1913, Liberty Head	NGC PF-64	Heritage	Jan 2010
23	3,737,500	Silver $1, 1804, Class I	NGC PF-62	Heritage	Apr 2008
24	3,600,000	10¢, 1873-CC, No Arrows	PCGS MS-65	Heritage	Jan 2023
25	3,600,000	$20, MCMVII, Ultra High Relief, Lettered Edge	NGC PF-68	Heritage	Feb 2021

KEY

Price: The sale price of the coin, including the appropriate buyer's fee.

Coin: The denomination/classification, date, and description of the coin, along with pertinent catalog or reference numbers. Abbreviations include: BD = Bass-Dannreuther; HR = High Relief; LE = Lettered Edge; Prefed = pre-federal issue.

Grade: The grade of the coin, plus the name of the grading firm (if independently graded). NGC = Numismatic Guaranty Company of America; PCGS = Professional Coin Grading Service.

Firm: The auction firm (or firms) that sold the coin. B&M = Bowers & Merena; Stack's Bowers = Stack's Bowers Galleries (the name under which Stack's and B&M merged in 2010; also encompasses the merger of Stack's and American Numismatic Rarities in 2006); Soth = Sotheby's.

Auction records compiled and edited by P. Scott Rubin.

Over the years coin collectors and dealers have developed a special jargon to describe coins. Here are some terms frequently used within the hobby.

altered date—A false date on a coin; a date fraudulently changed to make a coin appear to be one of a rarer or more valuable issue.

bag mark—A surface mark, usually a small nick, acquired by a coin through contact with others in a mint bag.

blank—The formed piece of metal on which a coin design will be stamped.

bullion—Uncoined silver, gold, or platinum in the form of bars, ingots, or plate.

certified coin—A coin that has been graded, authenticated, and encapsulated in plastic by an independent third-party (neither buyer nor seller) grading service.

circulation strike—A coin intended for eventual use in commerce, as opposed to a Proof coin.

clad coinage—U.S. dimes, quarters, half dollars, and some dollars made since 1965. Each coin has a center core of pure copper and a layer of copper-nickel or silver on both sides.

die—A piece of metal engraved with a negative-image design and used for stamping coins.

die variety—Any minor alteration in the basic design of a coin type.

dipped coin—A coin that has been chemically cleaned to remove oxidation or foreign matter from its surfaces.

doubled die—A die that has been given two misaligned impressions from a hub (positive-image punch); also, a coin made from such a die.

encapsulated coin—A coin that has been authenticated, graded, and sealed in plastic by a professional third-party grading service.

error coin—A mismade coin not intended for circulation.

field—The background portion of a coin's surface not used for a design or legends.

fineness—The purity of gold, silver, or other precious metal, expressed in terms of one thousand parts. A coin of 90% pure silver is described as being .900 fine.

gem—A coin of exceptionally high quality, typically considered MS-65 or PF-65 or better.

intrinsic value—The bullion or "melt" value of the actual silver or gold in a precious-metal coin.

junk silver—Common-date silver coins in circulated grades, worth only their bullion value.

key coin—One of the scarcer or more valuable coins in a series.

legend—A principal inscription on a coin (e.g., E PLURIBUS UNUM).

luster—The brilliant or "frosty" surface quality of an Uncirculated coin.

mintmark—A small letter or other mark on a coin, indicating the mint at which it was made.

Mint set—A set of Uncirculated coins, packaged and sold by the U.S. Mint, containing one of each of the coins made for circulation at each of the mints in a particular year.

Mint State—The grade of a circulation-strike coin that has never been used in commerce, and has retained its original surface and luster; also called Uncirculated.

obverse—The front or face ("heads") side of a coin.

planchet—The blank piece of metal on which a coin design is stamped.

Proof—A coin struck for collectors by the Mint using specially polished dies and planchets.

Proof set—A set of each of the Proof coins made during a given year, packaged by the Mint and sold to collectors.

raw coin—A coin that has not been encapsulated by an independent third-party grading service.

reeded edge—The edge of a coin with grooved lines that run vertically around its perimeter, as seen on modern U.S. silver and clad coins.

reverse—The back or "tails" side of a coin.

rim—The raised outer portion of a coin that protects the design from wear.

slab—A hard plastic case containing a coin that has been graded and encapsulated by a professional grading service.

spot price—The daily quoted market value of a precious metal in bullion form.

third-party grading service—A professional firm that authenticates and grades a coin, encapsulating it in a protective hard plastic case; called *third-party* because it is neither the buyer nor the seller of the coin.

token—A privately issued piece, similar to a coin but not official legal tender, typically with an exchange value for goods or services.

type—A series of coins defined by a shared distinguishing design, composition, denomination, and other elements. For example, Barber dimes or Morgan dollars.

type set—A collection consisting of one representative coin of each type, of a particular series or period.

Uncirculated coin—A circulation-strike coin that has never been used in commerce, and has retained its original surface and luster; also called Mint State.

variety—A coin with a die characteristic that sets it apart from the normal issues of its type.

Colonial Issues

Bowers, Q. David. *Whitman Encyclopedia of Colonial and Early American Coins.* (2nd ed.). Pelham, AL, 2020.

Cents

Bowers, Q. David. *A Guide Book of Half Cents and Large Cents.* Atlanta, GA, 2015.

Bowers, Q. David. *A Guide Book of Lincoln Cents* (3rd ed.). Pelham, AL, 2018.

Snow, Richard. *A Guide Book of Flying Eagle and Indian Head Cents* (3rd ed.). Atlanta, GA, 2016.

Nickels and Dimes

Bowers, Q. David. *A Guide Book of Barber Silver Coins* (2nd ed.). Atlanta, GA, 2019.

Bowers, Q. David. *A Guide Book of Buffalo and Jefferson Nickels* (2nd ed.). Pelham, AL, 2017.

Bowers, Q. David. *A Guide Book of Mercury Dimes, Standing Liberty Quarters, and Liberty Walking Half Dollars.* Atlanta, GA, 2015.

Bowers, Q. David. *A Guide Book of Shield and Liberty Head Nickels.* Atlanta, GA, 2006.

Quarter Dollars and Half Dollars

Bowers, Q. David. *A Guide Book of Barber Silver Coins* (2nd ed.). Atlanta, GA, 2019.

Bowers, Q. David. *A Guide Book of Mercury Dimes, Standing Liberty Quarters, and Liberty Walking Half Dollars.* Atlanta, GA, 2015.

Bowers, Q. David. *A Guide Book of Washington Quarters* (2nd ed.). Pelham, AL, 2017.

Tomaska, Rick. *A Guide Book of Franklin and Kennedy Half Dollars* (3rd ed.). Pelham, AL, 2018.

Silver Dollars

Bowers, Q. David. *A Guide Book of Morgan Silver Dollars* (7th ed.). Pelham, AL, 2022.

Burdette, Roger W. *A Guide Book of Peace Dollars* (4th ed.). Pelham, AL, 2020.

Newman, Eric P., and Kenneth E. Bressett. *The Fantastic 1804 Dollar, Tribute Edition.* Atlanta, GA, 2009.

Standish, Michael "Miles," and John B. Love. *Morgan Dollar: America's Love Affair With a Legendary Coin.* Atlanta, GA, 2014.

Gold Coins

Bowers, Q. David. *A Guide Book of Double Eagle Gold Coins.* Atlanta, GA, 2004.

Bowers, Q. David. *A Guide Book of Gold Dollars* (2nd ed.). Atlanta, GA, 2011.

Fivaz, Bill. *United States Gold Counterfeit Detection Guide.* Atlanta, GA, 2005.

Garrett, Jeff, and Ron Guth. *Encyclopedia of U.S. Gold Coins, 1795–1933* (2nd ed.). Atlanta, GA, 2008.

Commemoratives

Bowers, Q. David. *A Guide Book of United States Commemorative Coins* (2nd ed.). Pelham, AL, 2016.

Proof and Mint Sets

Lange, David W. *A Guide Book of Modern United States Proof Coin Sets* (2nd ed.). Atlanta, GA, 2010.

Bullion Coins

Mercanti, John M., with Michael Standish. *American Silver Eagles: A Guide to the U.S. Bullion Coin Program* (3rd ed.). Pelham, AL, 2018.

Moy, Edmund C. *American Gold and Platinum Eagles: A Guide to the U.S. Bullion Coin Programs.* Atlanta, GA, 2013.

Tucker, Dennis. *American Gold and Silver: U.S. Mint Collector and Investor Coins and Medals, Bicentennial to Date.* Atlanta, GA, 2016.

Tokens and Medals

Bowers, Q. David. *A Guide Book of Civil War Tokens* (3rd ed.). Pelham, AL, 2018.

Bowers, Q. David. *A Guide Book of Hard Times Tokens.* Atlanta, GA, 2015.

Jaeger, Katherine, and Q. David Bowers. *100 Greatest American Medals and Tokens.* Atlanta, GA, 2007.

Jaeger, Katherine. *A Guide Book of United States Tokens and Medals.* Atlanta, GA, 2008.

Tucker, Dennis. *American Gold and Silver: U.S. Mint Collector and Investor Coins and Medals, Bicentennial to Date.* Atlanta, GA, 2016.

U.S./Philippine Coins

Allen, Lyman L. *U.S. Philippine Coins.* Oakland Park, FL, 1998.

Shafer, Neil. *United States Territorial Coinage for the Philippine Islands.* Racine, WI, 1961.

Type Coins

Bowers, Q. David. *A Guide Book of United States Type Coins* (3rd ed.). Pelham, AL, 2019.

Guth, Ron, and Jeff Garrett. *United States Coinage: A Study by Type.* Atlanta, GA, 2005.

Garrett, Jeff, with Ron Guth. *100 Greatest U.S. Coins* (5th ed.), Pelham, AL, 2019.

Schechter, Scott, and Jeff Garrett. *100 Greatest U.S. Modern Coins* (3rd ed.), Atlanta, GA, 2014.

Die Varieties

Fivaz, Bill, and J.T. Stanton. *The Cherrypickers' Guide to Rare Die Varieties (various editions and volumes).* Atlanta, GA, and Pelham, AL.

281

282

283